The Writings of
Henry D. Thoreau

The Maine Woods

HENRY D. THOREAU

The Maine Woods

EDITED BY JOSEPH J. MOLDENHAUER

PRINCETON, NEW JERSEY

PRINCETON UNIVERSITY PRESS

MCMLXXII

CENTER FOR EDITIONS OF
AMERICAN AUTHORS
AN APPROVED TEXT
MODERN LANGUAGE
ASSOCIATION OF AMERICA
®

*The Center emblem means that one of a panel of textual
experts serving the Center has reviewed the text and
textual apparatus of the original volume by thorough and
scrupulous sampling, and has approved them for sound
and consistent editorial principles employed and
maximum accuracy attained. The accuracy of the text
has been guarded by careful and repeated proofreading
of printer's copy according to standards set by the Center.*

*Editorial expenses for this volume have been supported
by grants from the National Endowment for the Humanities
administered through the Center for Editions of
American Authors of the Modern Language Association*

Contents

The Maine Woods

Ktaadn.

On the 31st of August, 1846, I left Concord in Massachusetts for Bangor and the backwoods of Maine, by way of the railroad and steamboat, intending to accompany a relative of mine engaged in the lumber trade in Bangor, as far as a dam on the west branch of the Penobscot, in which property he was interested. From this place, which is about one hundred miles by the river above Bangor, thirty miles from the Houlton military road, and five miles beyond the last log hut, I proposed to make excursions to mount Ktaadn, the second highest mountain in New England, about thirty miles distant, and to some of the lakes of the Penobscot, either alone or with such company as I might pick up there. It is unusual to find a camp so far in the woods at that season, when lumbering operations have ceased, and I was glad to avail myself of the circumstance of a gang of men being employed there at that time in repairing the injuries caused by the great freshet in the spring. The mountain may be approached more easily and directly on horseback and on foot from the north-east side, by the Aroostook road, and the Wassataquoik river; but in that case you see much less of the wilderness, none of the glorious river and lake scenery, and have no experience of the batteau and the boatman's life. I was fortunate also in the season of the year, for in the summer myriads of black flies, mosquitoes, and midges, or, as the Indians call them, "no-see-ems," make travelling in the woods almost impossible; but now their reign was nearly over.

Ktaadn, whose name is an Indian word signifying highest land, was first ascended by white men in

1804. It was visited by Professor J. W. Bailey of West Point in 1836, by Dr. Charles T. Jackson, the State Geologist, in 1837, and by two young men from Boston in 1845. All these have given accounts of their expeditions. Since I was there, two or three other parties have made the excursion and told their stories. Besides these, very few, even among backwoodsmen and hunters, have ever climbed it, and it will be a long time before the tide of fashionable travel sets that way. The mountainous region of the State of Maine stretches from near the White Mountains, northeasterly one hundred and sixty miles, to the head of the Aroostook river, and is about sixty miles wide. The wild or unsettled portion is far more extensive. So that some hours only of travel in this direction will carry the curious to the verge of a primitive forest, more interesting, perhaps, on all accounts, than they would reach by going a thousand miles westward.

The next forenoon, Tuesday, Sept. 1st, I started with my companion in a buggy from Bangor for "up river," expecting to be overtaken the next day night, at Mattawamkeag Point, some sixty miles off, by two more Bangoreans, who had decided to join us in a trip to the mountain. We had each a knapsack or bag filled with such clothing and other articles as were indispensable, and my companion carried his gun.

Within a dozen miles of Bangor we passed through the villages of Stillwater and Oldtown, built at the falls of the Penobscot, which furnish the principal power by which the Maine woods are converted into lumber. The mills are built directly over and across the river. Here is a close jam, a hard rub, at all seasons; and then the once green tree, long since white, I need not say as the driven snow, but as a driven log, becomes lumber merely. Here your inch, your two and your three inch stuff begin to be, and Mr. Sawyer marks off those spaces which decide the destiny of so many prostrate forests. Through this steel riddle, more or less coarse, is the arrowy Maine forest, from Ktaadn and Chesuncook, and the head waters of the St. John, relentlessly sifted, till it comes out boards, clapboards, laths, and shingles such as the wind can take, still perchance to be slit and slit again, till men get a size that will suit. Think how stood the white-pine tree on the shore of Chesuncook, its branches soughing with the four winds, and every individual needle trembling in the sunlight—think how it stands with it now—sold, perchance to the New England Friction Match Company! There were in 1837, as I read, two hundred and fifty saw mills on the Penobscot and its tributaries above Bangor, the greater part of them in this immediate neighborhood, and they sawed two hundred millions of feet of boards annually. To this is to be added, the lumber of the Kennebeck, Androscoggin, Saco, Passamaquoddy, and other streams. No wonder that we hear so often of vessels which are becalmed off our coast, being surrounded a week at a time by floating lumber from the Maine woods. The mission of men there seems to be, like so many busy demons, to drive the forest all out of the country, from every solitary beaver swamp, and mountain side, as soon as possible.

At Oldtown we walked into a batteau manufactory. The making of batteaux is quite a business here for the supply of the Penobscot river. We examined some on the stocks. They are light and shapely vessels, calculated for rapid and rocky streams, and to be carried over long portages on men's shoulders, from twenty to thirty feet long, and only four or four and

a half wide, sharp at both ends like a canoe, though
broadest forward on the bottom, and reaching seven
or eight feet over the water, in order that they may
slip over rocks as gently as possible. They are made
very slight, only two boards to a side, commonly
secured to a few light maple or other hard-wood
knees, but inward are of the clearest and widest
white-pine stuff, of which there is a great waste on
account of their form, for the bottom is left perfectly
flat, not only from side to side, but from end to end.
Sometimes they become "hogging" even, after long
use, and the boatmen then turn them over and
straighten them by a weight at each end. They told
us that one wore out in two years, or often in a single
trip, on the rocks, and sold for from fourteen to sixteen dollars. There was something refreshing and
wildly musical to my ears in the very name of the
white man's canoe, reminding me of Charlevoix and
Canadian Voyageurs. The batteau is a sort of mongrel
between the canoe and the boat, a fur-trader's boat.

The ferry here took us past the Indian island. As
we left the shore, I observed a short shabby washer-
woman-looking Indian; they commonly have the woe-
begone look of the girl that cried for spilt milk—
just from "up river,"—land on the Oldtown side near
a grocery, and drawing up his canoe, take out a
bundle of skins in one hand, and an empty keg or
half-barrel in the other, and scramble up the bank
with them. This picture will do to put before the
Indian's history, that is, the history of his extinction.
In 1837, there were three hundred and sixty-two
souls left of this tribe. The island seemed deserted
to-day, yet I observed some new houses among the
weather-stained ones, as if the tribe had still a design
upon life; but generally they have a very shabby,
forlorn, and cheerless look, being all back side and

woodshed, not homesteads, even Indian homesteads, but instead of home or abroad-steads, for their life is *domi aut militiæ*, at home or at war, or now rather *venatus*, that is, a hunting, and most of the latter. The church is the only trim-looking building, but that is not Abenaki, that was Rome's doings. Good Canadian it may be, but it is poor Indian. These were once a powerful tribe. Politics are all the rage with them now. I even thought that a row of wigwams, with a dance of pow-wows, and a prisoner tortured at the stake, would be more respectable than this.

We landed in Milford, and rode along on the east side of the Penobscot, having a more or less constant view of the river, and the Indian islands in it, for they retain all the islands as far up as Nickatow, at the mouth of the East Branch. They are generally well-timbered, and are said to be better soil than the neighboring shores. The river seemed shallow and rocky, and interrupted by rapids, rippling and gleaming in the sun. We paused a moment to see a fish-hawk dive for a fish down straight as an arrow, from a great height, but he missed his prey this time. It was the Houlton Road on which we were now travelling, over which some troops were marched once towards Mars' Hill, though not to Mars' *field*, as it proved. It is the main, almost the only, road in these parts, as straight and well made, and kept in as good repair, as almost any you will find anywhere. Everywhere we saw signs of the great freshet—this house standing awry, and that where it was not founded, but where it was found, at any rate, the next day; and that other with a water-logged look, as if it were still airing and drying its basement, and logs with everybody's marks upon them, and sometimes the marks of their having served as bridges, strewn along the road. We crossed the Sunkhaze, a summery Indian name, the Olemmon, Passadumkeag, and other streams, which make a greater show on the map than they now did on the road. At Passadumkeag, we found anything but what the name implies, earnest politicians, to wit—white ones, I mean—on the alert, to know how the election was likely to go; men who talked rapidly, with subdued voice, and a sort of factitious earnestness, you could not help believing, hardly waiting for an introduction, one on each side of your buggy, endeavoring to say much in little, for they see you hold the whip impatiently, but always saying little in much. Caucuses they have had, it seems, and caucuses they are to have again—victory and defeat: somebody may be elected, somebody may not. One man, a total stranger, who stood by our carriage, in the dusk, actually frightened the horse with his asseverations, growing more solemnly positive as there was less in him to be positive about. So Passadumkeag did not look on the map. At sundown, leaving the river-road awhile for shortness, we went by way of Enfield, where we stopped for the night. This, like most of the localities bearing names on this road, was a place to name, which, in the midst of the unnamed and unincorporated wilderness, was to make a distinction without a difference, it seemed to me. Here, however, I noticed quite an orchard of healthy and well-grown apple trees, in a bearing state, it being the oldest settler's house in this region, but all natural fruit, and comparatively worthless for want of a grafter. And so it is generally lower down the river. It would be a good speculation, as well as a favor conferred on the settlers, for a Massachusetts boy to go down there with a trunk full of choice scions, and his grafting apparatus, in the spring.

The next morning we drove along through a high and hilly country, in view of Cold-Stream Pond, a beautiful lake, four or five miles long, and came into the Houlton road again, here called the Military road, at Lincoln, forty-five miles from Bangor, where there is quite a village, for this country—the principal one above Oldtown. Learning that there were several wigwams here, on one of the Indian islands, we left our horse and wagon, and walked through the forest half a mile, to the river, to procure a guide to the mountain. It was not till after considerable search that we discovered their habitations—small huts, in a retired place, where the scenery was unusually soft and beautiful, and the shore skirted with pleasant meadows and graceful elms. We paddled ourselves across to the island-side in a canoe, which we found on the shore. Near where we landed, sat an Indian girl, ten or twelve years old, on a rock in the water, in the sun, washing, and humming or moaning a song meanwhile. It was an aboriginal strain. A salmon-spear, made wholly of wood, lay on the shore, such as they might have used before white men came. It had an elastic piece of wood fastened to one side of its point, which slipped over and closed upon the fish, somewhat like the contrivance for holding a bucket at the end of a well-pole. As we walked up to the nearest house, we were met by a sally of a dozen wolfish-looking dogs, which may have been lineal descendants from the ancient Indian dogs, which the first voyageurs describe as "their wolves." I suppose they were. The occupant soon appeared, with a long pole in his hand, with which he beat off the dogs, while he parleyed with us. A stalwart, but dull and greasy-looking fellow, who told us, in his sluggish way, in answer to our questions, as if it were the first serious business he had to do that day, that there *were* Indians going "up river,"—he and one other—to-day, before noon. And who was the other? Louis Neptune, who lives in the next house. Well, let us go over and see Louis together. The same doggish reception, and Louis Neptune makes his appearance—a small, wiry man, with puckered and wrinkled face, yet he seemed the chief man of the two; the same, as I remembered, who had accompanied Jackson to the mountain in '37. The same questions were put to Louis, and the same information obtained, while the other Indian stood by. It appeared, that they were going to start by noon, with two canoes, to go up to Chesuncook, to hunt moose—to be gone a month. "Well, Louis, suppose you get to the Point, [to the Five Islands, just below Mattawamkeag,] to camp, we walk on up the West Branch to-morrow—four of us—and wait for you at the dam, or this side. You overtake us to-morrow or next day, and take us into your canoes. We stop for you, you stop for us. We pay you for your trouble." "Ye!" replied Louis, "may be you carry some provision for all—some pork—some bread—and so pay." He said, "Me sure get some moose;" and when I asked, if he thought Pomola would let us go up, he answered that we must plant one bottle of rum on the top, he had planted good many; and when he looked again, the rum was all gone. He had been up two or three times: he had planted letter—English, German, French, &c. These men were slightly clad in shirt and pantaloons, like laborers with us in warm weather. They did not invite us into their houses, but met us outside. So we left the Indians, thinking ourselves lucky to have secured such guides and companions.

There were very few houses along the road, yet they did not altogether fail, as if the law by which men are dispersed over the globe were a very stringent one, and not to be resisted with impunity or for slight reasons. There were even the germs of one or two villages just beginning to expand. The beauty of the road itself was remarkable. The various evergreens, many of which are rare with us—delicate and beautiful specimens of the larch, arbor-vitæ, ball spruce, and fir-balsam, from a few inches to many feet in height, lined its sides, in some places like a long front yard, springing up from the smooth grass-plots which uninterruptedly border it, and are made fertile by its wash; while it was but a step on either hand to the grim untrodden wilderness, whose tangled labyrinth of living, fallen, and decaying trees,—only the deer and moose, the bear and wolf, can easily penetrate. More perfect specimens than any front yard plot can show, grew there to grace the passage of the Houlton teams.

About noon we reached the Mattawamkeag, fifty-six miles from Bangor by the way we had come, and put up at a frequented house, still on the Houlton road, where the Houlton stage stops. Here was a substantial covered bridge over the Mattawamkeag, built, I think they said, some seventeen years before. We had dinner—where, by the way, and even at breakfast, as well as supper—at the public-houses on this road, the front rank is composed of various kinds of "sweet cakes," in a continuous line from one end of the table to the other. I think I may safely say that there was a row of ten or a dozen plates of this kind set before us two here. To account for which, they say, that when the lumberers come out of the woods, they have a craving for cakes and pies, and such sweet things, which there are almost unknown, and this is the *supply* to satisfy that *demand*—the supply is always equal to the demand,—and these hungry men think a good deal of getting their money's worth.

No doubt, the balance of victuals is restored by the time they reach Bangor: Mattawamkeag takes off the raw edge. Well, over this front rank, I say, you coming from the "sweet cake" side, with a cheap philosophic indifference though it may be, have to assault what there is behind, which I do not by any means mean to insinuate is insufficient in quantity or quality to supply that other demand of men not from the woods, but from the towns, for venison and strong country fare. After dinner, we strolled down to the "Point," formed by the junction of the two rivers, which is said to be the scene of an ancient battle between the Eastern Indians and the Mohawks, and searched there carefully for relics, though the men at the bar-room had never heard of such things; but we found only some flakes of arrow-head stone, some points of arrow-heads, one small leaden-bullet, and some colored beads, the last to be referred, perhaps, to early fur-trader days. The Mattawamkeag, though wide, was a mere river's bed, full of rocks and shallows at this time, so that you could cross it almost dry-shod in boots; and I could hardly believe my companion, when he told me that he had been fifty or sixty miles up it in a batteau, through distant and still uncut forests. A batteau could hardly find a harbor now at its mouth. Deer, and caribou, or reindeer, are taken here in the winter, in sight of the house.

Before our companions arrived, we rode on up the Houlton road seven miles, to Molunkus, where the Aroostook road comes into it, and where there is a spacious public house in the woods, called the "Molunkus House," kept by one Libbey, which looked as if it had its hall for dancing and for military drills. There was no other evidence of man but this huge shingle palace in this part of the world; but sometimes even this is filled with travellers. I looked off the piazza round the corner of the house up the Aroostook road, on which there was no clearing in sight. There was a man just adventuring upon it this evening, in a rude, original, what you may call Aroostook, wagon—a mere seat, with a wagon swung under it, a few bags on it, and a dog asleep to watch them. He offered to carry a message for us to anybody in that country, cheerfully. I suspect, that if you should go to the end of the world, you would find somebody there going further, as if just starting for home at sundown, and having a last word before he drove off. Here, too, *was* a small trader, whom I did not see at first, who kept a store—but no great store, certainly—in a small box over the way, behind the Molunkus sign-post. It looked like the balance-box of a patent hay-scales. As for his house, we could only conjecture where that was; he may have been a boarder in the Molunkus House. I saw him standing in his shop-door—his shop was so small, that, if a traveller should make demonstrations of entering in, *he* would have to go out by the back way, and confer with his customer through a window, about his goods in the cellar, or, more probably, bespoken, and yet on the way. I should have gone in, for I felt a real impulse to trade, if I had not stopped to consider what would become of him. The day before, we had walked into a shop, over against an inn where we stopped, the puny beginning of trade, which would grow at last into a firm copartnership, in the future town or city—indeed, it was already "Somebody & Co.," I forget who. The woman came forward from the penetralia of the attached house, for "Somebody & Co." was in the burning, and she sold us percussion-caps, canalés and smooth; and knew their prices and qualities, and which the hunters preferred. Here was a little of everything in a small compass to satisfy the wants and the ambition of the woods, a stock selected with what pains and care, and brought home in the wagon box, or a corner of the Houlton team; but there seemed to me, as usual, a preponderance of children's toys, dogs to bark, and cats to mew, and trumpets to blow, where natives there hardly are yet. As if a child, born into the Maine woods, among the pine cones and cedar berries, could not do without such a sugar-man, or skipping-jack, as the young Rothschild has.

I think that there was not more than one house on the road to Molunkus, or for seven miles. At that place we got over the fence into a new field, planted with potatoes, where the logs were still burning between the hills; and, pulling up the vines, found good-sized potatoes, nearly ripe, growing like weeds, and turnips mixed with them. The mode of clearing and planting, is, to fell the trees, and burn once what will burn, then cut them up into suitable lengths, roll into heaps, and burn again; then, with a hoe, plant potatoes where you can come at the ground between the stumps and charred logs, for a first crop, the ashes sufficing for manure, and no hoeing being necessary the first year. In the fall, cut, roll, and burn again, and so on, till the land is cleared; and soon it is ready for grain, and to be laid down. Let those talk of poverty and hard times who will, in the towns and cities; cannot the emigrant, who can pay his fare to New-York or Boston, pay five dollars more to get here,—I paid three, all told, for my passage from Boston to Bangor, 250 miles,—and be as rich as he pleases, where land virtually costs nothing, and houses only the labor of building, and he may begin life as Adam did? If he will still remember the distinction of poor and rich, let him bespeak him a narrower house forthwith.

When we returned to the Mattawamkeag, the Houlton stage had already put up there; and a Province man was betraying his greenness to the Yankees by his questions.—Why Province money won't pass here at par, when States' money is good at Frederickton—though this, perhaps, was sensible enough. From what I saw then, it appeared that the Province man was now the only real Jonathan, or raw country bumpkin, left so far behind by his enterprising neighbors, that he didn't know enough to put a question to them. No people can long continue provincial in character, who have the propensity for politics and whittling, and rapid travelling, which the Yankees have, and who are leaving the mother country behind in the variety of their notions and inventions. The possession and exercise of practical talent merely, are a sure and rapid means of intellectual culture and independence.

The last edition of Greenleaf's Map of Maine hung on the wall here, and, as we had no pocket map, we resolved to trace a map of the lake country: so dipping a wad of tow into the lamp, we oiled a sheet of paper on the oiled table-cloth, and, in good faith, traced what we afterwards ascertained to be a labyrinth of errors, carefully following the outlines of the imaginary lakes which that map contains. The Map of the Public Lands of Maine and Massachusetts is the only one I have seen that at all deserves the name. It was while we were engaged in this operation that our companions arrived. They had seen the Indians' fire on the Five Islands, and so we concluded that all was right.

Early the next morning we had mounted our

packs, and prepared for a tramp up the West Branch, my companion having turned his horse out to pasture for a week or ten days, thinking that a bite of fresh grass, and a taste of running water, would do him as much good as backwoods fare, and new country influences his master. Leaping over a fence, we began to follow an obscure trail up the northern bank of the Penobscot. There was now no road further, the river being the only highway, and but half a dozen log huts confined to its banks, to be met with for thirty miles; on either hand, and beyond, was a wholly uninhabited wilderness, stretching to Canada. Neither horse, nor cow, nor vehicle of any kind, had ever passed over this ground. The cattle, and the few bulky articles which the loggers use, being got up in the winter on the ice, and down again before it breaks up. The evergreen woods had a decidedly sweet and bracing fragrance; the air was a sort of diet-drink, and we walked on buoyantly in Indian file, stretching our legs. Occasionally there was a small opening on the bank, made for the purpose of log-rolling, where we got a sight of the river—always a rocky and rippling stream. The roar of the rapids, the note of a whistler-duck on the river, of the jay and chicadee around us, and of the pigeon-woodpecker in the openings, were the sounds that we heard. This was what you might call a bran new country; the only roads were of Nature's making, and the few houses were camps. Here, then, one could no longer accuse institutions and society, but must front the true source of evil.

There are three classes of inhabitants, who either frequent or inhabit the country which we had now entered; first, the loggers, who, for a part of the year, the winter and spring, are far the most numerous, but in the summer, except a few explorers for timber, completely desert it; second, the few settlers I have named, the only permanent inhabitants, who live on the verge of it, and help raise supplies for the former; third, the hunters, mostly Indians, who range over it in their season.

At the end of three miles we came to the Mattase-unk stream and mill, where there was even a rude wooden railroad running down to the Penobscot, the last railroad we were to see. We crossed one tract, on the bank of the river, of more than a hundred acres of heavy timber, which had just been felled and burnt over, and was still smoking. Our trail lay through the midst of it, and was well nigh blotted out. The trees lay at full length, four or five feet deep, and crossing each other in all directions, all black as charcoal, but perfectly sound within, still good for fuel or for timber; soon they would be cut into lengths and burnt again. Here were thousands of cords, enough to keep the poor of Boston and New-York amply warm for a winter, which only cumbered the ground, and were in the settler's way. And the whole of that solid and interminable forest is doomed to be gradually devoured thus by fire, like shavings, and no man be warmed by it. At Crocker's log hut, at the mouth of Salmon River, seven miles from the Point, one of the party commenced distributing a store of small cent picture-books among the children, to teach them to read; and also newspapers, more or less recent, among the parents, than which nothing can be more acceptable to a backwoods people. It was really an important item in our outfit, and, at times, the only currency that would circulate. I walked through Salmon River with my shoes on, it being low water, but not without wetting my feet. A few miles further we came to "Marm Howard's," at the end of an extensive clearing, where there were two or three log huts in sight at once, one on the opposite side of the river, and a few graves, even surrounded by a wooden paling, where already the rude forefathers of *a* hamlet lie; and a thousand years hence, perchance, some poet will write his "Elegy in a Country Churchyard." The "Village Hampdens," the "mute, inglorious Miltons," and Cromwells, "guiltless of" their "country's blood," were yet unborn.

> "Perchance in this *wild* spot *there will be* laid
>   Some heart once pregnant with celestial fire;
> Hands that the rod of empire might have swayed,
>   Or waked to ecstasy the living lyre."

The next house was Fisk's, ten miles from the Point, at the mouth of the East Branch, opposite to the island Nickatow, or the Forks, the last of the Indian islands. I am particular to give the names of the settlers and the distances, since every log hut in these woods is a public house, and such information is of no little consequence to those who may have occasion to travel this way. Our course here crossed the Penobscot, and followed the southern bank. One of the party, who entered the house in search of some one to set us over, reported a very neat dwelling, with plenty of books, and a new wife, just imported from Boston, wholly new to the woods. We found the East Branch a large and rapid stream at its mouth, and much deeper than it appeared. Having with some difficulty discovered the trail again, we kept up the south side of the West Branch, or main river, passing by some rapids called Rock-Ebeeme, the roar of which we heard through the woods, and, shortly after, in the thickest of the wood, some empty loggers' camps, still new, which were occupied the previous winter. Though we saw a few

more afterwards, I will make one account serve for
all. These were such houses as the lumberers of
Maine spend the winter in, in the wilderness. There
were the camps and the hovel for the cattle, hardly
distinguishable, except that the latter had no chimney. These camps were about twenty feet long by
fifteen wide, built of logs—hemlock, cedar, spruce, or
yellow birch—one kind alone, or all together, with
the bark on; two or three large ones first, one directly
above another, and notched together at the ends,
to the height of three or four feet, then of smaller
logs resting upon transverse ones at the ends, each
of the last successively shorter than the other, to
form the roof. The chimney was an oblong square
hole in the middle, three or four feet in diameter,
with a fence of logs as high as the ridge. The inter-
stices were filled with moss, and the roof was
shingled with long and handsome splints of cedar,
or spruce, or pine, rifted with a sledge and cleaver.
The fire-place, the most important place of all, was
in shape and size like the chimney, and directly
under it, defined by a log fence or fender on the
ground, and a heap of ashes a foot or two deep
within, with solid benches of split logs running round
it. Here the fire usually melts the snow, and dries
the rain before it can descend to quench it. The
faded beds of arbor-vitæ leaves extended under the
eaves on either hand. There was the place for the
water-pail, pork-barrel, and wash-basin, and generally a dingy pack of cards left on a log. Usually a
good deal of whittling was expended on the latch,
which was made of wood, in the form of an iron one.
These houses are made comfortable by the huge fires
that can be afforded night and day. Usually the
scenery about them is drear and savage enough; and
the logger's camp is as completely in the woods as

a fungus at the foot of a pine in a swamp; no outlook but to the sky overhead; no more clearing than
is made by cutting down the trees of which it is
built, and those which are necessary for fuel. If only
it be well sheltered and convenient to his work, and
near a spring, he wastes no thought on the prospect.
They are very proper forest houses, the stems of the
trees collected together and piled up around a man
to keep out wind and rain: made of living green logs,
hanging with moss and lichen, and with the curls
and fringes of the yellow-birch bark, and dripping
with resin, fresh and moist, and redolent of swampy
odors, with that sort of vigor and perennialness even
about them that toad-stools suggest.* The logger's
fare consists of tea, molasses, flour, pork,—sometimes
beef,—and beans. A great proportion of the beans
raised in Massachusetts find their market here. On
expeditions it is only hard bread and pork, often raw,
slice upon slice, with tea or water, as the case may be.

The primitive wood is always and everywhere
damp and mossy, so that I travelled constantly with
the impression that I was in a swamp; and only when
it was remarked that this or that tract, judging from
the quality of the timber on it, would make a profitable clearing, was I reminded, that if the sun were
let in it would make a dry field, like the few I had
seen, at once. The best shod for the most part travel

* Springer, in his "Forest Life" (1851), says that they first
remove the leaves and turf from the spot where they intend
to build a camp, for fear of fire; also, that "the spruce-tree
is generally selected for camp-building, it being light, straight,
and quite free from sap"; that "the roof is finally covered
with the boughs of the fir, spruce, and hemlock, so that when
the snow falls upon the whole, the warmth of the camp is
preserved in the coldest weather"; and that they make the
log seat before the fire, called the "Deacon's Seat," of a
spruce or fir split in halves, with three or four stout limbs
left on one side for legs, which are not likely to get loose.

with wet feet. If the ground was so wet and spongy at this, the driest part of a dry season, what must it be in the spring? The woods hereabouts abounded in beech and yellow-birch, of which last there were some very large specimens; also spruce, cedar, fir, and hemlock; but we saw only the stumps of the white pine here, some of them of great size, these having been already culled out, being the only tree much sought after, even as low down as this. Only a little spruce and hemlock beside had been logged here. The eastern wood, which is sold for fuel in Massachusetts, all comes from below Bangor. It was the pine alone, chiefly the white pine, that had tempted any but the hunter to precede us on this route.

Waite's farm, thirteen miles from the Point, is an extensive and elevated clearing, from which we got a fine view of the river, rippling and gleaming far beneath us. My companions had formerly had a good view of Ktaadn and the other mountains here, but to-day it was so smoky that we could see nothing of them. We could overlook an immense country of uninterrupted forest, stretching away up the East Branch toward Canada, on the north and northwest, and toward the Aroostook valley on the northeast: and imagine what wild life was stirring in its midst. Here was quite a field of corn for this region, whose peculiar dry scent we perceived a third of a mile off before we saw it.

Eighteen miles from the Point brought us in sight of McCauslin's, or "Uncle George's," as he was familiarly called by my companions, to whom he was well known, where we intended to break our long fast. His house was in the midst of an extensive clearing of intervale, at the mouth of the Little Schoodic River, on the opposite or north bank of the Penobscot. So we collected on a point of the shore, that we might be seen, and fired our gun as a signal, which brought out his dogs forthwith, and thereafter their master, who in due time took us across in his batteau. This clearing was bounded abruptly on all sides but the river, by the naked stems of the forest, as if you were to cut only a few feet square in the midst of a thousand acres of mowing, and set down a thimble therein. He had a whole heaven and horizon to himself, and the sun seemed to be journeying over his clearing only, the live-long day. Here we concluded to spend the night, and wait for the Indians, as there was no stopping place so convenient above. He had seen no Indians pass, and this did not often happen without his knowledge. He thought that his dogs sometimes gave notice of the approach of Indians, half an hour before they arrived.

McCauslin was a Kennebec man, of Scotch descent, who had been a waterman twenty-two years, and had driven on the lakes and head waters of the Penobscot five or six springs in succession, but was now settled here to raise supplies for the lumberers and for himself. He entertained us a day or two with true Scotch hospitality, and would accept no recompense for it. A man of a dry wit and shrewdness, and a general intelligence which I had not looked for in the backwoods. In fact, the deeper you penetrate into the woods, the more intelligent, and, in one sense, less countrified do you find the inhabitants; for always the pioneer has been a traveller, and, to some extent, a man of the world; and, as the distances with which he is familiar are greater, so is his information more general and far reaching than the villager's. If I were to look for a narrow, uninformed, and countrified mind, as opposed to the intelligence and refinement which are thought to emanate from cities, it would be among the rusty

inhabitants of an old-settled country, on farms all
run out and gone to seed with life-ever-lasting, in the
towns about Boston, even on the high road in Concord, and not in the backwoods of Maine.

Supper was got before our eyes, in the ample
kitchen, by a fire which would have roasted an ox;
many whole logs, four feet long, were consumed to
boil our tea-kettle—birch, or beech, or maple, the
same summer and winter; and the dishes were soon
smoking on the table, late the arm-chair, against the
wall, from which one of the party was expelled. The
arms of the chair formed the frame on which the
table rested; and, when the round top was turned up
against the wall, it formed the back of the chair, and
was no more in the way than the wall itself. This,
we noticed, was the prevailing fashion in these log
houses, in order to economize in room. There were
piping hot wheaten-cakes, the flour having been
brought up the river in batteaux,—no Indian bread,
for the upper part of Maine, it will be remembered,
is a wheat country,—and ham, eggs, and potatoes, and
milk and cheese, the produce of the farm; and, also,
shad and salmon, tea sweetened with molasses, and
sweet cakes in contradistinction to the hot cakes not
sweetened, the one white, the other yellow, to wind
up with. Such, we found, was the prevailing fare,
ordinary and extraordinary, along this river. Mountain cranberries (*Vaccinium Vitis-Idæa*), stewed and
sweetened, were the common dessert. Everything
here was in profusion, and the best of its kind. Butter
was in such plenty, that it was commonly used, before it was salted, to grease boots with.

In the night we were entertained by the sound of
rain-drops on the cedar splints which covered the
roof, and awaked the next morning with a drop or
two in our eyes. It had set in for a storm, and we

made up our minds not to forsake such comfortable quarters with this prospect, but wait for Indians and fair weather. It rained and drizzled, and gleamed by turns, the live-long day. What we did there, how we killed the time, would, perhaps, be idler to tell; how many times we buttered our boots, and how often a drowsy one was seen to sidle off to the bedroom. When it held up, I strolled up and down the bank and gathered the harebell and cedar berries, which grew there; or else we tried by turns the long-handled axe on the logs before the door. The axe-helves here were made to chop standing on the log—a primitive log of course—and were, therefore, nearly a foot longer than with us. One while we walked over the farm, and visited his well-filled barns with McCauslin. There were one other man and two women only here. He kept horses, cows, oxen, and sheep. I think he said that he was the first to bring a plough and a cow so far; and, he might have added, the last, with only two exceptions. The potato rot had found him out here, too, the previous year, and got half or two-thirds of his crop, though the seed was of his own raising. Oats, grass, and potatoes, were his staples; but he raised, also, a few carrots and turnips, and "a little corn for the hens," for this was all that he dared risk, for fear that it would not ripen. Melons, squashes, sweet-corn, beans, tomatoes, and many other vegetables, could not be ripened there.

The very few settlers along this stream were obviously tempted by the cheapness of the land mainly. When I asked McCauslin why more settlers did not come in, he answered, that one reason was, they could not buy the land, it belonged to individuals or companies who were afraid that their wild lands would be settled, and so incorporated into towns, and they be taxed for them; but to settling on the States' land there was no such hinderance. For his own part, he wanted no neighbors—he didn't wish to see any road by his house. Neighbors, even the best, were a trouble and expense, especially on the score of cattle and fences. They might live across the river, perhaps, but not on the same side.

The chickens here were protected by the dogs. As McCauslin said, "The old one took it up first, and she taught the pup, and now they had got it into their heads that it wouldn't do to have anything of the bird kind on the premises." A hawk hovering over was not allowed to alight, but barked off by the dogs circling underneath; and a pigeon, or a "yellow hammer," as they called the pigeon-woodpecker, on a dead limb or stump, was instantly expelled. It was the main business of their day, and kept them constantly coming and going. One would rush out of the house on the least alarm given by the other.

When it rained hardest, we returned to the house, and took down a tract from the shelf. There was the Wandering Jew, cheap edition, and fine print, the Criminal Calendar, and Parish's Geography, and flash novels two or three. Under the pressure of circumstances, we read a little in these. With such aid, the press is not so feeble an engine after all. This house, which was a fair specimen of those on this river, was built of huge logs, which peeped out everywhere, and were chinked with clay and moss. It contained four or five rooms. There were no sawed boards, or shingles, or clapboards, about it; and scarcely any tool but the axe had been used in its construction. The partitions were made of long clapboard-like splints, of spruce or cedar, turned to a delicate salmon color by the smoke. The roof and sides were covered with the same, instead of shingles and clapboards, and some of a much thicker and larger size were used for the floor. These were all so straight and smooth, that they answered the purpose admirably; and a careless observer would not have suspected that they were not sawed and planed. The chimney and hearth were of vast size, and made of stone. The broom was a few twigs of arbor-vitæ tied to a stick; and a pole was suspended over the hearth, close to the ceiling, to dry stockings and clothes on. I noticed that the floor was full of small, dingy holes, as if made with a gimlet, but which were, in fact, made by the spikes, nearly an inch long, which the lumberers wear in their boots to prevent their slipping on wet logs. Just above McCauslin's, there is a rocky rapid, where logs jam in the spring; and many "drivers" are there collected, who frequent his house for supplies: these were their tracks which I saw.

At sundown, McCauslin pointed away over the forest, across the river, to signs of fair weather amid the clouds—some evening redness there. For even there the points of compass held; and there was a quarter of the heavens appropriated to sunrise and another to sunset.

The next morning, the weather proving fair enough for our purpose, we prepared to start; and, the Indians having failed us, persuaded McCauslin, who was not unwilling to re-visit the scenes of his driving, to accompany us in their stead, intending to engage one other boatman on the way. A strip of cotton-cloth for a tent, a couple of blankets, which would suffice for the whole party, fifteen pounds of hard bread, ten pounds of "clear" pork, and a little tea, made up "Uncle George's" pack. The last three articles were calculated to be provision enough for six men for a week, with what we might pick up. A tea-kettle, a frying-pan and an axe, to be obtained at the last house, would complete our outfit.

We were soon out of McCauslin's clearing, and in the ever-green woods again. The obscure trail made by the two settlers above, which even the woodman is sometimes puzzled to discern, ere long crossed a narrow open strip in the woods overrun with weeds, called the Burnt Land, where a fire had raged formerly, stretching northward nine or ten miles, to Millinocket Lake. At the end of three miles we reached Shad Pond, or Noliseemack, an expansion of the river. Hodge, the Assistant State Geologist, who passed through this on the twenty-fifth of June, 1837, says, "We pushed our boat through an acre or more of buck-beans, which had taken root at the bottom, and bloomed above the surface in the greatest profusion and beauty." Thomas Fowler's house is four miles from McCauslin's, on the shore of the Pond, at the mouth of the Millinocket River, and eight miles from the lake of the same name, on the latter stream. This lake affords a more direct course to Ktaadn, but we preferred to follow the Penobscot and the Pamadum-cook Lakes. Fowler was just completing a new log hut, and was sawing out a window through the logs nearly two feet thick when we arrived. He had begun to paper his house with spruce bark, turned inside out, which had a good effect, and was in keeping with the circumstances. Instead of water we got here a draught of beer, which, it was allowed, would be better; clear and thin, but strong and stringent as the cedar sap. It was as if we sucked at the very teats of Nature's pine-clad bosom in these parts—the sap of all Millinocket botany commingled—the topmost most fantastic and spiciest sprays of the primitive wood, and whatever invigorating and stringent gum or essence it afforded, steeped and dissolved in it—a lumberer's drink, which would acclimate and naturalize a man at once—which would make him see green, and, if he slept, dream that he heard the wind sough among the pines. Here was a fife, praying to be played on, through which we breathed a few tuneful strains, —brought hither to tame wild beasts. As we stood upon the pile of chips by the door, fish-hawks were sailing over head; and here, over Shad Pond, might daily be witnessed, the tyranny of the bald-eagle over that bird. Tom pointed away over the Lake to a bald-eagle's nest, which was plainly visible more than a mile off, on a pine, high above the surrounding forest, and was frequented from year to year by the same pair, and held sacred by him. There were these two houses only there, his low hut, and the eagles' airy cart-load of fagots. Thomas Fowler, too, was persuaded to join us, for two men were necessary to manage the batteau, which was soon to be our carriage, and these men needed to be cool and skilful for the navigation of the Penobscot. Tom's pack was soon made, for he had not far to look for his waterman's boots, and a red flannel shirt. This is the favorite color with lumbermen; and red flannel is reputed to possess some mysterious virtues, to be most healthful and convenient in respect to perspiration. In every gang there will be a large proportion of red birds. We took here a poor and leaky batteau, and began to pole up the Millinocket two miles, to the elder Fowler's, in order to avoid the Grand Falls of the Penobscot, intending to exchange our batteau there for a better. The Millinocket is a small, shallow and sandy stream, full of what I took to be lamprey-eels' or suckers' nests, and lined with musquash cabins, but free from rapids, according to Fowler, excepting at its outlet from the Lake. He was at this time en-

rass—rush grass and
—on the meadows
tream. We noticed
either side, where,
ı the night before,
.s in these meadows.
.cket, six miles from
from the Point, is the
the Sowadnehunk, is the
that had proved a failure,
eserted. Fowler is the oldest
oods. He formerly lived a few
n the south side of the West
Branch, where he built his house sixteen years ago,
the first house built above the Five Islands. Here our
new batteau was to be carried over the first portage
of two miles, round the Grand Falls of the Penobscot,
on a horse-sled made of saplings, to jump the numerous rocks in the way, but we had to wait a couple of
hours for them to catch the horses, which were pastured at a distance, amid the stumps, and had wandered still further off. The last of the salmon for this
season had just been caught, and were still fresh in
pickle, from which enough was extracted to fill our
empty kettle, and so graduate our introduction to
simpler forest fare. The week before, they had lost
nine sheep here out of their first flock, by the wolves.
The surviving sheep came round the house, and
seemed frightened, which induced them to go and look
for the rest, when they found seven dead and lac-
erated, and two still alive. These last they carried
to the house, and, as Mrs. Fowler said, they were
merely scratched in the throat, and had no more
visible wound than would be produced by the prick
of a pin. She sheared off the wool from their throats,
and washed them and put on some salve, and turned

them out, but in a few moments they were missing, and had not been found since. In fact, they were all poisoned, and those that were found swelled up at once, so that they saved neither skin nor wool. This realized the old fables of the wolves and the sheep, and convinced me that that ancient hostility still existed. Verily, the shepherd boy did not need to sound a false alarm this time. There were steel traps by the door of various sizes, for wolves, otter, and bears, with large claws instead of teeth, to catch in their sinews. Wolves are frequently killed with poisoned bait.

At length, after we had dined here on the usual backwoods fare, the horses arrived, and we hauled our batteau out of the water, and lashed it to its wicker carriage, and, throwing in our packs, walked on before, leaving the boatmen and driver, who was Tom's brother, to manage the concern. The route, which led through the wild pasture where the sheep were killed, was in some places the roughest ever travelled by horses, over rocky hills, where the sled bounced and slid along, like a vessel pitching in a storm; and one man was as necessary to stand at the stern, to prevent the boat from being wrecked, as a helmsman in the roughest sea. The philosophy of our progress was something like this: when the runners struck a rock three or four feet high, the sled bounced back and upwards at the same time; but, as the horses never ceased pulling, it came down on the top of the rock, and so we got over. This portage probably followed the trail of an ancient Indian carry round these falls. By 2 o'clock we, who had walked on before, reached the river above the falls, not far from the outlet of Quakish Lake, and waited for the batteau to come up. We had been here but a short time, when a thunder-shower was seen coming up from the west, over the still invisible lakes, and that pleasant wilderness which we were so eager to become acquainted with; and soon the heavy drops began to patter on the leaves around us. I had just selected the prostrate trunk of a huge pine, five or six feet in diameter, and was crawling under it, when, luckily, the boat arrived. It would have amused a sheltered man to witness the manner in which it was unlashed, and whirled over, while the first water-spout burst upon us. It was no sooner in the hands of the eager company than it was abandoned to the first revolutionary impulse, and to gravity, to adjust it; and they might have been seen all stooping to its shelter, and wriggling under like so many eels, before it was fairly deposited on the ground. When all were under, we propped up the lee side, and busied our-selves there, whittling thole pins for rowing, when we should reach the lakes; and made the woods ring, between the claps of thunder, with such boat-songs as we could remember. The horses stood sleek and shin-ing with the rain, all drooping and crestfallen, while deluge after deluge washed over us; but the bottom of a boat may be relied on for a tight roof. At length, after two hours' delay at this place, a streak of fair weather appeared in the northwest, whither our course now lay, promising a serene evening for our voyage; and the driver returned with his horses, while we made haste to launch our boat, and com-mence our voyage in good earnest.

There were six of us, including the two boatmen. With our packs heaped up near the bows, and our-selves disposed as baggage to trim the boat, with in-structions not to move in case we should strike a rock, more than so many barrels of pork, we pushed out into the first rapid, a slight specimen of the stream we had to navigate. With Uncle George in the stern, and Tom in the bows, each using a spruce pole about twelve feet long, pointed with iron,* and poling on the same side, we shot up the rapids like a salmon, the water rushing and roaring around, so that only a practised eye could distinguish a safe course, or tell what was deep water and what rocks, frequently grazing the latter on one or both sides, with a hundred as narrow escapes as ever the Argo had in passing through the Symplegades. I, who had had some experience in boating, had never experienced any half so exhilarating before. We were lucky to have exchanged our Indians, whom we did not know, for these men, who, together with Tom's brother, were reputed the best boatmen on the river, and were at once indispensable pilots and pleasant companions. The canoe is smaller, more easily upset, and sooner worn out; and the Indian is said not to be so skilful in the management of the batteau. He is, for the most part, less to be relied on, and more disposed to sulks and whims. The utmost familiarity with dead streams, or with the ocean, would not prepare a man for this peculiar navigation; and the most skilful boatman anywhere else would here be obliged to take out his boat and carry round a hundred times, still with great risk, as well as delay, where the practised batteau man poles up with comparative ease and safety. The hardy "voyageur" pushes with incredible perseverance and success quite up to the foot of the falls, and then only carries round some perpendicular ledge, and launches again in "the torrent's smoothness, ere it dash below," to struggle with the boiling rapids above. The Indians say, that the river once ran both ways, one half up and the other down, but, that since the white man came, it all runs down, and now they must laboriously pole their canoes against the stream,

* The Canadians call it *picquer de fond*.

and carry them over numerous portages. In the summer, all stores, the grindstone and the plough of the pioneer, flour, pork, and utensils for the explorer, must be conveyed up the river in batteaux; and many a cargo and many a boatman is lost in these waters. In the winter, however, which is very equable and long, the ice is the great highway, and the loggers' team penetrates to Chesuncook Lake, and still higher up, even two hundred miles above Bangor. Imagine the solitary sled-track running far up into the snowy and evergreen wilderness, hemmed in closely for a hundred miles by the forest, and again stretching straight across the broad surfaces of concealed lakes!

We were soon in the smooth water of the Quakish Lake, and took our turns at rowing and paddling across it. It is a small, irregular, but handsome lake, shut in on all sides by the forest, and showing no traces of man but some low boom in a distant cove, reserved for spring use. The spruce and cedar on its shores, hung with gray lichens, looked at a distance like the ghosts of trees. Ducks were sailing here and there on its surface, and a solitary loon, like a more living wave—a vital spot on the lake's surface—laughed and frolicked, and showed its straight leg, for our amusement. Joe Merry Mountain appeared in the northwest, as if it were looking down on this lake especially; and we had our first, but a partial view of Ktaadn, its summit veiled in clouds, like a dark isthmus in that quarter, connecting the heavens with the earth. After two miles of smooth rowing across this lake, we found ourselves in the river again, which was a continuous rapid for one mile, to the dam, requiring all the strength and skill of our boatmen to pole up it.

This dam is a quite important and expensive work for this country, whither cattle and horses cannot penetrate in the summer, raising the whole river ten feet, and flooding, as they said, some sixty square miles by means of the innumerable lakes with which the river connects. It is a lofty and solid structure, with sloping piers some distance above, made of frames of logs filled with stones, to break the ice.* Here every log pays toll as it passes through the sluices.

We filed into the rude loggers' camp at this place, such as I have described, without ceremony, and the cook, at that moment the sole occupant, at once set about preparing tea for his visitors. His fire-place, which the rain had converted into a mud-puddle, was soon blazing again, and we sat down on the log benches around it to dry us. On the well-flattened, and somewhat faded beds of arbor-vitæ leaves, which stretched on either hand under the eaves behind us, lay an odd leaf of the Bible, some genealogical chapter out of the Old Testament; and, half buried by the leaves, we found Emerson's Address on West India Emancipation, which had been left here formerly by one of our company; and *had made two converts to the Liberty party here*, as I was told; also, an odd number of the Westminster Review, for 1834, and a pamphlet entitled History of the Erection of the Monument on the Grave of Myron Holley. This was the readable, or reading matter, in a lumberer's camp in the Maine woods, thirty miles from a road, which would be given up to the bears in a fortnight. These things were well thumbed and soiled. This gang was headed by one John Morrison, a good specimen of a Yankee; and was necessarily composed

---

* Even the Jesuit missionaries, accustomed to the St. Lawrence and other rivers of Canada, in their first expeditions to the Abnaquiois, speak of rivers *ferrées de rochers*, shod with rocks. See also No. 10 Relations, for 1647, p. 185.

of men not bred to the business of dam-building, but who were Jacks-at-all-trades, handy with the axe, and other simple implements, and well skilled in wood and water craft. We had hot cakes for our supper even here, white as snow-balls, but without butter, and the never-failing sweet cakes, with which we filled our pockets, foreseeing that we should not soon meet with the like again. Such delicate puffballs seemed a singular diet for backwoodsmen. There was also tea without milk, sweetened with molasses. And so, exchanging a word with John Morrison and his gang when we had returned to the shore, and also exchanging our batteau for a better still, we made haste to improve the little daylight that remained. This camp, exactly twenty-nine miles from Mattawamkeag Point, by the way we had come, and about one hundred from Bangor by the river, was the last human habitation of any kind in this direction. Beyond, there was no trail; and the river and lakes, by batteaux and canoes, was considered the only practicable route. We were about thirty miles by the river from the summit of Ktaadn, which was in sight, though not more than twenty, perhaps, in a straight line.

It being about the full of the moon, and a warm and pleasant evening, we decided to row five miles by moonlight to the head of the North Twin Lake, lest the wind should rise on the morrow. After one mile of river, or what the boatmen call "thoroughfare,"—for the river becomes at length only the connecting link between the lakes,—and some slight rapids which had been mostly made smooth water by the dam, we entered the North Twin Lake just after sundown, and steered across for the river "thoroughfare," four miles distant. This is a noble sheet of water, where one may get the impression which a new country and a "lake of the woods" are fitted to create. There was the smoke of no log-hut nor camp of any kind to greet us, still less was any lover of nature or musing traveller watching our batteau from the distant hills; not even the Indian hunter was there, for he rarely climbs them, but hugs the river like ourselves. No face welcomed us but the fine fantastic sprays of free and happy evergreen trees, waving one above another in their ancient home. At first the red clouds hung over the western shore as gorgeously as if over a city, and the lake lay open to the light with even a civilized aspect, as if expecting trade and commerce, and towns and villas. We could distinguish the inlet to the South Twin, which is said to be the larger, where the shore was misty and blue, and it was worth the while to look thus through a narrow opening across the entire expanse of a concealed lake to its own yet more dim and distant shore. The shores rose gently to ranges of low hills covered with forests; and though in fact the most valuable white pine timber, even about this lake, had been culled out, this would never have been suspected by the voyager. The impression, which indeed corresponded with the fact, was as if we were upon a high table land between the States and Canada, the northern side of which is drained by the St. John and Chaudiere, the southern by the Penobscot and Kennebec. There was no bold mountainous shore, as we might have expected, but only isolated hills and mountains rising here and there from the plateau. The country is an archipelago of lakes,—the lake-country of New England. Their levels vary but a few feet, and the boatmen, by short portages, or by none at all, pass easily from one to another. They say that at very high water the Penobscot and the Kennebec flow into each other, or at any rate, that you may lie with your face in the one and your toes in the other.

Even the Penobscot and St. John have been connected by a canal, so that the lumber of the Allagash, instead of going down the St. John, comes down the Penobscot; and the Indian's tradition that the Penobscot once ran both ways for his convenience, is, in one sense, partially realized to-day.

None of our party but McCauslin had been above this lake, so we trusted to him to pilot us, and we could not but confess the importance of a pilot on these waters. While it is river, you will not easily forget which way is up stream; but when you enter a lake, the river is completely lost, and you scan the distant shores in vain to find where it comes in. A stranger is, for the time at least, lost, and must set about a voyage of discovery first of all to find the river. To follow the windings of the shore when the lake is ten miles or even more in length, and of an irregularity which will not soon be mapped, is a wearisome voyage, and will spend his time and his provisions. They tell a story of a gang of experienced woodmen sent to a location on this stream, who were thus lost in the wilderness of lakes. They cut their way through thickets, and carried their baggage and their boats over from lake to lake, sometimes several miles. They carried into Millinocket lake, which is on another stream, and is ten miles square, and contains a hundred islands. They explored its shores thoroughly, and then carried into another and another, and it was a week of toil and anxiety before they found the Penobscot river again, and then their provisions were exhausted, and they were obliged to return.

While Uncle George steered for a small island near the head of the lake, now just visible like a speck on the water, we rowed by turns swiftly over its surface, singing such boat-songs as we could remember. The

shores seemed at an indefinite distance in the moonlight. Occasionally we paused in our singing and
rested on our oars, while we listened to hear if the
wolves howled, for this is a common serenade, and
my companions affirmed that it was the most dismal
and unearthly of sounds; but we heard none this
time.—If we did not *hear*, however, we did *listen*,
not without a reasonable expectation; that at least
I have to tell,—only some utterly uncivilized, big-
throated owl hooted loud and dismally in the drear
and boughy wilderness, plainly not nervous about his
solitary life, nor afraid to hear the echoes of his voice
there. We remembered also that possibly moose were
silently watching us from the distant coves, or some
surly bear, or timid caribou had been startled by our
singing. It was with new emphasis that we sang there
the Canadian boat-song—

> "Row, brothers, row, the stream runs fast,
> The Rapids are near and the daylight's past!"—

which described precisely our own adventure, and
was inspired by the experience of a similar kind of
life,—for the rapids were ever near, and the daylight
long past; the woods on shore looked dim, and many
an Utawas' tide here emptied into the lake.

> "Why should we yet our sail unfurl?
> There is not a breath the blue wave to curl!
> But, when the wind blows off the shore,
> O sweetly we'll rest our weary oar."

> "Utawas' tide! this trembling moon,
> Shall see us float o'er thy surges soon."

At last we glided past the "green isle" which had
been our landmark, all joining in the chorus; as if
by the watery links of rivers and of lakes we were
about to float over unmeasured zones of earth, bound
on unimaginable adventures.

"Saint of this green isle! hear our prayers,
  O grant us cool heavens and favoring airs!"

About nine o'clock we reached the river, and ran
our boat into a natural haven between some rocks,
and drew her out on the sand. This camping ground
McCauslin had been familiar with in his lumbering
days, and he now struck it unerringly in the moonlight, and we heard the sound of the rill which would
supply us with cool water emptying into the lake. The
first business was to make a fire, an operation which
was a little delayed by the wetness of the fuel and the
ground, owing to the heavy showers of the afternoon.
The fire is the main comfort of a camp, whether in
summer or winter, and is about as ample at one
season as at another. It is as well for cheerfulness,
as for warmth and dryness. It forms one side of the
camp; one bright side at any rate. Some were dispersed to fetch in dead trees and boughs, while
Uncle George felled the birches and beeches which
stood convenient, and soon we had a fire some ten
feet long by three or four high, which rapidly dried
the sand before it. This was calculated to burn all
night. We next proceeded to pitch our tent; which
operation was performed by sticking our two spike
poles into the ground in a slanting direction, about
ten feet apart, for rafters, and then drawing our
cotton cloth over them, and tying it down at the ends,
leaving it open in front, shed-fashion. But this evening the wind carried the sparks on to the tent and
burned it. So we hastily drew up the batteau just
within the edge of the woods before the fire, and
propping up one side three or four feet high, spread
the tent on the ground to lie on; and with the corner
of a blanket, or what more or less we could get to put
over us, lay down with our heads and bodies under
the boat, and our feet and legs on the sand toward

the fire. At first we lay awake, talking of our course, and finding ourselves in so convenient a posture for studying the heavens, with the moon and stars shining in our faces, our conversation naturally turned upon astronomy, and we recounted by turns the most interesting discoveries in that science. But at length we composed ourselves seriously to sleep. It was interesting, when awakened at midnight, to watch the grotesque and fiendlike forms and motions of some one of the party, who, not being able to sleep, had got up silently to arouse the fire, and add fresh fuel, for a change; now stealthily lugging a dead tree from out the dark, and heaving it on, now stirring up the embers with his fork, or tiptoeing about to observe the stars, watched, perchance, by half the prostrate party in breathless silence; so much the more intense because they were awake, while each supposed his neighbor sound asleep. Thus aroused, I too brought fresh fuel to the fire, and then rambled along the sandy shore in the moonlight, hoping to meet a moose come down to drink, or else a wolf. The little rill tinkled the louder, and peopled all the wilderness for me; and the glassy smoothness of the sleeping lake, laving the shores of a new world, with the dark, fantastic rocks rising here and there from its surface, made a scene not easily described. It has left such an impression of stern yet gentle wildness on my memory as will not soon be effaced. Not far from midnight, we were one after another awakened by rain falling on our extremities; and as each was made aware of the fact by cold or wet, he drew a long sigh and then drew up his legs, until gradually we had all sidled round from lying at right angles with the boat, till our bodies formed an acute angle with it, and were wholly protected. When next we awoke, the moon and stars were shining again, and there were

signs of dawn in the east. I have been thus particular
in order to convey some idea of a night in the woods.

We had soon launched and loaded our boat, and,
leaving our fire blazing, were off again before breakfast. The lumberers rarely trouble themselves to put
out their fires, such is the dampness of the primitive
forest; and this is one cause, no doubt, of the frequent fires in Maine, of which we hear so much on
smoky days in Massachusetts. The forests are held
cheap after the white pine has been culled out; and
the explorers and hunters pray for rain only to clear
the atmosphere of smoke. The woods were so wet to-
day, however, that there was no danger of our fire
spreading. After poling up half a mile of river, or
thoroughfare, we rowed a mile across the foot of
Pamadumcook Lake, which is the name given on the
map to this whole chain of lakes, as if there was but
one, though they are, in each instance, distinctly
separated by a reach of the river, with its narrow and
rocky channel and its rapids. This lake, which is one
of the largest, stretched north-west ten miles, to hills
and mountains in the distance. McCauslin pointed to
some distant and, as yet, inaccessible forests of white
pine, on the sides of a mountain in that direction.
The Joe Merry Lakes, which lay between us and
Moosehead, on the west, were recently, if they are not
still, "surrounded by some of the best timbered land
in the state." By another thoroughfare we passed
into Deep Cove, a part of the same lake, which makes
up two miles, toward the north-east, and rowing two
miles across this, by another short thoroughfare,
entered Ambejijis Lake.

At the entrance to a lake we sometimes observed
what is technically called "fencing stuff," or the un-
hewn timbers of which booms are formed, either
secured together in the water, or laid up on the rocks

and lashed to trees, for spring use. But it was always startling to discover so plain a trail of civilized man there. I remember that I was strangely affected when we were returning, by the sight of a ring-bolt well drilled into a rock, and fastened with lead, at the head of this solitary Ambejijis Lake.

It was easy to see, that driving logs must be an exciting as well as arduous and dangerous business. All winter long the logger goes on piling up the trees which he has trimmed and hauled in some dry ravine at the head of a stream, and then in the spring he stands on the bank, and whistles for Rain and Thaw, ready to wring the perspiration out of his shirt to swell the tide, till suddenly, with a whoop and halloo from him, shutting his eyes, as if to bid farewell to the existing state of things, a fair proportion of his winter's work goes scrambling down the country, followed by his faithful dogs, Thaw, and Rain, and Freshet, and Wind, the whole pack in full cry, toward the Orono Mills. Every log is marked with the owner's name, cut in the sapwood with an axe, or bored with an auger, so deep as not to be worn off in the driving, and yet not so as to injure the timber; and it requires considerable ingenuity to invent new and simple marks where there are so many owners. They have quite an alphabet of their own, which only the practised can read. One of my companions read off from his memorandum book some marks of his own logs, among which there were crosses, belts, crow's feet, girdles, &c., as Y—girdle—crow-foot, and various other devices. When the logs have run the gauntlet of innumerable rapids and falls, each on its own account, with more or less jamming and bruising, those bearing various owners' marks being mixed up together, since all must take advantage of the same freshet, they are collected together at the heads of the lakes, and surrounded by a boom fence of floating logs, to prevent their being dispersed by the wind, and are thus towed all together, like a flock of sheep, across the lake, where there is no current, by a windlass, or boom-head, such as we sometimes saw standing on an island or head-land, and, if circumstances permit, with the aid of sails and oars. Sometimes, notwithstanding, the logs are dispersed over many miles of lake surface in a few hours by winds and freshets, and thrown up on distant shores, where the driver can pick up only one or two at a time, and return with them to the thoroughfare; and, before he gets his flock well through Ambejijis or Pamadumcook, he makes many a wet and uncomfortable camp on the shore. He must be able to navigate a log as if it were a canoe, and be as indifferent to cold and wet as a muskrat. He uses a few efficient tools,— a lever commonly of rock-maple, six or seven feet long, with a stout spike in it, strongly ferruled on, and a long spike-pole, with a screw at the end of the spike to make it hold. The boys along shore learn to walk on floating logs as city boys on sidewalks. Sometimes the logs are thrown up on rocks in such positions as to be irrecoverable but by another freshet as high, or they jam together at rapids and falls, and accumulate in vast piles, which the driver must start at the risk of his life. Such is the lumber business, which depends on many accidents, as the early freezing of the rivers, that the teams may get up in season, a sufficient freshet in the spring, to fetch the logs down, and many others.* I quote Michaux on Lum-

* "A steady current or pitch of water is preferable to one either rising or diminishing; as, when rising rapidly, the water at the middle of the river is considerably higher than at the shores,—so much so as to be distinctly perceived by the eye of a spectator on the banks, presenting an appearance like a turnpike road. The lumber, therefore, is always

bering on the Kennebec, then the source of the best white-pine lumber carried to England. "The persons engaged in this branch of industry are generally emigrants from New Hampshire. . . . . In the summer they unite in small companies, and traverse these vast solitudes in every direction, to ascertain the places in which the pines abound. After cutting the grass and converting it into hay for the nourishment of the cattle to be employed in their labor, they return home. In the beginning of the winter they enter the forests again, establish themselves in huts covered with the bark of the canoe-birch, or the arborvitæ; and, though the cold is so intense that the mercury sometimes remains for several weeks from 40° to 50° [Fahr.] below the point of congelation, they persevere, with unabated courage, in their work." According to Springer, the company consists of choppers, swampers,—who make roads,—barker and loader, teamster, and cook. "When the trees are felled, they cut them into logs from fourteen to eighteen feet long, and, by means of their cattle, which they employ with great dexterity, drag them to the river, and after stamping on them a mark of property, roll them on its frozen bosom. At the breaking of the ice, in the spring, they float down with the current. . . . . The logs that are not sawn the first year," adds Michaux, "are attacked by large worms, which form holes about two lines in diameter, in every direction; but, if stripped of their bark, they will remain uninjured for thirty years."

Ambejijis, this quiet Sunday morning, struck me as the most beautiful lake we had seen. It is said to be one of the deepest. We had the fairest view of Joe

---

sure to incline from the centre of the channel toward either shore."—Springer.

Merry, Double Top, and Ktaadn, from its surface. The summit of the latter had a singularly flat table-land appearance, like a short highway, where a demigod might be let down to take a turn or two in an afternoon, to settle his dinner. We rowed a mile and a half to near the head of the lake, and, pushing through a field of lily pads, landed, to cook our breakfast by the side of a large rock, known to McCauslin. Our breakfast consisted of tea, with hard bread and pork, and fried salmon, which we ate with forks neatly whittled from alder-twigs, which grew there, off strips of birch-bark for plates. The tea was black tea, without milk to color or sugar to sweeten it, and two tin dippers were our tea cups. This beverage is as indispensable to the loggers as to any gossiping old women in the land, and they, no doubt, derive great comfort from it. Here was the site of an old loggers' camp, remembered by McCauslin, now overgrown with weeds and bushes. In the midst of a dense underwood, we noticed a whole brick, on a rock, in a small run, clean, and red, and square, as in a brick-yard, which had been brought thus far formerly for tamping. Some of us afterward regretted that we had not carried this on with us to the top of the mountain, to be left there for our mark. It would certainly have been a simple evidence of civilized man. McCauslin said, that large wooden crosses made of oak, still sound, were sometimes found standing in this wilderness, which were set up by the first Catholic missionaries who came through to the Kennebec.

In the next nine miles, which were the extent of our voyage, and which it took us the rest of the day to get over, we rowed across several small lakes, poled up numerous rapids and thoroughfares, and carried over four portages. I will give the names and distances, for the benefit of future tourists. First, after leaving Ambejijis Lake, we had a quarter of a mile of rapids to the portage, or carry of ninety rods around Ambejijis Falls; then a mile and a half through Passamagamet Lake, which is narrow and river-like, to the falls of the same name—Ambejijis stream coming in on the right; then two miles through Katepskonegan Lake to the portage of ninety rods around Katepskonegan Falls, which name signifies "carrying place"—Passamagamet stream coming in on the left; then three miles through Pockwockomus Lake, a slight expansion of the river, to the portage of forty rods around the falls of the same name—Katepskonegan stream coming in on the left; then three quarters of a mile through Aboljacarmegus Lake, similar to the last, to the portage of forty rods around the falls of the same name; then half a mile of rapid water to the Sowadnehunk dead-water, and the Aboljacknagesic stream.

This is generally the order of names as you ascend the river:—First, the lake, or, if there is no expansion, the dead-water; then the falls; then the stream emptying into the lake or river above, all of the same name. First we came to Passamagamet Lake, then to Passamagamet Falls, then to Passamagamet stream, emptying in. This order and identity of names, it will be perceived, is quite philosophical, since the dead-water or lake is always at least partially produced by the stream emptying in above; and the first fall below, which is the inlet of that lake, and where that tributary water makes its first plunge, also naturally bears the same name.

At the portage around Ambejijis Falls, I observed a pork-barrel on the shore, with a hole eight or nine inches square cut in one side, which was set against an upright rock; but the bears, without turning or upsetting the barrel, had gnawed a hole in the opposite side, which looked exactly like an enormous rat hole, big enough to put their heads in; and at the bottom of the barrel were still left a few mangled and slabbered slices of pork. It is usual for the lumberers to leave such supplies as they cannot conveniently carry along with them at carries or camps, to which the next comers do not scruple to help themselves, they being the property commonly not of an individual, but a company, who can afford to deal liberally.

I will describe particularly how we got over some of these portages and rapids, in order that the reader may get an idea of the boatman's life. At Ambejijis Falls, for instance, there was the roughest path imaginable cut through the woods; at first up hill at an angle of nearly forty-five degrees, over rocks and logs without end. This was the manner of the portage:— We first carried over our baggage, and deposited it on the shore at the other end; then returning to the batteau, we dragged it up the hill by the painter, and onward, with frequent pauses, over half the portage. But this was a bungling way, and would soon have worn out the boat. Commonly, three men walk over with a batteau weighing from three to five or six hundred pounds on their heads and shoulders, the tallest standing under the middle of the boat, which is turned over, and one at each end, or else there are two at the bows. More cannot well take hold at once. But this requires some practice, as well as strength, and is in any case extremely laborious, and wearing to the constitution, to follow. We were, on the whole, rather an invalid party, and could render our boatmen but little assistance. Our two men at length took the batteau upon their shoulders, and, while two of us steadied it, to prevent it from

rocking and wearing into their shoulders, on which
they placed their hats folded, walked bravely over the
remaining distance, with two or three pauses. In the
same manner they accomplished the other portages.
With this crushing weight they must climb and stum-
ble along over fallen trees and slippery rocks of all
sizes, where those who walked by the sides were continually brushed off, such was the narrowness of the
path. But we were fortunate not to have to cut our
path in the first place. Before we launched our boat,
we scraped the bottom smooth again with our knives,
where it had rubbed on the rocks, to save friction.

To avoid the difficulties of the portage, our men
determined to "warp up" the Passamagamet Falls: so
while the rest walked over the portage with the baggage, I remained in the batteau, to assist in warping
up. We were soon in the midst of the rapids, which
were more swift and tumultuous than any we had
poled up, and had turned to the side of the stream for
the purpose of warping, when the boatmen, who felt
some pride in their skill, and were ambitious to do
something more than usual, for my benefit, as I sur-
mised, took one more view of the rapids, or rather the
falls; and in answer to one's question, whether we
couldn't get up there, the other answered that he
guessed he'd try it: so we pushed again into the
midst of the stream, and began to struggle with the
current. I sat in the middle of the boat, to trim it,
moving slightly to the right or left as it grazed a rock.
With an uncertain and wavering motion we wound
and bolted our way up, until the bow was actually
raised two feet above the stern at the steepest pitch;
and then, when everything depended upon his exer-
tions, the bowman's pole snapped in two; but before
he had time to take the spare one, which I reached
him, he had saved himself with the fragment upon

a rock; and so we got up by a hair's breadth; and Uncle George exclaimed, that that was never done before; and he had not tried it, if he had not known whom he had got in the bow—nor he in the bow, if he had not known him in the stern. At this place there was a regular portage cut through the woods; and our boatmen had never known a batteau to ascend the falls. As near as I can remember, there was a perpendicular fall here, at the worst place, of the whole Penobscot River, two or three feet at least. I could not sufficiently admire the skill and coolness with which they performed this feat, never speaking to each other. The bowman, not looking behind, but knowing exactly what the other is about, works as if he worked alone; now sounding in vain for a bottom in fifteen feet of water, while the boat falls back several rods, held straight only with the greatest skill and exertion; or, while the sternman obstinately holds his ground, like a turtle, the bowman springs from side to side with wonderful suppleness and dexterity, scanning the rapids and the rocks with a thousand eyes; and now, having got a bite at last, with a lusty shove which makes his pole bend and quiver, and the whole boat tremble, he gains a few feet upon the river. To add to the danger, the poles are liable at any time to be caught between the rocks, and wrenched out of their hands, leaving them at the mercy of the rapids—the rocks, as it were, lying in wait, like so many alligators, to catch them in their teeth, and jerk them from your hands, before you have stolen an effectual shove against their palates. The pole is set close to the boat, and the prow is made to overshoot, and just turn the corners of the rocks, in the very teeth of the rapids. Nothing but the length and lightness, and the slight draught of the batteau, enables them to make any headway. The bowman must quickly choose his course; there is no time to deliberate. Frequently the boat is shoved between rocks where both sides touch, and the waters on either hand are a perfect maelstrom.

Half a mile above this, two of us tried our hands at poling up a slight rapid; and we were just surmounting the last difficulty, when an unlucky rock confounded our calculations; and while the batteau was sweeping round irrecoverably amid the whirlpool, we were obliged to resign the poles to more skilful hands.

Katepskonegan is one of the shallowest and weediest of the lakes, and looked as if it might abound in pickerel. The falls of the same name, where we stopped to dine, are considerable and quite picturesque. Here Uncle George had seen trout caught by the barrel-full; but they would not rise to our bait at this hour. Half way over this carry, thus far in the Maine wilderness on its way to the Provinces, we noticed a large flaming Oak Hall hand-bill, about two feet long, wrapped round the trunk of a pine, from which the bark had been stript, and to which it was fast glued by the pitch. This should be recorded among the advantages of this mode of advertising, that so, possibly, even the bears and wolves, moose, deer, otter, and beaver, not to mention the Indian, may learn where they can fit themselves according to the latest fashion, or, at least, recover some of their own lost garments. We christened this the Oak Hall carry.

The forenoon was as serene and placid on this wild stream in the woods as we are wont to imagine that Sunday in summer usually is in Massachusetts. We were occasionally startled by the scream of a bald-eagle, sailing over the stream in front of our batteau; or of the fish-hawks, on whom he levies his contributions. There were, at intervals, small meadows of a few acres on the sides of the stream, waving with uncut grass, which attracted the attention of our boatmen, who regretted that they were not nearer to their clearings, and calculated how many stacks they might cut. Two or three men sometimes spend the summer by themselves, cutting the grass in these meadows, to sell to the loggers in the winter, since it will fetch a higher price on the spot than in any market in the state. On a small isle, covered with this kind of rush, or cut grass, on which we landed, to consult about our further course, we noticed the recent track of a moose, a large, roundish hole, in the soft wet ground, evincing the great size and weight of the animal that made it. They are fond of the water, and visit all these island-meadows, swimming as easily from island to island as they make their way through the thickets on land. Now and then we passed what McCauslin called a pokelogan, an Indian term for what the drivers might have reason to call a poke-logs-in, an inlet that leads nowhere: if you get in you have got to get out again the same way. These, and the frequent "run-rounds," which come into the river again, would embarrass an inexperienced voyager not a little.

The carry around Pockwockomus Falls was exceedingly rough and rocky, the batteau having to be lifted directly from the water up four or five feet on to a rock, and launched again down a similar bank. The rocks on this portage were covered with the dents made by the spikes in the lumberers' boots while staggering over under the weight of their batteaux; and you could see where the surface of some large rocks on which they had rested their batteaux was worn quite smooth with use. As it was, we had carried over but half the usual portage at this place for this stage of the water, and launched our boat in the smooth wave just curving to the fall, prepared to struggle with the most violent rapid we had to encounter. The rest of the party walked over the remainder of the portage, while I remained with the boatmen to assist in warping up. One had to hold the boat while the others got in to prevent it from going over the falls. When we had pushed up the rapids as far as possible, keeping close to the shore, Tom seized the painter and leaped out upon a rock just visible in the water, but he lost his footing notwithstanding his spiked boots, and was instantly amid the rapids; but recovering himself by good luck, and reaching another rock, he passed the painter to me, who had followed him, and took his place again in the bows. Leaping from rock to rock in the shoal water close to the shore, and now and then getting a bite with the rope round an upright one, I held the boat while one reset his pole, and then all three forced it upward against any rapid. This was "warping up." When a part of us walked round at such a place, we generally took the precaution to take out the most valuable part of the baggage, for fear of being swamped.

As we poled up a swift rapid for half a mile above Aboljacarmegus Falls, some of the party read their own marks on the huge logs which lay piled up high and dry on the rocks on either hand, the relics probably of a jam which had taken place here in the Great Freshet in the spring. Many of these would have to wait for another great freshet, perchance, if they lasted so long, before they could be got off. It was singular enough to meet with property of theirs which they had never seen, and where they had never been before, thus detained by freshets and rocks when on its way to them. Methinks that must be where all my property lies, cast up on the rocks on some distant and unexplored stream, and waiting for an unheard-of freshet to fetch it down. O make haste, ye gods, with your winds and rains, and start the jam before it rots!

The last half mile carried us to the Sowadnehunk dead-water, so called from the stream of the same name, signifying "running between mountains," an important tributary which comes in a mile above. Here we decided to camp, about twenty miles from the Dam, at the mouth of Murch Brook and the Abol-jacknagesic, mountain streams, broad off from Ktaadn, and about a dozen miles from its summit; having made fifteen miles this day.

We had been told by McCauslin that we should here find trout enough: so while some prepared the camp, the rest fell to fishing. Seizing the birch poles which some party of Indians or white hunters had left on the shore, and baiting our hooks with pork, and with trout, as soon as they were caught, we cast our lines into the mouth of the Aboljacknagesic, a clear, swift, shallow stream, which came in from Ktaadn. Instantly a shoal of white chivin, (leucisci pulchelli,) silvery roaches, cousin-trout, or what not, large and small, prowling thereabouts, fell upon our bait, and one after another were landed amidst the bushes. Anon their cousins, the true trout, took their turn, and alternately the speckled trout, and the silvery roaches, swallowed the bait as fast as we could throw in; and the finest specimens of both that I have ever seen, the largest one weighing three pounds, were heaved upon the shore, though at first in vain, to wriggle down into the water again, for we stood in the boat; but soon we learned to remedy this evil: for one, who had lost his hook, stood on shore to catch them as they fell in a perfect shower

around him—sometimes, wet and slippery, full in his
face and bosom, as his arms were outstretched to
receive them. While yet alive, before their tints had
faded, they glistened like the fairest flowers, the
product of primitive rivers; and he could hardly trust
his senses, as he stood over them, that these jewels
should have swum away in that Aboljacknagesic
water for so long, so many dark ages;—these bright
fluviatile flowers, seen of Indians only, made beautiful, the Lord only knows why, to swim there! I
could understand better, for this, the truth of mythology, the fables of Proteus, and all those beautiful
sea-monsters,—how all history, indeed, put to a ter-
restrial use, is mere history; but put to a celestial, is
mythology always.

But there is the rough voice of Uncle George, who
commands at the frying-pan, to send over what
you've got, and then you may stay till morning. The
pork sizzles, and cries for fish. Luckily for the foolish
race, and this particularly foolish generation of trout,
the night shut down at last, not a little deepened by
the dark side of Ktaadn, which, like a permanent
shadow, reared itself from the eastern bank. Lescarbot, writing in 1609, tells us that the Sieur Champ-
doré, who, with one of the people of the Sieur de
Monts, ascended some fifty leagues up the St. John
in 1608, found the fish so plenty, "qu'en mettant
la chaudière sur le feu ils en avoient pris suffisam-
ment pour eux dîsner avant que l'eau fust chaude."
Their descendants here are no less numerous. So we
accompanied Tom into the woods, to cut cedar-twigs
for our bed. While he went ahead with the axe, and
lopped off the smallest twigs of the flat-leaved cedar,
the arbor-vitæ of the gardens, we gathered them up,
and returned with them to the boat, until it was
loaded. Our bed was made with as much care and

skill as a roof is shingled; beginning at the foot, and laying the twig end of the cedar upward, we advanced to the head, a course at a time, thus successively covering the stub-ends, and producing a soft and level bed. For us six it was about ten feet long by six in breadth. This time we lay under our tent, having pitched it more prudently with reference to the wind and the flame, and the usual huge fire blazed in front. Supper was eaten off a large log, which some freshet had thrown up. This night we had a dish of arbor-vitæ, or cedar tea, which the lumberer sometimes uses when other herbs fail,—

> "A quart of *arbor*-vitæ,
> To make him strong and mighty,"—

but I had no wish to repeat the experiment. It had too medicinal a taste for my palate. There was the skeleton of a moose here, whose bones some Indian hunters had picked on this very spot.

In the night I dreamed of trout-fishing; and, when at length I awoke, it seemed a fable, that this painted fish swam there so near my couch, and rose to our hooks the last evening—and I doubted if I had not dreamed it all. So I arose before dawn to test its truth, while my companions were still sleeping. There stood Ktaadn with distinct and cloudless outline in the moonlight; and the rippling of the rapids was the only sound to break the stillness. Standing on the shore, I once more cast my line into the stream, and found the dream to be real, and the fable true. The speckled trout and silvery roach, like flying fish, sped swiftly through the moonlight air, describing bright arcs on the dark side of Ktaadn, until moonlight, now fading into daylight, brought satiety to my mind, and the minds of my companions, who had joined me.

By six o'clock, having mounted our packs and a good blanket full of trout, ready dressed, and swung up such baggage and provision as we wished to leave behind upon the tops of saplings, to be out of the reach of bears, we started for the summit of the mountain, distant, as Uncle George said the boatmen called it, about four miles, but as I judged, and as it proved, nearer fourteen. He had never been any nearer the mountain than this, and there was not the slightest trace of man to guide us further in this direction. At first, pushing a few rods up the Aboljacknagesic, or "open-land stream," we fastened our batteau to a tree, and travelled up the north side, through burnt lands, now partially overgrown with young aspens, and other shrubbery; but soon, re-crossing this stream, where it was about fifty or sixty feet wide, upon a jam of logs and rocks, and you could cross it by this means almost anywhere, we struck at once for the highest peak, over a mile or more of comparatively open land still, very grad-ually ascending the while. Here it fell to my lot, as the oldest mountain-climber, to take the lead: so scanning the woody side of the mountain, which lay still at an indefinite distance, stretched out some seven or eight miles in length before us, we deter-mined to steer directly for the base of the highest peak, leaving a large slide, by which, as I have since learned, some of our predecessors ascended, on our left. This course would lead us parallel to a dark seam in the forest, which marked the bed of a torrent, and over a slight spur, which extended southward from the main mountain, from whose bare summit we could get an outlook over the country, and climb directly up the peak, which would then be close at hand. Seen from this point, a bare ridge at the ex-tremity of the open land, Ktaadn presented a different aspect from any mountain I have seen, there being a greater proportion of naked rock, rising abruptly from the forest; and we looked up at this blue barrier as if it were some fragment of a wall which anciently bounded the earth in that direction. Setting the compass for a north-east course, which was the bearing of the southern base of the highest peak, we were soon buried in the woods.

We soon began to meet with traces of bears and moose, and those of rabbits were everywhere visible. The tracks of moose, more or less recent, to speak literally covered every square rod on the sides of the mountain; and these animals are probably more numerous there now than ever before, being driven into this wilderness from all sides by the settlements. The track of a full-grown moose is like that of a cow, or larger, and of the young, like that of a calf. Sometimes we found ourselves travelling in faint paths, which they had made, like cow-paths in the woods, only far more indistinct, being rather openings, affording imperfect vistas through the dense underwood, than trodden paths; and everywhere the twigs had been browsed by them, clipt as smoothly as if by a knife. The bark of trees was stript up by them to the height of eight or nine feet, in long narrow strips, an inch wide, still showing the distinct marks of their teeth. We expected nothing less than to meet a herd of them every moment, and our Nimrod held his shooting-iron in readiness; but we did not go out of our way to look for them, and, though numerous, they are so wary, that the unskilful hunter might range the forest a long time before he could get sight of one. They are sometimes dangerous to encounter, and will not turn out for the hunter, but furiously rush upon him, and trample him to death, unless he is lucky enough to avoid them by dodging round a tree. The largest are nearly as large as a horse, and weigh sometimes one thousand pounds; and it is said that they can step over a five-foot gate in their ordinary walk. They are described as exceedingly awkward-looking animals, with their long legs and short bodies, making a ludicrous figure when in full run, but making great headway nevertheless. It seemed a mystery to us how they could thread these woods, which it required all our suppleness to accomplish, climbing, stooping, and winding, alternately. They are said to drop their long and branching horns, which usually spread five or six feet, on their backs, and make their way easily by the weight of their bodies. Our boatmen said, but I know not with how much truth, that their horns are apt to be gnawed away by vermin while they sleep. Their flesh, which is more like beef than venison, is common in Bangor market.

We had proceeded on thus seven or eight miles, till about noon, with frequent pauses to refresh the weary ones, crossing a considerable mountain stream, which we conjectured to be Murch Brook, at whose mouth we had camped, all the time in woods, without having once seen the summit, and rising very gradually, when the boatmen, beginning to despair a little, and fearing that we were leaving the mountain on one side of us, for they had not entire faith in the compass, McCauslin climbed a tree, from the top of which he could see the peak, when it appeared that we had not swerved from a right line, the compass down below still ranging with his arm, which pointed to the summit. By the side of a cool mountain rill, amid the woods, where the water began to partake of the purity and transparency of the air, we stopped to cook some of our fishes, which we had brought thus far in order to save our hard bread and pork, in the use of which we had put ourselves on short allowance. We soon had a fire blazing, and stood around it, under the damp and sombre forest of firs and birches, each with a sharpened stick, three or four feet in length, upon which he had spitted his trout, or roach, previously well gashed and salted, our sticks radiating like the spokes of a wheel from one centre, and each crowding his particular fish into the most desirable exposure, not with the truest regard always to his neighbor's rights. Thus we regaled ourselves, drinking meanwhile at the spring, till one man's pack, at least, was considerably lightened, when we again took up our line of march.

At length we reached an elevation sufficiently bare to afford a view of the summit, still distant and blue, almost as if retreating from us. A torrent, which proved to be the same we had crossed, was seen tumbling down in front, literally from out of the clouds. But this glimpse at our whereabouts was soon lost, and we were buried in the woods again. The wood was chiefly yellow birch, spruce, fir, mountain-ash, or round-wood, as the Maine people call it, and moose-wood. It was the worst kind of travelling; sometimes like the densest scrub-oak patches with us. The cornel, or bunch-berries, were very abundant, as well as Solomon's seal and moose-berries. Blue-berries were distributed along our whole route; and in one place the bushes were drooping with the weight of the fruit, still as fresh as ever. It was the seventh of September. Such patches afforded a grateful repast, and served to bait the tired party forward. When any lagged behind, the cry of "blue-berries" was most effectual to bring them up. Even at this elevation we passed through a moose-yard, formed by a large flat rock, four or five rods square, where they tread down the snow in winter. At length, fearing that if we held the direct course to the summit, we should not find any water near our camping-ground, we gradually swerved to the west, till, at four o'clock, we struck again the torrent which I have mentioned, and here, in view of the summit, the weary party decided to camp that night.

While my companions were seeking a suitable spot for this purpose, I improved the little daylight that was left in climbing the mountain alone. We were in a deep and narrow ravine, sloping up to the clouds, at an angle of nearly forty-five degrees, and hemmed in by walls of rock, which were at first covered with low trees, then with impenetrable thickets of scraggy birches and spruce-trees, and with moss, but at last bare of all vegetation but lichens, and almost continually draped in clouds. Following up the course of the torrent which occupied this—and I mean to lay some emphasis on this word *up*—pulling myself up by the side of perpendicular falls of twenty or thirty feet, by the roots of firs and birches, and then, perhaps, walking a level rod or two in the thin stream, for it took up the whole road, ascending by huge steps, as it were, a giant's stairway, down which a river flowed, I had soon cleared the trees, and paused on the successive shelves, to look back over the country. The torrent was from fifteen to thirty feet wide, without a tributary, and seemingly not diminishing in breadth as I advanced; but still it came rushing and roaring down, with a copious tide, over and amidst masses of bare rock, from the very clouds, as though a water-spout had just burst over the mountain. Leaving this at last, I began to work my way, scarcely less arduous than Satan's anciently through Chaos, up the nearest, though not the highest peak. At first scrambling on all fours over the tops of ancient black spruce-trees, (*Abies nigra*,) old as the flood, from two to ten or twelve feet in height, their tops flat and spreading, and their foliage blue and nipt with cold, as if for centuries they had ceased growing upward against the bleak sky, the solid cold. I walked some good rods erect upon the tops of these trees, which were overgrown with moss and mountain-cranberries. It seemed that in the course of time they had filled up the intervals between the huge rocks, and the cold wind had uniformly levelled all over. Here the principle of vegetation was hard put to it. There was apparently a belt of this kind running quite round the mountain, though, perhaps, nowhere so remarkable as here. Once, slumping through, I looked down ten feet, into a dark and cavernous region, and saw the stem of a spruce, on whose top I stood, as on a mass of coarse basket-work, fully nine inches in diameter at the ground. These holes were bears' dens, and the bears were even then at home. This was the sort of garden I made my way *over*, for an eighth of a mile, at the risk, it is true, of treading on some of the plants, not seeing any path *through* it—certainly the most treacherous and porous country I ever travelled.

> "——nigh founder'd, on he fares,
> Treading the crude consistence, half on foot,
> Half flying."

But nothing could exceed the toughness of the twigs, —not one snapped under my weight, for they had slowly grown. Having slumped, scrambled, rolled, bounced, and walked, by turns, over this scraggy country, I arrived upon a side-hill, or rather side-mountain, where rocks, gray, silent rocks, were the flocks and herds that pastured, chewing a rocky cud at sunset. They looked at me with hard gray eyes, without a bleat or a low. This brought me to the skirt of a cloud, and bounded my walk that night. But I had already seen that Maine country when I turned about, waving, flowing, rippling, down below.

When I returned to my companions, they had selected a camping-ground on the torrent's edge, and were resting on the ground; one was on the sick list, rolled in a blanket, on a damp shelf of rock. It was a savage and dreary scenery enough; so wildly rough, that they looked long to find a level and open space for the tent. We could not well camp higher, for want of fuel; and the trees here seemed so evergreen and sappy, that we almost doubted if they would acknowledge the influence of fire; but fire prevailed at last, and blazed here, too, like a good citizen of the world. Even at this height we met with frequent traces of moose, as well as of bears. As here was no cedar, we made our bed of coarser feathered spruce; but at any rate the feathers were plucked from the live tree. It was, perhaps, even a more grand and desolate place for a night's lodging than the summit would have been, being in the neighborhood of those wild trees, and of the torrent. Some more aerial and finer-spirited winds rushed and roared through the ravine all night, from time to time arousing our fire, and dispersing the embers about. It was as if we lay in the very nest of a young whirlwind. At midnight, one of my bedfellows, being startled in his dreams by the sudden blazing up to its top of a fir-tree, whose green boughs were dried by the heat, sprang up, with a cry, from his bed, thinking the world on fire, and drew the whole camp after him.

In the morning, after whetting our appetite on some raw pork, a wafer of hard bread, and a dipper of condensed cloud or water-spout, we all together began to make our way up the falls, which I have described; this time choosing the right hand, or highest peak, which was not the one I had approached before. But soon my companions were lost to my sight behind the mountain ridge in my rear, which still seemed ever retreating before me, and I climbed alone over huge rocks, loosely poised, a mile or more, still edging toward the clouds—for though the day was clear elsewhere, the summit was concealed by mist. The mountain seemed a vast aggregation of loose rocks, as if sometime it had rained rocks, and they lay as they fell on the mountain sides, nowhere fairly at rest, but leaning on each other, all rocking-stones, with cavities between, but scarcely any soil or smoother shelf. They were the raw materials of a planet dropped from an unseen quarry, which the vast chemistry of nature would anon work up, or work down, into the smiling and verdant plains and valleys of earth. This was an undone extremity of the globe; as in lignite we see coal in the process of formation.

At length I entered within the skirts of the cloud which seemed forever drifting over the summit, and yet would never be gone, but was generated out of that pure air as fast as it flowed away; and when, a quarter of a mile further, I reached the summit of the ridge, which those who have seen in clearer weather say is about five miles long, and contains a thousand acres of table-land, I was deep within the hostile ranks of clouds, and all objects were obscured by them. Now the wind would blow me out a yard of clear sunlight, wherein I stood; then a gray, dawning light was all it could accomplish, the cloud-line ever rising and falling with the wind's intensity. Sometimes it seemed as if the summit would be cleared in a few moments and smile in sunshine: but what was gained on one side was lost on another. It was like sitting in a chimney and waiting for the smoke to blow away. It was, in fact, a cloud-factory,—these were the cloud-works, and the wind turned them off done from the cool, bare rocks. Occasionally, when the windy columns broke in to me, I caught sight of a dark, damp crag to the right or left; the mist driving ceaselessly between it and me. It reminded me of the creations of the old epic and dramatic poets, of Atlas, Vulcan, the Cyclops, and Prometheus. Such was Caucasus and the rock where Prometheus was bound. Æschylus had no doubt visited such scenery as this. It was vast, Titanic, and such as man never inhabits. Some part of the beholder, even some vital part, seems to escape through the loose grating of his ribs as he ascends. He is more lone than you can imagine. There is less of substantial thought and fair understanding in him, than in the plains where men inhabit. His reason is dispersed and shadowy, more thin and subtile like the air. Vast, Titanic, inhuman Nature has got him at disadvantage, caught him alone, and pilfers him of some of his divine faculty. She does not smile on him as in the plains. She seems to say sternly, why came ye here before your time? This ground is not prepared for you. Is it not enough that I smile in the valleys? I have never made this soil for thy feet, this air for thy breathing, these rocks for thy neighbors. I cannot pity nor fondle thee here, but forever relentlessly drive thee hence to where I *am* kind. Why seek me where I have not called thee, and then complain because you find me but a stepmother? Shouldst thou freeze or starve, or shudder thy life away, here is no shrine, nor altar, nor any access to my ear.

> "Chaos and ancient Night, I come no spy
> With purpose to explore or to disturb
> The secrets of your realm, but * * *
> * * * * * * * as my way
> Lies through your spacious empire up to light."

The tops of mountains are among the unfinished parts of the globe, whither it is a slight insult to the gods to climb and pry into their secrets, and try their effect on our humanity. Only daring and insolent men, perchance, go there. Simple races, as savages, do not climb mountains—their tops are sacred and mysterious tracts never visited by them. Pomola is always angry with those who climb to the summit of Ktaadn.

According to Jackson, who in his capacity of geological surveyor of the state, has accurately measured it—the altitude of Ktaadn is 5,300 feet, or a little more than one mile above the level of the sea—and he adds: "It is then evidently the highest point in the State of Maine, and is the most abrupt granite mountain in New England." The peculiarities of that spacious table-land on which I was standing, as well as the remarkable semicircular precipice or basin on the eastern side, were all concealed by the mist. I had brought my whole pack to the top, not knowing but I should have to make my descent to the river, and possibly to the settled portion of the state alone and by some other route, and wishing to have a complete outfit with me. But at length, fearing that my companions would be anxious to reach the river before night, and knowing that the clouds might rest on the mountain for days, I was compelled to descend. Occasionally, as I came down, the wind would blow me a vista open through which I could see the country eastward, boundless forests, and lakes, and streams, gleaming in the sun, some of them emptying into the East Branch. There were also new mountains in sight in that direction. Now and then some small bird of the sparrow family would flit away before me, unable to command its course, like a fragment of the gray rock blown off by the wind.

I found my companions where I had left them, on the side of the peak, gathering the mountain cranberries, which filled every crevice between the rocks, together with blue berries, which had a spicier flavor the higher up they grew, but were not the less agreeable to our palates. When the country is settled and roads are made, these cranberries will perhaps become an article of commerce. From this elevation, just on the skirts of the clouds, we could overlook the country west and south for a hundred miles. There it was, the State of Maine, which we had seen on the map, but not much like that. Immeasurable forest for the sun to shine on, that eastern *stuff* we hear of in Massachusetts. No clearing, no house. It did not look as if a solitary traveller had cut so much as a walking-stick there. Countless lakes,—Moosehead in the southwest, forty miles long by ten wide, like a gleaming silver platter at the end of the table; Chesuncook, eighteen long by three wide, without an island; Millinocket, on the south, with its hundred islands; and a hundred others without a name; and mountains also, whose names, for the most part, are known only to the Indians. The forest looked like a firm grass sward, and the effect of these lakes in its midst has been well compared by one who has since visited this same spot, to that of a "mirror broken into a thousand fragments, and wildly scattered over the grass, reflecting the full blaze of the sun." It was a large farm for somebody, when cleared. According to the Gazetteer, which was printed before the boundary question was settled, this single Penobscot county in which we were, was larger than the whole State of Vermont, with its fourteen counties; and this was only a part of the wild lands of Maine. We are concerned now, however, about natural, not political limits. We were about eighty miles as the bird flies from Bangor, or one hundred and fifteen as we had ridden, and walked, and paddled. We had to console ourselves with the reflection that this view was probably as good as that from the peak, as far as it went, and what were a mountain without its attendant clouds and mists? Like ourselves, neither Bailey nor Jackson had obtained a clear view from the summit.

Setting out on our return to the river, still at an early hour in the day, we decided to follow the course of the torrent, which we supposed to be Murch Brook, as long as it would not lead us too far out of our way. We thus travelled about four miles in the very torrent itself, continually crossing and recrossing it, leaping from rock to rock, and jumping with the stream down falls of seven or eight feet, or sometimes sliding down on our backs in a thin sheet of water. This ravine had been the scene of an extraordinary freshet in the spring, apparently accompanied by a slide from the mountain. It must have been filled with a stream of stones and water, at least twenty feet above the present level of the torrent. For a rod or two on either side of its channel, the trees were barked and splintered up to their tops, the birches bent over, twisted, and sometimes finely split like a stable-broom; some a foot in diameter snapped off, and whole clumps of trees bent over with the weight of rocks piled on them. In one place we noticed a rock two or three feet in diameter, lodged nearly twenty feet high in the crotch of a tree. For the whole four miles, we saw but one rill emptying in, and the volume of water did not seem to be increased from the first. We travelled thus very rapidly with a downward impetus, and grew remarkably expert at leaping from rock to rock, for leap we must, and leap we did, whether there was any rock at the right distance or not. It was a pleasant picture when the foremost turned about and looked up the winding ravine, walled in with rocks and the green forest, to see at intervals of a rod or two, a red-shirted or green-jacketed mountaineer against the white torrent, leaping down the channel with his pack on his back, or pausing upon a convenient rock in the midst of the torrent to mend a rent in his clothes, or unstrap the dipper at his belt to take a draught of the water. At one place we were startled by seeing, on a little sandy shelf by the side of the stream, the fresh print of a man's foot, and for a moment realized how Robinson Crusoe felt in a similar case; but at last we remembered that we had struck this stream on our way up, though we could not have told where, and one had descended into the ravine for a drink. The cool air above, and the continual bathing of our bodies in mountain water, alternate foot, sitz, douche, and plunge baths, made this walk exceedingly refreshing, and we had travelled only a mile or two after leaving the torrent, before every thread of our clothes was as dry as usual, owing perhaps to a peculiar quality in the atmosphere.

After leaving the torrent, being in doubt about our course, Tom threw down his pack at the foot of the loftiest spruce tree at hand, and shinned up the bare trunk some twenty feet, and then climbed through the green tower, lost to our sight, until he held the topmost spray in his hand.* McCauslin, in his younger

---

* "The spruce-tree," says Springer in '51, "is generally selected, principally for the superior facilities which its numerous limbs afford the climber. To gain the first limbs of this tree, which are from twenty to forty feet from the ground, a smaller tree is undercut and lodged against it, clambering up which the top of the spruce is reached. In some cases, when a very elevated position is desired, the spruce-tree is lodged against the trunk of some lofty pine, up which we ascend to a height twice that of the surrounding forest."

days, had marched through the wilderness with a
body of troops, under General Somebody, and with
one other man did all the scouting and spying service. The General's word was: "Throw down the top
of that tree," and there was no tree in the Maine
woods so high that it did not lose its top in such a
case. I have heard a story of two men being lost
once in these woods, nearer to the settlements than
this, who climbed the loftiest pine they could find,
some six feet in diameter at the ground, from whose
top they discovered a solitary clearing and its smoke.
When at this height, some two hundred feet from the
ground, one of them became dizzy, and fainted in
his companion's arms, and the latter had to accomplish the descent with him, alternately fainting
and reviving, as best he could. To Tom we cried,
where away does the summit bear? where the burnt
lands? The last he could only conjecture; he descried, however, a little meadow and pond, lying
probably in our course, which we concluded to steer
for. On reaching this secluded meadow, we found
fresh tracks of moose on the shore of the pond, and
the water was still unsettled as if they had fled before us. A little further, in a dense thicket, we seemed
to be still on their trail. It was a small meadow, of
a few acres, on the mountain side, concealed by the
forest, and perhaps never seen by a white man before,
where one would think that the moose might browse
and bathe, and rest in peace. Pursuing this course,
we soon reached the open land, which went sloping
down some miles toward the Penobscot.

Perhaps I most fully realized that this was pri-
meval, untamed, and forever untameable *Nature*, or
whatever else men call it, while coming down this

To indicate the direction of pines, he throws down a
branch, and a man at the ground takes the bearing.

part of the mountain. We were passing over "Burnt Lands," burnt by lightning, perchance, though they showed no recent marks of fire, hardly so much as a charred stump, but looked rather like a natural pasture for the moose and deer, exceedingly wild and desolate, with occasional strips of timber crossing them, and low poplars springing up, and patches of blueberries here and there. I found myself traversing them familiarly, like some pasture run to waste, or partially reclaimed by man; but when I reflected what man, what brother or sister or kinsman of our race made it and claimed it, I expected the proprietor to rise up and dispute my passage. It is difficult to conceive of a region uninhabited by man. We habitually presume his presence and influence everywhere. And yet we have not seen pure Nature, unless we have seen her thus vast, and drear, and inhuman, though in the midst of cities. Nature was here something savage and awful, though beautiful. I looked with awe at the ground I trod on, to see what the Powers had made there, the form and fashion and material of their work. This was that Earth of which we have heard, made out of Chaos and Old Night. Here was no man's garden, but the unhandselled globe. It was not lawn, nor pasture, nor mead, nor woodland, nor lea, nor arable, nor waste-land. It was the fresh and natural surface of the planet Earth, as it was made forever and ever,—to be the dwelling of man, we say,—so Nature made it, and man may use it if he can. Man was not to be associated with it. It was Matter, vast, terrific,—not his Mother Earth that we have heard of, not for him to tread on, or be buried in,—no, it were being too familiar even to let his bones lie there—the home this of Necessity and Fate. There was there felt the presence of a force not bound to be kind to man. It was a place for heathenism and superstitious rites,—to be inhabited by men nearer of kin to the rocks and to wild animals than we. We walked over it with a certain awe, stopping from time to time to pick the blueberries which grew there, and had a smart and spicy taste. Perchance where *our* wild pines stand, and leaves lie on their forest floor in Concord, there were once reapers, and husbandmen planted grain; but here not even the surface had been scarred by man, but it was a specimen of what God saw fit to make this world. What is it to be admitted to a museum, to see a myriad of particular things, compared with being shown some star's surface, some hard matter in its home! I stand in awe of my body, this matter to which I am bound has become so strange to me. I fear not spirits, ghosts, of which I am one,—*that* my body might,—but I fear bodies, I tremble to meet them. What is this Titan that has possession of me? Talk of mysteries!—Think of our life in nature,— daily to be shown matter, to come in contact with it, —rocks, trees, wind on our cheeks! the *solid* earth! the *actual* world! the *common sense! Contact! Contact! Who* are we? *where* are we?

Ere long we recognized some rocks and other features in the landscape which we had purposely impressed on our memories, and quickening our pace, by two o'clock we reached the batteau.* Here we had expected to dine on trout, but in this glaring sunlight they were slow to take the bait, so we were compelled to make the most of the crumbs of our hard bread and our pork, which were both nearly exhausted. Meanwhile we deliberated whether we should go up the river a mile farther to Gibson's

* The bears had not touched things on our possessions. They sometimes tear a batteau to pieces for the sake of the tar with which it is besmeared.

clearing on the Sowadnehunk, where there was a deserted log hut, in order to get a half-inch auger, to mend one of our spike-poles with. There were young spruce trees enough around us, and we had a spare spike, but nothing to make a hole with. But as it was uncertain whether we should find any tools left there, we patched up the broken pole as well as we could for the downward voyage, in which there would be but little use for it. Moreover, we were unwilling to lose any time in this expedition, lest the wind should rise before we reached the larger lakes, and detain us, for a moderate wind produces quite a sea on these waters, in which a batteau will not live for a moment; and on one occasion McCauslin had been delayed a week at the head of the North Twin, which is only four miles across. We were nearly out of provisions, and ill prepared in this respect for what might possibly prove a week's journey round by the shore, fording innumerable streams, and threading a trackless forest, should any accident happen to our boat.

It was with regret that we turned our backs on Chesuncook, which McCauslin had formerly logged on, and the Allagash lakes. There were still longer rapids and portages above; among the last the Rippogenus Portage, which he described as the most difficult on the river, and three miles long. The whole length of the Penobscot is two hundred and seventy-five miles, and we are still nearly one hundred miles from its source. Hodge, the assistant State Geologist, passed up this river in 1837, and by a portage of only one mile and three-quarters, crossed over into the Allagash, and so went down that into the St. John, and up the Madawaska to the Grand Portage across to the St. Lawrence. His is the only account that I know, of an expedition through to Canada in this direction. He thus describes his first sight of the latter river, which, to compare small things with great, is like Balboa's first sight of the Pacific from the mountains of the Isthmus of Darien. "When we first came in sight of the St. Lawrence," he says, "from the top of a high hill, the view was most striking, and much more interesting to me from having been shut up in the woods for the two previous months. Directly before us lay the broad river, extending across nine or ten miles, its surface broken by a few islands and reefs; and two ships riding at anchor near the shore. Beyond, extended ranges of uncultivated hills, parallel with the river. The sun was just going down behind them, and gilding the whole scene with its parting rays."

About four o'clock the same afternoon, we commenced our return voyage, which would require but little if any poling. In shooting rapids, the boatmen use large and broad paddles, instead of poles, to guide the boat with. Though we glided so swiftly and often smoothly down, where it had cost us no slight effort to get up, our present voyage was attended with far more danger: for if we once fairly struck one of the thousand rocks by which we were surrounded, the boat would be swamped in an instant. When a boat is swamped under these circumstances, the boatmen commonly find no difficulty in keeping afloat at first, for the current keeps both them and their cargo up for a long way down the stream; and if they can swim, they have only to work their way gradually to the shore. The greatest danger is of being caught in an eddy behind some larger rock, where the water rushes up stream faster than elsewhere it does down, and being carried round and round under the surface till they are drowned. McCauslin pointed out some rocks which had been the scene of a fatal accident of this kind. Sometimes the body is not thrown out for several hours. He himself had performed such a circuit once, only his legs being visible to his companions; but he was fortunately thrown out in season to recover his breath.* In shooting the rapids, the boatman has this problem to solve: to choose a circuitous and safe course amid a thousand sunken rocks, scattered over a quarter or half a mile, at the same time that he is moving steadily on at the rate of fifteen miles an hour. Stop he cannot; the only question is, where will he go? The bow-man chooses the course with all his eyes about him, striking broad off with his paddle, and drawing the boat by main force into her course. The stern-man faithfully follows the bow.

We were soon at the Aboljacarmegus Falls. Anxious to avoid the delay as well as the labor of the portage here, our boatmen went forward first to reconnoitre, and concluded to let the batteau down the falls, carrying the baggage only over the portage. Jumping from rock to rock until nearly in the middle of the stream, we were ready to receive the boat and let her down over the first fall, some six or seven feet perpendicular. The boatmen stand upon the edge of a shelf of rock where the fall is perhaps nine or ten feet perpendicular, in from one to two feet of rapid water, one on each side of the boat, and let it slide gently over, till the bow is run out ten or twelve feet in the air; then letting it drop squarely, while one holds the painter, the other leaps in, and his com-

---

* I cut this from a newspaper. "On the 11th (instant?) [May, '49], on Rappogenes Falls, Mr. John Delantee, of Orono, Me., was drowned while running logs. He was a citizen of Orono, and was twenty-six years of age. His companions found his body, enclosed it in bark, and buried it in the solemn woods."

panion following, they are whirled down the rapids
to a new fall, or to smooth water. In a very few minutes they had accomplished a passage in safety,
which would be as fool-hardy for the unskilful to
attempt as the descent of Niagara itself. It seemed as
if it needed only a little familiarity, and a little more
skill, to navigate down such falls as Niagara itself
with safety. At any rate, I should not despair of such
men in the rapids above Table-Rock, until I saw them
actually go over the falls, so cool, so collected, so
fertile in resources are they. One might have thought
that these were falls, and that falls were not to be
waded through with impunity like a mud-puddle.
There was really danger of their losing their sublim-
ity in losing their power to harm us. Familiarity
breeds contempt. The boatman pauses, perchance, on
some shelf beneath a table-rock under the fall, standing in some cove of back-water two feet deep, and
you hear his rough voice come up through the spray,
coolly giving directions how to launch the boat this
time.

Having carried round Pockwockomus Falls, our
oars soon brought us to the Katepskonegan, or Oak
Hall carry, where we decided to camp half way over,
leaving our batteau to be carried over in the morning
on fresh shoulders. One shoulder of each of the boatmen showed a red spot as large as one's hand, worn
by the batteau on this expedition; and this shoulder,
as it did all the work, was perceptibly lower than its
fellow, from long service. Such toil soon wears out
the strongest constitution. The drivers are accustomed to work in the cold water in the spring, rarely
ever dry; and if one falls in all over, he rarely
changes his clothes till night, if then, even. One who
takes this precaution is called by a particular nick-
name, or is turned off. None can lead this life who

are not almost amphibious. McCauslin said soberly, what is at any rate a good story to tell, that he had seen where six men were wholly under water at once, at a jam, with their shoulders to handspikes. If the log did not start, then they had to put out their heads to breathe. The driver works as long as he can see, from dark to dark, and at night has not time to eat his supper and dry his clothes fairly, before he is asleep on his cedar bed. We lay that night on the very bed made by such a party, stretching our tent over the poles which were still standing, but reshingling the damp and faded bed with fresh leaves.

In the morning, we carried our boat over and launched it, making haste lest the wind should rise. The boatmen ran down Passamagamet, and, soon after, Ambejijis Falls, while we walked round with the baggage. We made a hasty breakfast at the head of Ambejijis lake, on the remainder of our pork, and were soon rowing across its smooth surface again, under a pleasant sky, the mountain being now clear of clouds in the northeast. Taking turns at the oars, we shot rapidly across Deep Cove, the Foot of Pamadumcook, and the North Twin, at the rate of six miles an hour, the wind not being high enough to disturb us, and reached the Dam at noon. The boatmen went through one of the log sluices in the batteau, where the fall was ten feet at the bottom, and took us in below. Here was the longest rapid in our voyage, and perhaps the running this was as dangerous and arduous a task as any. Shooting down sometimes at the rate, as we judged, of fifteen miles an hour, if we struck a rock, we were split from end to end in an instant. Now like a bait bobbing for some river monster amid the eddies, now darting to this side of the stream, now to that, gliding swift and smooth near to our destruction, or striking broad off with the paddle and drawing the boat to right or left with all our might, in order to avoid a rock. I suppose that it was like running the rapids of the Sault de Ste. Marie, at the outlet of Lake Superior, and our boatmen probably displayed no less dexterity than the Indians there do. We soon ran through this mile, and floated in Quakish lake.

After such a voyage, the troubled and angry waters, which once had seemed terrible and not to be trifled with, appeared tamed and subdued; they had been bearded and worried in their channels, pricked and whipped into submission with the spike-pole and paddle, gone through and through with impunity, and all their spirit and their danger taken out of them, and the most swollen and impetuous rivers seemed but playthings henceforth. I began, at length, to understand the boatman's familiarity with and contempt for the rapids. "Those Fowler boys," said Mrs. McCauslin, "are perfect ducks for the water." They had run down to Lincoln, according to her, thirty or forty miles, in a batteau, in the night, for a doctor, when it was so dark that they could not see a rod before them, and the river was swollen so as to be almost a continuous rapid, so that the doctor *cried*, when they brought him up by daylight, "Why, Tom, how did you see to steer?" "We didn't steer much,—only kept her straight." And yet they met with no accident. It is true, the more difficult rapids are higher up than this.

When we reached the Millinocket opposite to Tom's house, and were waiting for his folks to set us over, for we had left our batteau above the Grand Falls, we discovered two canoes with two men in each, turning up this stream from Shad Pond, one keeping the opposite side of a small island before us, while the other approached the side where we were standing, examining the banks carefully for muskrats as they came along. The last proved to be Louis Neptune and his companion, now at last on their way up to Chesuncook after moose; but they were so disguised that we hardly knew them. At a little distance, they might have been taken for Quakers, with their broad-brimmed hats, and overcoats with broad capes, the spoils of Bangor, seeking a settlement in this Sylvania,—or, nearer at hand, for fashionable gentlemen, the morning after a spree. Met face to face, these Indians in their native woods looked like the sinister and slouching fellows whom you meet picking up strings and paper in the streets of a city. There is, in fact, a remarkable and unexpected resemblance between the degraded savage and the lowest classes in a great city. The one is no more a child of nature than the other. In the progress of degradation, the distinction of races is soon lost. Neptune at first was only anxious to know what we "kill," seeing some partridges in the hands of one of the party, but we had assumed too much anger to permit of a reply. We thought Indians had some honor before. But—"Me been sick. O, me unwell now. You make bargain, then me go." They had in fact been delayed so long by a drunken frolic at the Five Islands, and they had not yet recovered from its effects. They had some young musquash in their canoes, which they dug out of the banks with a hoe for food, not for their skins, for musquash are their principal food on these expeditions. So they went on up the Millinocket, and we kept down the bank of the Penobscot, after recruiting ourselves with a draught of Tom's beer, leaving Tom at his home.

Thus a man shall lead his life away here on the edge of the wilderness, on Indian Millinocket stream, in a new world, far in the dark of a continent, and have a flute to play at evening here, while his strains echo to the stars, amid the howling of wolves; shall live, as it were, in the primitive age of the world, a primitive man. Yet he shall spend a sunny day, and in this century be my contemporary; perchance shall read some scattered leaves of literature, and sometimes talk with me. Why read history then if the ages and the generations are now? He lives three thousand years deep into time, an age not yet described by poets. Can you well go further back in history than this? Ay! ay!—for there turns up but now into the mouth of Millinocket stream a still more ancient and primitive man, whose history is not brought down even to the former. In a bark vessel sewn with the roots of the spruce, with horn-beam paddles he dips his way along. He is but dim and misty to me, obscured by the æons that lie between the bark canoe and the batteau. He builds no house of logs, but a wigwam of skins. He eats no hot-bread and sweet-cake, but musquash and moose-meat and the fat of bears. He glides up the Millinocket and is lost to my sight, as a more distant and misty cloud is seen flitting by behind a nearer, and is lost in space. So he goes about his destiny, the red face of man.

After having passed the night and buttered our boots for the last time at Uncle George's, whose dogs almost devoured him for joy at his return, we kept on down the river the next day about eight miles on foot, and then took a batteau with a man to pole it to Mattawamkeag, ten more. At the middle of that very night, to make a swift conclusion to a long story, we dropped our buggy over the half-finished bridge at Oldtown, where we heard the confused din and clink of a hundred saws which never rest, and at six o'clock the next morning one of the party was steaming his way to Massachusetts.

What is most striking in the Maine wilderness is, the continuousness of the forest, with fewer open intervals or glades than you had imagined. Except the few burnt lands, the narrow intervals on the rivers, the bare tops of the high mountains, and the lakes and streams, the forest is uninterrupted. It is even more grim and wild than you had anticipated, a damp and intricate wilderness, in the spring everywhere wet and miry. The aspect of the country indeed is universally stern and savage, excepting the distant views of the forest from hills, and the lake prospects, which are mild and civilizing in a degree. The lakes are something which you are unprepared for: they lie up so high exposed to the light, and the forest is diminished to a fine fringe on their edges, with here and there a blue mountain, like amethyst jewels set around some jewel of the first water,—so anterior, so superior to all the changes that are to take place on their shores, even now civil and refined, and fair, as they can ever be. These are not the artificial forests of an English king—a royal preserve merely. Here prevail no forest laws, but those of nature. The aborigines have never been dispossessed, nor nature disforested.

It is a country full of evergreen trees, of mossy silver birches and watery maples, the ground dotted with insipid, small red berries, and strewn with damp and moss-grown rocks—a country diversified with innumerable lakes and rapid streams, peopled with trout and various species of *leucisci*, with salmon, shad and pickerel, and other fishes; the forest resounding at rare intervals with the note of the chicadee, the blue-jay, and the woodpecker, the scream of the fish-hawk and the eagle, the laugh of the loon, and the whistle of ducks along the solitary streams; and at night, with the hooting of owls and howling of wolves; in summer, swarming with myriads of black flies and mosquitoes, more formidable than wolves to the white man. Such is the home of the moose, the bear, the caribou, the wolf, the beaver, and the Indian. Who shall describe the inexpressible tenderness and immortal life of the grim forest, where Nature, though it be mid-winter, is ever in her spring, where the moss-grown and decaying trees are not old, but seem to enjoy a perpetual youth; and blissful, innocent Nature, like a serene infant, is too happy to make a noise, except by a few tinkling, lisping birds and trickling rills?

What a place to live, what a place to die and be buried in! There certainly men would live forever, and laugh at death and the grave. There they could have no such thoughts as are associated with the village graveyard,—that make a grave out of one of those moist evergreen hummocks!

> Die and be buried who will,
> I mean to live here still;
> My nature grows ever more young
> The primitive pines among.

I am reminded by my journey how exceedingly new this country still is. You have only to travel for a few days into the interior and back parts even of many of the old states, to come to that very America which the Northmen, and Cabot, and Gosnold, and Smith and Raleigh visited. If Columbus was the first to discover the islands, Americus Vespucius, and Cabot, and the Puritans, and we their descendants, have discovered only the shores of America. While the republic has already acquired a history worldwide, America is still unsettled and unexplored. Like the English in New Holland, we live only on the shores of a continent even yet, and hardly know where the rivers come from which float our navy.

The very timber and boards, and shingles, of which our houses are made, grew but yesterday in a wilderness where the Indian still hunts and the moose runs wild. New-York has her wilderness within her own borders; and though the sailors of Europe are familiar with the soundings of her Hudson, and Fulton long since invented the steamboat on its waters, an Indian is still necessary to guide her scientific men to its head-waters in the Adirondac country.

Have we even so much as discovered and settled the shores? Let a man travel on foot along the coast, from the Passamaquoddy to the Sabine, or to the Rio Bravo, or to wherever the end is now, if he is swift enough to overtake it, faithfully following the windings of every inlet and of every cape, and stepping to the music of the surf—with a desolate fishing-town once a week, and a city's port once a month to cheer him, and putting up at the light-houses, when there are any, and tell me if it looks like a discovered and settled country, and not rather, for the most part, like a desolate island, and No-man's Land.

We have advanced by leaps to the Pacific, and left many a lesser Oregon and California unexplored behind us. Though the railroad and the telegraph have been established on the shores of Maine, the Indian still looks out from her interior mountains over all these to the sea. There stands the city of Bangor, fifty miles up the Penobscot, at the head of navigation for vessels of the largest class, the principal lumber depot on this continent, with a population of twelve thousand, like a star on the edge of night, still hewing at the forests of which it is built, already overflowing with the luxuries and refinement of Europe, and sending its vessels to Spain, to England, and to the West Indies for its groceries,—and yet only a few axe-men have gone "up river" into the howling wilderness which feeds it. The bear and deer are still found within its limits; and the moose, as he swims the Penobscot, is entangled amid its shipping and taken by foreign sailors in its harbor. Twelve miles in the rear, twelve miles of railroad, are Orono and the Indian Island, the home of the Penobscot tribe, and then commence the batteau and the canoe, and the military road; and, sixty miles above, the country is virtually unmapped and unexplored, and there still waves the virgin forest of the New World.

Chesuncook.

AT 5 P.M. September 13th 1853, I left Boston in the steamer for Bangor by the outside course. It was a warm and still night, warmer probably on the water than on the land, and the sea was as smooth as a small lake in summer, merely rippled. The passengers went singing on the deck, as in a parlor, till ten o'clock. We passed a vessel on her beam ends on a rock, just outside the islands, and some of us thought that she was the "rapt ship" which ran

> "on her side so low
> That she drank water, and her keel plowed air,"

not considering that there was no wind, and that she was under bare poles. Now we have left the islands behind and are off Nahant. We behold those features which the discoverers saw, apparently unchanged. Now we see the Cape Ann lights, and now pass near a small village-like fleet of mackerel fishers at anchor, probably off Gloucester. They salute us with a shout from their low decks; but I understand their "Good evening" to mean "Don't run against me Sir." From the wonders of the deep we go below to yet deeper sleep. And then the absurdity of being waked up in the night by a man who wants the job of blacking your boots! It is more inevitable than seasickness, and may have something to do with it. It is like the ducking you get on crossing the line the first time. I trusted that these old customs were abolished. They might with the same propriety insist on blacking your face. I heard of one man who complained that somebody had stolen his boots in the night, and when he found them he wanted to know what they had done to them—they had spoiled them—

he never put that stuff on them; and the blacker narrowly escaped paying damages.

Anxious to get out of the whale's belly, I rose early, and joined some old salts, who were smoking by a dim light on a sheltered part of the deck. We were just getting into the river. They knew all about it of course. I was proud to find that I had stood the voyage so well, and was not in the least digested. We brushed up and watched the first signs of dawn through an open port. But the day seemed to hang fire. We inquired the time; none of my companions had a chronometer. At length, an African prince rushed by, observing, "Twelve o'clock, gentlemen!" and blew out the light. It was moon-rise. So I slunk down into his bowels again.

The first land we make is Monhegan Island, before dawn, and next St. George's Islands, seeing two or three lights. Whitehead with its bare rocks and funereal bell, is interesting. Next I remember that the Camden Hills attracted my eyes, and afterward the hills about Frankfort. We reached Bangor about noon.

When I arrived, my companion that was to be had gone up river, and engaged an Indian, Joe Aitteon, a son of the Governor, to go with us to Chesuncook Lake. Joe had conducted two white men a-moose-hunting in the same direction the year before. He arrived by cars at Bangor that evening, with his canoe and a companion, Sabattis Solomon, who was going to leave Bangor the following Monday with Joe's father, by way of the Penobscot, and join Joe in moose-hunting at Chesuncook, when we had done with him. They took supper at my friend's house and lodged in his barn, saying that they should fare worse than that in the woods. They only made Watch bark a little, when they came to the door in the night for water, for he does not like Indians.

The next morning Joe and his canoe were put on board the stage for Moosehead Lake, sixty and odd miles distant, an hour before we started in an open wagon. We carried hard bread, pork, smoked beef, tea, sugar, &c., &c., seemingly enough for a regiment; the sight of which brought together reminded me by what ignoble means we had maintained our ground hitherto. We went by the Avenue Road, which is quite straight and very good, north-westward toward Moosehead Lake, through more than a dozen flourishing towns, with almost every one its academy; not one of which, however, is on my general atlas published, alas! in 1824; so much are they before the age, or I behind it. The earth must have been considerably lighter to the shoulders of General Atlas then. It rained all this day and till the middle of the next forenoon, concealing the landscape almost entirely; but we had hardly got out of the streets of Bangor before I began to be exhilarated by the sight of the wild fir and spruce tops, and those of other primitive evergreens, peering through the mist in the horizon. It was like the sight and odor of cake to a schoolboy. He who rides and keeps the beaten track studies the fences chiefly. Near Bangor, the fenceposts, on account of the frost's heaving them in the clayey soil, were not planted in the ground, but mortised into a transverse horizontal beam lying on the surface. Afterwards the prevailing fences were log ones, with sometimes a Virginia fence, or else rails slanted over crossed stakes, and these zigzagged or played leap-frog all the way to the lake, keeping just ahead of us. After getting out of the Penobscot Valley the country was unexpectedly level, or consisted of very even and equal swells, for twenty or thirty miles, never rising above the general level, but affording, it is said, a very good prospect in clear weather, with frequent

views of Katadn; straight roads and long hills. The
houses were far apart, commonly small and of one
story, but framed. There was very little land under
cultivation, yet the forest did not often border the
road. The stumps were frequently as high as one's
head, showing the depth of the snows. The white hay-
caps drawn over small stacks of beans or corn in the
fields, on account of the rain, were a novel sight to
me. We saw large flocks of pigeons, and several times
came within a rod or two of partridges in the road.
My companion said, that in one journey out of Bangor he and his son had shot sixty partridges from his
buggy. The mountain ash was now very handsome,
as also the wayfarer's tree or hobble bush, with its
ripe purple berries mixed with red. The Canada
thistle, an introduced plant, was the prevailing weed
all the way to the lake, the road-side in many places
and fields not long cleared being densely filled with
it as with a crop to the exclusion of everything else.
There were also whole fields full of ferns, now rusty
and withering, which in older countries are commonly confined to wet ground. There were very few
flowers, even allowing for the lateness of the season.
It chanced that I saw no asters in bloom along the
road for fifty miles, though they were so abundant
then in Massachusetts, except in one place one or
two of the aster acuminatus, and no golden-rods till
within twenty miles of Monson, where I saw one
three-ribbed one. There were many late buttercups,
however, and the two fire-weeds, erechthites and
epilobium, commonly where there had been a burning, and at last the pearly everlasting. I noticed occasionally very long troughs which supplied the road
with water, and my companion said that three dollars annually were granted by the state, to one man
in each school district, who provided and maintained

a suitable water-trough by the road-side, for the use of travellers; a piece of intelligence as refreshing to me as the water itself. That legislature did not sit in vain. It was an oriental act, which made me wish that I was still further down east—another Maine law, which I hope we may get in Massachusetts. That state is banishing bar-rooms from its highways, and conducting the mountain springs thither.

The country was first decidedly mountainous in Garland, Sangerville, and onwards, twenty-five or thirty miles from Bangor. At Sangerville, where we stopped at mid-afternoon to warm and dry ourselves, the landlord told us that he had found a wilderness where we found him. At a fork in the road between Abbot and Monson, about twenty miles from Moose-head Lake, I saw a guidepost surmounted by a pair of moose horns, spreading four or five feet, with the word Monson painted on one blade, and the name of some other town on the other. They are sometimes used for ornamental hat trees, together with deers' horns, in front entries; but, after the experience which I shall relate, I trust that I shall have a better excuse for killing a moose, than that I may hang my hat on his horns. We reached Monson, fifty miles from Bangor, and thirteen from the lake, after dark.

At four o'clock the next morning, in the dark, and still in the rain, we pursued our journey. Close to the academy in this town they have erected a sort of gallows for the pupils to practise on. I thought that they might as well hang at once all who need to go through such exercises in so new a country, where there is nothing to hinder their living an out-door life. Better omit Blair, and take the air. The country about the south end of the lake is quite mountainous, and the road began to feel the effects of it. There is one hill which, it is calculated, it takes twenty-five minutes to ascend. In many places the road was in that condition called *repaired*, having just been whittled into the required semi-cylindrical form with the shovel and scraper, with all the softest inequalities in the middle, like a hog's back with the bristles up, and Jehu was expected to keep astride of the spine. As you looked off each side of the bare sphere into the horizon the ditches were awful to behold—a vast hollowness like that between Saturn and his ring. At a tavern hereabouts the hostler greeted our horse as an old acquaintance, though he did not remember the driver. He said that he had taken care of that little mare for a short time, a year or two before, at the Mount Kineo house, and thought that she was not in as good condition as then. Every man to his trade. I am not acquainted with a single horse in the world, not even the one that kicked me.

Already we had thought that we saw Moosehead Lake from a hill-top, where an extensive fog filled the distant lowlands, but we were mistaken. It was not till we were within a mile or two of its south end that we got our first view of it—a suitably wild looking sheet of water, sprinkled with small low islands, which were covered with shaggy spruce and other wild wood; seen over the infant port of Greenville, with mountains on each side and far in the north, and a steamer's smoke-pipe rising above a roof. A pair of moose horns ornamented a corner of the public house where we left our horse, and a few rods distant lay the small steamer Moosehead, Captain King. There was no village nor any summer road any further in this direction, but a winter road, that is, one passable only when deep snow covers its inequalities, from Greenville up the east side of the lake to Lily Bay, about twelve miles.

I was here first introduced to Joe. He had ridden

all the way on the outside of the stage the day before, in the rain, giving way to ladies, and was well wetted. As it still rained, he asked if we were going to "put it through". He was a good looking Indian, twenty-four years old, apparently of unmixed blood, short and stout, with a broad face and reddish complexion, and eyes, methinks, narrower and more turned up at the outer corners than ours, answering to the description of his race. Beside his under clothing, he wore a red flannel shirt, woolen pants, and a black Kossuth hat, the ordinary dress of the lumberman, and to a considerable extent, of the Penobscot Indian. When afterward he had occasion to take off his shoes and stockings, I was struck with the smallness of his feet. He had worked a good deal as a lumberman, and appeared to identify himself with that class. He was the only one of the party who possessed an India-rubber jacket. The top strip or edge of his canoe was worn nearly through by friction on the stage.

At eight o'clock, the steamer with her bell and whistle, scaring the moose, summoned us on board. She was a well appointed little boat, commanded by a gentlemanly captain, with patent life-seats, and metallic life-boat, and dinner on board if you will. She is chiefly used by lumberers for the transportation of themselves, their boats and supplies, but also by hunters and tourists. There was another steamer named Amphitrite laid up close by; but, apparently, her name was not more trite than her hull. There were also two or three large sail-boats in port. These beginnings of commerce on a lake in the wilderness are very interesting; these larger white birds that come to keep company with the gulls. There were but few passengers and not one female among them; a St. Francis Indian, with his canoe and moose-hides, two explorers for lumber, three men who landed at

Sandbar Island, and a gentleman who lives on Deer Island eleven miles up the lake, and owns also Sugar Island, between which and the former the steamer runs; these, I think, were all beside ourselves. In the saloon was some kind of musical instrument, cherubim or seraphim, to soothe the angry waves, and there, very properly, was tacked up the map of the Public Lands of Maine and Massachusetts, a copy of which I had in my pocket.

The heavy rain confining us to the saloon awhile, I discoursed with the proprietor of Sugar Island on the condition of the world in Old Testament times. But at length, leaving this subject as fresh as we found it, he told me that he had lived about this lake twenty or thirty years, and yet had not been to the head of it for twenty-one years. He faces the other way. The explorers had a fine new birch on board, larger than ours, in which they had come up the Piscataquis from Howland, and they had had several messes of trout already. They were going to the neighborhood of Eagle and Chamberlain Lakes, or the headwaters of the St. John, and offered to keep us company as far as we went. The lake to-day was rougher than I found the ocean either going or returning, and Joe remarked that it would swamp his birch. Off Lily Bay it is a dozen miles wide, but it is much broken by islands. The scenery is not merely wild, but varied and interesting; mountains were seen further or nearer on all sides but the north-west, their summits now lost in the clouds, but Mount Kineo is the principal feature of the lake, and more exclusively belongs to it. After leaving Greenville at the foot, which is the nucleus of a town some eight or ten years old, you see but three or four houses for the whole length of the lake, or about forty miles, three of them the public houses at which the steamer is advertised to stop, and the shore is an unbroken wilderness. The prevailing wood seemed to be spruce, fir, birch, and rock maple. You could easily distinguish the hard wood from the soft, or "black growth", as it is called, at a great distance, the former being smooth, round-topped and light green, with a bowery and cultivated look.

Mount Kineo, at which the boat touched, is a peninsula with a narrow neck, about mid-way the lake on the east side. The celebrated precipice is on the east or land side of this, and is so high and perpendicular that you can jump from the top many hundred feet into the water which makes up behind the point. A man on board told us that an anchor had been sunk ninety fathoms at its base before reaching bottom! Probably it will be discovered ere-long that some Indian maiden jumped off it for love once, for true love never could have found a path more to its mind. We passed quite close to the rock here, since it is a very bold shore, and I observed marks of a rise of four or five feet on it. The St. Francis Indian expected to take in his boy here, but he was not at the landing. The father's sharp eyes, however, detected a canoe with his boy in it far away under the mountain, though no one else could see it. "Where is the canoe?" asked the captain, "I don't see it;" but he held on nevertheless, and by and by it hove in sight.

We reached the head of the lake about noon. The weather had in the meanwhile cleared up, though the mountains were still capped with clouds. Seen from this point Mount Kineo, and two other allied mountains ranging with it north-easterly, presented a very strong family likeness, as if all cast in one mould. The steamer here approached a long pier projecting from the northern wilderness and built of some of its logs—and whistled, where not a cabin nor a mortal was to be seen. The shore was quite low, with flat rocks on it, overhung with black ash, arborvitae &c., which, at first, did not look as if they cared a whistle for us. There was not a single cabman to cry "coach", or inveigle us to the United States Hotel. At length a Mr. Hinckley, who has a camp at the other end of the carry, appeared with a truck drawn by an ox and a horse over a rude log railway through the woods. The next thing was to get our canoe and effects over the carry from this lake, one of the heads of the Kennebec, into the Penobscot River. This railway from the lake to the river occupied the middle of a clearing two or three rods wide and perfectly straight through the forest. We walked across while our baggage was drawn behind. My companion went ahead to be ready for partridges, while I followed, looking at the plants.

This was an interesting botanical locality for one coming from the south to commence with, for many plants which are rather rare, and one or two which are not found at all, in the eastern part of Massachusetts, grew abundantly between the rails; as Labrador tea, Kalmia glauca, Canada blueberry, which was still in fruit and a second time in bloom, Clintonia and Linnaea borealis, which last (?) a lumberer called *moxon*, creeping snowberry, painted trillium, large-flowered bellwort &c., &c. I fancied that the aster radula, diplopappus umbellatus, solidago lanceolata, red trumpet weed, and many others, which were conspicuously in bloom on the shore of the lake and on the carry, had a peculiarly wild and primitive look there. The spruce and fir trees crowded to the track on each side to welcome us, the arborvitae with its changing leaves prompted us to make haste, and the sight of the canoe birch gave us spirits to do so. Sometimes an evergreen just fallen lay across the track with its rich burden of cones, looking, still, fuller of life than our trees in the most favorable positions. You did not expect to find such *spruce* trees in the wild woods, but they evidently attend to their toilets each morning even there. Through such a front yard did we enter that wilderness.

There was a very slight rise above the lake, the country appearing like and perhaps being partly a swamp, and at length a gradual descent to the Penobscot; which I was surprised to find here a large stream, from twelve to fifteen rods wide, flowing from west to east, or at right angles with the lake, and not more than two and a half miles from it. The distance is nearly twice too great on the map of the Public Lands, and on Colton's Map of Maine, and Russell Stream is placed too far down. Jackson makes Moosehead Lake to be nine hundred and sixty feet above high water in Portland harbor. It is higher than Chesuncook, for the lumberers consider the Penobscot, where we struck it, twenty-five feet lower than Moosehead, though eight miles above it is said to be the highest, so that the water can be made to flow either way, and the river falls a good deal between here and Chesuncook. The carry-man called this about one hundred and forty miles above Bangor by the river, or two hundred from the ocean, and fifty-five miles below Hilton's on the Canada road, the first clearing above, which is four and a half miles from the source of the Penobscot.

At the north end of the carry, in the midst of a clearing of sixty acres or more, there was a log camp of the usual construction, with something more like a house adjoining, for the accommodation of the carry-man's family and passing lumberers. The bed of withered fir twigs smelled very sweet, though really very dirty. There was also a storehouse on the bank of the river, containing pork, flour, iron, batteaux, and birches, locked up. We now proceeded to get our dinner, which always turned out to be tea, and to pitch canoes, for which purpose a large iron pot lay permanently on the bank. This we did in company with the explorers. Both Indians and whites use a mixture of rosin and grease for this purpose—that is, for the pitching, not the dinner. Joe took a small brand from the fire, and blew the heat and flame against the pitch on his birch, and so melted and spread it. Sometimes he put his mouth over the place and sucked, to see if it admitted air, and at one place, where we stopped, he placed his canoe high on crossed stakes, and poured water into it. I narrowly watched his motions, and listened attentively to his observations, for we had employed an Indian mainly that I might have an opportunity to study his ways. I heard him swear once mildly during this operation, about his knife being as dull as a hoe, an accomplishment which he owed to his intercourse with the whites, and he remarked, "We ought to have some tea before we start. We shall be hungry before we kill that moose."

At mid afternoon we embarked on the Penobscot. Our birch was nineteen and a half feet long by two and a half at the widest part, and fourteen inches deep within, both ends alike, and painted green, which Joe thought affected the pitch and made it leak. This, I think, was a middling sized one. That of the explorers was much larger, though probably not much longer. This carried us three with our baggage, weighing in all between five hundred and fifty and six hundred pounds. We had two heavy, though slender, rock maple paddles, one of them of bird's-eye maple. Joe placed birch bark on the bottom for us to sit on, and slanted cedar splints against the cross-bars to protect our backs, while he himself sat upon a cross-bar in the stern. The baggage occupied the middle or widest part of the canoe. We also paddled by turns in the bows, now sitting with our legs extended, now sitting upon our legs, and now rising upon our knees, but I found none of these positions endurable, and was reminded of the complaints of the old Jesuit missionaries, of the torture they endured from long confinement in constrained positions in canoes, in their long voyages from Quebec to the Huron country. But afterwards I sat on the cross-bars, or stood up, and experienced no inconvenience.

It was deadwater for a couple of miles. The river had been raised about two feet by the rain, and lumberers were hoping for a flood sufficient to bring down the logs that were left in the spring. Its banks were seven or eight feet high, and densely covered with white and black spruce, which I think must be the commonest trees thereabouts, fir, arbor-vitae, canoe, yellow, and black birch, rock, mountain, and a few red maples, beech, black and mountain ash, the common and rarely the large-toothed aspen, many civil looking elms now imbrowned along the stream, and at first a few hemlocks also. We had not gone far before I was startled by seeing what I thought was an Indian encampment, covered with a red flag, on the bank, and exclaimed "camp"! to my comrades. I was slow to discover that it was a red maple changed by the frost. The immediate shores were also densely covered with the speckled alder, red osier, shrubby willows or sallows, and the like. There were a few yellow-lily pads still left half-drowned along the sides, and sometimes a white one. Many fresh tracks of moose were visible where the water was shallow and on the shore, and the lily stems were freshly bitten off by them.

After paddling about two miles, we parted company with the explorers, and turned up Lobster Stream, which comes in on the right, from the southeast. This was six or eight rods wide, and appeared to run nearly parallel with the Penobscot. Joe said that it was so called from small fresh-water lobsters found in it. It is the Matahumkeag of the maps. My companion wished to look for moose signs, and intended, if it proved worth the while, to camp up that way, since the Indian advised it. On account of the rise of the Penobscot, the water ran up this stream quite to the pond of the same name, or two miles. The Spencer Mts., east of the north end of Moosehead Lake, were now in plain sight in front of us. The king-fisher flew before us, the pigeon woodpecker was seen and heard, and nuthatches and chicadees close at hand. Joe said that they called the chicadee *Kecunnilessu* in his language. I will not vouch for the spelling of what possibly was never spelt before, but I pronounced after him till he said it would do. We passed close to a woodcock which stood perfectly still on the shore, with feathers puffed up, as if sick. This, Joe said, they called *Nipsquecohossus*. The king-fisher was *Skuscumonsuck*, bear was *Wassus*; Indian Devil *lunxus*; the mountain ash *Upahsis*. This was very abundant and beautiful. Moose tracks were not so fresh along this stream, except in a small creek about a mile up it, where a large log had lodged in the spring, marked W-cross-girdle-crowfoot. We saw a pair of moose-horns on the shore, and I asked Joe if a moose had shed them; but he said there was a head attached to them, and I knew that they did not shed their heads more than once in their lives.

After ascending about a mile and a half, to within a short distance of Lobster Lake, we returned to the Penobscot. Just below the mouth of the Lobster we found quick water, and the river expanded to twenty or thirty rods in width. The moose tracks were quite numerous and fresh here. We noticed in a great many places narrow and well trodden paths by which they had come down to the river, and where they had slid on the steep and clayey bank. Their tracks were either close to the edge of the stream, those of the calves distinguishable from the others, or in shallow water; the holes made by their feet in the soft bottom being visible for a long time. They were particularly numerous where there was a small bay or *pokelogan*, as it is called, bordered by a strip of meadow, or separated from the river by a low peninsula covered with coarse grass, wool-grass, &c., wherein they had waded back and forth and eaten the pads. We detected the remains of one in such a place. At one place where we landed to pick up a summer duck, which my companion had shot, Joe peeled a canoe birch for bark for his hunting horn. He then asked if we were not going to get the other duck, for his sharp eyes had seen another fall in the bushes a little further along, and my companion obtained it. I now began to notice the bright red berries of the tree cranberry, which grows eight or ten feet high, mingled with the alders and cornel along the shore. There was less hard wood than at first.

After proceeding a mile and three quarters below the mouth of the Lobster, we reached, about sundown, a small island at the head of what Joe called the Moosehorn Dead-water (the Moosehorn, in which he was going to hunt that night, coming in about three miles below,) and on the upper end of this we decided to camp. On a point at the lower end lay the carcass of a moose killed a month or more be-fore. We concluded merely to prepare our camp, and leave our baggage here, that all might be ready when we returned from moose-hunting. Though I had not come a-hunting, and felt some compunctions about accompanying the hunters, I wished to see a moose near at hand, and was not sorry to learn how the Indian managed to kill one. I went as reporter or chaplain to the hunters—and the chaplain has been known to carry a gun himself. After clearing a small space amid the dense spruce and fir trees, we covered the damp ground with a shingling of fir twigs, and while Joe was preparing his birch horn and pitching his canoe,—for this had to be done whenever we stopped long enough to build a fire, and was the principal labor which he took upon himself at such times—we collected fuel for the night, large wet and rotting logs, which had lodged at the head of the island, for our hatchet was too small for effective chopping; but we did not kindle a fire, lest the moose should smell it. Joe set up a couple of forked stakes, and prepared half a dozen poles, ready to cast one of our blankets over, in case it rained in the night, which precaution however was omitted the next night. We also plucked the ducks which had been killed for breakfast.

While we were thus engaged in the twilight, we heard faintly, from far down the stream, what sounded like two strokes of a woodchopper's axe, echoing dully through the grim solitude. We are wont to liken many sounds heard at a distance in the forest to the stroke of an axe, because they resemble each other under those circumstances, and that is the one we commonly hear there. When we told Joe of this, he exclaimed, "By George, I'll bet that was moose! They make a noise like that." These sounds affected us strangely, and by their very resemblance to a familiar one, where they probably had so different an origin, enhanced the impression of solitude and wildness.

At starlight we dropped down the stream, which was a dead-water for three miles, or as far as the Moosehorn; Joe telling us that we must be very silent, and he himself made no noise with his paddle, while he urged the canoe along with effective impulses. It was a still night and suitable for this purpose, for if there is wind the moose will smell you, and Joe was very confident that he should get some. The harvest moon had just risen, and its level rays began to light up the forest on our right, while we glided downward in the shade on the same side, against the little breeze that was stirring. The lofty spiring tops of the spruce and fir were very black against the sky, and more distinct than by day, close bordering this broad avenue on each side, and the beauty of the scene, as the moon rose above the forest, it would not be easy to describe. A bat flew over our heads, and we heard a few faint notes of birds from time to time, perhaps the myrtle bird for one, or the sudden plunge of a musquash, or saw one crossing the stream before us, or heard the sound of a rill emptying in, swollen by the recent rain. About a mile below the island, when the solitude seemed to be growing more complete every moment, we suddenly saw the light and heard the crackling of a fire on the bank, and discovered the camp of the two explorers; they standing before it in their red shirts, and talking aloud of the adventures and profits of the day. They were just then speaking of a bargain in which, as I understood, somebody had cleared twenty-five dollars. We glided by without speaking, close under the bank, within a couple of rods of them, and Joe taking his horn imitated the call of the moose, till we suggested that they might fire on us. This was the last we saw of them, and we never knew whether they detected or suspected us.

I have often wished since that I was with them. They search for timber over a given section, climbing hills and often high trees to look off, explore the streams by which it is to be driven, and the like, spend five or six weeks in the woods, they two alone, a hundred miles or more from any town, roaming about and sleeping on the ground where night over-takes them, depending chiefly on the provisions they carry with them, though they do not decline what game they come across; and then in the fall they return and make report to their employers, deter-mining the number of teams that will be required the following winter. Experienced men get three or four dollars a day for this work. It is a solitary and ad-venturous life, and comes nearest to that of the trapper of the west, perhaps. Working ever with a gun as well as an axe, letting their beards grow, without neighbors, not on an open plain, but far within a wilderness.

This discovery accounted for the sounds which we had heard, and destroyed the prospect of seeing moose yet awhile. At length, when we had left the explorers far behind, Joe laid down his paddle, drew forth his birch horn—a straight one about fifteen inches long and three or four wide at the mouth, tied round with strips of the same bark—and standing up, imitated the call of the moose—*ugh ugh ugh*, or *oo oo oo oo*, and then a prolonged *oo o o o o o o*, and listened attentively for several minutes. We asked him what kind of noise he expected to hear. He said that if a moose heard it, he guessed we should find out; we should hear him coming half a mile off. He would come close to, perhaps into the water, and my companion must wait till he got fair sight, and then aim just behind the shoulder.

The moose venture out to the river side to feed and drink at night. Earlier in the season the hunters do not use a horn to call them out, but steal upon them as they are feeding along the sides of the stream, and often the first notice they have of one is the sound of the water dropping from its muzzle. An Indian whom I heard imitate the voice of the moose, and also the caribou and deer, using a much longer horn than Joe's, told me that the first could be heard eight or ten miles sometimes. It was a loud sort of bellowing sound, clearer and more sonorous than the lowing of cattle; the caribou's a sort of snort, and the small deer's like that of a lamb.

At length we turned up the Moosehorn, where the Indians at the carry had told us that they killed a moose the night before. This was a very meandering stream, only a rod or two in width, but comparatively deep, coming in on the right, fitly enough named Moosehorn, whether from its windings or its inhabitants. It was bordered here and there by narrow meadows between the stream and the endless forest, which afforded favorable places for the moose to feed, and to call them out on. We proceeded half a mile up this, as through a narrow winding canal, where the tall dark spruce and firs and arbor-vitae, towered on both sides in the moonlight, forming a perpendicular forest edge of great height, like the spires of a Venice in the forest. In two places stood a small stack of hay on the bank, ready for the lumberer's use in the winter, looking strange enough there. We thought of the day when this might be a brook winding through smooth shaven meadows on some gentleman's grounds; and seen by moonlight *then*, excepting the forest that now hems it in, how little changed it would appear.

Again and again Joe called the moose, placing the canoe close by some favorable point of meadow for them to come out on, but listened in vain to hear one come rushing through the woods, and concluded that they had been hunted too much thereabouts. We saw many times what to our imaginations looked like a gigantic moose, with his horns, peering from out the forest edge, but we saw the forest only, and not its inhabitant that night. So at last we turned about. There was now a little fog on the water, though it was a fine clear night above. There were very few sounds to break the stillness of the forest. Several times we heard the hooting of a great horned owl, as at home, and told Joe that he would call out the moose for him, for he made a sound considerably like the horn, but Joe answered that the moose had heard that sound a thousand times, and knew better; and oftener still we were startled by the plunge of a musquash. Once, when Joe had *called* again, and we were listening for moose, we heard come faintly echoing or creeping from far through the moss-clad aisles, a dull dry rushing sound, with a solid core to it, yet as if half smothered under the grasp of the luxuriant and fungus-like forest, like the shutting of a door in some distant entry of the damp and shaggy wilderness. If we had not been there no mortal had heard it. When we asked Joe in a whisper what it was, he answered, "Tree fall." There is something singularly grand and impressive in the sound of a tree falling in a perfectly calm night like this, as if the agencies which overthrow it did not need to be excited, but worked with a subtle, deliberate, and conscious force, like a boa constrictor, and more effectively then than even in a windy day. If there is any such difference, perhaps it is because trees with the dews of the night on them are heavier than by day.

Having reached the camp, about ten o'clock, we kindled our fire and went to bed. Each of us had a blanket, in which he lay on the fir twigs, with his extremities toward the fire, but nothing over his head. It was worth the while to lie down in a country where you could afford such great fires; that was one whole side, and the bright side, of our world. We had first rolled up a large log some eighteen inches through and ten feet long, for a back log to last all night, and then piled on the trees to the height of three or four feet, no matter how green or damp. In fact, we burned as much wood that night as would, with economy and an air-tight stove, last a poor family in one of our cities all winter. It was very agreeable, as well as independent, this lying in the open air, and the fire kept our uncovered extremities warm enough. The Jesuit missionaries used to say, that in their journeys with the Indians in Canada, they lay on a bed which has never been shaken up since the creation, unless by earthquakes. It is surprising with what impunity and comfort one who has always lain in a warm bed in a close apartment, and studiously avoided drafts of air, can lie down on the ground without a shelter, roll himself in a blanket, and sleep before a fire, in a frosty autumn night, just after a long rain-storm, and even come soon to enjoy and value the fresh air.

I lay awake awhile watching the ascent of the sparks through the firs, and sometimes their descent in half extinguished cinders on to my blanket. They were as interesting as fire-works, going up in endless successive crowds, each after an explosion, in an eager serpentine course, some to five or six rods above the tree tops before they went out. We do not suspect how much our chimneys have concealed; and now air-tight stoves have come to conceal all the rest. In the course of the night, I got up once or twice and put fresh logs on the fire, making my companions curl up their legs.

When we awoke in the morning (Saturday Sep. 17th) there was considerable frost whitening the leaves. We heard the sound of the chickaree, and a few faintly lisping birds, and also of ducks in the water about the island. I took a botanical account of stock of our domains, before the dew was off, and found that the ground hemlock, or American yew, was the prevailing under shrub. We breakfasted on tea, hard bread and ducks.

Before the fog had fairly cleared away we paddled down the stream again, and were soon past the mouth of the Moosehorn. These twenty miles of the Penobscot, between Moosehead and Chesuncook Lakes, are comparatively smooth and a great part dead-water, but from time to time it is shallow and rapid, with rocks or gravel beds where you can wade across. There is no expanse of water, and no break in the forest, and the meadow is a mere edging here and there. There are no hills near the river nor within sight, except one or two distant mountains seen in a few places. The banks are from six to ten feet high, but once or twice rise gently to higher ground. In many places the forest on the bank was but a thin strip, letting the light through from some alder swamp or meadow behind. The conspicuous berry-bearing bushes and trees along the shore, were the red osier, with its whitish fruit, hobble bush, mountain ash, tree cranberry, choke-cherry, now ripe, alternate cornel, and naked viburnum. Following Joe's example I ate the fruit of the last, and also of the hobble bush, but found them rather insipid and seedy. I looked very narrowly at the vegetation, as we glided along close to the shore, and frequently made Joe turn aside for me to pluck a plant, that I might see by comparison what was primitive about my native river. Horehound, horsemint, and the sensitive fern grew close to the edge, under the willows and alders, and wool-grass on the islands, as along the Assabet River in Concord. It was too late for flowers, except a few asters, golden-rods, &c. In several places we noticed the slight frame of a camp, such as we had prepared to set up, amid the forest by the river side, where some lumberers or hunters had passed a night, and sometimes steps cut in the muddy or clayey bank in front of it.

We stopped to fish for trout at the mouth of a small stream called Ragmuff, which came in from the west, about two miles below the Moosehorn. Here were the ruins of an old lumbering camp, and a small space, which had formerly been cleared and burned over, was now densely overgrown with the red cherry and raspberries. While we were trying for trout, Joe, Indian like, wandered off up the Ragmuff on his own errands, and when we were ready to start was far beyond call. So we were compelled to make a fire and get our dinner here, not to lose time. Some dark reddish birds, with greyer females, (perhaps purple finches), and myrtle birds in their summer dress, hopped within six or eight feet of us and our smoke. Perhaps they smelled the frying pork. The latter bird, or both, made the lisping notes which I had heard in the forest. They suggested that the few small birds found in the wilderness are on more familiar terms with the lumberman and hunter than those of the orchard and clearing with the farmer. I have since found the Canada jay, and partridges, both the black and the common, equally tame there, as if they had not yet learned to mistrust man entirely. The chicadee, which is at home alike in the primitive woods and in our wood-lots, still retains its confidence in the towns to a remarkable degree.

Joe at length returned, after an hour and a half, and said that he had been two miles up the stream exploring, and had seen a moose, but, not having the gun, he did not get him. We made no complaint, but concluded to look out for Joe the next time. However, this may have been a mere mistake, for we had no reason to complain of him afterwards. As we continued down the stream, I was surprised to hear him whistling "O Susanna," and several other such airs, while his paddle urged us along. Once he said, "Yes, Sir-ee." His common word was "Sartain." He paddled, as usual, on one side only, giving the birch an impulse by using the side as a fulcrum. I asked him how the ribs were fastened to the side rails. He answered, "I don't know, I never noticed." Talking with him about subsisting wholly on what the woods yielded, game, fish, berries, etc., I suggested that his ancestors did so; but he answered, that he had been brought up in such a way that he could not do it. "Yes," said he, "that's the way they got a living, like wild fellows, wild as bears. By George! I shan't go into the woods without provision,—hard bread, pork, etc." He had brought on a barrel of hard bread and stored it at the carry for his hunting. However, though he was a Governor's son, he had not learned to read.

At one place below this, on the east side, where the bank was higher and drier than usual, rising gently from the shore to a slight elevation, some one had felled the trees over twenty or thirty acres, and left them drying in order to burn. This was the only preparation for a house between the Moosehead carry and Chesuncook, but there was no hut nor inhabitants there yet. The pioneer thus selects a site for his house, which will, perhaps, prove the germ of a town.

My eyes were all the while on the trees, distinguishing between the black and white spruce and the fir. You paddle along in a narrow canal through an endless forest, and the vision I have in my mind's eye, still, is of the small dark and sharp tops of tall fir and spruce trees, and pagoda-like arbor-vitæs, crowded together on each side, with various hard woods intermixed. Some of the arbor-vitæs were at least sixty feet high. The hard woods, occasionally occurring exclusively, were less wild to my eye. I fancied them ornamental grounds, with farm-houses in the rear. The canoe and yellow birch, beech, maple, and elm are Saxon and Norman; but the spruce and fir, and pines generally, are Indian. The soft engravings which adorn the annuals give no idea of a stream in such a wilderness as this. The rough sketches in Jackson's Reports on the Geology of Maine answer much better. At one place we saw a small grove of slender sapling white-pines, the only collection of pines that I saw on this voyage. Here and there, however, was a full-grown, tall, and slender, but defective one, what lumbermen call a *konchus* tree, which they ascertain with their axes, or by the knots. I did not learn whether this word was Indian or English. It reminded me of the Greek κόγχη, a conch or shell, and I amused myself with fancying that it might signify the dead sound which the trees yield when struck. All the rest of the pines had been driven off.

How far men go for the material of their houses! The inhabitants of the most civilized cities, in all ages, send into far, primitive forests, beyond the bounds of their civilization, where the moose and bear and savage dwell, for their pine-boards for ordinary use. And, on the other hand, the savage soon receives from cities iron arrow-points, hatchets, and guns to point his savageness with.

The solid and well-defined fir-tops, like sharp and regular spear-heads, black against the sky, gave a peculiar, dark, and sombre look to the forest. The spruce-tops have a similar, but more ragged outline,— their shafts also merely feathered below. The firs were somewhat oftener regular and dense pyramids. I was struck by this universal spiring upward of the forest evergreens. The tendency is to slender, spiring tops, while they are narrower below. Not only the spruce and fir, but even the arbor-vitae and white pine, unlike the soft spreading second growth, of which I saw none, all spire upwards, lifting a dense spear-head of cones to the light and air, at any rate, while their branches straggle after as they may; as Indians lift the ball over the heads of the crowd in their desperate game. In this they resemble grasses, as also palms somewhat. The hemlock is commonly a tent-like pyramid from the ground to its summit.

After passing through some long rips and by a large island, we reached an interesting part of the river called the Pine Stream Dead-water, about six miles below Ragmuff, where the river expanded to thirty rods in width and had many islands in it, with elms and canoe birches, now yellowing, along the shore, and we got our first sight of Katadn.

Here, about two o'clock, we turned up a small branch three or four rods wide, which comes in on the right from the south, called Pine Stream, to look for moose signs. We had gone but a few rods before we saw very recent signs along the water's edge, the

mud lifted up by their feet being quite fresh, and Joe
declared that they had gone along there but a short
time before. We soon reached a small meadow on
the east side, at an angle in the stream, which was
for the most part densely covered with alders. As
we were advancing along the edge of this, rather
more quietly than usual, perhaps, on account of the
freshness of the signs,—the design being to camp up
this stream, if it promised well,—I heard a slight
crackling of twigs deep in the alders, and turned Joe's
attention to it. Whereupon he began to push the canoe back rapidly, and we had receded thus half a
dozen rods, when we suddenly spied two moose standing just on the edge of the open part of the meadow
which we had passed, not more than six or seven
rods distant, looking round the alders at us. They
made me think of great frightened rabbits, with their
long ears and half inquisitive half frightened looks;
the true denizens of the forest, (I saw at once),
filling a vacuum which now first I discovered had not
been filled for me—*Moose* men, *wood eaters*, the word
is said to mean—clad in a sort of Vermont gray or
homespun. Our Nimrod, owing to the retrograde
movement, was now the furthest from the game, but
being warned of its neighborhood, he hastily stood
up, and while we ducked, fired over our heads, one
barrel at the foremost, which alone he saw, though
he did not know what kind of creature it was;
whereupon this one dashed across the meadow and
up a high bank on the north-east, so rapidly as to
leave but an indistinct impression of its outlines on
my mind. At the same instant, the other, a young
one, but as tall as a horse, leaped out into the stream,
in full sight, and there stood cowering for a moment,
or rather its disproportionate lowness behind gave it
that appearance, and uttering two or three trumpet-

ing squeaks. I have an indistinct recollection of seeing the old one pause an instant on the top of the
bank in the woods, look toward its shivering young,
and then dash away again. The second barrel was
levelled at the calf, and when we expected to see it
drop in the water, after a little hesitation, it too got
out of the water, and dashed up the hill, though in
a somewhat different direction. All this was the work
of a few seconds, and our hunter having never seen a
moose before, did not know but they were deer, for
they stood partly in the water, nor whether he had
fired at the same one twice or not. From the style in
which they went off, and the fact that he was not
used to standing up and firing from a canoe, I judged
that we should not see anything more of them. The
Indian said that they were a cow and her calf—a
yearling or perhaps two years old, for they accompany their dams so long,—but for my part I had not
noticed much difference in their size. It was but two
or three rods across the meadow to the foot of the
bank, which like all the world thereabouts was densely wooded, but I was surprised to notice, that as soon
as the moose had passed behind the veil of the woods,
there was no sound of footsteps to be heard from the
soft damp moss which carpets that forest, and long
before we landed perfect silence reigned. Joe said,
"If you wound em moose me sure get 'em".

We all landed at once. My companion reloaded; the
Indian fastened his birch, threw off his hat—ad-
justed his waistband, seized the hatchet, and set out.
He told me afterward, casually, that before we landed
he had seen a drop of blood on the bank, when it was
two or three rods off. He proceeded rapidly up the
bank and through the woods, with a peculiar, elastic,
noiseless and stealthy tread, looking to right and
left on the ground, and stepping in the faint tracks

of the wounded moose, now and then pointing in silence to a single drop of blood on the handsome shining leaves of the Clintonia borealis, which on every side covered the ground, or to a dry fern stem freshly broken, all the while chewing some leaf or else the spruce gum. I followed, watching his motions more than the trail of the moose. After following the trail about forty rods in a pretty direct course, stepping over fallen trees and winding between standing ones, he at length lost it, for there were many other moose tracks there, and returning once more to the last blood stain traced it a little way and lost it again, and, too soon, I thought, for a good hunter, gave it up entirely. He traced a few steps also the tracks of the calf, but seeing no blood, soon relinquished the search.

I observed while he was tracking the moose a certain reticence or moderation in him. He did not communicate several observations of interest which he made, as a white man would have done, though they may have leaked out afterward. At another time, when we heard a slight crackling of twigs and he landed to reconnoitre, he stepped lightly and gracefully, stealing through the bushes with the least possible noise, in a way in which no white man does, as it were, finding a place for his foot each time.

About half an hour after seeing the moose, we pursued our voyage up Pine Stream, and soon, coming to a part which was very shoal and also rapid, we took out the baggage, and proceeded to carry it round, while Joe got up with the canoe alone. We were just completing our portage, and I was absorbed in the plants, admiring the leaves of the aster macrophyllus, ten inches wide, and plucking the seeds of the great round-leaved orchis, when Joe exclaimed from the stream that he had killed a moose. He had found the cow moose lying dead, but quite warm, in the middle of the stream, which was so shallow that it rested on the bottom, with hardly a third of its body above water. It was about an hour after it was shot, and it was swollen with water. It had run about a hundred rods and sought the stream again, cutting off a slight bend. No doubt a better hunter would have tracked it to this spot at once. I was surprised at its great size, horse-like, but Joe said it was not a large cow moose. My companion went in search of the calf again. I took hold of the ears of the moose, while Joe pushed his canoe down stream toward a favorable shore, and so we made out, though with some difficulty, its long nose frequently sticking in the bottom, to drag it into still shallower water. It was a brownish black, or perhaps a dark iron-gray, on the back and sides, but lighter beneath and in front. I took the cord which served for the canoe's painter, and with Joe's assistance measured it carefully, the greatest distances first, making a knot each time. The painter being wanted, I reduced these measures that night with equal care to lengths and fractions of my umbrella, beginning with the smallest measures, and untying the knots as I proceeded; and when we arrived at Chesuncook the next day, finding a two-foot rule there, I reduced the last to feet and inches; and, moreover, I made myself a two-foot rule of a thin and narrow strip of black ash, which would fold up conveniently to six inches. All this pains I took because I did not wish to be obliged to say merely that the moose was very large. Of the various dimensions which I obtained I will mention only two. The distance from the tips of the hoofs of the fore feet *stretched out* to the top of the back between the shoulders was seven feet and five inches. I can hardly believe my own measure, for this is about two feet greater than the height of a tall horse. [Indeed, I am now satisfied that this measurement was incorrect, but the other measures given here I can warrant to be correct, having proved them in a more recent visit to those woods.] The extreme length was eight feet and two inches. Another cow moose which I have since measured in those woods with a tape, was just six feet from the tip of the hoof to the shoulders, and eight feet long as she lay.

When afterward I asked an Indian at the carry how much taller the male was, he answered eighteen inches, and made me observe the height of a cross-stake over the fire, more than four feet from the ground to give me an idea of the depth of his chest! Another Indian, at Oldtown, told me that they were nine feet high to the top of the back, and that one which he tried weighed eight hundred pounds. The length of the spinal projections between the shoulders is very great. A white hunter, who was the best authority among hunters that I could have, told me that the male was not eighteen inches taller than the female, yet he agreed that he was sometimes nine feet high to the top of the back and weighed a thousand pounds. Only the male has horns, and they rise two feet or more above the shoulders, spreading three or four, and sometimes six feet, which would make him in all, sometimes, eleven feet high! According to this calculation, the moose is as tall, though it may not be as large, as the great Irish elk, Megaceros Hibernicus, of a former period, of which Mantell says, that it "very far exceeded in magnitude any living species. The skeleton" being "upwards of ten feet high from the ground to the highest point of the antlers." Joe said that though the moose shed the whole horn annually each new horn has an additional prong; but I have noticed that they sometimes have more prongs on one side than on the other. I was struck with the delicacy and tenderness of the hoofs which divide very far up, and the one half could be pressed very much behind the other, thus probably making the animal surer footed on the uneven ground and slippery moss-covered logs of the primitive forest. They were very unlike the stiff and battered feet of our horses and oxen. The bare horny part of the fore foot was just six inches long, and the two portions could be separated four inches at the extremities.

The moose is singularly grotesque and awkward to look at. Why should it stand so high at the shoulders? Why have so long a head? Why have no tail to speak of? for in my examination I overlooked it entirely. Naturalists say it is one inch and a half long. It reminded me at once of the camelopard, high before and low behind, and no wonder, for like it it is fitted to browse on trees. The upper lip projected two inches beyond the lower for this purpose.—This was the kind of man that was at home there, for as near as I can learn, that has never been the residence, but rather the hunting ground of the Indian. The moose will perhaps one day become extinct, but how naturally then, when it exists only as a fossil relic, and unseen as that, may the poet or sculptor invent a fabulous animal with similar branching and leafy horns—a sort of fucus or lichen in bone—to be the inhabitant of such a forest as this!

Here, just at the head of the murmuring rapids, Joe now proceeded to skin the moose with a pocket knife, while I looked on, and a tragical business it was; to see that still warm and palpitating body pierced with a knife, to see the warm milk stream from the rent udder, and the ghastly naked red carcass appearing from within its seemly robe, which was made to *hide* it. The ball had passed through the shoulder-blade diagonally and lodged under the skin on the opposite side, and was partially flattened. My companion keeps it to show to his grandchildren. He has the shanks of another moose, which he has since shot, skinned and stuffed, ready to be made into boots by putting in a thick leather sole. Joe said, if a moose stood fronting you you must not fire, but advance toward him, for he will turn slowly and give you a fair shot. In the bed of this narrow wild and rocky stream, between two lofty walls of spruce and firs, a mere cleft in the forest which the stream had made, this work went on. At length Joe had stripped off the hide and dragged it trailing to the shore, declaring that it weighed a hundred pounds, though probably fifty would have been nearer the truth. He cut off a large mass of the meat to carry along, and another, together with the tongue and nose, he put with the hide on the shore to lie there all night, or till we returned. I was surprised that he thought of leaving this meat thus exposed by the side of the carcass, as the simplest course, not fearing that any creature would touch it; but nothing did. This could hardly have happened on the bank of one of our rivers in the eastern part of Massachusetts; but I suspect that fewer small wild animals are prowling there than with us. Twice however in this excursion I had a glimpse of a species of large mouse.

This stream was so withdrawn, and the moose tracks were so fresh, that my companions, still bent on hunting, concluded to go further up it and camp, and then hunt up or down at night. Half a mile above this, at a place where I saw the aster puniceus and the beaked hazel, as we paddled along, Joe hearing a slight rustling amid the alders, and seeing something black about two rods off, jumped up and whispered "bear"! but before the hunter had discharged his piece he corrected himself to "beaver!"—"hedgehog"! The bullet killed a large hedgehog more than two feet and eight inches long. The quills were rayed out and flattened on the hinder part of its back, even as if it had lain on that part, but were erect and long between this and the tail. Their points, closely examined, were seen to be finely bearded or barbed, and shaped like an awl, that is, a little concave to give the barbs effect. After about a mile of still water, we prepared our camp on the right side, just at the foot of a considerable fall. Little chopping was done that night for fear of scaring the moose. We had moose meat fried for supper. It tasted like tender beef, with perhaps more flavor; sometimes like veal.

After supper, the moon having risen, we proceeded to hunt a mile up this stream, first carrying about the falls. We made a picturesque sight wending single-file along the shore, climbing over rocks and logs, Joe, who brought up the rear, twirling his canoe in his hands as if it were a feather, in places where it was difficult to get along without a burden. We launched the canoe again from the ledge over which the stream fell, but after half a mile of still water suitable for hunting, it became rapid again, and we were compelled to make our way along the shore, while Joe endeavored to get up in the birch alone, though it was still very difficult for him to pick his way amid the rocks in the night. We on the shore found the worst of walking, a perfect chaos of fallen and drifted trees, and of bushes projecting far over the water, and now and then we made our way across the mouth of a small tributary on a kind of net-work of alders. So we went tumbling on in the dark, being on the shady side, effectually scaring all

the moose and bears that might be thereabouts. At
length we came to a standstill, and Joe went forward
to reconnoitre, but he reported that it was still a
continuous rapid as far as he went, or half a mile,
with no prospect of improvement, as if it were coming down from a mountain. So we turned about,
hunting back to the camp through the still water. It
was a splendid moonlight night, and I, getting
sleepy as it grew late, for I had nothing to do, found
it difficult to realize where I was. This was much
more unfrequented than the main stream, lumbering
operations being no longer carried on in this quarter.
It was only three or four rods wide, but the firs and
spruce through which it trickled seemed yet taller by
contrast. Being in this dreamy state, which the moonlight enhanced, I did not clearly discern the shore,
but seemed, most of the time, to be floating through
ornamental grounds, for I associated the fir tops
with such scenes—very high up some Broadway, and
beneath or between their tops I thought I saw an
endless succession of porticoes and columns, cornices
and facades, verandas and churches. I did not merely
fancy this, but in my drowsy state such was the illusion. I fairly lost myself in sleep several times,
still dreaming of that architecture and the nobility
that dwelt behind and might issue from it; but all
at once I would be aroused and brought back to a
sense of my actual position, by the sound of Joe's
birch horn in the midst of all this silence calling the
moose—*ugh, ugh oo, oo, oo oo oo oo*, and I prepared
to hear a furious moose come rushing and crashing
through the forest, and see him burst out on to the
little strip of meadow by our side.

But on more accounts than one I had had enough
of moose-hunting. I had not come to the woods for
this purpose, nor had I foreseen it, though I had

been willing to learn how the Indian manoeuvred; but one moose killed was as good, if not as bad, as a dozen. The afternoon's tragedy, and my share in it, as it affected the innocence, destroyed the pleasure of my adventure. It is true, I came as near to being a hunter and miss it, as possible myself, and as it is, I think that I could spend a year in the woods fishing and hunting just enough to sustain myself, with satisfaction. This would be next to living like a philosopher on the fruits of the earth which you had raised, which also attracts me. But this hunting of the moose merely for the satisfaction of killing him—not even for the sake of his hide, without making any extraordinary exertion or running any risk yourself, is too much like going out by night to some woodside pasture and shooting your neighbor's horses. These are God's own horses, poor timid creatures that will run fast enough as soon as they smell you, though they *are* nine feet high. Joe told us of some hunters who a year or two before had shot down several oxen by night, somewhere in the Maine woods, mistaking them for moose. And so might any of the hunters; and what is the difference in the sport, but the name? In the former case, having killed one of God's and *your own* oxen, you strip off its hide, because that is the common trophy, and moreover you have heard that it may be sold for moccasins, cut a steak from its haunches, and leave the huge carcass to smell to heaven for you. It is no better, at least, than to assist at a slaughter house.

This afternoon's experience suggested to me how base or coarse are the motives which commonly carry men into the wilderness. The explorers, and lumberers generally, are all hirelings, paid so much a day for their labor, and as such, they have no more love for wild nature, than wood-sawyers have for forests.

Other white men and Indians who come here are for the most part hunters, whose object is to slay as many moose and other wild animals as possible. But, pray, could not one spend some weeks or years in the solitude of this vast wilderness with other employments than these—employments perfectly sweet and innocent and ennobling? For one that comes with a pencil to sketch or sing, a thousand come with an axe or rifle. What a coarse and imperfect use Indians and hunters make of nature! No wonder that their race is so soon exterminated. I already and for weeks afterward felt my nature the coarser for this part of my woodland experience, and was reminded that our life should be lived as tenderly and daintily as one would pluck a flower.

With these thoughts, when we reached our camping ground I decided to leave my companions to continue moose hunting down the stream, while I prepared the camp, though they requested me not to chop much nor make a large fire, for fear I should scare their game. In the midst of the damp fir wood, high on the mossy bank, about nine o'clock of this bright moonlight night, I kindled a fire, when they were gone, and sitting on the fir-twigs, within sound of the falls, examined by its light the botanical specimens which I had collected that afternoon, and wrote down some of the reflections which I have here expanded; or I walked along the shore and gazed up the stream, where the whole space above the falls was filled with mellow light. As I sat before the fire on my fir twig seat, without walls above or around me, I remembered how far on every hand that wilderness stretched, before you came to cleared or cultivated fields, and wondered if any bear or moose was watching the light of my fire, for nature looked sternly upon me on account of the murder of the moose.

Strange that so few ever come to the woods to see how the pine lives and grows and spires, lifting its evergreen arms to the light—to see its perfect success, but most are content to behold it in the shape of many broad boards brought to market, and deem *that* its true success! But the pine is no more lumber than man is, and to be made into boards and houses is no more its true and highest use than the truest use of a man is to be cut down and made into manure. There is a higher law affecting our relation to pines as well as to men. A pine cut down, a dead pine, is no more a pine than a dead human carcass is a man. Can he who has discovered only some of the values of whalebone and whale oil be said to have discovered the true use of the whale? Can he who slays the elephant for his ivory be said to have "seen the elephant"? These are petty and accidental uses; just as if a stronger race were to kill us in order to make buttons and flageolets of our bones; for everything may serve a lower as well as a higher use. Every creature is better alive than dead, men and moose and pine-trees, and he who understands it aright will rather preserve its life than destroy it.

Is it the lumberman then who is the friend and lover of the pine—stands nearest to it and understands its nature best? Is it the tanner who has barked it, or he who has boxed it for turpentine, whom posterity will fable was changed into a pine at last? No! no! it is the poet; he it is who makes the truest use of the pine—who does not fondle it with an axe, nor tickle it with a saw, nor stroke it with a plane; who knows whether its heart is false without cutting into it; who has not bought the stumpage of the township on which it stands. All the pines shudder and heave a sigh when *that* man steps on the forest floor. No, it is the poet, who loves them as his own shadow in the air, and lets them stand. I have been into the lumber yard, and the carpenter's shop, and the tannery, and the lampblack factory, and the turpentine clearing; but when at length I saw the tops of the pines waving and reflecting the light at a distance high over all the rest of the forest, I realized that the former were not the highest use of the pine. It is not their bones or hide or tallow that I love most. It is the living spirit of the tree, not its spirit of turpentine, with which I sympathize, and which heals my cuts. It is as immortal as I am, and perchance will go to as high a heaven, there to tower above me still.

Ere-long the hunters returned, not having seen a moose, but in consequence of my suggestions bringing a quarter of the dead one, which, with ourselves, made quite a load for the canoe.

After breakfasting on moose-meat, we returned down Pine Stream on our way to Chesuncook Lake, which was about five miles distant. We could see the red carcass of the moose lying in Pine Stream when nearly half a mile off. Just below the mouth of this stream were the most considerable rapids between the two lakes, called Pine-Stream Falls, where were large flat rocks washed smooth, and at this time you could easily wade across above them. Joe ran down alone while we walked over the portage, my companion collecting spruce gum for his friends at home, and I looking for flowers. Near the lake, which we were approaching with as much expectation as if it had been a university,—for it is not often that the stream of our life opens into such expansions,— were islands, and a low and meadowy shore with scattered trees, birches, white and yellow, slanted over the water, and maples,—many of the white birches killed, apparently by inundations. There was considerable native grass; and even a few cattle—whose movements we heard, though we did not see them, mistaking them at first for moose—were pastured there.

On entering the lake, where the stream runs southeasterly, and for some time before, we had a view of the mountains about Katadn, (*Katahdinauguoh* one says they are called,) like a cluster of blue fungi of rank growth, apparently twenty-five or thirty miles distant, in a southeast direction, their summits concealed by clouds. Joe called some of them the *Souadneunk* mountains. This is the name of a stream there, which another Indian told us meant "Running between mountains." Though some lower summits were afterward uncovered, we got no more complete view of Katadn while we were in the woods. The clearing to which we were bound was on the right of the mouth of the river, and was reached by going round a low point, where the water was shallow to a great distance from the shore. Chesuncook Lake extends northwest and southeast, and is called eighteen miles long and three wide, without an island. We had entered the northwest corner of it, and when near the shore could see only part way down it. The principal mountains visible from the land here were those already mentioned, between southeast and east, and a few summits a little west of north, but generally the north and northwest horizon about the St. John and the British boundary was comparatively level.

Ansell Smith's, the oldest and principal clearing about this lake, appeared to be quite a harbor for batteaux and canoes; seven or eight of the former were lying about, and there was a small scow for hay, and a capstan on a platform, now high and dry, ready to be floated and anchored to tow rafts with. It was a very primitive kind of harbor, where boats were drawn up amid the stumps,—such a one, me-thought, as the Argo might have been launched in. There were five other huts with small clearings on the opposite side of the lake, all at this end and vis-ible from this point. One of the Smiths told me that it was so far cleared that they came here to live and built the present house four years before, though the family had been here but a few months.

I was interested to see how a pioneer lived on this side of the country. His life is in some respects more adventurous than that of his brother in the West; for he contends with winter as well as the wilderness, and there is a greater interval of time at least be-tween him and the army which is to follow. Here immigration is a tide which may ebb when it has swept away the pines; there it is not a tide, but an inundation, and roads and other improvements come steadily rushing after.

As we approached the log-house, a dozen rods from the lake, and considerably elevated above it, the projecting ends of the logs lapping over each other irregularly several feet at the corners gave it a very rich and picturesque look, far removed from the meanness of weather-boards. It was a very spacious, low building, about eighty feet long, with many large apartments. The walls were well clayed between the logs, which were large and round, except on the upper and under sides, and as visible inside as out, successive bulging cheeks gradually lessening up-wards and tuned to each other with the axe, like Pandean pipes. Probably the musical forest-gods had

not yet cast them aside; they never do till they are
split or the bark is gone. It was a style of architecture not described by Vitruvius, I suspect, though
possibly hinted at in the biography of Orpheus; none
of your frilled or fluted columns, which have cut
such a false swell, and support nothing but a gable
end and their builder's pretensions,—that is, with the
multitude; and as for "ornamentation," one of those
words with a dead tail which architects very properly use to describe their flourishes, there were the
lichens and mosses and fringes of bark, which nobody troubled himself about. We certainly leave the
handsomest paint and clapboards behind in the
woods, when we strip off the bark and poison ourselves with white-lead in the towns. We get but half
the spoils of the forest. For beauty, give me trees
with the fur on. This house was designed and con-
structed with the freedom of stroke of a forester's
axe, without other compass and square than Nature
uses. Wherever the logs were cut off by a window or
door, that is, were not kept in place by alternate
overlapping, they were held one upon another by
very large pins driven in diagonally on each side,
where branches might have been, and then cut off
so close up and down as not to project beyond the
bulge of the log, as if the logs clasped each other
in their arms. These logs were posts, studs, boards,
clapboards, laths, plaster, and nails, all in one.
Where the citizen uses a mere sliver or board, the
pioneer uses the whole trunk of a tree. The house
had large stone chimneys, and was roofed with
spruce-bark. The windows were imported, all but the
casings. One end was a regular logger's camp, for
the boarders, with the usual fir floor and log benches.
Thus this house was but a slight departure from the

hollow tree, which the bear still inhabits,—being a hollow made with trees piled up, with a coating of bark like its original.

The cellar was a separate building, like an ice-house, and it answered for a refrigerator at this season, our moose-meat being kept there. It was a potato-hole with a permanent roof. Each structure and institution here was so primitive that you could at once refer it to its source; but our buildings commonly suggest neither their origin nor their purpose. There was a large, and what farmers would call handsome, barn, part of whose boards had been sawed by a whip-saw; and the saw-pit, with its great pile of dust, remained before the house. The long split shingles on a portion of the barn were laid a foot to the weather, suggesting what kind of weather they have there. Grant's barn at Caribou Lake was said to be still larger, the biggest ox-nest in the woods, fifty feet by a hundred. Think of a monster barn in that primitive forest lifting its gray back above the tree-tops! Man makes very much such a nest for his domestic animals, of withered grass and fodder, as the squirrels and many other wild creatures do for themselves.

There was also a blacksmith's shop, where plainly a good deal of work was done. The oxen and horses used in lumbering operations were shod, and all the iron-work of sleds, etc., was repaired or made here. I saw them load a batteau at the Moosehead carry, the next Tuesday, with about thirteen hundred weight of bar iron for this shop. This reminded me how primitive and honorable a trade was Vulcan's. I do not hear that there was any carpenter or tailor among the gods. The smith seems to have preceded these and every other mechanic at Chesuncook as well as on Olympus, and his family is the most widely dispersed, whether he be christened John or Ansell.

Smith owned two miles down the lake by half a mile in width. There were about one hundred acres cleared here. He cut seventy tons of English hay this year on this ground, and twenty more on another clearing, and he uses it all himself in lumbering operations. The barn was crowded with pressed hay and a machine to press it. There was a large garden full of roots, turnips, beets, carrots, potatoes, etc., all of great size. They said that they were worth as much here as in New York. I suggested some currants for sauce, especially as they had no apple-trees set out, and showed how easily they could be obtained.

There was the usual long-handled axe of the primitive woods by the door, three and a half feet long,— for my new black-ash rule was in constant use,—and a large, shaggy dog, whose nose, report said, was full of porcupine quills. I can testify that he looked very sober. This is the usual fortune of pioneer dogs, for they have to face the brunt of the battle for their race, and act the part of Arnold Winkelried without intending it. If he should invite one of his town friends up this way, suggesting moose-meat and unlimited freedom, the latter might pertinently inquire, "What is that sticking in your nose?" When a generation or two have used up all the enemies' darts, their successors lead a comparatively easy life. We owe to our fathers analogous blessings. Many old people receive pensions for no other reason, it seems to me, but as a compensation for having lived a long time ago. No doubt, our town dogs still talk, in a snuffling way, about the days that tried dogs' noses. How they got a cat up there I do not know, for they are as shy as my aunt about entering a canoe. I wondered that she did not run up a tree on the way; but perhaps she was bewildered by the very crowd of opportunities.

Twenty or thirty lumberers, Yankee and Canadian, were coming and going,—Aleck among the rest,—and from time to time an Indian touched here. In the winter there are sometimes a hundred men lodged here at once. The most interesting piece of news that circulated among them appeared to be, that four horses belonging to Smith, worth seven hundred dollars, had passed by further into the woods a week before.

The white-pine-tree was at the bottom or further end of all this. It is a war against the pines, the only real Aroostook or Penobscot war. I have no doubt that they lived pretty much the same sort of life in the Homeric age, for men have always thought more of eating than of fighting; then, as now, their minds ran chiefly on the "hot bread and sweet cakes"; and the fur and lumber trade is an old story to Asia and Europe. I doubt if men ever made a trade of heroism. In the days of Achilles, even, they delighted in big barns, and perchance in pressed hay, and he who possessed the most valuable team was the best fellow.

We had designed to go on at evening up the Caucomgomoc, whose mouth was a mile or two distant, to the lake of the same name, about ten miles off; but some Indians of Joe's acquaintance, who were making canoes on the Caucomgomoc, came over from that side, and gave so poor an account of the moose-hunting, so many had been killed there lately, that my companions concluded not to go there. Joe spent this Sunday and the night with his acquaintances. The lumberers told me that there were many moose hereabouts, but no caribou or deer. A man from Old-town had killed ten or twelve moose, within a year, so near the house that they heard all his guns. His name may have been Hercules, for aught I know, though I should rather have expected to hear the rattling of his club; but, no doubt, he keeps pace with the improvements of the age, and uses a Sharps rifle now; probably he gets all his armor made and repaired at Smith's shop. One moose had been killed and another shot at within sight of the house within two years. I do not know whether Smith has yet got a poet to look after the cattle, which, on account of the early breaking up of the ice, are compelled to summer in the woods, but I would suggest this office to such of my acquaintances as love to write verses and go a-gunning.

After a dinner, at which apple-sauce was the greatest luxury to me, but our moose-meat was oftenest called for by the lumberers, I walked across the clearing into the forest, southward, returning along the shore. For my dessert, I helped myself to a large slice of the Chesuncook woods, and took a hearty draught of its waters with all my senses. The woods were as fresh and full of vegetable life as a lichen in wet weather, and contained many interesting plants; but unless they are of white pine, they are treated with as little respect here as a mildew, and in the other case they are only the more quickly cut down. The shore was of coarse, flat, slate rocks, often in slabs, with the surf beating on it. The rocks and bleached drift-logs, extending some way into the shaggy woods, showed a rise and fall of six or eight feet, caused partly by the dam at the outlet. They said that in winter the snow was three feet deep on a level here, and sometimes four or five,—that the ice on the lake was two feet thick, clear, and four feet, including the snow-ice. Ice had already formed in vessels.

We lodged here this Sunday night in a comfortable

bed-room, apparently the best one; and all that I noticed unusual in the night—for I still kept taking notes, like a spy in the camp—was the creaking of the thin split boards, when any of our neighbors stirred.

Such were the first rude beginnings of a town. They spoke of the practicability of a winter-road to the Moosehead carry, which would not cost much, and would connect them with steam and staging and all the busy world. I almost doubted if the lake would be then the self-same lake,—preserve its form and identity, when the shores should be cleared and settled; as if these lakes and streams which explorers report never awaited the advent of the citizen.

The sight of one of these frontier-houses, built of these great logs, whose inhabitants have unflinchingly maintained their ground many summers and winters in the wilderness, reminds me of famous forts, like Ticonderoga, or Crown Point, which have sustained memorable sieges. They are especially winter-quarters, and at this season this one had a partially deserted look, as if the siege were raised a little, the snow-banks being melted from before it, and its garrison accordingly reduced. I think of their daily food as rations,—it is called "supplies"; a Bible and a great coat are munitions of war, and a single man seen about the premises is a sentinel on duty. You expect that he will require the countersign, and will perchance take you for Ethan Allen, come to demand the surrender of his fort in the name of the Continental Congress. It is a sort of ranger service. Arnold's expedition is a daily experience with these settlers. They can prove that they were out at almost any time; and I think that all the first generation of them deserve a pension more than any that went to the Mexican war.

Early the next morning we started on our return

up the Penobscot, my companion wishing to go about twenty-five miles above the Moosehead carry to a camp near the junction of the two forks, and look for moose there. Our host allowed us something for the quarter of the moose which we had brought, and which he was glad to get. Two explorers from Chamberlain Lake started at the same time that we did. Red flannel shirts should be worn in the woods, if only for the fine contrast which this color makes with the evergreens and the water. Thus I thought when I saw the forms of the explorers in their birch, poling up the rapids before us, far off against the forest. It is the surveyor's color also, most distinctly seen under all circumstances. We stopped to dine at Ragmuff, as before. My companion it was who wandered up the stream to look for moose this time, while Joe went to sleep on the bank, so that we felt sure of him; and I improved the opportunity to botanize and bathe. Soon after starting again, while Joe was gone back in the canoe for the frying-pan, which had been left, we picked a couple of quarts of tree-cranberries for a sauce.

I was surprised by Joe's asking me how far it was to the Moosehorn. He was pretty well acquainted with this stream, but he had noticed that I was curious about distances, and had several maps. He, and Indians generally, with whom I have talked, are not able to describe dimensions or distances in our measures with any accuracy. He could tell, perhaps, at what time we should arrive, but not how far it was. We saw a few wood-ducks, sheldrakes, and black ducks, but they were not so numerous there at that season as on our river at home. We scared the same family of wood-ducks before us, going and returning. We also heard the note of one fish-hawk, somewhat like that of a pigeon-woodpecker, and soon after saw him perched near the top of a dead white-pine against the island where we had first camped, while a company of peetweets were twittering and teetering about over the carcass of a moose on a low sandy spit just beneath. We drove the fish-hawk from perch to perch, each time eliciting a scream or whistle, for many miles before us. Our course being up-stream, we were obliged to work much harder than before, and had frequent use for a pole. Some-times all three of us paddled together, standing up, small and heavily laden as the canoe was. About six miles from Moosehead, we began to see the moun-tains east of the north end of the lake, and at four o'clock we reached the carry.

The Indians were still encamped here. There were three, including the St. Francis Indian who had come in the steamer with us. One of the others was called Sabattis. Joe and the St. Francis Indian were plainly clear Indian, the other two apparently mixed Indian and white; but the difference was confined to their features and complexions, for all that I could see. We here cooked the tongue of the moose for supper,—having left the nose, which is esteemed the choicest part, at Chesuncook, boiling, it being a good deal of trouble to prepare it. We also stewed our tree-cran-berries, (*Viburnum opulus*,) sweetening them with sugar. The lumberers sometimes cook them with molasses. They were used in Arnold's expedition. This sauce was very grateful to us who had been confined to hard bread, pork, and moose-meat, and, notwith-standing their seeds, we all three pronounced them equal to the common cranberry; but perhaps some allowance is to be made for our forest appetites. It would be worth the while to cultivate them, both for beauty and for food. I afterward saw them in a garden in Bangor. Joe said that they were called *ebeemenar*.

While we were getting supper, Joe commenced curing the moose-hide, on which I had sat a good part of the voyage, he having already cut most of the hair off with his knife at the Caucomgomoc. He set up two stout forked poles on the bank, seven or eight feet high, and as much asunder east and west, and having cut slits eight or ten inches long, and the same distance apart, close to the edge, on the sides of the hide, he threaded poles through them, and then, placing one of the poles on the forked stakes, tied the other down tightly at the bottom. The two ends also were tied with cedar bark, their usual string, to the upright poles, through small holes at short intervals. The hide, thus stretched, and slanted a little to the north, to expose its flesh side to the sun, measured, in the extreme, eight feet long by six high. Where any flesh still adhered, Joe boldly scored it with his knife to lay it open to the sun. It now appeared somewhat spotted and injured by the duck shot. You may see the old frames on which hides have been stretched at many camping-places in these woods.

For some reason or other, the going to the forks of the Penobscot was given up, and we decided to stop here, my companion intending to hunt down the stream at night. The Indians invited us to lodge with them, but my companion inclined to go to the log-camp on the carry. This camp was close and dirty, and had an ill smell, and I preferred to accept the Indians' offer, if we did not make a camp for ourselves; for, though they were dirty, too, they were more in the open air, and were much more agreeable, and even refined company, than the lumberers. The most interesting question entertained at the lumberers' camp was, which man could "handle" any other on the carry; and, for the most part, they possessed no qualities which you could not lay hands on. So we went to the Indians' camp or wigwam.

It was rather windy, and therefore Joe concluded to hunt after midnight, if the wind went down, which the other Indians thought it would not do, because it was from the south. The two mixed bloods, however, went off up the river for moose at dark, before we arrived at their camp. This Indian camp was a slight, patched-up affair, which had stood there several weeks, built shed-fashion, open to the fire on the west. If the wind changed, they could turn it round. It was formed by two forked stakes and a cross-bar, with rafters slanted from this to the ground. The covering was partly an old sail, partly birch-bark, quite imperfect, but securely tied on, and coming down to the ground on the sides. A large log was rolled up at the back side for a headboard, and two or three moose-hides were spread on the ground with the hair up. Various articles of their wardrobe were tucked around the sides and corners, or under the roof. They were smoking moose-meat on just such a crate as is represented by With in De Bry's "Collectio Peregrinationum," published in 1592, and which the natives of Brazil called *boucan*, (whence buccaneer,) on which were frequently shown pieces of human flesh drying along with the rest. It was erected in front of the camp over the usual large fire, in the form of an oblong square. Two stout forked stakes, four or five feet apart and five feet high, were driven into the ground at each end, and then two poles ten feet long were stretched across over the fire, and smaller ones laid transversely on these a foot apart. On the last hung large, thin slices of moose-meat smoking and drying, a space being left open over the centre of the fire. There was the whole heart, black as a thirty-two pound ball, hanging at one corner.

They said, that it took three or four days to cure this meat, and it would keep a year or more. Refuse pieces lay about on the ground in different stages of decay, and some pieces also in the fire, half buried and sizzling in the ashes, as black and dirty as an old shoe. These last I at first thought were thrown away, but afterwards found that they were being cooked. Also a tremendous rib-piece was roasting before the fire, being impaled on an upright stake forced in and out between the ribs. There was a moose-hide stretched and curing on poles like ours, and quite a pile of cured skins close by. They had killed twenty-two moose within two months, but, as they could use but very little of the meat, they left the carcasses on the ground. Altogether it was about as savage a sight as was ever witnessed, and I was carried back at once three hundred years. There were many torches of birch-bark, shaped like straight tin horns, lying ready for use on a stump outside.

For fear of dirt, we spread our blankets over their hides, so as not to touch them anywhere. The St. Francis Indian and Joe alone were there at first, and we lay on our backs talking with them till midnight. They were very sociable, and, when they did not talk with us, kept up a steady chatting in their own language. We heard a small bird just after dark, which, Joe said, sang at a certain hour in the night,— at ten o'clock, he believed. We also heard the hylodes and tree-toads, and the lumberers singing in their camp a quarter of a mile off. I told them that I had seen pictured in old books pieces of human flesh drying on these crates; whereupon they repeated some tradition about the Mohawks eating human flesh, what parts they preferred, etc., and also of a battle with the Mohawks near Moosehead, in which many of the latter were killed; but I found that they knew but little of the history of their race, and could be entertained by stories about their ancestors as readily as any way. At first I was nearly roasted out, for I lay against one side of the camp, and felt the heat reflected not only from the birch-bark above, but from the side; and again I remembered the sufferings of the Jesuit missionaries, and what extremes of heat and cold the Indians were said to endure. I struggled long between my desire to remain and talk with them, and my impulse to rush out and stretch myself on the cool grass; and when I was about to take the last step, Joe, hearing my murmurs, or else being uncomfortable himself, got up and partially dispersed the fire. I suppose that that is Indian manners,—to defend yourself.

While lying there listening to the Indians, I amused myself with trying to guess at their subject by their gestures, or some proper name introduced. There can be no more startling evidence of their being a distinct and comparatively aboriginal race, than to hear this unaltered Indian language, which the white man cannot speak nor understand. We may suspect change and deterioration in almost every other particular, but the language which is so wholly unintelligible to us. It took me by surprise, though I had found so many arrow-heads, and convinced me that the Indian was not the invention of historians and poets. It was a purely wild and primitive American sound, as much as the barking of a *chickaree*, and I could not understand a syllable of it; but Paugus, had he been there, would have understood it. These Abenakis gossiped, laughed, and jested, in the language in which Eliot's Indian Bible is written, the language which has been spoken in New England who shall say how long? These were the sounds that issued from the wigwams of this country before Columbus was born; they have not yet died away; and, with remarkably few exceptions, the language of their forefathers is still copious enough for them. I felt that I stood, or rather lay, as near to the primitive man of America, that night, as any of its discoverers ever did.

In the midst of their conversation, Joe suddenly appealed to me to know how long Moosehead Lake was.

Meanwhile, as we lay there, Joe was making and trying his horn, to be ready for hunting after midnight. The St. Francis Indian also amused himself with sounding it, or rather calling through it; for the sound is made with the voice, and not by blowing through the horn. The latter appeared to be a speculator in moose-hides. He bought my companion's for two dollars and a quarter, green. Joe said that it was worth two and a half at Oldtown. Its chief use is for moccasins. One or two of these Indians wore them. I was told, that, by a recent law of Maine, foreigners are not allowed to kill moose there at any season; white Americans can kill them only at a particular season, but the Indians of Maine at all seasons. The St. Francis Indian accordingly asked my companion for a *wighiggin*, or bill, to show, since he was a foreigner. He lived near Sorel. I found that he could write his name very well, *Tahmunt Swasen*. One Ellis, an old white man of Guilford, a town through which we passed, not far from the south end of Moosehead, was the most celebrated moose-hunter of those parts. Indians and whites spoke with equal respect of him. Tahmunt said, that there were more moose here than in the Adirondack country in New York, where he had hunted; that three years before there were a great many about, and there were a great many now in the woods, but they did not come out to the water. It was of no use to hunt them at midnight,—they would not come out then. I asked Sabattis, after he came home, if the moose never attacked him. He answered, that you must not fire many times so as to mad him. "I fire once and hit him in the right place, and in the morning I find him. He won't go far. But if you keep firing, you mad him. I fired once five bullets, every one through the heart, and he did not mind 'em at all; it only made him more mad." I asked him if they did not hunt them with dogs. He said, that they did so in winter, but never in the summer, for then it was of no use; they would run right off straight and swiftly a hundred miles.

Another Indian said, that the moose, once scared, would run all day. A dog will hang to their lips, and be carried along till he is swung against a tree and drops off. They cannot run on a "glaze," though they can run in snow four feet deep; but the caribou can run on ice. They commonly find two or three moose together. They cover themselves with water, all but their noses, to escape flies. He had the horns of what he called "the black moose that goes in low lands." These spread three or four feet. The "red moose" was another kind, "running on mountains," and had horns which spread six feet. Such were his distinctions. Both can move their horns. The broad flat blades are covered with hair, and are so soft, when the animal is alive, that you can run a knife through them. They regard it as a good or bad sign, if the horns turn this way or that. His caribou horns had been gnawed by mice in his wigwam, but he thought that the horns neither of the moose nor of the caribou were ever gnawed while the creature was alive, as some have asserted. An Indian, whom I met after this at Oldtown, who had carried about a bear and other animals of Maine to exhibit, told me that thirty years ago there were not so many moose in Maine as now; also, that the moose were very easily tamed, and would come back when once fed, and so would deer, but not caribou. The Indians of this neighborhood are about as familiar with the moose as we are with the ox, having associated with them for so many generations. Father Rasles, in his Dictionary of the Abenaki Language, gives not only a word for the male moose, (*aianbé*,) and another for the female, (*hèrar*,) but for the bone which is in the middle of the heart of the moose (!), and for his left hind-leg.

There were none of the small deer up there; they are more common about the settlements. One ran into the city of Bangor two years before, and jumped through a window of costly plate glass, and then into a mirror, where it thought it recognized one of its kind, and out again, and so on, leaping over the heads of the crowd, until it was captured. This the inhabitants speak of as the deer that went a-shopping. The last-mentioned Indian spoke of the *lunxus* or Indian devil, (which I take to be the cougar, and not the *Gulo luscus*,) as the only animal in Maine which man need fear; it would follow a man, and did not mind a fire. He also said, that beavers were getting to be pretty numerous again, where we went, but their skins brought so little now that it was not profitable to hunt them.

I had put the ears of our moose, which were ten inches long, to dry along with the moose-meat over the fire, wishing to preserve them; but Sabattis told me that I must skin and cure them, else the hair would all come off. He observed, that they made tobacco-pouches of the skins of their ears, putting the two together inside to inside. I asked him how he got fire; and he produced a little cylindrical box of friction-matches. He also had flints and steel, and some punk, which was not dry; I think it was from the yellow birch. "But suppose you upset, and all these and your powder get wet." "Then," said he, "we wait till we get to where there is some fire." I produced from my pocket a little vial, containing matches, stoppled water-tight, and told him, that, though we were upset, we should still have some dry matches; at which he stared without saying a word.

We lay awake thus a long while talking, and they gave us the meaning of many Indian names of lakes and streams in the vicinity,—especially Tahmunt. I asked the Indian name of Moosehead Lake. Joe answered, *Sebamook*; Tahmunt pronounced it *Sebemook*. When I asked what it meant, they answered, Moosehead Lake. At length, getting my meaning, they alternately repeated the word over to themselves, as a philologist might,—*Sebamook*,—*Sebamook*, —now and then comparing notes in Indian; for there was a slight difference in their dialects; and finally Tahmunt said, "Ugh! I know,"—and he rose up partly on the moose-hide,—"like as here is a place, and there is a place," pointing to different parts of the hide, "and you take water from there and fill this, and it stays here; that is *Sebamook*." I understood him to mean that it was a reservoir of water which did not run away, the river coming in on one side and passing out again near the same place, leaving a permanent bay. Another Indian said, that it meant Large-Bay Lake, and that *Sebago* and *Sebec*, the names of other lakes, were kindred words, meaning large open water. Joe said that *Seboois* meant Little River. I observed their inability, often described, to convey an abstract idea. Having got the idea, though indistinctly, they groped about in vain for words with which to express it. Tahmunt thought that the whites called it Moosehead Lake, because Mount Kineo, which commands it, is shaped like a moose's head, and that Moose River was so called "because the mountain points right across the lake to its mouth." John Josselyn, writing about 1673, says, "Twelve miles from Casco Bay, and passable for men and horses, is a lake, called by the Indians Sebug. On the brink thereof, at one end, is the famous rock, shaped like a moose deer or helk, diaphanous, and called the Moose Rock." He appears to have confounded Sebamook with Sebago, which is nearer, but has no "diaphanous" rock on its shore.

I give more of their definitions, for what they are worth,—partly *because* they differ sometimes from the commonly received ones. They never analyzed these words before. After long deliberation and repeating of the word, for it gave much trouble, Tahmunt said that *Chesuncook* meant a place where many streams emptied in (?), and he enumerated them,—Penobscot, Umbazookskus, Cusabexsex, Red Brook, etc.—"*Caucomgomoc*,—what does that mean?" "What are those large white birds?" he asked. "Gulls," said I. "Ugh! Gull Lake."—*Pammadumcook*, Joe thought, meant the Lake with Gravelly Bottom or Bed.—*Kenduskeag*, Tahmunt concluded at last, after asking if birches went up it, for he said that he was not much acquainted with it, meant something like this: "You go up Penobscot till you come to *Kenduskeag*, and you go by, you don't turn up there. That is *Kenduskeag*." (?) Another Indian, however, who knew the river better, told us afterward that it meant Little Eel River.—*Mattawamkeag* was a place where two rivers meet. (?)—*Penobscot* was Rocky River. One writer says, that this was "originally the name of only a section of the main channel, from the head of the tide-water to a short distance above Oldtown."

A very intelligent Indian, whom we afterward met, son-in-law of Neptune, gave us also these other definitions:—*Umbazookskus*, Meadow Stream; *Millinoket*, Place of Islands; *Aboljacarmegus*, Smooth-Ledge Falls (and Dead-Water); *Aboljacarmeguscook*, the stream emptying in; (the last was the word he gave when I asked about *Aboljacknagesic*, which he did not recognize;) *Mattahumkeag*, Sand-Creek Pond; *Piscataquis*, Branch of a River.

I asked our hosts what *Musketaquid*, the Indian name of Concord, Mass., meant; but they changed it to *Musketicook*, and repeated that, and Tahmunt said that it meant Dead Stream, which is probably true. *Cook* appears to mean stream, and perhaps *quid* signifies the place or ground. When I asked the meaning of the names of two of our hills, they answered that they were another language. As Tahmunt said that he traded at Quebec, my companion inquired the meaning of the word *Quebec*, about which there has been so much question. He did not know, but began to conjecture. He asked what those great ships were called that carried soldiers. "Men-of-war," we answered. "Well," he said, "when the English ships came up the river, they could not go any further, it was so narrow there; they must go back,—go-back,— that's Que-bec." I mention this to show the value of his authority in the other cases.

Late at night the other two Indians came home from moose-hunting, not having been successful, aroused the fire again, lighted their pipes, smoked awhile, took something strong to drink, and ate some moose-meat, and, finding what room they could, lay down on the moose-hides; and thus we passed the night, two white men and four Indians, side by side.

When I awoke in the morning the weather was drizzling. One of the Indians was lying outside, rolled in his blanket, on the opposite side of the fire, for want of room. Joe had neglected to awake my companion, and he had done no hunting that night. Tahmunt was making a cross-bar for his canoe with a singularly shaped knife, such as I have since seen other Indians using. The blade was thin, about three quarters of an inch wide, and eight or nine inches long, but curved out of its plane into a hook, which he said made it more convenient to shave with. As the Indians very far north and northwest use the same kind of knife, I suspect that it was made according to an aboriginal pattern, though some white artisans may use a similar one. The Indians baked a loaf of flour bread in a spider on its edge before the fire for their breakfast; and while my companion was making tea, I caught a dozen sizable fishes in the Penobscot, two kinds of sucker and one trout. After we had breakfasted by ourselves, one of our bedfellows, who had also breakfasted, came along, and, being invited, took a cup of tea, and finally, taking up the common platter, licked it clean. But he was nothing to a white fellow, a lumberer, who was continually stuffing himself with the Indians' moosemeat, and was the butt of his companions accordingly. He seems to have thought that it was a feast "to eat all." It is commonly said that the white man finally surpasses the Indian on his own ground, and it was proved true in this case. I cannot swear to his employment during the hours of darkness, but I saw him at it again as soon as it was light, though he came a quarter of a mile to his work.

The rain prevented our continuing any longer in the woods; so giving some of our provisions and utensils to the Indians, we took leave of them. This being the steamer's day, I set out for the lake at once.

I walked over the carry alone and waited at the

head of the lake. An eagle, or some other large bird, flew screaming away from its perch by the shore at my approach. For an hour after I reached the shore there was not a human being to be seen, and I had all that wide prospect to myself. I thought that I heard the sound of the steamer before she came in sight on the open lake. I noticed at the landing, when the steamer came in, one of our bedfellows, who had been a-moose-hunting the night before, now very sprucely dressed in a clean white shirt and fine black pants, a true Indian dandy, who had evidently come over the carry to show himself to any arrivers on the north shore of Moosehead Lake, just as New York dandies take a turn up Broadway and stand on the steps of a hotel.

Midway the lake we took on board two manly-looking middle-aged men, with their batteau, who had been exploring for six weeks as far as the Canada line, and had let their beards grow. They had the skin of a beaver, which they had recently caught, stretched on an oval hoop, though the fur was not good at that season. I talked with one of them, telling him that I had come all this distance partly to see where the white-pine, the Eastern stuff of which our houses are built, grew, but that on this and a previous excursion into another part of Maine I had found it a scarce tree; and I asked him where I must look for it. With a smile, he answered, that he could hardly tell me. However, he said that he had found enough to employ two teams the next winter in a place where there was thought to be none left. What was considered a "tip-top" tree now was not looked at twenty years ago, when he first went into the business; but they succeeded very well now with what was considered quite inferior timber then. The explorer used to cut into a tree higher and higher up, to see if it was false-hearted, and if there was a rotten heart as big as his arm, he let it alone; but now they cut such a tree, and sawed it all around the rot, and it made the very best of boards, for in such a case they were never shaky.

One connected with lumbering operations at Bangor told me that the largest pine belonging to his firm, cut the previous winter, "scaled" in the woods four thousand five hundred feet, and was worth ninety dollars in the log at the Bangor boom in Oldtown. They cut a road three and a half miles long for this tree alone. He thought that the principal locality for the white-pine that came down the Penobscot now was at the head of the East Branch and the Allegash, about Webster Stream and Eagle and Chamberlain Lakes. Much timber has been stolen from the public lands. (Pray, what kind of forest-warden is the Public itself?) I heard of one man who, having discovered some particularly fine trees just within the boundaries of the public lands, and not daring to employ an accomplice, cut them down, and by means of block and tackle, without cattle, tumbled them into a stream, and so succeeded in getting off with them without the least assistance. Surely, stealing pine-trees in this way is not so mean as robbing hen-roosts.

We reached Monson that night, and the next day rode to Bangor, all the way in the rain again, varying our route a little. Some of the taverns on this road, which were particularly dirty, were plainly in a transition state from the camp to the house.

The next forenoon we went to Oldtown. One slender old Indian on the Oldtown shore, who recognized my companion, was full of mirth and gestures, like a Frenchman. A Catholic priest crossed to the island in the same batteau with us. The Indian houses are framed, mostly of one story, and in rows one behind another, at the south end of the island, with a few scattered ones. I counted about forty, not including the church and what my companion called the council-house. The last, which I suppose is their town-house, was regularly framed and shingled like the rest. There were several of two stories, quite neat, with front-yards inclosed, and one at least had green blinds. Here and there were moose-hides stretched and drying about them. There were no cart-paths, nor tracks of horses, but foot-paths; very little land cultivated, but an abundance of weeds, indigenous and naturalized; more introduced weeds than useful vegetables, as the Indian is said to cultivate the vices rather than the virtues of the white man. Yet this village was cleaner than I expected, far cleaner than such Irish villages as I have seen. The children were not particularly ragged nor dirty. The little boys met us with bow in hand and arrow on string, and cried, "Put up a cent." Verily, the Indian has but a feeble hold on his bow now; but the curiosity of the white man is insatiable, and from the first he has been eager to witness this forest accomplishment. That elastic piece of wood with its feathered dart, so sure to be unstrung by contact with civilization, will serve for the type, the coat-of-arms of the savage. Alas for the Hunter Race! the white man has driven off their game, and substituted a cent in its place. I saw an Indian woman washing at the water's edge. She stood on a rock, and, after dipping the clothes in the stream, laid them on the rock, and beat them with a short club. In the grave-yard, which was crowded with graves, and overrun with weeds, I noticed an inscription in Indian, painted on a wooden grave-board. There was a large wooden cross on the island.

Since my companion knew him, we called on Governor Neptune, who lived in a little "ten-footer," one of the humblest of them all. Personalities are allowable in speaking of public men, therefore I will give the particulars of our visit. He was a-bed. When we entered the room, which was one half of the house, he was sitting on the side of the bed. There was a clock hanging in one corner. He had on a black frock-coat, and black pants, much worn, white cotton shirt, socks, a red silk handkerchief about his neck, and a straw hat. His black hair was only slightly grayed. He had very broad cheeks, and his features were decidedly and refreshingly different from those of any of the upstart Native American party whom I have seen. He was no darker than many old white men. He told me that he was eighty-nine; but he was going a-moose-hunting that fall, as he had been the previous one. Probably his companions did the hunting. We saw various squaws dodging about. One sat on the bed by his side and helped him out with his stories. They were remarkably corpulent, with smooth, round faces, apparently full of good-humor. Certainly our much-abused climate had not dried up their adipose substance. While we were there,—for we stayed a good while,—one went over to Oldtown, returned and cut out a dress, which she had bought, on another bed in the room. The Governor said, that "he could remember when the moose were much larger; that they did not use to be in the woods, but came out of the water, as all deer did. Moose was whale once. Away down Merrimack way, a whale came ashore in a shallow bay. Sea went out and left him, and he came up on land a moose. What made them know he was a whale was, that at first, before he began to run in bushes, he had no bowels inside, but"———and then the squaw who sat on the bed by his side, as the

Governor's aid, and had been putting in a word now and then and confirming the story, asked me what we called that soft thing we find along the sea-shore. "Jelly-fish," I suggested. "Yes," said he, "no bowels, but jelly-fish."

There may be some truth in what he said about the moose growing larger formerly; for the quaint John Josselyn, a physician who spent many years in this very district of Maine in the seventeenth century, says, that the tips of their horns "are sometimes found to be two fathoms asunder,"—and he is particular to tell us that a fathom is six feet,—"and [they are] in height, from the toe of the fore-foot to the pitch of the shoulder, twelve foot, both which hath been taken by some of my sceptique readers to be monstrous lies"; and he adds,—"There are certain transcendentia in every creature, which are the indelible characters of God, and which discover God." This is a greater dilemma to be caught in than is presented by the cranium of the young Bechuana ox, apparently another of the *transcendentia*, in the collection of Thomas Steel, Upper Brook Street, London, whose "entire length of horn, from tip to tip, along the curve, is 13 ft. 5 in.; distance (straight) between the tips of the horns, 8 ft. 8½ in." However, the size both of the moose and the cougar, as I have found, is generally rather underrated than overrated, and I should be inclined to add to the popular estimate a part of what I subtracted from Josselyn's.

But we talked mostly with the Governor's son-in-law, a very sensible Indian; and the Governor, being so old and deaf, permitted himself to be ignored, while we asked questions about him. The former said, that there were two political parties among them,—one in favor of schools, and the other opposed to them, or rather they did not wish to resist the priest, who was opposed to them. The first had just prevailed at the election and sent their man to the legislature. Neptune and Aitteon and he himself were in favor of schools. He said, "If Indians got learning, they would keep their money." When we asked where Joe's father, Aitteon, was, he knew that he must be at Lincoln, though he was about going a-moose-hunting, for a messenger had just gone to him there to get his signature to some papers. I asked Neptune if they had any of the old breed of dogs yet. He answered, "Yes." "But that," said I, pointing to one that had just come in, "is a Yankee dog." He assented. I said that he did not look like a good one. "Oh, yes!" he said, and he told, with much gusto, how, the year before, he had caught and held by the throat a wolf. A very small black puppy rushed into the room and made at the Governor's feet, as he sat in his stockings with his legs dangling from the bedside. The Governor rubbed his hands and dared him to come on, entering into the sport with spirit. Nothing more that was significant transpired, to my knowledge, during this interview. This was the first time that I ever called on a governor, but, as I did not ask for an office, I can speak of it with the more freedom.

An Indian who was making canoes behind a house, looking up pleasantly from his work,—for he knew my companion,—said that his name was Old John Pennyweight. I had heard of him long before, and I inquired after one of his contemporaries, Joe Fourpence-ha'penny; but, alas! he no longer circulates. I made a faithful study of canoe-building, and I thought that I should like to serve an apprenticeship at that trade for one season, going into the woods for bark with my "boss," making the canoe there, and returning in it at last.

While the batteau was coming over to take us off, I picked up some fragments of arrow-heads on the shore, and one broken stone chisel, which were greater novelties to the Indians than to me. After this, on Old Fort Hill, at the bend of the Penobscot, three miles above Bangor, looking for the site of an Indian town which some think stood thereabouts, I found more arrow-heads, and two little dark and crumbling fragments of Indian earthenware, in the ashes of their fires. The Indians on the Island appeared to live quite happily and to be well treated by the inhabitants of Oldtown.

We visited Veazie's mills, just below the Island, where were sixteen sets of saws,—some gang saws, sixteen in a gang, not to mention circular saws. On one side, they were hauling the logs up an inclined plane by water-power; on the other, passing out the boards, planks, and sawed timber, and forming them into rafts. The trees were literally drawn and quartered there. In forming the rafts, they use the lower three feet of hard-wood saplings, which have a crooked and knobbed but-end, for bolts, passing them up through holes bored in the corners and sides of the rafts, and keying them. In another apartment they were making fence-slats, such as stand all over New England, out of odds and ends,— and it may be that I saw where the picket-fence behind which I dwell at home came from. I was surprised to find a boy collecting the long edgings of boards as fast as cut off, and thrusting them down a hopper, where they were *ground up* beneath the mill, that they might be out of the way; otherwise they accumulate in vast piles by the side of the building, increasing the danger from fire, or, floating off, they obstruct the river. This was not only a saw-mill, but a grist-mill, then. The inhabitants of Oldtown,

Stillwater, and Bangor cannot suffer for want of kindling-stuff, surely. Some get their living exclusively by picking up the drift-wood and selling it by the cord in the winter. In one place I saw where an Irishman, who keeps a team and a man for the purpose, had covered the shore for a long distance with regular piles, and I was told that he had sold twelve hundred dollars' worth in a year. Another, who lived by the shore, told me that he got all the material of his out-buildings and fences from the river; and in that neighborhood I perceived that this refuse wood was frequently used instead of sand to fill hollows with, being apparently cheaper than dirt.

I got my first clear view of Katadn, on this excursion, from a hill about two miles northwest of Bangor, whither I went for this purpose. After this I was ready to return to Massachusetts.

Humboldt has written an interesting chapter on the primitive forest, but no one has yet described for me the difference between that wild forest which once occupied our oldest townships, and the tame one which I find there to-day. It is a difference which would be worth attending to. The civilized man not only clears the land permanently to a great extent, and cultivates open fields, but he tames and cultivates to a certain extent the forest itself. By his mere presence, almost, he changes the nature of the trees as no other creature does. The sun and air, and perhaps fire, have been introduced, and grain raised where it stands. It has lost its wild, damp, and shaggy look, the countless fallen and decaying trees are gone, and consequently that thick coat of moss which lived on them is gone too. The earth is comparatively bare and smooth and dry. The most primitive places left with us are the swamps, where the

spruce still grows shaggy with usnea. The surface of
the ground in the Maine woods is everywhere spongy
and saturated with moisture. I noticed that the plants
which cover the forest floor there are such as are
commonly confined to swamps with us,—the *Clintonia
borealis*, orchises, creeping snowberry, and others;
and the prevailing aster there is the *Aster acuminatus*,
which with us grows in damp and shady woods. The
asters *cordifolius* and *macrophyllus* also are common, asters of little or no color, and sometimes without petals. I saw no soft, spreading, second-growth
white-pines, with smooth bark, acknowledging the
presence of the wood-chopper, but even the young
white-pines were all tall and slender rough-barked
trees.

Those Maine woods differ essentially from ours.
There you are never reminded that the wilderness
which you are threading is, after all, some villager's
familiar wood-lot, some widow's thirds, from which
her ancestors have sledded fuel for generations, mi-
nutely described in some old deed which is recorded,
of which the owner has got a plan too, and old
bound-marks may be found every forty rods, if you
will search. 'Tis true, the map may inform you that
you stand on land granted by the State to some
academy, or on Bingham's purchase; but these names
do not impose on you, for you see nothing to remind
you of the academy or of Bingham. What were the
"forests" of England to these? One writer relates of
the Isle of Wight, that in Charles the Second's time
"there were woods in the island so complete and
extensive, that it is said a squirrel might have travelled
in several parts many leagues together on the tops of
the trees." If it were not for the rivers, (and he might
go round their heads,) a squirrel could here travel
thus the whole breadth of the country.

We have as yet had no adequate account of a primitive pine-forest. I have noticed that in a physical atlas lately published in Massachusetts, and used in our schools, the "wood land" of North America is limited almost solely to the valleys of the Ohio and some of the Great Lakes, and the great pine-forests of the globe are not represented. In our vicinity, for instance, New Brunswick and Maine are exhibited as bare as Greenland. It may be that the children of Greenville, at the foot of Moosehead Lake, who surely are not likely to be scared by an owl, are referred to the valley of the Ohio to get an idea of a forest; but they would not know what to do with their moose, bear, caribou, beaver, etc., there. Shall we leave it to an Englishman to inform us, that "in North America, both in the United States and Canada, are the most extensive pine-forests in the world"? The greater part of New Brunswick, the northern half of Maine, and adjacent parts of Canada, not to mention the north-eastern part of New York and other tracts further off, are still covered with an almost unbroken pine-forest.

But Maine, perhaps, will soon be where Massachusetts is. A good part of her territory is already as bare and common-place as much of our neighborhood, and her villages generally are not so well shaded as ours. We seem to think that the earth must go through the ordeal of sheep-pasturage before it is habitable by man. Consider Nahant, the resort of all the fashion of Boston,—which peninsula I saw but indistinctly in the twilight, when I steamed by it, and thought that it was unchanged since the discovery. John Smith described it in 1614 as "the Mattahunts, two pleasant isles of groves, gardens, and cornfields"; and others tell us that it was once well wooded, and even furnished timber to build the wharves of Boston. Now it is difficult to make a tree grow there, and the visitor comes away with a vision of Mr. Tudor's ugly fences a rod high, designed to protect a few pear-shrubs. And what are we coming to in our Middlesex towns?—a bald, staring town-house, or meeting-house, and a bare liberty-pole, as leafless as it is fruitless, for all I can see. We shall be obliged to import the timber for the last, hereafter, or splice such sticks as we have;—and our ideas of liberty are equally mean with these. The very willow-rows lopped every three years for fuel or powder,—and every sizable pine and oak, or other forest tree, cut down within the memory of man! As if individual speculators were to be allowed to export the clouds out of the sky, or the stars out of the firmament, one by one. We shall be reduced to gnaw the very crust of the earth for nutriment.

They have even descended to smaller game. They have lately, as I hear, invented a machine for chopping up huckleberry-bushes fine, and so converting them into fuel!—bushes which, for fruit alone, are worth all the pear-trees in the country many times over. (I can give you a list of the three best kinds, if you want it.) At this rate, we shall all be obliged to let our beards grow at least, if only to hide the nakedness of the land and make a sylvan appearance. The farmer sometimes talks of "brushing up," simply as if bare ground looked better than clothed ground, than that which wears its natural vesture,—as if the wild hedges, which, perhaps, are more to his children than his whole farm beside, were *dirt*. I know of one who deserves to be called the Tree-hater, and, perhaps, to leave this for a new patronymic to his children. You would think that he had been warned by an oracle that he would be killed by the fall of a tree, and so was resolved to anticipate them.

The journalists think that they cannot say too much in favor of such "improvements" in husbandry; it is a safe theme, like piety; but as for the beauty of one of these "model farms," I would as lief see a patent churn and a man turning it. They are, commonly, places merely where somebody is making money, it may be counterfeiting. The virtue of making two blades of grass grow where only one grew before does not begin to be superhuman.

Nevertheless, it was a relief to get back to our smooth, but still varied landscape. For a permanent residence, it seemed to me that there could be no comparison between this and the wilderness, necessary as the latter is for a resource and a background, the raw material of all our civilization. The wilderness is simple, almost to barrenness. The partially cultivated country it is which chiefly has inspired, and will continue to inspire, the strains of poets, such as compose the mass of any literature. Our woods are sylvan, and their inhabitants woodmen and rustics,—that is, *selvaggia*, and the inhabitants are *salvages*. A civilized man, using the word in the ordinary sense, with his ideas and associations, must at length pine there, like a cultivated plant, which clasps its fibres about a crude and undissolved mass of peat. At the extreme North, the voyagers are obliged to dance and act plays for employment. Perhaps our own woods and fields,—in the best wooded towns, where we need not quarrel about the huckleberries,—with the primitive swamps scattered here and there in their midst, but not prevailing over them, are the perfection of parks and groves, gardens, arbors, paths, vistas, and landscapes. They are the natural consequence of what art and refinement we as a people have,—the common which each village possesses, its true paradise, in comparison with which all elaborately and wilfully wealth-constructed parks and gardens are paltry imitations. Or, I would rather say, such *were* our groves twenty years ago. The poet's, commonly, is not a logger's path, but a wood-man's. The logger and pioneer have preceded him, like John the Baptist; eaten the wild honey, it may be, but the locusts also; banished decaying wood and the spongy mosses which feed on it, and built hearths and humanized Nature for him.

But there are spirits of a yet more liberal culture, to whom no simplicity is barren. There are not only stately pines, but fragile flowers, like the orchises, commonly described as too delicate for cultivation, which derive their nutriment from the crudest mass of peat. These remind us, that, not only for strength, but for beauty, the poet must, from time to time, travel the logger's path and the Indian's trail, to drink at some new and more bracing fountain of the Muses, far in the recesses of the wilderness.

The kings of England formerly had their forests "to hold the king's game," for sport or food, some-times destroying villages to create or extend them; and I think that they were impelled by a true in-stinct. Why should not we, who have renounced the king's authority, have our national preserves, where no villages need be destroyed, in which the bear and panther, and some even of the hunter race, may still exist, and not be "civilized off the face of the earth," —our forests, not to hold the king's game merely, but to hold and preserve the king himself also, the lord of creation,—not for idle sport or food, but for inspiration and our own true recreation? or shall we, like villains, grub them all up, poaching on our own national domains?

The Allegash and East Branch

I STARTED on my 3^d excursion to the Maine Woods Monday July 20th 1857, with one companion, arriving at Bangor the next day at noon. We had hardly left the steamer when we passed Molly Molasses in the street. As long as she lives the Penobscots may be considered extant as a tribe. The succeeding morning a relative of mine, who is well acquainted with the Penobscot Indians, and who had been my companion in my two previous excursions into the Maine Woods, took me in his wagon to Oldtown, to assist me in obtaining an Indian for this expedition.

We were ferried across to the Indian Island in a batteau. The ferryman's boy had got the key to it, but the father, who was a blacksmith, after a little hesitation, cut the chain with a cold chisel on a rock. He told us that the Indians were nearly all gone, to the sea-board and to Massachusetts, partly on account of the small pox, of which they are very much afraid, having broken out in Oldtown, and it was doubtful whether we should find a suitable one at home. The old chief Neptune, however, was there still. The first man we saw on the Island was an Indian named Joseph Polis, whom my relative had known from a boy, and now addressed familiarly as "Joe". He was dressing a deer skin in his yard. The skin was spread over a slanting log, and he was scraping it with a stick held by both hands. He was stoutly built, perhaps a little above the middle height, with a broad face and as others said perfect Indian features and complexion. His house was a 2-story white one with blinds, the best looking that I noticed there, and as good as an average one on a New Eng-

land village street. It was surrounded by a garden
and fruit trees, single corn-stalks standing thinly
amid the beans. We asked him if he knew any good
Indian who would like to go into the woods with us,
that is, to the Allegash Lakes, by way of Moosehead,
and return by the East Branch of the Penobscot, or
vary from this as we pleased. To which he answered,
out of that strange remoteness in which the Indian
ever dwells to the white man, "Me like to go myself;
me want to get some moose;" and kept on scraping
the skin. His brother had been into the woods with
my relative only a year or two before, and the Indian
now inquired what the latter had done to him, that
he did not come back, for he had not seen nor heard
from him since.

At length we got round to the more interesting
topic again. The ferry-man had told us that all the
best Indians were gone except Polis, who was one of
the aristocracy. He, to be sure, would be the best man
we could have, but if he went at all would want a
great price; so we did not expect to get him.

Polis asked at first $2 00 a day, but agreed to go
for a dollar and a half, and 50 cents a week for his
canoe. He would come to Bangor with his canoe by
the 7 o'clock train that evening—we might depend on
him. We thought ourselves lucky to secure the serv-
ices of this man, who was known to be particularly
steady and reliable.

I spent the afternoon with my companion, who
had remained in Bangor, in preparing for our expedition, purchasing provisions, hard bread, pork, coffee, sugar, &c. and some India-rubber clothing.

We had at first thought of exploring the St. John
from its source to its mouth; or else to go up the
Penobscot by its East Branch to the lakes of the St.
John and return by way of Chesuncook and Moose-

head. We had finally inclined to the last route, only reversing the order of it, going by way of Moosehead, and returning by the Penobscot, otherwise it would have been all the way up stream, and taken twice as long.

At evening Polis arrived in the cars, and I led the way while he followed me ¾ of a mile to my friend's house, with the canoe on his head. I did not know the exact route myself, but steered by the lay of the land, as I do in Boston, and I tried to enter into conversation with him, but as he was puffing under the weight of his canoe, not having the usual apparatus for carrying it, but, above all, was an Indian, I might as well have been thumping on the bottom of his birch the while. In answer to the various observations which I made by way of breaking the ice, he only grunted vaguely from beneath his canoe once or twice, so that I knew he was there.

Early the next morning, (July 23ᵈ) the stage called for us, the Indian having breakfasted with us, and already placed the baggage in the canoe to see how it would go. My companion and I had each a large knapsack as full as it would hold, and we had 2 large India rubber bags which held our provision and utensils. As for the Indian, all the baggage he had, beside his axe and gun, was a blanket which he brought loose in his hand. However, he had laid in a store of tobacco and a new pipe for the excursion. The canoe was securely lashed diagonally across the top of the stage, with bits of carpet tucked under the edge to prevent its chafing. The very accommodating driver appeared as much accustomed to carrying canoes in this way as band boxes.

At the Bangor House we took in 4 men bound on a hunting excursion, one of the men going as cook. They had a dog, a middling sized brindled cur which ran by the side of the stage, his master showing his head and whistling from time to time; but after we had gone about 3 miles, the dog was suddenly missing, and two of the party went back for him while the stage, which was full of passengers, waited. I suggested that he had taken the back track for the Bangor House. At length one man came back, while the other kept on. This whole party of hunters declared their intention to stop till the dog was found, but the very obliging driver was ready to wait a spell longer. He was evidently unwilling to lose so many passengers, who would have taken a private conveyance, or perhaps the other line of stages the next day. Such progress did we make, with a journey of over 60 miles to be accomplished that day, and a rainstorm just setting in. We discussed the subject of dogs and their instincts till it was threadbare, while we waited there, and the scenery of the suburbs of Bangor is still distinctly impressed on my memory. After full half an hour the man returned, leading the dog by a rope. He had overtaken him just as he was entering the Bangor House. He was then tied on the top of the stage, but being wet and cold, several times in the course of the journey he jumped off, and I saw him dangling by his neck. This dog was depended on to stop bears with. He had already stopped one somewhere in New Hampshire, and I can testify that he stopped a stage in Maine. This party of four probably paid nothing for the dog's ride, nor for his run, while our party of three paid nine dollars, and were charged four for the light canoe which lay still on the top.

It soon began to rain, and grew more and more stormy as the day advanced. This was the third time that I had passed over this route, and it rained steadily each time all day. We accordingly saw but little of the country. The stage was crowded all the way, and I attended the more to my fellow-travellers. If you had looked inside this coach you would have thought that we were prepared to run the gauntlet of a band of robbers, for there were four or five guns on the front seat, the Indian's included, and one or two on the back one, each man holding his darling in his arms. One had a gun which carried twelve to a pound. It appeared that this party of hunters was going our way, but much further down the Allegash and St. John, and thence up some other stream, and across to the Ristigouche and the Bay of Chaleur, to be gone six weeks. They had canoes, axes, and supplies deposited some distance along the route. They carried flour, and were to have new bread made every day. Their leader was a handsome man about thirty years old, of good height, but not apparently robust, of gentlemanly dress and faultless toilet; such a one as you might expect to meet on Broadway. In fact, in the popular sense of the word, he was the most "gentlemanly" appearing man in the stage, or that we saw on the road. He had a fair white complexion, as if he had always lived in the shade, and an intellectual face, and with his quiet manners might have passed for a divinity student who had seen something of the world. I was surprised to find, on talking with him in the course of the day's journey, that he was a hunter at all,—for his gun was not much exposed,—and yet more to find that he was probably the chief white hunter of Maine, and was known all along the road. He had also hunted in some of the States further south and west. I afterwards heard him spoken of as one who could endure a great deal of exposure and fatigue without showing the effect of it; and he could not only use guns, but make them, being himself a gunsmith. In

the spring, he had saved a stage-driver and two passengers from drowning in the backwater of the
Piscataquis in Foxcroft on this road, having swum
ashore in the freezing water and made a raft and
got them off,—though the horses were drowned,—at
great risk to himself, while the only other man who
could swim withdrew to the nearest house to prevent
freezing. He could now ride over this road for nothing. He knew our man, and remarked that we had a
good Indian there, a good hunter; adding that he
was said to be worth $6,000. The Indian also knew
him, and said to me, "the great hunter."

The former told me that he practised a kind of still
hunting, new or uncommon in those parts, that the
caribou, for instance, fed round and round the same
meadow, returning on the same path, and he lay in
wait for them.

The Indian sat on the front seat, saying nothing to
anybody, with a stolid expression of face, as if barely
awake to what was going on. Again I was struck by
the peculiar vagueness of his replies when addressed
in the stage, or at the taverns. He really never said
anything on such occasions. He was merely stirred
up, like a wild beast, and passively muttered some
insignificant response. His answer, in such cases, was
never the consequence of a positive mental energy,
but vague as a puff of smoke, suggesting no *responsibility*, and if you considered it, you would find that
you had got nothing out of him. This was instead of
the conventional palaver and smartness of the white
man, and equally profitable. Most get no more than
this out of the Indian, and pronounce him stolid
accordingly. I was surprised to see what a foolish and
impertinent style a Maine man, a passenger, used in
addressing him, as if he were a child, which only
made his eyes glisten a little. A tipsy Canadian asked

him at a tavern, in a drawling tone, if he smoked, to which he answered with an indefinite "yes." "Won't you lend me your pipe a little while?" asked the other. He replied, looking straight by the man's head, with a face singularly vacant to all neighboring interests, "Me got no pipe"; yet I had seen him put a new one, with a supply of tobacco, into his pocket that morning.

Our little canoe, so neat and strong, drew a favorable criticism from all the wiseacres among the tavern loungers along the road. By the roadside, close to the wheels, I noticed a splendid great purple-fringed orchis with a spike as big as an epilobium, which I would fain have stopped the stage to pluck, but as this had never been known to stop a bear, like the cur on the stage, the driver would probably have thought it a waste of time.

When we reached the lake, about half past eight in the evening, it was still steadily raining, and harder than before; and, in that fresh, cool atmosphere, the hylodes were peeping and the toads ringing about the lake universally, as in the spring with us. It was as if the seasons had revolved backward two or three months, or I had arrived at the abode of perpetual spring.

We had expected to go upon the lake at once, and after paddling up two or three miles, to camp on one of its islands; but on account of the steady and increasing rain, we decided to go to one of the taverns for the night, though, for my own part, I should have preferred to camp out.

About four o'clock the next morning, (July 24th,) though it was quite cloudy, accompanied by the landlord to the water's edge, in the twilight, we launched our canoe from a rock on the Moosehead Lake. When I was there four years before we had a rather small canoe for three persons, and I had thought that this time I would get a larger one, but the present one was even smaller than that. It was 18¼ feet long by 2 feet 6½ inches wide in the middle, and one foot deep within, as I found by measurement, and I judged that it would weigh not far from eighty pounds. The Indian had recently made it himself, and its smallness was partly compensated for by its newness, as well as stanchness and solidity, it being made of very thick bark and ribs. Our baggage weighed about 166 pounds, so that the canoe carried about 600 pounds in all, or the weight of four men. The principal part of the baggage was, as usual, placed in the middle of the broadest part, while we stowed ourselves in the chinks and crannies that were left before and behind it, where there was no room to extend our legs, the loose articles being tucked into the ends. The canoe was thus as closely packed as a market-basket, and might possibly have been upset without spilling any of its contents. The Indian sat on a cross-bar in the stern, but we flat on the bottom, with a splint or chip behind our backs, to protect them from the cross-bar, and one of us commonly paddled with the Indian. He foresaw that we should not want a pole till we reached the Umbazookskus River, it being either dead water or down stream so far, and he was prepared to make a sail of his blanket in the bows, if the wind should be fair; but we never used it.

It had rained more or less the four previous days, so that we thought we might count on some fair weather. The wind was at first southwesterly.

Paddling along the eastern side of the lake in the still of the morning, we soon saw a few sheldrakes, which the Indian called *Shecorways*, and some peet-weets *Naramekechus*, on the rocky shore; we also saw and heard loons, *medawisla*, which he said was a sign of wind. It was inspiriting to hear the regular dip of the paddles, as if they were our fins or flippers, and to realize that we were at length fairly embarked. We who had felt strangely as stage-passengers and tavern-lodgers were suddenly naturalized there and presented with the freedom of the lakes and the woods. Having passed the small rocky isles within two or three miles of the foot of the lake, we had a short consultation respecting our course, and inclined to the western shore for the sake of its lee; for otherwise, if the wind should rise, it would be impossible for us to reach Mount Kineo, which is about midway up the lake on the east side, but at its narrowest part, where probably we could recross if we took the western side. The wind is the chief obstacle to crossing the lakes, especially in so small a canoe. The Indian remarked several times that he did not like to cross the lakes "in littlum canoe," but nevertheless, "just as we say, it made no odds to him." He sometimes took a straight course up the middle of the lake between Sugar and Deer Islands, when there was no wind.

Measured on the map, Moosehead Lake is twelve miles wide at the widest place, and thirty miles long in a direct line, but longer as it lies. The captain of the steamer called it thirty-eight miles as he steered. We should probably go about forty. The Indian said that it was called "*Mspame*, because large water." Squaw Mountain rose darkly on our left, near the outlet of the Kennebec, and what the Indian called Spencer Bay Mountain, on the east, and already we saw Mount Kineo before us in the north.

Paddling near the shore, we frequently heard the *pe-pe* of the olive-sided fly-catcher, also the wood-pewee, and the kingfisher, thus early in the morning.

The Indian reminding us that he could not work without eating, we stopped to breakfast on the main shore, southwest of Deer Island, at a spot where the *Mimulus ringens* grew abundantly. We took out our bags, and the Indian made a fire under a very large bleached log, using white-pine bark from a stump, though he said that hemlock was better, and kindling with canoe-birch bark. Our table was a large piece of freshly peeled birch-bark, laid wrong-side-up, and our breakfast consisted of hard bread, fried pork, and strong coffee, well sweetened, in which we did not miss the milk.

While we were getting breakfast a brood of twelve black dippers, half grown, came paddling by within three or four rods, not at all alarmed; and they loitered about as long as we stayed, now huddled close together, within a circle of eighteen inches in diameter, now moving off in a long line, very cunningly. The Indian thought that the mother had perhaps been killed. Yet they bore a certain proportion to the great Moosehead Lake on whose bosom they floated, and I felt as if they were under its protection.

Looking northward from this place it appeared as if we were entering a large bay, and we did not know whether we should be obliged to diverge from our course and keep outside a point which we saw, or should find a passage between this and the mainland. I consulted my map and used my glass, and the Indian did the same, but we could not find our place exactly on the map, nor could we detect any break in the shore. When I asked the Indian the way, he answered "I don't know," which I thought remarkable, since he had said that he was familiar with the lake; but it appeared that he had never been up this side. It was misty dog-day weather, and we had already penetrated a smaller bay of the same kind, and knocked the bottom out of it, though we had been obliged to pass over a small bar, between an island and the shore, where there was but just breadth and depth enough to float the canoe, and the Indian had observed, "Very easy makum bridge here," but now it seemed that, if we held on, we should be fairly embayed. Presently, however, though we had not stirred, the mist lifted somewhat, and revealed a break in the shore northward, showing that the point was a portion of Deer Island, and that our course lay westward of it. Where it had seemed a continuous shore even through a glass, one portion was now seen by the naked eye to be much more distant than the other which overlapped it, merely by the greater thickness of the mist which still rested on it, while the nearer or island portion was comparatively bare and green. The line of separation was very distinct, and the Indian immediately remarked, "I guess you and I go there,—I guess there's room for my canoe there." This was his common expression instead of saying we. He never addressed us by our names, though curious to know how they were spelled and what they meant, while we called him Polis. He had already guessed very accurately at our ages, and said that he was forty-eight.

After breakfast I emptied the melted pork that was left into the lake, making what sailors call a "slick," and watching to see how much it spread over and smoothed the agitated surface. The Indian looked at it a moment and said, "That make hard paddlum thro'; hold 'em canoe. So say old times."

We hastily reloaded, putting the dishes loose in the bows, that they might be at hand when wanted, and set out again. The western shore, near which we paddled along, rose gently to a considerable height, and was everywhere densely covered with the forest, in which was a large proportion of hard wood to enliven and relieve the fir and spruce.

The Indian said that the usnea lichen which we saw hanging from the trees was called *chorchorque.* We asked him the names of several small birds which we heard this morning. The wood-thrush, which was quite common, and whose note he imitated, he said was called *Adelungquamooktum*; but sometimes he could not tell the name of some small bird which I heard and knew, but he said, "I tell all the birds about here,—this country; can't tell littlum noise, but I see 'em, then I can tell."

I observed that I should like to go to school to him to learn his language, living on the Indian island the while; could not that be done? "O, yer," he replied, "good many do so." I asked how long he thought it would take. He said one week. I told him that in this voyage I would tell him all I knew, and he should tell me all he knew, to which he readily agreed.

The birds sang quite as in our woods,—the red-eye, red-start, veery, wood-pewee, etc., but we saw no bluebirds in all our journey, and several told me in Bangor that they had not the bluebird there. Mt. Kineo, which was generally visible, though occasionally concealed by islands or the mainland in front, had a level bar of cloud concealing its summit, and all the mountain-tops about the lake were cut off at the same height. Ducks of various kinds—sheldrake, summer ducks, etc.—were quite common, and ran over the water before us as fast as a horse trots. Thus they were soon out of sight.

The Indian asked the meaning of *reality*, as near as I could make out the word, which he said one of us had used; also of "*interrent*," that is, intelligent. I observed that he could rarely sound the letter r, but used l, as also r for l sometimes; as *load* for road, *pickelel* for pickerel, *Soogle* Island for Sugar Island, *lock* for rock, etc. Yet he trilled the r pretty well after me.

He generally added the syllable *um* to his words when he could,—as padl*um*, etc. I have once heard a Chippewa lecture, who made his audience laugh unintentionally by putting *m* after the word *too*, which word he brought in continually and unnecessarily, accenting and prolonging this sound into *m–ar* sonorously as if it were necessary to bring in so much of his vernacular as a relief to his organs, a compensation for twisting his jaws about, and putting his tongue into every corner of his mouth, as he complained that he was obliged to do when he spoke English. There was so much of the Indian accent resounding through his English, so much of the "bow-arrow tang" as my neighbor calls it, and I have no doubt that word seemed to him the best pronounced. It was a wild and refreshing sound, like that of the wind among the pines, or the booming of the surf on the shore.

I asked him the meaning of the word *Musketicook*, the Indian name of Concord River. He pronounced it *Muskéeticook*, emphasizing the second syllable with a peculiar guttural sound, and said that it meant "Dead-water," which it is, and in this definition he agreed exactly with the St. Francis Indian with whom I talked in 1853.

On a point on the mainland some miles southwest of Sand-bar Island, where we landed to stretch our legs and look at the vegetation, going inland a few steps, I discovered a fire still glowing beneath its ashes, where somebody had breakfasted, and a bed of twigs prepared for the following night. So I knew not only that they had just left, but that they designed to return, and by the breadth of the bed that there was more than one in the party. You might have gone within six feet of these signs without seeing them. There grew the beaked hazel, the only hazel which I saw on this journey, the *Diervilla*, rue seven feet high, which was very abundant on all the lake and river shores, and *Cornus stolonifera*, or red osier, whose bark, the Indian said, was good to smoke, and was called *maquoxigill*, "tobacco before white people came to this country, Indian tobacco."

The Indian was always very careful in approaching the shore, lest he should injure his canoe on the rocks, letting it swing round slowly sidewise, and was still more particular that we should not step into it on shore, nor till it floated free, and then should step gently lest we should open its seams, or make a hole in the bottom. He said that he would tell us when to jump.

Soon after leaving this point we passed the mouth of the Kennebec, and heard and saw the falls at the dam there, for even Moosehead Lake is dammed. After passing Deer Island, we saw the little steamer from Greenville, far east in the middle of the lake, and she appeared nearly stationary. Sometimes we could hardly tell her from an island which had a few trees on it. Here we were exposed to the wind from over the whole breadth of the lake, and ran a little risk of being swamped. While I had my eye fixed on the spot where a large fish had leaped, we took in a gallon or two of water, which filled my lap; but we soon reached the shore and took the canoe over the bar, at Sand-bar Island, a few feet wide only, and so saved a considerable distance. One landed first at a more sheltered place, and walking round caught the canoe by the prow, to prevent it being injured against the shore.

Again we crossed a broad bay opposite the mouth

of Moose River, before reaching the narrow strait at
Mount Kineo, made what the voyageurs call a *traverse*, and found the water quite rough. A very little
wind on these broad lakes raises a sea which will
swamp a canoe. Looking off from a lee shore, the
surface may appear to be very little agitated, almost
smooth, a mile distant, or if you see a few white
crests they appear nearly level with the rest of the
lake; but when you get out so far, you may find quite
a sea running, and erelong, before you think of it,
a wave will gently creep up the side of the canoe
and fill your lap, like a monster deliberately covering
you with its slime before it swallows you, or it will
strike the canoe violently and break into it. The
same thing may happen when the wind rises suddenly, though it were perfectly calm and smooth
there a few minutes before; so that nothing can save
you, unless you can swim ashore, for it is impossible
to get into a canoe again when it is upset. Since you
sit flat on the bottom, though the danger should not
be imminent, a little water is a great inconvenience,
not to mention the wetting of your provisions. We
rarely crossed even a bay directly, from point to
point, when there was wind, but made a slight curve
corresponding somewhat to the shore, that we might
the sooner reach it if the wind increased.

When the wind is aft, and not too strong, the Indian makes a spritsail of his blanket. He thus easily
skims over the whole length of this lake in a day.

The Indian paddled on one side, and one of us on
the other, to keep the canoe steady, and when he
wanted to change hands he would say "t'other side."
He asserted, in answer to our questions, that he had
never upset a canoe himself, though he may have
been upset by others.

Think of our little egg-shell of a canoe tossing

across that great lake, a mere black speck to the eagle soaring above it!

My companion trailed for trout as we paddled along, but the Indian warning him that a big fish might upset us, for there are some very large ones there, he agreed to pass the line quickly to him in the stern if he had a bite. Beside trout, I heard of cusk, white-fish, &c., as found in this lake.

While we were crossing this bay, where Mount Kineo rose dark before us, within two or three miles, the Indian repeated the tradition respecting this mountain's having anciently been a cow moose,—how a mighty Indian hunter, whose name I forget, succeeded in killing this queen of the moose tribe with great difficulty, while her calf was killed somewhere among the islands in Penobscot Bay, and, to his eyes, this mountain had still the form of the moose in a reclining posture, its precipitous side presenting the outline of her head. He told this at some length, though it did not amount to much, and with apparent good faith, and asked us how we supposed the hunter could have killed such a mighty moose as that,—how we could do it. Whereupon a man-of-war to fire broadsides into her was suggested, etc. An Indian tells such a story as if he thought it deserved to have a good deal said about it, only he has not got it to say, and so he makes up for the deficiency by a drawling tone, long-windedness, and a dumb wonder which he hopes will be contagious.

We approached the land again through pretty rough water, and then steered directly across the lake, at its narrowest part, to the eastern side, and were soon partly under the lee of the mountain, about a mile north of the Kineo House, having paddled about twenty miles. It was now about noon. We designed to stop there that afternoon and night, and spent half an hour looking along the shore northward for a suitable place to camp. We took out all our baggage at one place in vain, it being too rocky and uneven, and while engaged in this search we made our first acquaintance with the moose-fly. At length, half a mile further north, by going half a dozen rods into the dense spruce and fir wood on the side of the mountain, almost as dark as a cellar, we found a place sufficiently clear and level to lie down on, after cutting away a few bushes. We required a space only seven feet by six for our bed, the fire being four or five feet in front, though it made no odds how rough the hearth was; but it was not always easy to find this in those woods. The Indian first cleared a path to it from the shore with his axe, and we then carried up all our baggage, pitched our tent, and made our bed, in order to be ready for foul weather, which then threatened us, and for the night. He gathered a large armful of fir twigs, breaking them off, which he said were the best for our bed, partly, I thought, because they were the largest and could be most rapidly collected. It had been raining more or less for four or five days, and the wood was even damper than usual, but he got dry bark for the fire from the under-side of a dead leaning hemlock, which, he said, he could always do.

This noon his mind was occupied with a law question, and I referred him to my companion, who was a lawyer. It appeared that he had been buying land lately, (I think it was a hundred acres,) but there was probably an incumbrance to it, somebody else claiming to have bought some grass on it for this year. He wished to know to whom the grass belonged, and was told that if the other man could prove that he bought the grass before he, Polis, bought the land, the former could take it, whether the latter knew it or not. To which he only answered, "Strange!" He went over this several times, fairly sat down to it, with his back to a tree, as if he meant to confine us to this topic henceforth; but as he made no headway, only reached the jumping-off place of his wonder at white men's institutions after each explanation, we let the subject die.

He said that he had fifty acres of grass, potatoes, &c., somewhere above Oldtown, beside some about his house; that he hired a good deal of his work, hoeing, &c., and preferred white men to Indians, because "they keep steady, and know how."

After dinner we returned southward along the shore, in the canoe, on account of the difficulty of climbing over the rocks and fallen trees, and began to ascend the mountain along the edge of the precipice. But a smart shower coming up just then, the Indian crept under his canoe, while we, being protected by our rubber coats, proceeded to botanize. So we sent him back to the camp for shelter, agreeing that he should come there for us with his canoe toward night. It had rained a little in the forenoon, and we trusted that this would be the clearing-up shower, which it proved; but our feet and legs were thoroughly wet by the bushes. The clouds breaking away a little, we had a glorious wild view, as we ascended, of the broad lake with its fluctuating surface and numerous forest-clad islands, extending beyond our sight both north and south, and the boundless forest undulating away from its shores on every side, as densely packed as a rye-field, and enveloping nameless mountains in succession; but above all, looking westward over a large island was visible a very distant part of the lake, though we did not then suspect it to be Moosehead,—at first a mere broken white line seen through the tops of the island trees, like hay-caps, but spreading to a lake when we got higher. Beyond this we saw what appears to be called Bald Mountain on the map, some twenty-five miles distant, near the sources of the Penobscot. It was a perfect lake of the woods. But this was only a transient gleam, for the rain was not quite over.

Looking southward, the heavens were completely overcast, the mountains capped with clouds, and the lake generally wore a dark and stormy appearance, but from its surface just north of Sugar Island, six or eight miles distant, there was reflected upward to us through the misty air a bright blue tinge from the distant unseen sky of another latitude beyond. They probably had a clear sky then at Greenville, the south end of the lake. Standing on a mountain in the midst of a lake, where would you look for the first sign of approaching fair weather? Not into the heavens, it seems, but into the lake.

Again we mistook a little rocky islet seen through the "drisk," with some taller bare trunks or stumps on it, for the steamer with its smoke-pipes, but as it had not changed its position after half an hour, we were undeceived. So much do the works of man resemble the works of nature. A moose might mistake a steamer for a floating isle, and not be scared till he heard its puffing or its whistle.

If I wished to see a mountain or other scenery under the most favorable auspices, I would go to it in foul weather, so as to be there when it cleared up; we are then in the most suitable mood, and nature is most fresh and inspiring. There is no serenity so fair as that which is just established in a tearful eye.

Jackson, in his Report on the Geology of Maine, in 1838, says of this mountain: "Hornstone, which will answer for flints, occurs in various parts of the

State, where trap-rocks have acted upon silicious slate. The largest mass of this stone known in the world is Mount Kineo, upon Moosehead Lake, which appears to be entirely composed of it, and rises seven hundred feet above the lake level. This variety of hornstone I have seen in every part of New England in the form of Indian arrow-heads, hatchets, chisels, etc., which were probably obtained from this mountain by the aboriginal inhabitants of the country." I have myself found hundreds of arrow-heads made of the same material. It is generally slate-colored, with white specks, becoming a uniform white where exposed to the light and air, and it breaks with a conchoidal fracture, producing a ragged cutting edge. I noticed some conchoidal hollows more than a foot in diameter. I picked up a small thin piece which had so sharp an edge that I used it as a dull knife, and to see what I could do, fairly cut off an aspen one inch thick with it, by bending it and making many cuts; though I cut my fingers badly with the back of it in the meanwhile.

From the summit of the precipice which forms the southern and eastern sides of this mountain peninsula, and is its most remarkable feature, being described as five or six hundred feet high, we looked, and probably might have jumped down to the water, or to the seemingly dwarfish trees on the narrow neck of land which connects it with the main. It is a dangerous place to try the steadiness of your nerves. Hodge says that these cliffs descend "perpendicularly ninety feet" below the surface of the water.

The plants which chiefly attracted our attention on this mountain were the mountain cinquefoil (*Potentilla tridentata*), abundant and in bloom still at the very base, by the water-side, though it is usually confined to the summits of mountains in our latitude; very beautiful harebells overhanging the precipice; bear-berry; the Canada blueberry (*Vaccinium Canadense*), similar to the *V. Pennsylvanicum*, our earliest one, but entire leaved and with a downy stem and leaf; I have not seen it in Massachusetts; *Diervilla trifida; Microstylis ophioglossoides*, an orchidaceous plant new to us; wild holly (*Nemopanthes Canadensis*); the great round-leaved orchis (*Platanthera orbiculata*), not long in bloom; *Spiranthes cernua*, at the top; bunch-berry, reddening as we ascended, green at the base of the mountain, red at the top; and the small fern, *Woodsia ilvensis*, growing in tufts, now in fruit. I have also received *Liparis liliifolia*, or twayblade, from this spot. Having explored the wonders of the mountain, and the weather being now entirely cleared up, we commenced the descent. We met the Indian, puffing and panting, about one third of the way up, but thinking that he must be near the top, and saying that it took his breath away. I thought that superstition had something to do with his fatigue. Perhaps he believed that he was climbing over the back of a tremendous moose. He said that he had never ascended Kineo. On reaching the canoe we found that he had caught a lake trout weighing about three pounds, at the depth of twenty-five or thirty feet, while we were on the mountain.

When we got to the camp, the canoe was taken out and turned over, and a log laid across it to prevent its being blown away. The Indian cut some large logs of damp and rotten hard wood to smoulder and keep fire through the night. The trout was fried for supper. Our tent was of thin cotton cloth and quite small, forming with the ground a triangular prism closed at the rear end, six feet long, seven wide, and

four high, so that we could barely sit up in the middle. It required two forked stakes, a smooth ridge-
pole, and a dozen or more pins to pitch it. It kept off
dew and wind, and an ordinary rain, and answered
our purpose well enough. We reclined within it till
bedtime, each with his baggage at his head, or else
sat about the fire, having hung our wet clothes on a
pole before the fire for the night.

As we sat there, just before night, looking out
through the dusky wood, the Indian heard a noise
which he said was made by a snake. He imitated it
at my request, making a low whistling note,—*pheet—
pheet*,—two or three times repeated, somewhat like
the peep of the hylodes, but not so loud. In answer
to my inquiries, he said that he had never seen them
while making it, but going to the spot he finds the
snake. This, he said on another occasion, was a sign
of rain. When I had selected this place for our camp,
he had remarked that there were snakes there,—he
saw them. But they won't do any hurt, I said. "O no,"
he answered, "just as you say, it makes no difference
to me."

He lay on the right side of the tent, because, as he
said, he was partly deaf in one ear, and he wanted
to lie with his good ear up. As we lay there, he inquired if I ever heard "Indian sing." I replied that I
had not often, and asked him if he would not favor
us with a song. He readily assented, and lying on his
back, with his blanket wrapped around him, he commenced a slow, somewhat nasal, yet musical chant,
in his own language, which probably was taught his
tribe long ago by the Catholic missionaries. He translated it to us, sentence by sentence, afterward, wishing to see if we could remember it. It proved to be a
very simple religious exercise or hymn, the burden
of which was, that there was only one God who ruled

all the world. This was hammered (or sung) out very thin, so that some stanzas wellnigh meant nothing at all, merely keeping up the idea. He then said that he would sing us a Latin song; but we did not detect any Latin, only one or two Greek words in it,—the rest may have been Latin with the Indian pronunciation.

His singing carried me back to the period of the discovery of America, to San Salvador and the Incas, when Europeans first encountered the simple faith of the Indian. There was, indeed, a beautiful simplicity about it; nothing of the dark and savage, only the mild and infantile. The sentiments of humility and reverence chiefly were expressed.

It was a dense and damp spruce and fir wood in which we lay, and, except for our fire, perfectly dark; and when I awoke in the night, I either heard an owl from deeper in the forest behind us, or a loon from a distance over the lake. Getting up some time after midnight to collect the scattered brands together, while my companions were sound asleep, I observed, partly in the fire, which had ceased to blaze, a perfectly regular elliptical ring of light, about five inches in its shortest diameter, six or seven in its longer, and from one eighth to one quarter of an inch wide. It was fully as bright as the fire, but not reddish or scarlet like a coal, but a white and slumbering light, like the glowworm's. I could tell it from the fire only by its whiteness. I saw at once that it must be phosphorescent wood, which I had so often heard of, but never chanced to see. Putting my finger on it, with a little hesitation, I found that it was a piece of dead moose-wood (*Acer striatum*) which the Indian had cut off in a slanting direction the evening before. Using my knife, I discovered that the light proceeded from that portion of the sap-wood immediately under the bark, and thus presented a regular ring at the end, which, indeed, appeared raised above the level of the wood, and when I pared off the bark and cut into the sap, it was all aglow along the log. I was surprised to find the wood quite hard and apparently sound, though probably decay had commenced in the sap, and I cut out some little triangular chips, and placing them in the hollow of my hand, carried them into the camp, waked my companion, and showed them to him. They lit up the inside of my hand, revealing the lines and wrinkles, and appearing exactly like coals of fire raised to a white heat, and I saw at once how, probably, the Indian jugglers had imposed on their people and on travellers, pretending to hold coals of fire in their mouths.

I also noticed that part of a decayed stump within four or five feet of the fire, an inch wide and six inches long, soft and shaking wood, shone with equal brightness.

I neglected to ascertain whether our fire had anything to do with this, but the previous day's rain and long-continued wet weather undoubtedly had.

I was exceedingly interested by this phenomenon, and already felt paid for my journey. It could hardly have thrilled me more if it had taken the form of letters, or of the human face. If I had met with this ring of light while groping in this forest alone, away from any fire, I should have been still more surprised. I little thought that there was such a light shining in the darkness of the wilderness for me.

The next day the Indian told me their name for this light,—*Artoosoqu'*,—and on my inquiring concerning the will-o'-the-wisp, and the like phenomena, he said that his "folks" sometimes saw fires passing along at various heights, even as high as the trees, and making a noise. I was prepared after this to hear of the most startling and unimagined phenomena witnessed by "his folks," they are abroad at all hours and seasons in scenes so unfrequented by white men. Nature must have made a thousand revelations to them which are still secrets to us.

I did not regret my not having seen this before, since I now saw it under circumstances so favorable. I was in just the frame of mind to see something wonderful, and this was a phenomenon adequate to my circumstances and expectation, and it put me on the alert to see more like it. I exulted like "a pagan suckled in a creed" that had never been worn at all, but was bran new, and adequate to the occasion. I let science slide, and rejoiced in that light as if it had been a fellow-creature. I saw that it was excellent, and was very glad to know that it was so cheap. A scientific *explanation*, as it is called, would have been altogether out of place there. That is for pale daylight. Science with its *retorts* would have put me to sleep; it was the opportunity to be ignorant that I improved. It suggested to me that there was something to be seen if one had eyes. It made a believer of me more than before. I believed that the woods were not tenantless, but choke-full of honest spirits as good as myself any day,—not an empty chamber, in which chemistry was left to work alone, but an inhabited house,—and for a few moments I enjoyed fellowship with them. Your so-called wise man goes trying to persuade himself that there is no entity there but himself and his traps, but it is a great deal easier to believe the truth. It suggested, too, that the same experience always gives birth to the same sort of belief or religion. One revelation has been made to the Indian, another to the white man. I have much to learn of the Indian, nothing of the missionary. I am

not sure but all that would tempt me to teach the
Indian my religion would be his promise to teach
me *his*. Long enough I had heard of irrelevant things;
now at length I was glad to make acquaintance with
the light that dwells in rotten wood. Where is all
your knowledge gone to? It evaporates completely,
for it has no depth.

I kept those little chips and wet them again the
next night, but they emitted no light.

SATURDAY, JULY 25.

At breakfast this Saturday morning, the Indian,
evidently curious to know what would be expected of
him the next day, whether we should go along or
not, asked me how I spent the Sunday when at home.
I told him that I commonly sat in my chamber reading, etc., in the forenoon, and went to walk in the
afternoon. At which he shook his head and said,
"Er, that is ver bad." "How do you spend it?" I asked.
He said that he did no work, that he went to church
at Oldtown when he was at home; in short, he did
as he had been taught by the whites. This led to a
discussion in which I found myself in the minority.
He stated that he was a Protestant, and asked me if
I was. I did not at first know what to say, but I
thought that I could answer with truth that I was.

When we were washing the dishes in the lake,
many fishes, apparently chivin, came close up to us
to get the particles of grease.

The weather seemed to be more settled this morning, and we set out early in order to finish our voyage up the lake before the wind arose. Soon after
starting the Indian directed our attention to the
Northeast Carry, which we could plainly see, about
thirteen miles distant in that direction as measured
on the map, though it is called much further. This

carry is a rude wooden railroad, running north and south about two miles, perfectly straight, from the lake to the Penobscot, through a low tract, with a clearing three or four rods wide; but low as it is, it passes over the height of land there. This opening appeared as a clear bright, or light point in the horizon, resting on the edge of the lake, whose breadth a hair could have covered at a considerable distance from the eye, and of no appreciable height. We should not have suspected it to be visible if the Indian had not drawn our attention to it. It was a remarkable kind of light to steer for,—daylight seen through a vista in the forest,—but visible as far as an ordinary beacon by night.

We crossed a deep and wide bay which makes eastward north of Kineo, leaving an island on our left, and keeping up the eastern side of the lake. This way or that led to some Tomhegan or *Socatarian* stream, up which the Indian had hunted, and whither I longed to go. The last name, however, had a bogus sound, too much like sectarian for me, as if a missionary had tampered with it; but I know that the Indians were very liberal. I think I should have inclined to the Tomhegan first.

We then crossed another broad bay, which, as we could no longer observe the shore particularly, afforded ample time for conversation. The Indian said that he had got his money by hunting, mostly high up the west branch of the Penobscot, and toward the head of the St. John; he had hunted there from a boy, and knew all about that region. His game had been, beaver, otter, black cat (or fisher), sable, moose, &c. Loup cervier (or Canada lynx) were plenty yet in burnt grounds. For food in the woods, he uses partridges, ducks, dried moose-meat, hedge-hog, &c. Loons, too, were good, only "bile 'em good." He told us at some length how he had suffered from starvation when a mere lad, being overtaken by winter when hunting with two grown Indians in the northern part of Maine, and obliged to leave their canoe on account of ice.

Pointing into the bay, he said that it was the way to various lakes which he knew. Only solemn bear-haunted mountains, with their great wooded slopes, were visible; where, as man is not, we suppose some other power to be. My imagination personified the slopes themselves, as if by their very length they would waylay you, and compel you to camp again on them before night. Some invisible glutton would seem to drop from the trees and gnaw at the heart of the solitary hunter who threaded those woods; and yet I was tempted to walk there. The Indian said that he had been along there several times.

I asked him how he guided himself in the woods. "O," said he, "I can tell good many ways." When I pressed him further, he answered, "Sometimes I lookum side hill," and he glanced toward a high hill or mountain on the eastern shore, "great difference between the north and south, see where the sun has shone most. So trees,—the large limbs bend toward south. Sometimes I lookum locks" (rocks). I asked what he saw on the rocks, but he did not describe anything in particular, answering vaguely, in a mysterious or drawling tone, "Bare locks on lake shore,— great difference between north, south, east, west side, —can tell what the sun has shone on." "Suppose," said I, "that I should take you in a dark night, right up here into the middle of the woods a hundred miles, set you down, and turn you round quickly twenty times, could you steer straight to Oldtown?" "O yer," said he, "have done pretty much same thing. I will tell you. Some years ago I met an old white hunter at Millinocket; very good hunter. He said he could go anywhere in the woods. He wanted to hunt with me that day, so we start. We chase a moose all the forenoon, round and round, till middle of afternoon, when we kill him. Then I said to him, now you go straight to camp. Don't go round and round where we've been, but go straight. He said, I can't do that, I don't know where I am. Where you think camp? I asked. He pointed so. Then I laugh at him. I take the lead and go right off the other way, cross our tracks many times, straight camp." "How do you do that?" asked I. "O, I can't tell *you*," he replied. "Great difference between me and white man."

It appeared as if the sources of information were so various that he did not give a distinct, conscious attention to any one, and so could not readily refer to any when questioned about it, but he found his way very much as an animal does. Perhaps what is commonly called instinct in the animal, in this case is merely a sharpened and educated sense. Often, when an Indian says, "I don't know," in regard to the route he is to take, he does not mean what a white man would by those words, for his Indian instinct may tell him still as much as the most confident white man knows. He does not carry things in his head, nor remember the route exactly, like a white man, but relies on himself at the moment. Not having experienced the need of the other sort of knowledge, all labelled and arranged, he has not acquired it.

The white hunter with whom I talked in the stage knew some of the resources of the Indian. He said that he steered by the wind, or by the limbs of the hemlocks, which were largest on the south side; also sometimes, when he knew that there was a lake near, by firing his gun and listening to hear the direction and distance of the echo from over it.

The course we took over this lake, and others afterward, was rarely direct, but a succession of curves from point to point, digressing considerably into each of the bays; and this was not merely on account of the wind, for the Indian, looking toward the middle of the lake, said it was hard to go there, easier to keep near the shore, because he thus got over it by successive reaches and saw by the shore how he got along.

The following will suffice for a common experience in crossing lakes in a canoe. As the forenoon advanced the wind increased. The last bay which we crossed before reaching the desolate pier at the northeast carry, was two or three miles over, and the wind was southwesterly. After going a third of the way, the waves had increased so as occasionally to wash into the canoe, and we saw that it was worse and worse ahead. At first we might have turned about, but were not willing to. It would have been of no use to follow the curve of the shore, for not only the distance would have been much greater, but the waves ran still higher there on account of the greater sweep the wind had. At any rate it would have been dangerous now to alter our course, because the waves would have struck us at an advantage. It will not do to meet them at right angles, for then they will wash in both sides, but you must take them quartering. So the Indian stood up in the canoe, and exerted all his skill and strength for a mile or two, while I paddled right along in order to give him more steerage-way. For more than a mile he did not allow a single wave to strike the canoe as it would, but turned it quickly from this side to that, so that it would always be on or near the crest of a wave when it broke, where all its force was spent, and we merely settled down with it. At length I jumped out on to the end of the pier, against which the waves were dashing violently, in order to lighten the canoe, and catch it at the landing, which was not much sheltered; but just as I jumped we took in two or three gallons of water. I remarked to the Indian, "You managed that well," to which he replied: "Ver few men do that. Great many waves; when I look out for one, another come quick."

While the Indian went to get cedar-bark, &c., to carry his canoe with, we cooked the dinner on the shore, at this end of the carry, in the midst of a sprinkling rain.

He prepared his canoe for carrying in this wise. He took a cedar shingle or splint eighteen inches long and four or five wide, rounded at one end, that the corners might not be in the way, and tied it with cedar-bark by two holes made midway, near the edge on each side, to the middle crossbar of the canoe. When the canoe was lifted upon his head bottom up, this shingle, with its rounded end uppermost, distributed the weight over his shoulders and head, while a band of cedar-bark, tied to the cross-bar on each side of the shingle, passed round his breast, and another longer one, outside of the last, round his forehead; also a hand on each side rail served to steer the canoe and keep it from rocking. He thus carried it with his shoulders, head, breast, forehead, and both hands, as if the upper part of his body were all one hand to clasp and hold it. If you know of a better way, I should like to hear of it. A cedar-tree furnished all the gear in this case, as it had the woodwork of the canoe. One of the paddles rested on the crossbars in the bows. I took the canoe upon my head and found that I could carry it with ease, though the straps were not fitted to my shoulders; but I let him carry it, not caring to establish a different precedent, though he said that if I would carry the canoe, he would take all the rest of the baggage, except my companion's. This shingle remained tied to the cross-bar throughout the voyage, was always ready for the carries, and also served to protect the back of one passenger.

We were obliged to go over this carry twice, our load was so great. But the carries were an agreeable variety, and we improved the opportunity to gather the rare plants which we had seen, when we returned empty-handed.

We reached the Penobscot about four o'clock, and found there some St. Francis Indians encamped on the bank, in the same place where I camped with four Indians four years before. They were making a canoe, and, as then, drying moose-meat. The meat looked very suitable to make a *black* broth at least. Our Indian said it was not good. Their camp was covered with spruce-bark. They had got a young moose, taken in the river a fortnight before, confined in a sort of cage of logs piled up cob-fashion, seven or eight feet high. It was quite tame, about four feet high, and covered with moose-flies. There was a large quantity of cornel (*C. stolonifera*), red maple, and also willow and aspen boughs, stuck through between the logs on all sides, but-ends out, and on their leaves it was browsing. It looked at first as if it were in a bower rather than a pen.

Our Indian said that *he* used *black* spruce-roots to sew canoes with, obtaining it from high lands or mountains. The St. Francis Indian thought that *white* spruce-roots might be best. But the former said, "No good, break, can't split 'em"; also that they were hard to get, deep in ground, but the black were near the surface, on higher land, as well as tougher. He said that the white spruce was *subekoondark*, black, *skusk*. I told him I thought that I could make a canoe, but he expressed great doubt of it; at any rate, he thought that my work would not be "neat" the first time. An Indian at Greenville had told me that the winter bark, that is, bark taken off before the sap flows in May, was harder and much better than summer bark.

Having reloaded, we paddled down the Penobscot, which, as the Indian remarked, and even I detected, remembering how it looked before, was uncommonly full. We soon after saw a splendid yellow lily (*Lilium Canadense*) by the shore, which I plucked. It was six feet high, and had twelve flowers, in two whorls, forming a pyramid, such as I have seen in Concord. We afterward saw many more thus tall along this stream, and also still more numerous on the East Branch, and, on the latter, one which I thought approached yet nearer to the *Lilium superbum*. The Indian asked what we called it, and said that the "loots" (roots) were good for soup, that is, to cook with meat, to thicken it, taking the place of flour. They get them in the fall. I dug some, and found a mass of bulbs pretty deep in the earth, two inches in diameter, looking, and even tasting, somewhat like raw green corn on the ear.

When we had gone about three miles down the Penobscot, we saw through the tree-tops a thunder-shower coming up in the west, and we looked out a camping-place in good season, about five o'clock, on the west side, not far below the mouth of what Joe Aitteon, in '53, called Lobster Stream, coming from Lobster Pond. Our present Indian, however, did not admit this name, nor even that of *Matahumkeag*, which is on the map, but called the lake *Beskabekuk*.

I will describe, once for all, the routine of camping at this season. We generally told the Indian that we would stop at the first suitable place, so that he might be on the lookout for it. Having observed a clear, hard, and flat beach to land on, free from mud, and from stones which would injure the canoe, one would run up the bank to see if there were open and level space enough for the camp between the trees, or if it could be easily cleared, preferring at the same time a cool place, on account of insects. Sometimes we paddled a mile or more before finding one to our minds, for where the shore was suitable, the bank would often be too steep, or else too low and grassy, and therefore mosquitoey. We then took out the baggage and drew up the canoe, sometimes turning it over on shore for safety. The Indian cut a path to the spot we had selected, which was usually within two or three rods of the water, and we carried up our baggage. One, perhaps, takes canoe-birch bark, always at hand, and dead dry wood or bark, and kindles a fire five or six feet in front of where we intend to lie. It matters not, commonly, on which side this is, because there is little or no wind in so dense a wood at that season; and then he gets a kettle of water from the river, and takes out the pork, bread, coffee, &c., from their several packages.

Another, meanwhile, having the axe, cuts down the nearest dead rock-maple or other dry hard wood, collecting several large logs to last through the night, also a green stake, with a notch or fork to it, which is slanted over the fire, perhaps resting on a rock or forked stake, to hang the kettle on, and two forked stakes and a pole for the tent.

The third man pitches the tent, cuts a dozen or more pins with his knife, usually of moose-wood, the common underwood, to fasten it down with, and then collects an armful or two of fir-twigs,* arbor-vitæ, spruce, or hemlock, whichever is at hand, and makes

---

* These twigs are called in Rasles' Dictionary, *Sediak.*

the bed, beginning at either end, and laying the twigs wrong-side up, in regular rows, covering the stub-ends of the last row; first, however, filling the hollows, if there are any, with coarser material. Wrangel says that his guides in Siberia first strewed a quantity of dry brushwood on the ground, and then cedar twigs on that.

Commonly, by the time the bed is made, or within fifteen or twenty minutes, the water boils, the pork is fried, and supper is ready. We eat this sitting on the ground, or a stump, if there is any, around a large piece of birch-bark for a table, each holding a dipper in one hand and a piece of ship-bread or fried pork in the other, frequently making a pass with his hand, or thrusting his head into the smoke, to avoid the mosquitoes.

Next, pipes are lit by those who smoke, and veils are donned by those who have them, and we hastily examine and dry our plants, anoint our faces and hands, and go to bed,—and—the mosquitoes.

Though you have nothing to do but see the country, there's rarely any time to spare, hardly enough to examine a plant, before the night or drowsiness is upon you.

Such was the ordinary experience, but this evening we had camped earlier on account of the rain, and had more time.

We found that our camp to-night was on an old, and now more than usually indistinct, supply-road, running along the river. What is called a road there shows no ruts or trace of wheels, for they are not used; nor, indeed, of runners, since they are used only in the winter, when the snow is several feet deep. It is only an indistinct vista through the wood, which it takes an experienced eye to detect.

We had no sooner pitched our tent than the thunder-shower burst on us, and we hastily crept under it, drawing our bags after us, curious to see how much of a shelter our thin cotton roof was going to be in this excursion. Though the violence of the rain forced a fine shower through the cloth before it was fairly wetted and shrunk, with which we were well be-dewed, we managed to keep pretty dry, only a box of matches having been left out and spoiled, and before we were aware of it the shower was over, and only the dripping trees imprisoned us.

Wishing to see what fishes there were in the river there, we cast our lines over the wet bushes on the shore, but they were repeatedly swept down the swift stream in vain. So, leaving the Indian, we took the canoe just before dark, and dropped down the river a few rods to fish at the mouth of a sluggish brook on the opposite side. We pushed up this a rod or two, where, perhaps, only a canoe had been before. But though there were a few small fishes, mostly *chivin*, there, we were soon driven off by the mosquitoes. While there we heard the Indian fire his gun twice in such rapid succession that we thought it must be double-barrelled, though we observed afterward that it was single. His object was to clean out and dry it after the rain, and he then loaded it with ball, being now on ground where he expected to meet with large game. This sudden, loud, crashing noise in the still aisles of the forest, affected me like an insult to na-ture, or ill manners at any rate, as if you were to fire a gun in a hall or temple. It was not heard far, however, except along the river, the sound being rapidly hushed up or absorbed by the damp trees and mossy ground.

The Indian made a little smothered fire of damp leaves close to the back of the camp, that the smoke might drive through and keep out the mosquitoes;

but just before we fell asleep this suddenly blazed up, and came near setting fire to the tent. We were considerably molested by mosquitoes at this camp.

SUNDAY, JULY 26.

The note of the white-throated sparrow, a very inspiriting but almost wiry sound, was the first heard in the morning, and with this all the woods rang. This was the prevailing bird in the northern part of Maine. The forest generally was all alive with them at this season, and they were proportionally numerous and musical about Bangor. They evidently breed in that State. Though commonly unseen, their simple *ah, te-te-te, te-te-te, te-te-te*, so sharp and piercing, was as distinct to the ear as the passage of a spark of fire shot into the darkest of the forest would be to the eye. I thought that they commonly uttered it as they flew. I hear this note for a few days only in the spring, as they go through Concord, and in the fall see them again going southward, but then they are mute. We were commonly aroused by their lively strain very early. What a glorious time they must have in that wilderness, far from mankind and election day!

I told the Indian that we would go to church to Chesuncook this (Sunday) morning, some fifteen miles. It was settled weather at last. A few swallows flitted over the water, we heard the white throats along the shore, the phebe notes of the chicadee, and, I believe, red-starts, and moose-flies of large size pursued us in mid-stream.

The Indian thought that we should lie by on Sunday. Said he, "We come here lookum things, look all round; but come Sunday, lock up all that, and then Monday look again." He spoke of an Indian of his acquaintance who had been with some ministers to

Ktaadn, and had told him how they conducted. This he described in a low and solemn voice. "They make a long prayer every morning and night, and at every meal. Come Sunday," said he, "they stop 'em, no go at all that day,—keep still,—preach all day,— first one then another, just like church. O, ver good men." "One day," said he, "going along a river, they came to the body of a man in the water, drowned good while, all ready fall to pieces. They go right ashore,—stop there, go no further that day,—they have meeting there, preach and pray just like Sunday. Then they get poles and lift up the body, and they go back and carry the body with them. O, they ver good men."

I judged from this account that their every camp was a camp-meeting, and they had mistaken their route,—they should have gone to Eastham; that they wanted an opportunity to preach somewhere more than to see Ktaadn. I read of another similar party that seem to have spent their time there singing the songs of Zion. I was glad that I did not go to that mountain with such slow coaches.

However, the Indian added, plying the paddle all the while, that if we would go along, he must go with us, he our man, and he suppose that if he no takum pay for what he do Sunday, then there's no harm, but if he takum pay, then wrong. I told him that he was stricter than white men. Nevertheless, I noticed that he did not forget to reckon in the Sundays at last.

He appeared to be a very religious man, and said his prayers in a loud voice, in Indian, kneeling before the camp, morning and evening,—sometimes scrambling up again in haste when he had forgotten this, and saying them with great rapidity. In the course of the day, he remarked, not very originally, "Poor man rememberum God more than rich."

We soon passed the island where I had camped four years before, and I recognized the very spot. The dead water, a mile or two below it, the Indian called, *Beskabekukskishtuk*, from the lake *Beskabekuk*, which empties in above. This dead water, he said, was "a great place for moose always." We saw the grass bent where a moose came out the night before, and the Indian said that he could smell one as far as he could see him; but, he added, that if he should see five or six to-day close by canoe, he no shoot 'em. Accordingly, as he was the only one of the party who had a gun, or had come a-hunting, the moose were safe.

Just below this, a cat-owl flew heavily over the stream, and he, asking if I knew what it was, imitated very well the common *hoo, hoo, hoo, hoorer, hoo*, of our woods; making a hard, guttural sound, "Ugh, ugh, ugh,–ugh, ugh." When we passed the Moose-horn, he said that it had no name. What Joe Aitteon had called Ragmuff, he called *Paytaytequick*, and said that it meant Burnt Ground Stream. We stopped there, where I had stopped before, and I bathed in this tributary. It was shallow but cold, apparently too cold for the Indian, who stood looking on. As we were pushing away again, a white-headed eagle sailed over our heads. A reach some miles above Pine Stream, where there were several islands, the Indian said was *Nonglangyis* dead-water. Pine Stream he called Black River, and said that its Indian name was *Karsaootuk*. He could go to Caribou Lake that way.

We carried a part of the baggage about Pine Stream Falls, while the Indian went down in the canoe. A

Bangor merchant had told us that two men in his employ were drowned some time ago while passing these falls in a batteau, and a third clung to a rock all night, and was taken off in the morning. There were magnificent great purple-fringed orchises on this carry and the neighboring shores. I measured the largest canoe-birch which I saw in this journey near the end of the carry. It was 14½ feet in circumference at two feet from the ground, but at five feet divided into three parts. The canoe-birches thereabouts were commonly marked by conspicuous dark spiral ridges, with a groove between, so that I thought at first that they had been struck by lightning, but, as the Indian said, it was evidently caused by the grain of the tree. He cut a small, woody knob, as big as a filbert, from the trunk of a fir, apparently an old balsam vesicle filled with wood, which he said was good medicine.

After we had embarked and gone half a mile, my companion remembered that he had left his knife, and we paddled back to get it, against the strong and swift current. This taught us the difference between going up and down the stream, for while we were working our way back a quarter of a mile, we should have gone down a mile and a half at least. So we landed, and while he and the Indian were gone back for it, I watched the motions of the foam, a kind of white water-fowl near the shore, forty or fifty rods below. It alternately appeared and disappeared behind the rock, being carried round by an eddy. Even this semblance of life was interesting on that lonely river.

Immediately below these falls was the Chesuncook dead-water, caused by the flowing back of the lake. As we paddled slowly over this, the Indian told us a story of his hunting thereabouts, and something more interesting about himself. It appeared that he had represented his tribe at Augusta, and also once at Washington, where he had met some Western chiefs. He had been consulted at Augusta, and gave advice, which he said was followed, respecting the eastern boundary of Maine, as determined by highlands and streams, at the time of the difficulties on that side. He was employed with the surveyors on the line. Also he had called on Daniel Webster in Boston, at the time of his Bunker Hill oration.

I was surprised to hear him say that he liked to go to Boston, New York, Philadelphia, &c., &c.; that he would like to live there. But then, as if relenting a little, when he thought what a poor figure he would make there, he added, "I suppose, I live in New York, I be poorest hunter, I expect." He understood very well both his superiority and his inferiority to the whites. He criticised the people of the United States as compared with other nations, but the only distinct idea with which he labored was, that they were "very strong," but, like some individuals, "too fast." He must have the credit of saying this just before the general breaking down of railroads and banks. He had a great idea of education, and would occasionally break out into such expressions as this, "Kademy —a-cad-e-my—good thing—I suppose they usum Fifth Reader there. . . . . You been college?"

From this dead-water the outlines of the mountains about Ktaadn were visible. The top of Ktaadn was concealed by a cloud, but the Souneunk Mountains were nearer, and quite visible. We steered across the northwest end of the lake, from which we looked down south-southeast, the whole length to Joe Merry Mountain, seen over its extremity. It is an agreeable change to cross a lake, after you have been shut up in the woods, not only on account of the greater expanse of water, but also of sky. It is one of the surprises which Nature has in store for the traveller in the forest. To look down, in this case, over eighteen miles of water, was liberating and civilizing even. No doubt, the short distance to which you can see in the woods, and the general twilight, would at length react on the inhabitants, and make them *salvages*. The lakes also reveal the mountains, and give ample scope and range to our thought. The very gulls which we saw sitting on the rocks, like white specks, or circling about, reminded me of custom-house officers. Already there were half a dozen log-huts about this end of the lake, though so far from a road. I perceive that in these woods the earliest settlements are, for various reasons, clustering about the lakes, but partly, I think, for the sake of the neighborhood as the oldest clearings. They are forest schools already established,—great centres of light. Water is a pioneer which the settler follows, taking advantage of its improvements.

Thus far only I had been before. About noon we turned northward, up a broad kind of estuary, and at its northeast corner found the Caucomgomoc River, and after going about a mile from the lake, reached the Umbazookskus, which comes in on the right at a point where the former river, coming from the west, turns short to the south. Our course was up the Umbazookskus, but as the Indian knew of a good camping-place, that is, a cool place where there were few mosquitoes, about half a mile further up the Caucomgomoc, we went thither. The latter river, judging from the map, is the longer and principal stream, and, therefore, its name must prevail below the junction. So quickly we changed the civilizing sky of Chesuncook for the dark wood of the Caucomgomoc. On reaching the Indian's camping-ground, on the south side, where the bank was about a dozen feet high, I read on the trunk of a fir-tree blazed by an axe an inscription in charcoal which had been left by him. It was surmounted by a drawing of a bear paddling a canoe, which he said was the sign which had been used by his family always. The drawing, though rude, could not be mistaken for anything but a bear, and he doubted my ability to copy it. The inscription ran thus, *verbatim et literatim*. I interline the English of his Indian as he gave it to me.

July 26,
1853.

Niasoseb
We alone Joseph

Polis	*elioi*
Polis	start
sia	*olta*
for	Oldtown
onke	*ni*
right	away.
quambi	

July 15,
1855.
Niasoseb.

He added now below:—

1857,
July 26.
Io.   Polis.

This was one of his homes. I saw where he had sometimes stretched his moose-hides on the opposite or sunny north side of the river, where there was a narrow meadow.

After we had selected a place for our camp, and kindled our fire, almost exactly on the site of the Indian's last camp here, he, looking up, observed, "That tree danger." It was a dead part, more than a foot in diameter, of a large canoe-birch, which branched at the ground. This branch, rising thirty feet or more, slanted directly over the spot which we had chosen for our bed. I told him to try it with his axe; but he could not shake it perceptibly, and, therefore, seemed inclined to disregard it, and my companion expressed his willingness to run the risk. But it seemed to me that we should be fools to lie under it, for though the lower part was firm, the top, for aught we knew, might be just ready to fall, and we should at any rate be very uneasy if the wind arose in the night. It is a common accident for men camping in the woods to be killed by a falling tree. So the camp was moved to the other side of the fire.

It was, as usual, a damp and shaggy forest, that Caucomgomoc one, and the most you knew about it was, that on this side it stretched toward the settlements, and on that to still more unfrequented regions. You carried so much topography in your mind always,—and sometimes it seemed to make a considerable difference whether you sat or lay nearer the settlements, or further off, than your companions,—were the rear or frontier man of the camp. But there is really the same difference between our positions wherever we may be camped, and some are nearer the frontiers on feather-beds in the towns than others on fir-twigs in the backwoods.

The Indian said that the Umbazookskus, being a

dead stream with broad meadows, was a good place for moose, and he frequently came a-hunting here, being out alone three weeks or more from Oldtown. He sometimes, also, went a-hunting to the Seboois Lakes, taking the stage, with his gun and ammunition, axe and blanket, hard bread and pork, perhaps for a hundred miles of the way, and jumped off at the wildest place on the road, where he was at once at home, and every rod was a tavern-site for him. Then, after a short journey through the woods, he would build a spruce-bark canoe in one day, putting but few ribs into it, that it might be light, and after doing his hunting with it on the lakes, would return with his furs the same way he had come. Thus you have an Indian availing himself cunningly of the advantages of civilization, without losing any of his woodcraft, but proving himself the more successful hunter for it.

This man was very clever and quick to learn anything in his line. Our tent was of a kind new to him; but when he had once seen it pitched it was surprising how quickly he would find and prepare the pole and forked stakes to pitch it with, cutting and placing them right the first time, though I am sure that the majority of white men would have blundered several times.

This river came from Caucomgomoc Lake, about ten miles further up. Though it was sluggish here, there were falls not far above us, and we saw the foam from them go by from time to time. The Indian said that *Caucomgomoc* meant Big-gull Lake, (i.e. Herring-gull, I suppose,) *gomoc* meaning lake. Hence this was *Caucomgomoc-took*, or the river from that lake. This was the Penobscot *Caucomgomoc-took*; there was another St. John one not far north. He finds the eggs of this gull, sometimes twenty together, as big as hen's eggs, on rocky ledges on the west side of Millinocket River, for instance, and eats them.

Now I thought I would observe how he spent his Sunday. While I and my companion were looking about at the trees and river, he went to sleep. Indeed, he improved every opportunity to get a nap, whatever the day.

Rambling about the woods at this camp, I noticed that they consisted chiefly of firs, black spruce, and some white, red maple, canoe-birch, and, along the river, the hoary alder, *Alnus incana*. I name them in the order of their abundance. The *Viburnum nudum* was a common shrub, and of smaller plants, there were the dwarf-cornel, great round-leaved orchis, abundant and in bloom (a greenish-white flower growing in little communities), *Uvularia grandiflora*, whose stem tasted like a cucumber, *Pyrola secunda*, apparently the commonest Pyrola in those woods, now out of bloom, *Pyrola elliptica*, and *Chiogenes hispidula*. The *Clintonia borealis*, with ripe berries, was very abundant, and perfectly at home there. Its leaves, disposed commonly in triangles about its stem, were just as handsomely formed and green, and its berries as blue and glossy, as if it grew by some botanist's favorite path.

I could trace the outlines of large birches that had fallen long ago, collapsed and rotted and turned to soil, by faint yellowish-green lines of feather-like moss, eighteen inches wide and twenty or thirty feet long, crossed by other similar lines.

I heard a Maryland yellow-throat's midnight strain, wood-thrush, kingfisher, tweezer bird or parti-colored warbler, and a night-hawk. I also heard and saw red squirrels, and heard a bull-frog. The Indian said that he heard a snake.

Wild as it was, it was hard for me to get rid of the associations of the settlements. Any steady and monotonous sound, to which I did not distinctly attend, passed for a sound of human industry. The waterfalls which I heard were not without their dams and mills to my imagination,—and several times I found that I had been regarding the steady rushing sound of the wind from over the woods beyond the rivers as that of a train of cars,—the cars at Quebec. Our minds anywhere, when left to themselves, are always thus busily drawing conclusions from false premises.

I asked the Indian to make us a sugar-bowl of birch-bark, which he did, using the great knife which dangled in a sheath from his belt; but the bark broke at the corners when he bent it up, and he said it was not good; that there was a great difference in this respect between the bark of one canoe-birch and that of another, i.e. one cracked more easily than another. I used some thin and delicate sheets of this bark which he split and cut, in my flower-book; thinking it would be good to separate the dried specimens from the green.

My companion, wishing to distinguish between the black and white spruce, asked Polis to show him a twig of the latter, which he did at once, together with the black; indeed, he could distinguish them about as far as he could see them; but as the two twigs appeared very much alike, my companion asked the Indian to point out the difference; whereupon the latter, taking the twigs, instantly remarked, as he passed his hand over them successively in a stroking manner, that the white was rough (i.e. the needles stood up nearly perpendicular), but the black smooth (i.e. as if bent or combed down). This was an obvious difference, both to sight and touch. However, if I remember rightly, this would not serve to distinguish the white spruce from the light-colored variety of the black.

I asked him to let me see him get some black spruce root, and make some thread. Whereupon, without looking up at the trees overhead, he began to grub in the ground, instantly distinguishing the black spruce roots, and cutting off a slender one, three or four feet long, and as big as a pipe-stem, he split the end with his knife, and taking a half between the thumb and forefinger of each hand, rapidly separated its whole length into two equal semi-cylindrical halves; then giving me another root, he said, "You try." But in my hands it immediately ran off one side, and I got only a very short piece. In short, though it looked very easy, I found that there was a great art in splitting these roots. The split is skilfully humored by bending short with this hand or that, and so kept in the middle. He then took off the bark from each half, pressing a short piece of cedar bark against the convex side with both hands, while he drew the root upward with his teeth. An Indian's teeth are strong, and I noticed that he used his often where we should have used a hand. They amounted to a third hand. He thus obtained, in a moment, a very neat, tough, and flexible string, which he could tie into a knot, or make into a fish-line even. It is said that in Norway and Sweden the roots of the Norway spruce (*Abies excelsa*) are used in the same way for the same purpose. He said that you would be obliged to give half a dollar for spruce root enough for a canoe, thus prepared. He had hired the sewing of his own canoe, though he made all the rest. The root in his canoe was of a pale slate color, probably acquired by exposure to the weather, or perhaps from being boiled in water first.

He had discovered the day before that his canoe leaked a little, and said that it was owing to stepping into it violently, which forced the water under the edge of the horizontal seams on the side. I asked him where he would get pitch to mend it with, for they commonly use hard-pitch, obtained of the whites at Oldtown. He said that he could make something very similar, and equally good, not of spruce gum, or the like, but of material which we had with us; and he wished me to guess what. But I could not, and he would not tell me, though he showed me a ball of it when made, as big as a pea, and like black pitch, saying, at last, that there were some things which a man did not tell even his wife. It may have been his own discovery. In Arnold's expedition the pioneers used for their canoe "the turpentine of the pine, and the scrapings of the pork-bag."

Being curious to see what kind of fishes there were in this dark, deep, sluggish river, I cast in my line just before night, and caught several small somewhat yellowish sucker-like fishes, which the Indian at once rejected, saying that they were *Michigan* fish (i.e. *soft* and *stinking* fish) and good for nothing. Also, he would not touch a pout, which I caught, and said that neither Indians nor whites thereabouts ever ate them, which I thought was singular, since they are esteemed in Massachusetts, and he had told me that he ate hedgehogs, loons, &c. But he said that some small silvery fishes, which I called white chivin, which were similar in size and form to the first, were the best fish in the Penobscot waters, and if I would toss them up the bank to him, he would cook them for me. After cleaning them, not very carefully, leaving the heads on, he laid them on the coals and so broiled them.

Returning from a short walk, he brought a vine in

his hand, and asked me if I knew what it was, saying that it made the best tea of anything in the woods. It was the Creeping Snowberry (*Chiogenes hispidula*), which was quite common there, its berries just grown. He called it *cowosnebagosar*, which name implies that it grows where old prostrate trunks have collapsed and rotted. So we determined to have some tea made of this to-night. It had a slight checkerberry flavor, and we both agreed that it was really better than the black tea which we had brought. We thought it quite a discovery, and that it might well be dried, and sold in the shops. I, for one, however, am not an old tea-drinker, and cannot speak with authority to others. It would have been particularly good to carry along for a cold drink during the day, the water thereabouts being invariably warm. The Indian said that they also used for tea a certain herb which grew in low ground, which he did not find there, and *Ledum*, or Labrador tea, which I have since found and tried in Concord; also hemlock leaves, the last especially in the winter, when the other plants were covered with snow; and various other things; but he did not approve of *arbor vitæ*, which I said I had drunk in those woods. We could have had a new kind of tea every night.

Just before night we saw a *musquash*, (he did not say muskrat,) the only one we saw in this voyage, swimming downward on the opposite side of the stream. The Indian, wishing to get one to eat, hushed us, saying, "Stop, me call 'em"; and sitting flat on the bank, he began to make a curious squeaking, wiry sound with his lips, exerting himself considerably. I was greatly surprised,—thought that I had at last got into the wilderness, and that he was a wild man indeed, to be talking to a musquash! I did not know which of the two was the strangest to me. He seemed suddenly to have quite forsaken humanity, and gone over to the musquash side. The musquash, however, as near as I could see, did not turn aside, though he may have hesitated a little, and the Indian said that he saw our fire; but it was evident that he was in the habit of calling the musquash to him, as he said. An acquaintance of mine who was hunting moose in those woods a month after this, tells me that his Indian in this way repeatedly called the musquash within reach of his paddle in the moonlight, and struck at them.

The Indian said a particularly long prayer this Sunday evening, as if to atone for working in the morning.

MONDAY, JULY 27.

Having rapidly loaded the canoe, which the Indian always carefully attended to, that it might be well trimmed, and each having taken a look, as usual, to see that nothing was left, we set out again, descending the Caucomgomoc, and turning northeasterly up the *Umbazookskus*. This name, the Indian said, meant *Much Meadow River*. We found it a very meadowy stream, and dead water, and now very wide on account of the rains, though, he said, it was sometimes quite narrow. The space between the woods, chiefly bare meadow, was from fifty to two hundred rods in breadth, and is a rare place for moose. It reminded me of the Concord; and what increased the resemblance, was one old musquash house almost afloat.

In the water on the meadows grew sedges, woolgrass, the common blue-flag abundantly, its flower just showing itself above the high water, as if it were a blue water-lily, and higher in the meadows a great many clumps of a peculiar narrow-leaved willow (*Salix petiolaris*), which is common in our river meadows. It was the prevailing one here, and the Indian said that the musquash ate much of it; and here also grew the red osier (*Cornus stolonifera*), its large fruit now whitish.

Though it was still early in the morning, we saw night-hawks circling over the meadow, and as usual heard the *Pepe* (*Muscicapa Cooperi*), which is one of the prevailing birds in these woods, and the robin.

It was unusual for the woods to be so distant from the shore, and there was quite an echo from them, but when I was shouting in order to awake it, the Indian reminded me that I should scare the moose, which he was looking out for, and which we all wanted to see. The word for echo was *Pockadunk-quaywayle*.

A broad belt of dead larch-trees along the distant edge of the meadow, against the forest on each side, increased the usual wildness of the scenery. The Indian called these juniper, and said that they had been killed by the back water caused by the dam at the outlet of Chesuncook Lake, some twenty miles distant. I plucked at the water's edge the *Asclepias incarnata*, with quite handsome flowers, a brighter red than our variety (the *pulchra*). It was the only form of it which I saw there.

Having paddled several miles up the Umbazook-skus, it suddenly contracted to a mere brook, narrow and swift, the larches and other trees approaching the bank and leaving no open meadow, and we landed to get a black-spruce pole for pushing against the stream. This was the first occasion for one. The one selected was quite slender, cut about ten feet long, merely whittled to a point, and the bark shaved off. The stream, though narrow and swift, was still deep, with a muddy bottom, as I proved by diving to it. Beside the plants which I have mentioned, I observed on the bank here the *Salix cordata* and *rostrata, Ranunculus recurvatus*, and *Rubus triflorus* with ripe fruit.

While we were thus employed, two Indians in a canoe hove in sight round the bushes, coming down stream. Our Indian knew one of them, an old man, and fell into conversation with him in Indian. He belonged at the foot of Moosehead. The other was of another tribe. They were returning from hunting. I asked the younger if they had seen any moose, to which he said no; but I, seeing the moose-hides sticking out from a great bundle made with their blankets in the middle of the canoe, added, "Only their hides." As he was a foreigner, he may have wished to deceive me, for it is against the law for white men and foreigners to kill moose in Maine at this season. But, perhaps, he need not have been alarmed, for the moose-wardens are not very particular. I heard quite directly of one, who being asked by a white man going into the woods what he would say if he killed a moose, answered, "If you bring me a quarter of it, I guess you won't be troubled." His duty being, as he said, only to prevent the "indiscriminate" slaughter of them for their hides. I suppose that he would consider it an *indiscriminate* slaughter when a quarter was not reserved for himself. Such are the perquisites of this office.

We continued along through the most extensive larch wood which I had seen,—tall and slender trees with fantastic branches. But though this was the prevailing tree here, I do not remember that we saw any afterward. You do not find straggling trees of this species here and there throughout the wood, but rather a little forest of them. The same is the case with the white and red pines, and some other trees, greatly to the convenience of the lumberer. They are of a social habit, growing in "veins," "clumps," "groups," or "communities," as the explorers call them, distinguishing them far away, from the top of a hill or a tree, the white pines towering above the surrounding forest, or else they form extensive forests by themselves. I would have liked to come across a large community of pines, which had never been invaded by the lumbering army.

We saw some fresh moose tracks along the shore, but the Indian said that the moose were not driven out of the woods by the flies, as usual at this season, on account of the abundance of water everywhere. The stream was only from one and one half to three rods wide, quite winding, with occasional small islands, meadows, and some very swift and shallow places. When we came to an island, the Indian never hesitated which side to take, as if the current told him which was the shortest and deepest. It was lucky for us that the water was so high. We had to walk but once on this stream, carrying a part of the load, at a swift and shallow reach, while he got up with the canoe, not being obliged to take out, though he said it was very strong water. Once or twice we passed the red wreck of a batteau which had been stove some spring.

While making this portage I saw many splendid specimens of the great purple-fringed orchis, three feet high. It is remarkable that such delicate flowers should here adorn these wilderness paths.

Having resumed our seats in the canoe, I felt the Indian wiping my back, which he had accidentally spat upon. He said it was a sign that I was going to be married.

The Umbazookskus River is called ten miles long. Having poled up the narrowest part some three or four miles, the next opening in the sky was over Umbazookskus Lake, which we suddenly entered about eleven o'clock in the forenoon. It stretches northwesterly four or five miles, with what the Indian called the Caucomgomoc Mountain seen far beyond it. It was an agreeable change.

This lake was very shallow a long distance from the shore, and I saw stone heaps on the bottom, like those in the Assabet at home. The canoe ran into one. The Indian thought that they were made by an eel. Joe Aitteon in 1853 thought that they were made by chub. We crossed the southeast end of the lake to the carry into Mud Pond.

Umbazookskus Lake is the head of the Penobscot in this direction, and Mud Pond is the nearest head of the Allegash, one of the chief sources of the St. John. Hodge, who went through this way to the St. Lawrence in the service of the State, calls the portage here a mile and three quarters long, and states that Mud Pond has been found to be fourteen feet higher than Umbazookskus Lake. As the west branch of the Penobscot at the Moosehead carry is considered about twenty-five feet lower than Moosehead Lake, it appears that the Penobscot in the upper part of its course runs in a broad and shallow valley, between the Kennebec and St. John's, and lower than either of them, though, judging from the map, you might expect it to be the highest.

Mud Pond is about half-way from Umbazookskus to Chamberlain Lake, into which it empties, and to which we were bound. The Indian said that this was the wettest carry in the State, and as the season was a very wet one, we anticipated an unpleasant walk. As usual he made one large bundle of the pork-keg, cooking utensils, and other loose traps, by tying them up in his blanket. We should be obliged to go over the carry twice, and our method was to carry one half part way, and then go back for the rest.

Our path ran close by the door of a log-hut in a clearing at this end of the carry, which the Indian, who alone entered it, found to be occupied by a Canadian and his family, and that the man had been blind for a year. He seemed peculiarly unfortunate to be taken blind there, where there were so few eyes to see for him. He could not even be led out of that country by a dog, but must be taken down the rapids as passively as a barrel of flour. This was the first house above Chesuncook, and the last on the Penobscot waters, and was built here, no doubt, because it was the route of the lumberers in the winter and spring.

After a slight ascent from the lake through the springy soil of the Canadian's clearing, we entered on a level and very wet and rocky path through the universal dense evergreen forest, a loosely paved gutter merely, where we went leaping from rock to rock and from side to side, in the vain attempt to keep out of the water and mud. We concluded that it was yet Penobscot water, though there was no flow to it. It was on this carry that the white hunter whom I met in the stage, as he told me, had shot two bears a few months before. They stood directly in the path, and did not turn out for him. They might be excused for not turning out there, or only taking the right as the law directs. He said that at this season bears were found on the mountains and hillsides, in search of berries, and were apt to be saucy,—that we might come across them up Trout Stream; and he added, what I hardly credited, that many Indians slept in their canoes, not daring to sleep on land, on account of them.

Here commences what was called, twenty years ago, the best timber land in the State. This very spot was described as "covered with the greatest abundance of pine," but now this appeared to me, comparatively, an uncommon tree there,—and yet you did not see where any more could have stood, amid the dense growth of cedar, fir, &c. It was then proposed to cut a canal from lake to lake here, but the outlet was finally made further east, at Telos Lake, as we shall see.

The Indian with his canoe soon disappeared before us; but erelong he came back and told us to take a path which turned off westward, it being better walking, and, at my suggestion, he agreed to leave a bough in the regular carry at that place, that we might not pass it by mistake. Thereafter, he said, we were to keep the main path, and he added, "You see 'em my tracks." But I had not much faith that we could distinguish his tracks, since others had passed over the carry within a few days.

We turned off at the right place, but were soon confused by numerous logging-paths, coming into the one we were on, by which lumberers had been to pick out those pines which I have mentioned. However, we kept what we considered the main path, though it was a winding one, and in this, at long intervals, we distinguished a faint trace of a footstep. This, though comparatively unworn, was at first a better, or, at least, a drier road, than the regular carry which we had left. It led through an arbor-vitæ wilderness of the grimmest character. The great fallen and rotting trees had been cut through and rolled aside, and their huge trunks abutted on the path on each side, while others still lay across it two or three feet high. It was impossible for us to discern the Indian's trail in the elastic moss, which, like a thick carpet, covered every rock and fallen tree, as well as the earth. Nevertheless, I did occasionally detect the track of a man, and I gave myself some credit for it. I carried my whole load at once, a heavy knapsack, and a large India-rubber bag, containing our bread and a blanket, swung on a paddle; in all, about sixty pounds; but my companion preferred to make two journeys, by short stages, while I waited for him. We could not be sure that we were not depositing our loads each time further off from the true path.

As I sat waiting for my companion, he would seem to be gone a long time, and I had ample opportunity to make observations on the forest. I now first began to be seriously molested by the black-fly, a very small but perfectly formed fly of that color, about one tenth of an inch long, which I first felt, and then saw, in swarms about me, as I sat by a wider and more than usually doubtful fork in this dark forest-path. The hunters tell bloody stories about them,—how they settle in a ring about your neck, before you know it, and are wiped off in great numbers with your blood. But remembering that I had a wash in my knapsack, prepared by a thoughtful hand in Bangor, I made haste to apply it to my face and hands, and was glad to find it effectual, as long as it was fresh, or for twenty minutes, not only against black-flies, but all the insects that molested us. They would not alight on the part thus defended. It was composed of sweet-oil and oil of turpentine, with a little oil of spearmint, and camphor. However, I finally concluded that the remedy was worse than the disease. It was so disagreeable and inconvenient to have your face and hands covered with such a mixture.

Three large slate-colored birds of the jay genus (*Garrulus Canadensis*), the Canada-jay, moose-bird, meat-bird, or what not, came flitting silently and by degrees toward me, and hopped down the limbs inquisitively to within seven or eight feet. They were more clumsy and not nearly so handsome as the blue-jay. Fish-hawks, from the lake, uttered their sharp whistling notes low over the top of the forest near me, as if they were anxious about a nest there.

After I had sat there some time, I noticed at this fork in the path a tree which had been blazed, and the letters "Chamb. L." written on it with red chalk. This I knew to mean Chamberlain Lake. So I concluded that on the whole we were on the right course, though as we had come nearly two miles, and saw no signs of Mud Pond, I did harbor the suspicion that we might be on a direct course to Chamberlain Lake, leaving out Mud Pond. This I found by my map would be about five miles northeasterly, and I then took the bearing by my compass.

My companion having returned with his bag, and also defended his face and hands with the insect-wash, we set forward again. The walking rapidly grew worse, and the path more indistinct, and at length, after passing through a patch of *calla palustris*, still abundantly in bloom, we found ourselves in a more open and regular swamp, made less passable than ordinary by the unusual wetness of the season. We sank a foot deep in water and mud at every step, and sometimes up to our knees, and the trail was almost obliterated, being no more than that a musquash leaves in similar places, when he parts the floating sedge. In fact, it probably was a musquash trail in some places. We concluded that if Mud Pond was as muddy as the approach to it was wet, it certainly deserved its name. It would have been amusing to behold the dogged and deliberate pace at which we entered that swamp, without interchanging a word, as if determined to go through it, though it should come up to our necks. Having penetrated a considerable distance into this, and found a tussuck on which we could deposit our loads, though there was no place to sit, my companion went back for the rest of his pack. I had thought to observe on this carry when we crossed the dividing line between the Penobscot and St. John, but as my feet had hardly been out of water the whole distance, and it was all level and stagnant, I began to despair of finding it. I remembered hearing a good deal about the "highlands" dividing the waters of the Penobscot from those of the St. John, as well as the St. Lawrence, at the time of the northeast boundary dispute, and I observed by my map, that the line claimed by Great Britain as the boundary prior to 1842 passed between Umbazookskus Lake and Mud Pond, so that we had either crossed or were then on it. These, then, according to *her* interpretation of the treaty of '83, were the "highlands which divide those rivers that empty themselves into the St. Lawrence from those which fall into the Atlantic Ocean." Truly an interesting spot to stand on,—if that were it,—though you could not sit down there. I thought that if the commissioners themselves, and the king of Holland with them, had spent a few days here, with their packs upon their backs, looking for that "highland," they would have had an interesting time, and perhaps it would have modified their views of the question somewhat. The king of Holland would have been in his element. Such were my meditations while my companion was gone back for his bag.

It was a cedar swamp, through which the peculiar note of the white-throated sparrow rang loud and clear. There grew the side-saddle flower, Labrador tea, *Kalmia glauca*, and, what was new to me, the Low Birch (*Betula pumila*), a little round-leafed shrub, two or three feet high only. We thought to name this swamp after the latter.

After a long while my companion came back, and the Indian with him. We had taken the wrong road, and the Indian had lost us. He had very wisely gone back to the Canadian's camp, and asked him which way we had probably gone, since he could better understand the ways of white men, and he told him correctly that we had undoubtedly taken the supply road to Chamberlain Lake (slender supplies they would get over such a road at this season). The Indian was greatly surprised that we should have taken what he called a "tow" (i.e. tote or toting or supply) road, instead of a carry path,—that we had not followed his tracks,—said it was "strange," and evidently thought little of our woodcraft.

Having held a consultation, and eaten a mouthful of bread, we concluded that it would, perhaps, be nearer for us two now to keep on to Chamberlain Lake, omitting Mud Pond, than to go back and start anew for the last place, though the Indian had never been through this way, and knew nothing about it. In the meanwhile he would go back and finish carrying over his canoe and bundle to Mud Pond, cross that, and go down its outlet and up Chamberlain Lake, and trust to meet us there before night. It was now a little after noon. He supposed that the water in which we stood had flowed back from Mud Pond, which could not be far off eastward, but was unapproachable through the dense cedar swamp.

Keeping on, we were erelong agreeably disappointed by reaching firmer ground, and we crossed a ridge where the path was more distinct, but there was never any outlook over the forest. While descending the last, I saw many specimens of the great round-leaved orchis, of large size; one which I measured had leaves, as usual, flat on the ground, nine and a half inches long, and nine wide, and was two feet high. The dark, damp wilderness is favorable to some of these orchidaceous plants, though they are too delicate for cultivation. I also saw the swamp gooseberry (*Ribes lacustre*), with green fruit, and in all the low ground, where it was not too wet, the *Rubus triflorus* in fruit. At one place I heard a very clear and piercing note from a small hawk, like a single note from a white-throated sparrow, only very much louder, as he dashed through the tree-tops over my head. I wondered that he allowed himself to be disturbed by our presence, since it seemed as if he could not easily find his nest again himself in that wilderness. We also saw and heard several times the red squirrel, and often, as before observed, the bluish scales of the fir cones which it had left on a rock or fallen tree. This, according to the Indian, is the only squirrel found in those woods, except a very few striped ones. It must have a solitary time in that dark evergreen forest, where there is so little life, seventy-five miles from a road as we had come. I wondered how he could call any particular tree there his home; and yet he would run up the stem of one out of the myriads, as if it were an old road to him. How can a hawk ever find him there? I fancied that he must be glad to see us, though he did seem to chide us. One of those sombre fir and spruce woods is not complete unless you hear from out its cavernous mossy and twiggy recesses his fine alarum,—his spruce voice, like the working of the sap through some crack in a tree,— the working of the spruce-beer. Such an impertinent fellow would occasionally try to alarm the wood about me. "O," said I, "I am well acquainted with your family, I know your cousins in Concord very well. Guess the mail's irregular in these parts, and you'd like to hear from 'em." But my overtures were vain, for he would withdraw by his aerial turnpikes into a more distant cedar-top, and spring his rattle again.

We then entered another swamp, at a necessarily slow pace, where the walking was worse than ever, not only on account of the water, but the fallen timber, which often obliterated the indistinct trail entirely. The fallen trees were so numerous, that for long distances the route was through a succession of small yards, where we climbed over fences as high as our heads, down into water often up to our knees, and then over another fence into a second yard, and so on; and going back for his bag my companion once lost his way and came back without it. In many places the canoe would have run if it had not been for the fallen timber. Again it would be more open, but equally wet, too wet for trees to grow, and no place to sit down. It was a mossy swamp, which it required the long legs of a moose to traverse, and it is very likely that we scared some of them in our transit, though we saw none. It was ready to echo the growl of a bear, the howl of a wolf, or the scream of a panther; but when you get fairly into the middle of one of these grim forests, you are surprised to find that the larger inhabitants are not at home commonly, but have left only a puny red squirrel to bark at you. Generally speaking, a howling wilderness does not howl: it is the imagination of the traveller that does the howling. I did, however, see one dead porcupine; perhaps he had succumbed to the difficulties of the way. These bristly fellows are a very suitable small fruit of such unkempt wildernesses.

Making a logging-road in the Maine woods is called "swamping" it, and they who do the work are called "swampers." I now perceived the fitness of the term. This was the most perfectly swamped of all the roads I ever saw. Nature must have co-operated with art here. However, I suppose they would tell you that this name took its origin from the fact that the chief work of road-makers in those woods is to make the swamps passable. We came to a stream where the bridge, which had been made of logs tied together with cedar bark, had been broken up, and we got over as we could. This probably emptied into Mud Pond, and perhaps the Indian might have come up it and taken us in there if he had known it. Such as it was, this ruined bridge was the chief evidence that we were on a path of any kind.

We then crossed another low rising ground, and I, who wore shoes, had an opportunity to wring out my stockings, but my companion, who used boots, had found that this was not a safe experiment for him, for he might not be able to get his wet boots on again. He went over the whole ground, or water, three times, for which reason our progress was very slow; beside that the water softened our feet, and to some extent unfitted them for walking. As I sat waiting for him, it would naturally seem an unaccountable time that he was gone. Therefore, as I could see through the woods that the sun was getting low, and it was uncertain how far the lake might be, even if we were on the right course, and in what part of the world we should find ourselves at nightfall, I proposed that I should push through with what speed I could, leaving boughs to mark my path, and find the lake and the Indian, if possible, before night, and send the latter back to carry my companion's bag.

Having gone about a mile, and got into low ground again, I heard a noise like the note of an owl, which I soon discovered to be made by the Indian, and answering him, we soon came together. He had reached the lake, after crossing Mud Pond, and running some rapids below it, and had come up about a mile and a half on our path. If he had not come back to meet us, we probably should not have found him that night, for the path branched once or twice before reaching this particular part of the lake. So he went back for my companion and his bag, while I kept on. Having waded through another stream where the bridge of logs had been broken up and half floated away,—and this was not altogether worse than our ordinary walking, since it was less muddy,—we continued on, through alternate mud and water, to the shore of Apmoojenegamook Lake, which we reached in season for a late supper, instead of dining there, as we had expected, having gone without our dinner. It was at least five miles by the way we had come, and as my companion had gone over most of it three times, he had walked full a dozen miles, bad as it was. In the winter, when the water is frozen, and the snow is four feet deep, it is no doubt a tolerable path to a footman. As it was, I would not have missed that walk for a good deal. If you want an exact recipe for making such a road, take one part Mud Pond, and dilute it with equal parts of Umbazookskus and Apmoojenegamook; then send a family of musquash through to locate it, look after the grades and culverts, and finish it to their minds, and let a hurricane follow to do the fencing.

We had come out on a point extending into Apmoojenegamook, or Chamberlain Lake, west of the outlet of Mud Pond, where there was a broad, gravelly, and rocky shore, encumbered with bleached logs and trees. We were rejoiced to see such dry things in that part of the world. But at first we did not attend to dryness so much as to mud and wetness. We all three walked into the lake up to our middle to wash our clothes.

This was another noble lake, called twelve miles long, east and west; if you add Telos Lake, which, since the dam was built, has been connected with it by dead water, it will be twenty; and it is apparently from a mile and a half to two miles wide. We were about midway its length, on the south side. We could see the only clearing in these parts, called the "Chamberlain Farm," with two or three log buildings close together, on the opposite shore, some two and a half miles distant. The smoke of our fire on the shore brought over two men in a canoe from the farm, that being a common signal agreed on when one wishes to cross. It took them about half an hour to come over, and they had their labor for their pains this time. Even the English name of the lake had a wild, woodland sound, reminding me of that Chamberlain who killed Paugus at Lovewell's fight.

After putting on such dry clothes as we had, and hanging the others to dry on the pole which the Indian arranged over the fire, we ate our supper, and lay down on the pebbly shore with our feet to the fire, without pitching our tent, making a thin bed of grass to cover the stones.

Here first I was molested by the little midge called the No-see-em (*Simulium nocivum*, the latter word is not the Latin for no-see-em), especially over the sand at the water's edge, for it is a kind of sand-fly. You would not observe them but for their light-colored wings. They are said to get under your clothes, and produce a feverish heat, which I suppose was what I felt that night.

Our insect foes in this excursion, to sum them up, were, first, mosquitoes, the chief ones, but only troublesome at night, or when we sat still on shore by day; second, black flies (*Simulium molestum*), which molested us more or less on the carries by day, as I have before described, and sometimes in narrower parts of the stream. Harris mistakes when he says that they are not seen after June. Third, mooseflies. The big ones, Polis said, were called *Bososquasis*. It is a stout brown fly, much like a horse-fly, about eleven sixteenths of an inch long, commonly rusty colored beneath, with unspotted wings. They can bite smartly, according to Polis, but are easily avoided or killed. Fourth, the No-see-ems above mentioned. Of all these, the mosquitoes are the only ones that troubled me seriously; but, as I was provided with a wash and a veil, they have not made any deep impression.

The Indian would not use our wash to protect his face and hands, for fear that it would hurt his skin, nor had he any veil; he, therefore, suffered from insects now, and throughout this journey, more than either of us. I think that he suffered more than I did, when neither of us was protected. He regularly tied up his face in his handkerchief, and buried it in his blanket, and he now finally lay down on the sand between us and the fire for the sake of the smoke, which he tried to make enter his blanket about his face, and for the same purpose he lit his pipe and breathed the smoke into his blanket.

As we lay thus on the shore, with nothing between us and the stars, I inquired what stars he was acquainted with, or had names for. They were the Great Bear, which he called by this name, the Seven Stars, which he had no English name for, "the morning star," and "the north star."

In the middle of the night, as indeed each time that we lay on the shore of a lake, we heard the voice of the loon, loud and distinct, from far over the lake. It is a very wild sound, quite in keeping with the place and the circumstances of the traveller, and very unlike the voice of a bird. I could lie awake for hours listening to it, it is so thrilling. When camping in such a wilderness as this, you are prepared to hear sounds from some of its inhabitants which will give voice to its wildness. Some idea of bears, wolves, or panthers runs in your head naturally, and when this note is first heard very far off at midnight, as you lie with your ear to the ground,—the forest being perfectly still about you, you take it for granted that it is the voice of a wolf or some other wild beast, for only the last part is heard when at a distance,—you conclude that it is a pack of wolves baying the moon, or, perchance, cantering after a moose. Strange as it may seem, the "mooing" of a cow on a mountain-side comes nearest to my idea of the voice of a bear; and this bird's note resembled that. It was the unfailing and characteristic sound of those lakes. We were not so lucky as to hear wolves howl, though that is an occasional serenade. Some friends of mine, who two years ago went up the Caucomgomoc River, were serenaded by wolves while moose-hunting by moonlight. It was a sudden burst, as if a hundred demons had broke loose,—a startling sound enough, which, if any, would make your hair stand on end, and all was still again. It lasted but a moment, and you'd have thought there were twenty of them, when probably there were only two or three. They heard it twice only, and they said that it gave expression to the wilderness which it lacked before. I heard of some men who, while skinning a moose lately in those woods, were driven off from the carcass by a pack of wolves, which ate it up.

This of the loon—I do not mean its laugh, but its looning—is a long-drawn call, as it were, sometimes singularly human to my ear,—*hoo-hoo-ooooo*, like the hallooing of a man on a very high key, having thrown his voice into his head. I have heard a sound exactly like it when breathing heavily through my own nostrils, half awake at ten at night, suggesting my affinity to the loon; as if its language were but a dialect of my own, after all. Formerly, when lying awake at midnight in those woods, I had listened to hear some words or syllables of their language, but it chanced that I listened in vain until I heard the cry of the loon. I have heard it occasionally on the ponds of my native town, but there its wildness is not enhanced by the surrounding scenery.

I was awakened at midnight by some heavy, low-flying bird, probably a loon, flapping by close over my head, along the shore. So, turning the other side of my half-clad body to the fire, I sought slumber again.

TUESDAY, JULY 28.

When we awoke we found a heavy dew on our blankets. I lay awake very early, and listened to the clear, shrill *ah-tette-tette-te*, of the white-throated sparrow, repeated at short intervals, without the least variation, for half an hour, as if it could not enough express its happiness. Whether my companions heard it or not, I know not, but it was a kind of matins to me, and the event of that forenoon.

It was a pleasant sunrise, and we had a view of the mountains in the southeast. Ktaadn appeared about southeast by south. A double-topped mountain, about southeast by east, and another portion of the same, east-southeast. The last the Indian called Nerlum-skeechticook, and said that it was at the head of the East Branch, and we should pass near it on our return that way.

We did some more washing in the lake this morning, and with our clothes hung about on the dead trees and rocks, the shore looked like washing-day at home. The Indian, taking the hint, borrowed the soap, and walking into the lake, washed his only cotton shirt on his person, then put on his pants and let it dry on him.

I observed that he wore a cotton shirt, originally white, a greenish flannel one over it, but no waist-coat, flannel drawers, and strong linen or duck pants, which also had been white, blue woollen stockings, cowhide boots, and a Kossuth hat. He carried no change of clothing, but putting on a stout, thick jacket, which he laid aside in the canoe, and seizing a full-sized axe, his gun and ammunition, and a blanket, which would do for a sail or knapsack, if wanted, and strapping on his belt, which contained a large sheath-knife, he walked off at once, ready to be gone all summer. This looked very independent; a few simple and effective tools, and no India rubber clothing. He was always the first ready to start in the morning, and if it had not held some of our property would not have been obliged to roll up his blanket. Instead of carrying a large bundle of his own extra clothing &c. he brought back the great coats of moose tied up in his blanket. I found that his outfit was the result of a long experience, and in the main, was hardly to be improved on unless by washing or an extra shirt. Wanting a button here, he walked off to a place where some Indians had recently encamped, and searched for one, but I believe, in vain.

Having softened our stiffened boots and shoes with the pork fat—the usual disposition of what was left at breakfast—we crossed the lake early, steering in a diagonal direction north-westerly about 4 miles, to the outlet, which was not to be discerned till we were close to it. The Indian name, *Apmoojenegamook*, means Lake that is crossed, because the usual course lies across and not along it. This is the largest of the

Alleguash Lakes, and was the first St. John's water
that we floated on. It is shaped in the main like
Chesuncook. There are no mountains or high hills
very near it. At Bangor we had been told of a township many miles further north-west, containing the
highest land thereabouts, where, by climbing a particular tree in the forest, we could get a general idea
of the country. I have no doubt that the last was good
advice, but we did not go there. We did not now intend to go far down the Allegash, but merely to get a
view of the great lakes which are its source and then
return this way to the East Branch of the Penobscot.
The water now by "good rights" flowed northward—if
it could be said to flow at all. After reaching the
middle of the lake, we found the waves as usual
pretty high, and Polis warned my companion, who
was nodding, that he must not allow himself to fall
asleep in the canoe lest he should upset us, adding
that when Indians want to sleep in a canoe they lie
down straight on the bottom. But in this crowded one
that was impossible. However, he said that he would
nudge him if he saw him nodding.

A belt of dead trees stood all around the lake, some
far out in the water, with others prostrate behind
them, and they made the shore for the most part
almost inaccessible. This is the effect of the dam at
the outlet. Thus the natural sandy or rocky shore,
with its green fringe, was concealed and destroyed.
We coasted westward along the north side, searching
for the outlet, about ¼ of a mile distant from this
savage looking shore, on which the waves were breaking violently—knowing that it might easily be concealed amid this rubbish, or by the overlapping of the
shore. It is remarkable how little these important
gates to a lake are blazoned. There is no triumphal
arch over the modest inlet or outlet, but at some

undistinguished point it trickles in or out through the uninterrupted forest, almost as through a sponge.

We reached the outlet in about an hour, and carried over the dam there, which is quite a solid structure, and about ¼ of a mile further there was a 2nd dam. The reader will perceive that the result of this particular damming about Chamberlain Lake is that the head waters of the St. John are made to flow by Bangor.

They have thus dammed all the larger lakes, raising their broad surfaces many feet; Moosehead for instance, some 40 miles long, with its steamer on it; thus turning the forces of Nature against herself, that they might float their spoils out of the country. They rapidly run out of these immense forests all the finer and more accessible pine timber, and then leave the bears to watch the decaying dams. Not clearing nor cultivating the land, nor making roads, nor building houses, but leaving it a wilderness, as they found it. In many parts only these dams remain, like deserted beaver dams. Think how much land they have flowed without asking Nature's leave!

The wilderness experiences a sudden rise of all her streams and lakes, she feels 10000 vermin gnawing at the base of her noblest trees. Many combining drag them off jarring over the roots of the survivors, and tumble them into the nearest stream, till, the fairest having fallen, they scamper off to ransack some new wilderness, and all is still again. It is as when a migrating army of mice girdles a forest of pines. The chopper fells trees from the same motive that the mouse gnaws them—to get his living. You tell me that he has a more interesting family than the mouse. That is as it happens. He speaks of a "berth" of timber—a good place for him to get into—just as a worm might.

When the chopper would praise a pine, he will commonly tell you, that the one he cut was so big that a yoke of oxen stood on its stump. As if that were what the pine had grown for—to become the footstool of oxen! In my mind's eye, I can see these unwieldly tame deer, with a yoke binding them together, and brazen-tipped horns betraying their servitude, taking their stand on the stump of each giant pine in succession throughout this whole forest, and chewing their cud there, until it is nothing but an ox pasture and run out at that. As if it were good for the oxen—and some terebinthine or other medicinal quality ascended into their nostrils. Or is their elevated position intended merely as a symbol of the fact that the pastoral comes next in order to the sylvan or hunter life?

The character of the logger's admiration is betrayed by his very mode of expressing it. If he told all that was in his mind, he would say—It was so big that I cut it down and then a yoke of oxen could stand on its stump. He admires the log, the carcass or corpse, more than the tree. Why, my dear sir, the tree might have stood on its own stump, and a great deal more comfortably and firmly than a yoke of oxen can, if you had not cut it down. What right have you to celebrate the virtues of the man you murdered?

The Anglo American can indeed cut down and grub up all this waving forest and make a stump speech and vote for Buchanan on its ruins, but he cannot converse with the spirit of the tree he fells—he cannot read the poetry and mythology which retire as he advances. He ignorantly erases mythological tablets in order to print his handbills and town meeting warrants on them.

Before he has learned his a b c in the beautiful but

mystic lore of the wilderness, which Spenser and Dante had just begun to read, he cuts it down—coins a *pine-tree* shilling—(as if to signify the pine's value to him) puts up a *dee*strict school house, and introduces Webster's spelling book. When the state wishes to endow an academy or university it grants it a tract of forest land; one saw represents an academy, a gang a university.

Below the last dam, the river being swift and shallow, though broad enough, we two walked about half a mile to lighten the canoe. I made it a rule to carry my Knapsack when I walked, and also to keep it tied to a cross-bar when in the canoe, that it might be found with the canoe if we should upset.

I heard the dog-day locust here, and afterward on the carries, a sound which I had associated only with more open, if not settled countries. The area for locusts must be small in the Maine woods.

We were now fairly on the Allegash River, which name our Indian said meant hemlock bark. These waters flow northward about 100 miles, at first very feebly, then southeasterly 250 more to the Bay of Fundy. After perhaps two miles of river, we entered Heron Lake, called on the map *Pongokwahem*, scaring up forty or fifty young *shecorways*, sheldrakes, at the entrance, which ran over the water with great rapidity, as usual in a long line.

This was the fourth great lake, lying northwest and southeast, like Chesuncook, and most of the long lakes in that neighborhood, and, judging from the map, it is about ten miles long. We had entered it on the southwest side, and saw a dark mountain northeast over the lake, not very far off nor high, which the Indian said was called *Peaked Mountain*, and used by explorers to look for timber from. There was also some other high land more easterly. The shores were in the same ragged and unsightly condition, encumbered with dead timber, both fallen and standing, as in the last lake, owing to the dam on the Allegash below. Some low points or islands were almost drowned.

I saw something white a mile off on the water, which turned out to be a great gull on a rock in the middle, which the Indian would have been glad to kill and eat, but it flew away long before we were near; and also a flock of summer ducks that were about the rock with it. I asking him about herons, since this was Heron Lake, he said that he found the blue heron's nests in the hard-wood trees. I thought that I saw a light-colored object move along the opposite or northern shore, four or five miles distant. He did not know what it could be, unless it were a moose, though he had never seen a white one; but he said that he could distinguish a moose "anywhere on shore, clear across the lake."

Rounding a point, we stood across a bay for a mile and a half or two miles, toward a large island, three or four miles down the lake. We met with ephemeræ (shad-fly) midway, about a mile from the shore, and they evidently fly over the whole lake. On Moosehead I had seen a large devil's-needle half a mile from the shore, coming from the middle of the lake, where it was three or four miles wide at least. It had probably crossed. But at last, of course, you come to lakes so large that an insect cannot fly across them; and this, perhaps, will serve to distinguish a large lake from a small one.

We landed on the southeast side of the island, which was rather elevated, and densely wooded, with a rocky shore, in season for an early dinner. Somebody had camped there not long before, and left the frame on which they stretched a moose-hide, which our Indian criticised severely, thinking it showed but little woodcraft. Here were plenty of the shells of crayfish, or fresh-water lobsters, which had been washed ashore, such as have given a name to some ponds and streams. They are commonly four or five inches long. The Indian proceeded at once to cut a canoe-birch, slanted it up against another tree on the shore, tying it with a withe, and lay down to sleep in its shade.

When we were on the Caucomgomoc, he recommended to us a new way home, the very one which we had first thought of, by the St. John. He even said that it was easier, and would take but little more time than the other, by the east branch of the Penobscot, though very much further round; and taking the map, he showed where we should be each night, for he was familiar with the route. According to his calculation, we should reach the French settlements the next night after this, by keeping northward down the Allegash, and when we got into the main St. John the banks would be more or less settled all the way; as if that were a recommendation. There would be but one or two falls, with short carrying-places, and we should go down the stream very fast, even a hundred miles a day, if the wind allowed; and he indicated where we should carry over into Eel River to save a bend below Woodstock in New Brunswick, and so into the Schoodic Lake, and thence to the Mattawamkeag. It would be about three hundred and sixty miles to Bangor this way, though only about one hundred and sixty by the other; but in the former case we should explore the St. John from its source through two thirds of its course, as well as the Schoodic Lake and Mattawamkeag,—and we were again tempted to go that way. I feared, however, that the banks of the St. John were too much settled.

When I asked him which course would take us through the wildest country, he said the route by the East Branch. Partly from this consideration, as also from its shortness, we resolved to adhere to the latter route, and perhaps ascend Ktaadn on the way. We made this island the limit of our excursion in this direction.

We had now seen the largest of the Allegash Lakes. The next dam "was about fifteen miles" further north, down the Allegash, and it was dead water so far. We had been told in Bangor of a man who lived alone, a sort of hermit, at that dam, to take care of it, who spent his time tossing a bullet from one hand to the other, for want of employment,—as if we might want to call on him. This sort of tit-for-tat intercourse between his two hands, bandying to and fro a leaden subject, seems to have been his symbol for society.

This island, according to the map, was about a hundred and ten miles in a straight line north-north-west from Bangor, and about ninety-nine miles east-southeast from Quebec. There was another island visible toward the north end of the lake, with an elevated clearing on it; but we learned afterward that it was not inhabited, had only been used as a pasture for cattle which summered in these woods, though our informant said that there was a hut on the mainland near the outlet of the lake. This unnaturally smooth-shaven, squarish spot, in the midst of the otherwise uninterrupted forest, only reminded us how uninhabited the country was. You would sooner expect to meet with a bear than an ox in such a clearing. At any rate, it must have been a surprise to the bears when they came across it. Such, seen far or near, you know at once to be man's work, for Nature never does it. In order to let in the light to the earth as on a lake, he clears off the forest on the hillsides and plains, and sprinkles fine grass-seed, like an enchanter, and so carpets the earth with a firm sward.

Polis had evidently more curiosity respecting the few settlers in those woods than we. If nothing was said, he took it for granted that we wanted to go straight to the next log-hut. Having observed that we came by the log-huts at Chesuncook, and the blind Canadian's at the Mud Pond carry, without stopping to communicate with the inhabitants, he took occasion now to suggest that the usual way was, when you came near a house, to go to it, and tell the inhabitants what you had seen or heard, and then they tell you what they had seen; but we laughed, and said that we had had enough of houses for the present, and had come here partly to avoid them.

In the mean while, the wind, increasing, blew down the Indian's birch and created such a sea that we found ourselves prisoners on the island, the nearest shore, which was the western, being perhaps a mile distant, and we took the canoe out to prevent its drifting away. We did not know but we should be compelled to spend the rest of the day and the night there. At any rate, the Indian went to sleep again in the shade of his birch, my companion busied himself drying his plants, and I rambled along the shore westward, which was quite stony, and obstructed with fallen bleached or drifted trees for four or five rods in width. I found growing on this broad rocky and gravelly shore the *Salix rostrata, discolor,* and *lucida, Ranunculus recurvatus, Potentilla Norvegica, Scutellaria lateriflora, Eupatorium purpureum, Aster Tradescanti, Mentha Canadensis, Epilobium angustifolium,* abundant, *Lycopus sinuatus, Solidago lanceolata, Spiræa salicifolia, Antennaria margaritacea, Prunella, Rumex acetosella,* Raspberries, Wool-grass, *Onoclea,* &c. The nearest trees were *Betula papyracea* and *excelsa,* and *Populus tremuloides.* I give these names because it was my furthest northern point.

Our Indian said that he was a doctor, and could tell me some medicinal use for every plant I could show him. I immediately tried him. He said that the inner bark of the aspen (*Populus tremuloides*) was good for sore eyes; and so with various other plants, proving himself as good as his word. According to his account, he had acquired such knowledge in his youth from a wise old Indian with whom he associated, and he lamented that the present generation of Indians "had lost a great deal."

He said that the caribou was a "very great runner," that there were none about this lake now, though there used to be many, and pointing to the belt of dead trees caused by the dams, he added, "No likum stump,—when he sees that he scared."

Pointing southeasterly over the lake and distant forest, he observed, "Me go Oldtown in three days." I asked how he would get over the swamps and fallen trees. "O," said he, "in winter all covered, go anywhere on snow-shoes, right across lakes." When I asked how he went, he said, "First I go Ktaadn, west side, then I go Millinocket, then Pamadumcook, then Nickatou, then Lincoln, then Oldtown," or else he went a shorter way by the Piscataquis. What a wilderness walk for a man to take alone! None of your half-mile swamps, none of your mile-wide woods merely, as on the skirts of our towns, without hotels, only a dark mountain or a lake for guide-board and station, over ground much of it impassable in summer!

It reminded me of Prometheus Bound. Here was travelling of the old heroic kind over the unaltered face of nature. From the Allegash, or Hemlock River, and Pongoquahem Lake, across great Apmoojenegamook, and leaving the Nerlumskeechticook Mountain on his left, he takes his way under the bear-haunted slopes of Souneunk and Ktaadn Mountains to Pamadumcook and Millinocket's inland seas, (where often gulls'-eggs may increase his store,) and so on to the forks at Nickatou, (*nia soseb* "we alone Joseph" seeing what our folks see,) ever pushing the boughs of the fir and spruce aside, with his load of furs, contending day and night, night and day, with the shaggy demon Vegetation, travelling through the mossy graveyard of trees. Or he could go by "that rough tooth of the sea," Kineo, great source of arrows and of spears to the ancients, when weapons of stone were used. Seeing and hearing moose, caribou, bears, porcupines, lynxes, wolves, and panthers. Places where he might live and die and never hear of the United States, which make such a noise in the world, —never hear of America, so called from the name of a European gentleman.

There is a lumberer's road called the Eagle Lake road, from the Seboois to the east side of this lake. It may seem strange that any road through such a wilderness should be passable, even in winter, when the snow is three or four feet deep, but at that season, wherever lumbering operations are actively carried on, teams are continually passing on the single track, and it becomes as smooth almost as a railway. I am told that in the Aroostook country the sleds are required by law to be of one width, (four feet,) and sleighs must be altered to fit the track, so that one runner may go in one rut and the other follow the horse. Yet it is very bad turning out.

We had for some time seen a thunder-shower coming up from the west over the woods of the island, and heard the muttering of the thunder, though we were in doubt whether it would reach us; but now the darkness rapidly increasing, and a fresh breeze rustling the forest, we hastily put up the plants which we had been drying, and with one consent made a rush for the tent material and set about pitching it. A place was selected and stakes and pins cut in the shortest possible time, and we were pinning it down lest it should be blown away, when the storm suddenly burst over us.

As we lay huddled together under the tent, which leaked considerably about the sides, with our baggage at our feet, we listened to some of the grandest thunder which I ever heard,–rapid peals, round and plump, bang, bang, bang, in succession, like artillery from some fortress in the sky; and the lightning was proportionally brilliant. The Indian said, "It must be good powder." All for the benefit of the moose and us, echoing far over the concealed lakes. I thought it must be a place which the thunder loved, where the lightning practised to keep its hand in, and it would do no harm to shatter a few pines. What had become of the ephemeræ and devil's-needles then? Were they prudent enough to seek harbor before the storm? Perhaps their motions might guide the voyageur.

Looking out I perceived that the violent shower falling on the lake had almost instantaneously flattened the waves,–the commander of that fortress had smoothed it for us so,–and it clearing off, we resolved to start immediately, before the wind raised them again.

Going outside, I said that I saw clouds still in the southwest, and heard thunder there. The Indian asked if the thunder went "lound" (round), saying that if it did we should have more rain. I thought that it did. We embarked, nevertheless, and paddled rapidly back toward the dams. The white-throated sparrows on the shore were about, singing *Ah te, e, e, te, e, e, te,* or else *ah te, e, e, te, e, e, te, e, e, te, e, e.*

At the outlet of Chamberlain Lake we were overtaken by another gusty rain-storm, which compelled
us to take shelter, the Indian under his canoe on the
bank, and we under the edge of the dam. However,
we were more scared than wet. From my covert I
could see the Indian peeping out from beneath his
canoe to see what had become of the rain. When we
had taken our respective places thus once or twice,
the rain not coming down in earnest, we commenced
rambling about the neighborhood, for the wind had
by this time raised such waves on the lake that we
could not stir, and we feared that we should be
obliged to camp there. We got an early supper on the
dam and tried for fish there, while waiting for the
tumult to subside. The fishes were not only few, but
small and worthless, and the Indian declared that
there were no good fishes in the St. John's waters;
that we must wait till we got to the Penobscot waters.

At length, just before sunset, we set out again. It
was a wild evening when we coasted up the north
side of this Apmoojenegamook Lake. One thunder-
storm was just over, and the waves which it had
raised were still running with violence, and another
storm was now seen coming up in the southwest, far
over the lake; but it might be worse in the morning,
and we wished to get as far as possible on our way
up the lake while we might. It blowed hard against
the northern shore about an eighth of a mile distant
on our left, and there was just as much sea as our
shallow canoe would bear, without our taking unusual care. That which we kept off, and toward
which the waves were driving, was as dreary and
harborless a shore as you can conceive. For half a
dozen rods in width it was a perfect maze of sub-
merged trees, all dead and bare and bleaching, some
standing half their original height, others prostrate,

and criss-across, above or beneath the surface, and mingled with them were loose trees and limbs and stumps, beating about. Imagine the wharves of the largest city in the world, decayed, and the earth and planking washed away, leaving the spiles standing in loose order, but often of twice the ordinary height, and mingled with and beating against them the wreck of ten thousand navies, all their spars and timbers, while there rises from the water's edge the densest and grimmest wilderness, ready to supply more material when the former fails, and you may get a faint idea of that coast. We could not have landed if we would, without the greatest danger of being swamped; so blow as it might, we must depend on coasting by it. It was twilight, too, and that stormy cloud was advancing rapidly in our rear. It was a pleasant excitement, yet we were glad to reach, at length, in the dusk, the cleared shore of the Chamberlain Farm.

We landed on a low and thinly wooded point there, and while my companions were pitching the tent, I ran up to the house to get some sugar, our six pounds being gone;—it was no wonder they were, for Polis had a sweet tooth. He would first fill his dipper nearly a third full of sugar, and then add the coffee to it. Here was a clearing extending back from the lake to a hill-top, with some dark-colored log buildings and a storehouse in it, and half a dozen men standing in front of the principal hut, greedy for news. Among them was the man who tended the dam on the Allegash and tossed the bullet. He having charge of the dams, and learning that we were going to Webster Stream the next day, told me that some of their men, who were haying at Telos Lake, had shut the dam at the canal there in order to catch trout, and if we wanted more water to take us through the canal we might raise the gate, for he would like to have it raised. The Chamberlain Farm is no doubt a cheerful opening in the woods, but such was the lateness of the hour that it has left but a dusky impression on my mind. As I have said, the influx of light merely is civilizing, yet I fancied that they walked about on Sundays in their clearing somewhat as in a prison-yard.

They were unwilling to spare more than four pounds of brown sugar,—unlocking the storehouse to get it,—since they only kept a little for such cases as this, and they charged twenty cents a pound for it, which certainly it was worth to get it up there.

When I returned to the shore it was quite dark, but we had a rousing fire to warm and dry us by, and a snug apartment behind it. The Indian went up to the house to inquire after a brother who had been absent hunting a year or two, and while another shower was beginning, I groped about cutting spruce and arbor-vitæ twigs for a bed. I preferred the arbor-vitæ on account of its fragrance, and spread it particularly thick about the shoulders. It is remarkable with what pure satisfaction the traveller in these woods will reach his camping-ground on the eve of a tempestuous night like this, as if he had got to his inn, and, rolling himself in his blanket, stretch himself on his six feet by two bed of dripping fir-twigs, with a thin sheet of cotton for roof, snug as a meadow-mouse in its nest. Invariably our best nights were those when it rained, for then we were not troubled with mosquitoes.

You soon come to disregard rain on such excursions, at least in the summer, it is so easy to dry yourself, supposing a dry change of clothing is not to be had. You can much sooner dry you by such a fire as you can make in the woods than in anybody's kitchen, the fireplace is so much larger, and wood so much more abundant. A shed-shaped tent will catch and reflect the heat like a Yankee-baker, and you may be drying while you are sleeping.

Some who have leaky roofs in the towns may have been kept awake, but we were soon lulled asleep by a steady, soaking rain, which lasted all night. To-night, the rain not coming at once with violence, the twigs were soon dried by the reflected heat.

WEDNESDAY, JULY 29.

When we awoke it had done raining, though it was still cloudy. The fire was put out, and the Indian's boots, which stood under the eaves of the tent, were half full of water. He was much more improvident in such respects than either of us, and he had to thank us for keeping his powder dry. We decided to cross the lake at once, before breakfast, or while we could; and before starting I took the bearing of the shore which we wished to strike, S. S. E. about three miles distant, lest a sudden misty rain should conceal it when we were midway. Though the bay in which we were was perfectly quiet and smooth, we found the lake already wide awake outside, but not dangerously or unpleasantly so; nevertheless, when you get out on one of those lakes in a canoe like this, you do not forget that you are completely at the mercy of the wind, and a fickle power it is. The playful waves may at any time become too rude for you in their sport, and play right on over you. We saw a few *shecorways* and a *fish-hawk* thus early, and after much steady paddling and dancing over the dark waves of Apmoojenegamook, we found ourselves in the neighborhood of the southern land, heard the waves breaking on it, and turned our thoughts wholly to that side. After coasting eastward along this shore a mile or two, we breakfasted on a rocky point, the first convenient place that offered.

It was well enough that we crossed thus early, for the waves now ran quite high, and we should have been obliged to go round somewhat, but beyond this point we had comparatively smooth water. You can commonly go along one side or the other of a lake, when you cannot cross it.

The Indian was looking at the hard-wood ridges from time to time, and said that he would like to buy a few hundred acres somewhere about this lake, asking our advice. It was to buy as near the crossing place as possible.

My companion and I having a minute's discussion on some point of ancient history, were amused by the attitude which the Indian, who could not tell what we were talking about, assumed. He constituted himself umpire, and, judging by our air and gesture, he very seriously remarked from time to time, "you beat," or "he beat."

Leaving a spacious bay, a northeasterly prolongation of Chamberlain Lake, on our left, we entered through a short strait into a small lake a couple of miles over, called on the map *Telasinis*, but the Indian had no distinct name for it, and thence into *Telos* Lake, which he called *Paytaywecongomec*, or Burnt-Ground Lake. This curved round toward the northeast, and may have been three or four miles long as we paddled. He had not been here since 1825. He did not know what Telos meant; thought it was not Indian. He used the word *"Spokelogan"* (for an inlet in the shore which led nowhere), and when I asked its meaning said that there was "no Indian in 'em." There was a clearing, with a house and barn, on the southwest shore, temporarily occupied by some men who were getting the hay, as we had been told;

also a clearing for a pasture on a hill on the west side of the lake.

We landed on a rocky point on the northeast side, to look at some Red Pines (*Pinus resinosa*), the first we had noticed, and get some cones, for our few which grow in Concord do not bear any.

The outlet from the lake into the East Branch of the Penobscot is an artificial one, and it was not very apparent where it was exactly, but the lake ran curving far up northeasterly into two narrow valleys or ravines, as if it had for a long time been groping its way toward the Penobscot waters, or remembered when it anciently flowed there; by observing where the horizon was lowest, and following the longest of these, we at length reached the dam, having come about a dozen miles from the last camp. Somebody had left a line set for trout, and the jackknife with which the bait had been cut on the dam beside it, an evidence that man was near, and in a deserted log hut close by a loaf of bread baked in a Yankee-baker. These proved the property of a solitary hunter, whom we soon met, and canoe and gun and traps were not far off. He told us that it was twenty miles further on our route to the foot of Grand Lake, where you could catch as many trout as you wanted, and that the first house below the foot of the lake, on the East Branch, was Hunt's, about forty-five miles further; though there was one about a mile and a half up Trout stream, some fifteen miles ahead, but it was rather a blind route to it. It turned out that, though the stream was in our favor, we did not reach the next house till the morning of the third day after this. The nearest permanently inhabited house behind us was now a dozen miles distant, so that the interval between the two nearest houses on our route was about sixty miles.

This hunter, who was a quite small, sunburnt man, having already carried his canoe over, and baked his loaf, had nothing so interesting and pressing to do as to observe our transit. He had been out a month or more alone. How much more wild and adventurous his life than that of the hunter in Concord woods, who gets back to his house and the mill-dam every night! Yet they in the towns who have wild oats to sow commonly sow them on cultivated and comparatively exhausted ground. And as for the rowdy world in the large cities, so little enterprise has it that it never adventures in this direction, but like vermin clubs together in alleys and drinking-saloons, its highest accomplishment, perchance, to run beside a fire-engine and throw brickbats. But the former is comparatively an independent and successful man, getting his living in a way that he likes, without disturbing his human neighbors. How much more respectable also is the life of the solitary pioneer or settler in these, or any woods,—having real difficulties, not of his own creation, drawing his subsistence directly from nature,—than that of the helpless multitudes in the towns who depend on gratifying the extremely artificial wants of society and are thrown out of employment by hard times!

Here for the first time we found the raspberries really plenty,—that is, on passing the height of land between the Allegash and the East Branch of the Penobscot; the same was true of the blueberries.

Telos Lake, the head of the St. John on this side, and Webster Pond, the head of the East Branch of the Penobscot, are only about a mile apart, and they are connected by a ravine, in which but little digging was required to make the water of the former, which is the highest, flow into the latter. This canal, which is something less than a mile long and about four rods wide, was made a few years before my first visit to Maine. Since then the lumber of the upper Allegash and its lakes has been run down the Penobscot, that is, up the Allegash, which here consists principally of a chain of large and stagnant lakes, whose thoroughfares, or river-links, have been made nearly equally stagnant by damming, and then down the Penobscot. The rush of the water has produced such changes in the canal that it has now the appearance of a very rapid mountain stream flowing through a ravine, and you would not suspect that any digging had been required to persuade the waters of the St. John to flow into the Penobscot here. It was so winding that one could see but little way down.

It is stated by Springer, in his "Forest Life," that the cause of this canal being dug was this. According to the treaty of 1842 with Great Britain, it was agreed that all the timber run down the St. John, which rises in Maine, "when within the Province of New Brunswick . . . . shall be dealt with as if it were the produce of the said Province," which was thought by our side to mean that it should be free from taxation. Immediately, the Province, wishing to get something out of the Yankees, levied a duty on all the timber that passed down the St. John; but to satisfy its own subjects "made a corresponding discount on the stumpage charged those hauling timber from the crown lands." The result was that the Yankees made the St. John run the other way, or down the Penobscot, so that the Province lost both its duty and its water, while the Yankees, being greatly enriched, had reason to thank it for the suggestion.

It is wonderful how well watered this country is. As you paddle across a lake, bays will be pointed out to you, by following up which, and perhaps the tributary stream which empties in, you may, after a short

portage, or possibly, at some seasons, none at all, get
into another river, which empties far away from the
one you are on. Generally, you may go in any direction in a canoe, by making frequent but not very long
portages. You are only realizing once more what all
nature distinctly remembers here, for no doubt the
waters flowed thus in a former geological period, and
instead of being a lake country, it was an archipelago.
It seems as if the more youthful and impressible
streams can hardly resist the numerous invitations
and temptations to leave their native beds and run
down their neighbors' channels. Your carries are often
over half-submerged ground, on the dry channels of
a former period. In carrying from one river to another, I did not go over such high and rocky ground
as in going about the falls of the same river. For in
the former case I was once lost in a swamp, as I
have related, and, again, found an artificial canal
which appeared to be natural.

I remember once dreaming of pushing a canoe up
the rivers of Maine, and that, when I had got so high
that the channels were dry, I kept on through the
ravines and gorges, nearly as well as before, by pushing a little harder, and now it seemed to me that my
dream was partially realized.

Wherever there is a channel for water, there is a
road for the canoe. The pilot of the steamer which
ran from Oldtown up the Penobscot in 1853 told me
that she drew only fourteen inches, and would run
easily in two feet of water, though they did not like
to. It is said that some Western steamers can run on
a heavy dew, whence we can imagine what a canoe
may do. Montresor, who was sent from Quebec by the
English about 1760 to explore the route to the Kennebec, over which Arnold afterward passed, supplied
the Penobscot near its source with water by opening

the beaver-dams, and he says, "This is often done." He afterward states that the Governor of Canada had forbidden to molest the beaver about the outlet of the Kennebec from Moosehead Lake, on account of the service which their dams did by raising the water for navigation.

This canal, so called, was a considerable and extremely rapid and rocky river. The Indian decided that there was water enough in it without raising the dam, which would only make it more violent, and that he would run down it alone, while we carried the greater part of the baggage. Our provision being about half consumed, there was the less left in the canoe. We had thrown away the pork-keg, and wrapt its contents in birch bark, which is the unequalled wrapping-paper of the woods.

Following a moist trail through the forest, we reached the head of Webster Pond about the same time with the Indian, notwithstanding the velocity with which he moved, our route being the most direct. The Indian name of Webster Stream, of which this pond is the source, is, according to him, *Madunkehunk*, i.e. Height of Land, and of the pond, *Madunkehunk-gamooc*, or Height of Land Pond. The latter was two or three miles long. We passed near a pine on its shore which had been splintered by lightning, perhaps the day before. This was the first proper East Branch Penobscot water that we came to.

At the outlet of Webster Lake was another dam, at which we stopped and picked raspberries, while the Indian went down the stream a half-mile through the forest, to see what he had got to contend with. There was a deserted log camp here, apparently used the previous winter, with its "hovel" or barn for cattle. In the hut was a large fir-twig bed, raised two feet from the floor, occupying a large part of the single apartment, a long narrow table against the wall, with a stout log bench before it, and above the table a small window, the only one there was, which admitted a feeble light. It was a simple and strong fort erected against the cold, and suggested what valiant trencher work had been done there. I discovered one or two curious wooden traps, which had not been used for a long time, in the woods near by. The principal part consisted of a long and slender pole.

We got our dinner on the shore, on the upper side of the dam. As we were sitting by our fire, concealed by the earth bank of the dam, a long line of sheldrake, half grown, came waddling over it from the water below, passing within about a rod of us, so that we could almost have caught them in our hands. They were very abundant on all the streams and lakes which we visited, and every two or three hours they would rush away in a long string over the water before us, twenty to fifty of them at once, rarely ever flying, but running with great rapidity up or down the stream, even in the midst of the most violent rapids, and apparently as fast up as down, or else crossing diagonally, the old, as it appeared, behind, and driving them, and flying to the front from time to time, as if to direct them. We also saw many small black dippers, which behaved in a similar manner, and, once or twice, a few black ducks.

An Indian at Oldtown had told us that we should be obliged to carry ten miles between Telos Lake on the St. John's and Second Lake on the East Branch of the Penobscot; but the lumberers whom we met assured us that there would not be more than a mile of carry. It turned out that the Indian, who had lately been over this route, was nearest right, as far as we were concerned. However, if one of us could have assisted the Indian in managing the canoe in the rapids, we might have run the greater part of the way; but as he was alone in the management of the canoe in such places, we were obliged to walk the greater part. I did not feel quite ready to try such an experiment on Webster Stream, which has so bad a reputation. According to my observation, a batteau, properly manned, shoots rapids as a matter of course, which a single Indian with a canoe carries round.

My companion and I carried a good part of the baggage on our shoulders, while the Indian took that which would be least injured by wet in the canoe. We did not know when we should see him again, for he had not been this way since the canal was cut, nor for more than thirty years. He agreed to stop when he got to smooth water, come up and find our path if he could, and halloo for us, and after waiting a reasonable time go on and try again,—and we were to look out in like manner for him.

He commenced by running through the sluice-way and over the dam, as usual, standing up in his tossing canoe, and was soon out of sight behind a point in a wild gorge. This Webster Stream is well known to lumbermen as a difficult one. It is exceedingly rapid and rocky, and also shallow, and can hardly be considered navigable, unless that may mean that what is launched in it is sure to be carried swiftly down it, though it may be dashed to pieces by the way. It is somewhat like navigating a thunder-spout. With commonly an irresistible force urging you on, you have got to choose your own course each moment, between the rocks and shallows, and to get into it, moving forward always with the utmost possible moderation, and often holding on, if you can, that you may inspect the rapids before you.

By the Indian's direction we took an old path on

the south side, which appeared to keep down the
stream, though at a considerable distance from it,
cutting off bends, perhaps to Second Lake, having
first taken the course from the map with a compass,
which was northeasterly, for safety. It was a wild
wood-path, with a few tracks of oxen which had been
driven over it, probably to some old camp clearing,
for pasturage, mingled with the tracks of moose
which had lately used it. We kept on steadily for
about an hour without putting down our packs, occasionally winding around or climbing over a fallen
tree, for the most part far out of sight and hearing of
the river; till, after walking about three miles, we
were glad to find that the path came to the river
again at an old camp ground, where there was a
small opening in the forest, at which we paused.
Swiftly as the shallow and rocky river ran here, a
continuous rapid with dancing waves, I saw, as I sat
on the shore, a long string of sheldrakes, which
something scared, run up the opposite side of the
stream by me, with the same ease that they commonly did down it, just touching the surface of the
waves, and getting an impulse from them as they
flowed from under them; but they soon came back,
driven by the Indian, who had fallen a little behind
us, on account of the windings. He shot round a point
just above, and came to land by us with considerable
water in his canoe. He had found it, as he said, "very
strong water," and had been obliged to land once
before to empty out what he had taken in. He complained that it strained him to paddle so hard in
order to keep his canoe straight in its course, having
no one in the bows to aid him, and, shallow as it was,
said that it would be no joke to upset there, for the
force of the water was such that he had as lief I
would strike him over the head with a paddle as have

that water strike him. Seeing him come out of that gap was as if you should pour water down an inclined and zigzag trough, then drop a nutshell into it, and taking a short cut to the bottom, get there in time to see it come out, notwithstanding the rush and tumult, right side up, and only partly full of water.

After a moment's breathing space, while I held his canoe, he was soon out of sight again around another bend, and we, shouldering our packs, resumed our course.

We did not at once fall into our path again, but made our way with difficulty along the edge of the river, till at length, striking inland through the forest, we recovered it. Before going a mile we heard the Indian calling to us. He had come up through the woods and along the path to find us, having reached sufficiently smooth water to warrant his taking us in. The shore was about one fourth of a mile distant, through a dense, dark forest, and as he led us back to it, winding rapidly about to the right and left, I had the curiosity to look down carefully, and found that he was following his steps backward. I could only occasionally perceive his trail in the moss, and yet he did not appear to look down nor hesitate an instant, but led us out exactly to his canoe. This surprised me, for without a compass, or the sight or noise of the river to guide us, we could not have kept our course many minutes, and could have retraced our steps but a short distance, with a great deal of pains and very slowly, using a laborious circumspection. But it was evident that he could go back through the forest wherever he had been during the day.

After this rough walking in the dark woods it was an agreeable change to glide down the rapid river in the canoe once more. This river, which was about the size of our Assabet (in Concord), though still very swift, was almost perfectly smooth here, and showed a very visible declivity, a regularly inclined plane, for several miles, like a mirror set a little aslant, on which we coasted down. This very obvious regular descent, particularly plain when I regarded the water-line against the shores, made a singular impression on me, which the swiftness of our motion probably enhanced, so that we seemed to be gliding down a much steeper declivity than we were, and that we could not save ourselves from rapids and falls if we should suddenly come to them. My companion did not perceive this slope, but I have a surveyor's eyes, and I satisfied myself that it was no ocular illusion. You could tell at a glance on approaching such a river, which way the water flowed, though you might perceive no motion. I observed the angle at which a level line would strike the surface, and calculated the amount of fall in a rod, which did not need to be remarkably great to produce this effect.

It was very exhilarating, and the perfection of travelling, quite unlike floating on our dead Concord River, the coasting down this inclined mirror, which was now and then gently winding, down a mountain, indeed, between two evergreen forests, edged with lofty dead white pines, sometimes slanted half-way over the stream, and destined soon to bridge it. I saw some monsters there, nearly destitute of branches, and scarcely diminishing in diameter for eighty or ninety feet.

As we thus swept along, our Indian repeated in a deliberate and drawling tone the words "Daniel Webster, great lawyer," apparently reminded of him by the name of the stream, and he described his calling on him once in Boston, at what he supposed was his boarding-house. He had no business with him, but merely went to pay his respects, as we should say. In answer to our questions, he described his person well enough. It was on the day after Webster delivered his Bunker Hill oration, which I believe Polis heard. The first time he called he waited till he was tired without seeing him, and then went away. The next time, he saw him go by the door of the room in which he was waiting several times, in his shirt-sleeves, without noticing him. He thought that if he had come to see Indians, they would not have treated him so. At length, after very long delay, he came in, walked toward him, and asked in a loud voice, gruffly, "What do you want?" and he, thinking at first, by the motion of his hand, that he was going to strike him, said to himself, "You'd better take care, if you try that I shall know what to do." He did not like him, and declared that all he said "was not worth talk about a musquash." We suggested that probably Mr. Webster was very busy, and had a great many visitors just then.

Coming to falls and rapids, our easy progress was suddenly terminated. The Indian went along shore to inspect the water, while we climbed over the rocks, picking berries. The peculiar growth of blueberries on the tops of large rocks here made the impression of high land, and indeed this was the Height-of-land stream. When the Indian came back, he remarked, "You got to walk; ver strong water." So, taking out his canoe, he launched it again below the falls, and was soon out of sight. At such times, he would step into the canoe, take up his paddle, and, with an air of mystery, start off, looking far down stream, and keeping his own counsel, as if absorbing all the intelligence of forest and stream into himself; but I sometimes detected a little fun in his face, which could yield to my sympathetic smile, for he was thoroughly good-humored. We meanwhile scrambled along the shore with our packs, without any path. This was the last of *our* boating for the day.

The prevailing rock here was a kind of slate, standing on its edges, and my companion, who was recently from California, thought it exactly like that in which the gold is found, and said that if he had had a pan he would have liked to wash a little of the sand here.

The Indian now got along much faster than we, and waited for us from time to time. I found here the only cool spring that I drank at anywhere on this excursion, a little water filling a hollow in the sandy bank. It was a quite memorable event, and due to the elevation of the country, for wherever else we had been the water in the rivers and the streams emptying in was dead and warm, compared with that of a mountainous region. It was very bad walking along the shore over fallen and drifted trees and bushes, and rocks, from time to time swinging ourselves round over the water, or else taking to a gravel bar or going inland. At one place, the Indian being ahead, I was obliged to take off all my clothes in order to ford a small but deep stream emptying in, while my companion, who was inland, found a rude bridge, high up in the woods, and I saw no more of him for some time. I saw there very fresh moose tracks, found a new golden-rod to me (perhaps *Solidago thyrsoidea*), and I passed one white-pine log, which had lodged, in the forest near the edge of the stream, which was quite five feet in diameter at the but. Probably its size detained it.

Shortly after this, I overtook the Indian at the edge of some burnt land, which extended three or four miles at least, beginning about three miles above Second Lake, which we were expecting to reach that night, and which is about ten miles from

Telos Lake. This burnt region was still more rocky than before, but, though comparatively open, we could not yet see the lake. Not having seen my companion for some time, I climbed, with the Indian, a singular high rock on the edge of the river, forming a narrow ridge only a foot or two wide at top, in order to look for him; and after calling many times, I at length heard him answer from a considerable distance inland, he having taken a trail which led off from the river, perhaps directly to the lake, and was now in search of the river again. Seeing a much higher rock, of the same character, about one third of a mile further east, or down stream, I proceeded toward it, through the burnt land, in order to look for the lake from its summit, supposing that the Indian would keep down the stream in his canoe, and hallooing all the while that my companion might join me on the way. Before we came together, I noticed where a moose, which possibly I had scared by my shouting, had apparently just run along a large rotten trunk of a pine, which made a bridge, thirty or forty feet long, over a hollow, as convenient for him as for me. The tracks were as large as those of an ox, but an ox could not have crossed there. This burnt land was an exceedingly wild and desolate region. Judging by the weeds and sprouts, it appeared to have been burnt about two years before. It was covered with charred trunks, either prostrate or standing, which crocked our clothes and hands, and we could not easily have distinguished a bear there by his color. Great shells of trees, sometimes unburnt without, or burnt on one side only, but black within, stood twenty or forty feet high. The fire had run up inside, as in a chimney, leaving the sap-wood. Sometimes we crossed a rocky ravine fifty feet wide, on a fallen trunk; and there were great fields of fire-weed (*Epilobium angustifolium*) on all sides, the most extensive that I ever saw, which presented great masses of pink. Intermixed with these were blueberry and raspberry bushes.

Having crossed a second rocky ridge, like the first, when I was beginning to ascend the third, the Indian, whom I had left on the shore some fifty rods behind, beckoned to me to come to him, but I made sign that I would first ascend the highest rock before me, whence I expected to see the lake. My companion accompanied me to the top. This was formed just like the others. Being struck with the perfect parallelism of these singular rock-hills, however much one might be in advance of another, I took out my compass and found that they lay northwest and southeast, the rock being on its edge, and sharp edges they were. This one, to speak from memory, was perhaps a third of a mile in length, but quite narrow, rising gradually from the northwest to the height of about eighty feet, but steep on the southeast end. The southwest side was as steep as an ordinary roof, or as we could safely climb; the northeast was an abrupt precipice from which you could jump clean to the bottom, near which the river flowed; while the level top of the ridge, on which you walked along, was only from one to three or four feet in width. For a rude illustration, take the half of a pear cut in two lengthwise, lay it on its flat side, the stem to the northwest, and then halve it vertically in the direction of its length, keeping the southwest half. Such was the general form.

There was a remarkable series of these great rock-waves revealed by the burning; breakers, as it were. No wonder that the river that found its way through them was rapid and obstructed by falls. No doubt the absence of soil on these rocks, or its dryness where there was any, caused this to be a very thorough burning. We could see the lake over the woods, two or three miles ahead, and that the river made an abrupt turn southward around the northwest end of the cliff on which we stood, or a little above us, so that we had cut off a bend, and that there was an important fall in it a short distance below us. I could see the canoe a hundred rods behind, but now on the opposite shore, and supposed that the Indian had concluded to take out and carry round some bad rapids on that side, and that that might be what he had beckoned to me for; but after waiting a while I could still see nothing of him, and I observed to my companion that I wondered where he was, though I began to suspect that he had gone inland to look for the lake from some hill-top on that side, as we had done. This proved to be the case; for after I had started to return to the canoe, I heard a faint halloo, and descried him on the top of a distant rocky hill on that side. But as, after a long time had elapsed, I still saw his canoe in the same place, and he had not returned to it, and appeared in no hurry to do so, and, moreover, as I remembered that he had previously beckoned to me, I thought that there might be something more to delay him than I knew, and began to return northwest, along the ridge, toward the angle in the river. My companion, who had just been separated from us, and had even contemplated the necessity of camping alone, wishing to husband his steps, and yet to keep with us, inquired where I was going; to which I answered, that I was going far enough back to communicate with the Indian, and that then I thought we had better go along the shore together, and keep him in sight.

When we reached the shore, the Indian appeared from out the woods on the opposite side, but on account of the roar of the water it was difficult to communicate with him. He kept along the shore westward to his canoe, while we stopped at the angle where the stream turned southward around the precipice. I again said to my companion, that we would keep along the shore and keep the Indian in sight. We started to do so, being close together, the Indian behind us having launched his canoe again, but just then I saw the latter, who had crossed to our side, forty or fifty rods behind, beckoning to me, and I called to my companion, who had just disappeared behind large rocks at the point of the precipice, three or four rods before me, on his way down the stream, that I was going to help the Indian a moment. I did so,—helped get the canoe over a fall, lying with my breast over a rock, and holding one end while he received it below,—and within ten or fifteen minutes at most I was back again at the point where the river turned southward, in order to catch up with my companion, while Polis glided down the river alone, parallel with me. But to my surprise, when I rounded the precipice, though the shore was bare of trees (not of rocks) for a quarter of a mile at least, my companion was not to be seen. It was as if he had sunk into the earth. This was the more unaccountable to me, because I knew that his feet were since our swamp walk very sore, and that he wished to keep with the party; and besides this was very bad walking, climbing over or about the rocks. I hastened along, hallooing and searching for him, thinking he might be concealed behind a rock, yet doubting if he had not taken the other side of the precipice, but the Indian had got along still faster in his canoe, till he was arrested by the falls, about a quarter of a mile below. He then landed, and said that we could go no further that night. The sun was setting, and on account of falls and rapids we should be obliged to leave this river and carry a good way into another further east. The first thing then was to find my companion, for I was now very much alarmed about him, and I sent the Indian along the shore down stream, which began to be covered with unburnt wood again just below the falls, while I searched backward about the precipice which we had passed. The Indian showed some unwillingness to exert himself, complaining that he was very tired, in consequence of his day's work, that it had strained him very much getting down so many rapids alone; but he went off calling somewhat like an owl. I remembered that my companion was near-sighted, and I feared that he had either fallen from the precipice, or fainted and sunk down amid the rocks beneath it. I shouted and searched above and below this precipice in the twilight till I could not see, expecting nothing less than to find his body beneath it. For half an hour I anticipated and believed only the worst. I thought what I should do the next day, if I did not find him, what I *could* do in such a wilderness, and how his relatives would feel, if I should return without him. I felt that if he were really lost away from the river there, it would be a desperate undertaking to find him; and where were they who could help you? What would it be to raise the country, where there were only two or three camps, twenty or thirty miles apart, and no road, and perhaps nobody at home? Yet we must try the harder, the less the prospect of success.

I rushed down from this precipice to the canoe in order to fire the Indian's gun, but found that my companion had the caps. I was still thinking of getting it off when the Indian returned. He had not found him, but he said that he had seen his tracks once or twice along the shore. This encouraged me very much. He objected to firing the gun, saying that if my companion heard it, which was not likely, on account of the roar of the stream, it would tempt him to come toward us, and he might break his neck in the dark. For the same reason we refrained from lighting a fire on the highest rock. I proposed that we should both keep down the stream to the lake, or that I should go at any rate, but the Indian said, "No use, can't do anything in the dark; come morning, then we find 'em. No harm,—he make 'em camp. No bad animals here, no gristly bears, such as in California, where he's been,—warm night,—he well off as you and I." I considered that if he was well he could do without us. He had just lived eight years in California, and had plenty of experience with wild beasts and wilder men, was peculiarly accustomed to make journeys of great length, but if he were sick or dead, he was near where we were. The darkness in the woods was by this so thick that it alone decided the question. We must camp where we were. I knew that he had his knapsack, with blanket and matches, and, if well, would fare no worse than we, except that he would have no supper nor society.

This side of the river being so encumbered with rocks, we crossed to the eastern or smoother shore, and proceeded to camp there, within two or three rods of the Falls. We pitched no tent, but lay on the sand, putting a few handfuls of grass and twigs under us, there being no evergreen at hand. For fuel we had some of the charred stumps. Our various bags of provisions had got quite wet in the rapids, and I arranged them about the fire to dry. The fall close by was the principal one on this stream, and it shook the earth under us. It was a cool, because dewy, night; the more so, probably, owing to the nearness of the falls. The Indian complained a good deal, and thought afterward that he got a cold there which occasioned a more serious illness. We were not much troubled by mosquitoes at any rate. I lay awake a good deal from anxiety, but, unaccountably to myself, was at length comparatively at ease respecting him. At first I had apprehended the worst, but now I had little doubt but that I should find him in the morning. From time to time I fancied that I heard his voice calling through the roar of the falls from the opposite side of the river; but it is doubtful if we could have heard him across the stream there. Sometimes I doubted whether the Indian had really seen his tracks, since he manifested an unwillingness to make much of a search, and then my anxiety returned.

It was the most wild and desolate region we had camped in, where, if anywhere, one might expect to meet with befitting inhabitants, but I heard only the squeak of a night-hawk flitting over. The moon in her first quarter, in the fore part of the night, setting over the bare rocky hills, garnished with tall, charred, and hollow stumps or shells of trees, served to reveal the desolation.

THURSDAY, JULY 30.

I aroused the Indian early this morning to go in search of our companion, expecting to find him within a mile or two, further down the stream. The Indian wanted his breakfast first, but I reminded him that my companion had had neither breakfast nor supper. We were obliged first to carry our canoe and baggage over into another stream, the main East Branch, about three fourths of a mile distant, for Webster Stream was no further navigable. We went twice over this carry, and the dewy bushes wet us through like water up to the middle; I hallooed in a high key from time to time, though I had little expectation that I could be heard over the roar of the rapids, and moreover we were necessarily on the opposite side of the stream to him. In going over this portage the last time, the Indian, who was before me with the canoe on his head, stumbled and fell heavily once, and lay for a moment silent, as if in pain. I hastily stepped forward to help him, asking if he was much hurt, but after a moment's pause, without replying, he sprang up and went forward. He was all the way subject to taciturn fits, but they were harmless ones.

We had launched our canoe and gone but little way down the East Branch, when I heard an answering shout from my companion, and soon after saw him standing on a point where there was a clearing a quarter of a mile below, and the smoke of his fire was rising near by. Before I saw him I naturally shouted again and again, but the Indian curtly remarked, "He hears you," as if once was enough. It was just below the mouth of Webster Stream. When we arrived, he was smoking his pipe, and said that he had passed a pretty comfortable night, though it was rather cold, on account of the dew.

It appeared that when we stood together the previous evening, and I was shouting to the Indian across the river, he, being near-sighted, had not seen the Indian nor his canoe, and when I went back to the Indian's assistance, did not see which way I went, and supposed that we were below and not above him, and so, making haste to catch up, he ran away from us. Having reached this clearing, a mile or more below our camp, the night overtook him, and he made a fire in a little hollow, and lay down by it in his blanket, still thinking that we were ahead of him. He thought it likely that he had heard the Indian call once the evening before, but mistook it for an owl. He had seen one botanical rarity before it was dark,—

pure white *Epilobium angustifolium* amidst the fields of pink ones, in the burnt lands. He had already stuck up the remnant of a lumberer's shirt, found on the point, on a pole by the water-side, for a signal, and attached a note to it, to inform us that he had gone on to the lake, and that if he did not find us there, he would be back in a couple of hours. If he had not found us soon, he had some thoughts of going back in search of the solitary hunter whom we had met at Telos Lake, ten miles behind, and, if successful, hire him to take him to Bangor. But if this hunter had moved as fast as we, he would have been twenty miles off by this time, and who could guess in what direction? It would have been like looking for a needle in a hay-mow, to search for him in these woods. He had been considering how long he could live on berries alone.

We substituted for his note a card containing our names and destination, and the date of our visit, which Polis neatly enclosed in a piece of birch-bark to keep it dry. This has probably been read by some hunter or explorer ere this.

We all had good appetites for the breakfast which we made haste to cook here, and then, having partially dried our clothes, we glided swiftly down the winding stream toward Second Lake.

As the shores became flatter with frequent gravel and sand bars, and the stream more winding in the lower land near the lake, elms and ash trees made their appearance; also the yellow land Lily, (Lilium Canadense) some of whose bulbs I collected for a soup. On some ridges the burnt land extended as far as the lake.

This was a very beautiful lake, 2 or 3 miles long, with high mountains on the S. W. side—the, as our Indian said, *Nerlumskeechticook* i.e. Dead Water Mt.

It appears to be the same called Carbuncle Mt. on the map. (According to Polis it extends in separate elevations all along this and the next lake which is much larger.) The lake too, I think, is called by the same name or perhaps with the addition of *gamoc* or *mooc*. The morning was a bright one and perfectly still and serene, the lake as smooth as glass, we making the only ripples as we paddled into it. The dark mountains about it were seen through a glaucous mist, and the brilliant white stems of canoe-birches were seen mingled with the other woods around it. The wood-thrush sang on the distant shore, and the laugh of some loons sporting in a concealed western bay, as if inspired by the morning, came distinct over the lake to us, and, what was remarkable, the echo which ran round the lake, was much louder than the original note; probably, because, the loons, being in a regularly curving bay under the mountain, we were exactly in the focus of many echoes, the sound being reflected like light from a concave mirror. The beauty of the scene may have been enhanced to our eyes by the fact that we had just come together again after a night of some anxiety.

This reminded me of Ambejijis Lake on the West Branch, which I crossed in my first coming to Maine.

Having paddled ¾ down the lake, we came to a standstill, while my companion let down a line for fish. A white (or whitish) gull sat on a rock, which rose above the surface in mid lake not far off, quite in harmony with the scene; and as we rested there in the warm sun, we heard one loud crashing or crackling sound from the forest, 40 or 50 rods distant, as of a stick broken by the foot of some large animal. Even this was an interesting incident there. In the midst of our dream of giant lake trout, even then supposed to be nibbling, our fisherman drew up a diminutive red perch, and we took up our paddles again in haste.

It was not apparent where the outlet of this lake was, and while the Indian thought it was in one direction, I thought it was in another. He said "I bet you fourpence it is there," but he still held on in my direction, which proved to be the right one. As we were approaching the outlet, it being still early in the forenoon, he suddenly exclaimed, "Moose! moose!" and told us to be still. He put a cap on his gun, and standing up in the stern, rapidly pushed the canoe straight toward the shore and the moose. It was a cow moose, about 30 rods off, standing in the water by the side of the outlet, partly behind some fallen timber and bushes, and at that distance she did not look very large. She was flapping her large ears, and from time to time poking off the flies with her nose from some part of her body. She did not appear much alarmed by our neighborhood, only occasionally turned her head and looked straight at us, and then gave her attention to the flies again. As we approached nearer, she got out of the water, stood higher, and regarded us more suspiciously. Polis pushed the canoe steadily forward in the shallow water; and I for a moment forgot the moose in attending to some pretty rose-colored polygonums just rising above the surface,—but the canoe soon grounded in the mud 8 or 10 rods distant from the moose, and the Indian seized his gun, and prepared to fire. After standing still a moment, she turned slowly, as usual, so as to expose her side, and he improved this moment to fire, over our heads. She thereupon moved off 8 or 10 rods at a moderate pace, across a shallow bay, to an old standing place of hers, behind some fallen red maples, on the opposite shore, and there she stood still again, a dozen or 14 rods from us, while the Indian hastily loaded and fired twice at her, without her moving. My companion who passed him his caps and bullets, said that Polis was as excited as a boy of 15, that his hand trembled, and he once put his ramrod back upside-down. This was remarkable for so experienced a hunter. Perhaps he was anxious to make a good shot before us. The white hunter had told me that the Indians were not good shots, because they were excited, though he said that we had got a good hunter with us.

The Indian now pushed quickly and quietly back, and a long distance round, in order to get into the outlet,—for he had fired over the neck of a peninsula between it and the lake—till we approached the place where the moose had stood, when he exclaimed, "She's a goner", and was surprised that we did not see her as soon as he did. There, to be sure, she lay perfectly dead, with her tongue hanging out, just where she had stood to receive the last shots, looking unexpectedly large and horse-like, and we saw where the bullets had scored the trees.

Using a tape, I found that the moose measured just six feet from the shoulder to the tip of the hoof, and was 8 feet long as she lay. Some portions of the body for a foot in diameter, were almost completely covered with flies—apparently the common fly of our woods with a dark spot on the wing—and not the very large ones which occasionally pursued us in mid stream, though both are called moose flies.

Polis, preparing to skin the moose, asked me to help him find a stone on which to sharpen his large knife. It being all a flat alluvial ground where the moose had fallen, covered with red maples &c.—this was no easy matter;—we searched far and wide a long time, till at length I found a flat kind of slate stone, and soon after he returned with a similar one, on which he soon made his knife very sharp.

While he was skinning the moose I proceeded to ascertain what kind of fishes were to be found in the sluggish and muddy outlet. The greatest difficulty was as usual to obtain a pole. It was almost impossible to find a slender straight pole 10 or 12 feet long in those woods. You might search half an hour in vain. They are commonly spruce—arbor vitae—fir &c.— short stout and branchy—and do not make good fish-poles, even after you have patiently cut off all their tough and scraggy branches. The fishes were red perch and chivin.

The Indian having cut off a large piece of sirloin, the upper lip and the tongue, wrapped them in the hide and placed them in the bottom of the canoe, observing that there was "one man", meaning the weight of one. Our load had previously been reduced some 30 lbs., but 100 lbs. were now added—a serious addition, which made our quarters still more narrow, and considerably increased the danger on the lakes and rapids, as well as the labor of the carries. The skin was ours according to custom, since the Indian was in our employ, but we did not think of claiming it. He being a skilful dresser of moose-hides, would make it worth 7 or 8 dollars to him, as I was told. He said that he sometimes earned 50 or 60 dollars in a day at them; he had killed 10 moose in one day, though the skinning and all took 2 days. This was the way he had got his property. There were the tracks of a calf thereabouts which he said would come "by by", and he could get it if we cared to wait— but I cast cold water on the project.

We continued along the outlet toward Grand Lake —through a swampy region, by a long winding and narrow dead water, very much choked up by wood, where we were obliged to land sometimes in order to get the canoe over a log. It was hard to find any channel and we did not know but we should be lost in the swamp. It abounded in ducks, as usual. At length we reached Grand Lake which the Indian called *Matungamook.*

At the head of this we saw coming in from the S.W.—with a sweep, apparently from a gorge in the mountains Trout Stream, or, *Uncardnerheese*, which name, the Indian said, had something to do with mountains.

We stopped to dine on an interesting high rocky island soon after entering Matungamook lake, securing our canoe to the cliffy shore. It is always pleasant to step from a boat on to a large rock or cliff. Here was a good opportunity to dry our dewy blankets on the open sunny rock. Indians had recently camped here and accidentally burned over the western end of the island—and Polis picked up a guncase of blue broadcloth, saying that he knew the Indian it belonged to, and would carry it to him. His tribe is not so large but he may know all its effects. We proceeded to make a fire and cook our dinner amid some pines, where our predecessors had done the same, while the Indian busied himself about his moose hide on the shore, for he said that he thought it a good plan for one to do all the cooking, i.e. I suppose, if that one were not himself. A peculiar evergreen overhung our fire which at first glance looked like a pitch pine (P. rigida) with leaves little more than an inch long—spruce-like; but we found it to be the "*Pinus Banksiana*—Banks' or the Labrador Pine" also called Scrub Pine, Grey Pine &c., a new tree to us. These must have been good specimens, for several were 30 or 35 feet high, which is 2 or 3 times the height commonly assigned them. Michaux says that it grows further north than any of our pines, but he did not find it any where more than 10 feet high. Richardson found it 40 feet high and upward, and states that the porcupine feeds on its bark. Here also grew the Red Pine (Pinus resinosa).

I saw where the Indians had made canoes in a little secluded hollow in the woods, on the top of the rock, where they were out of the wind, and large piles of whittlings remained. This must have been a favorite resort for their ancestors, and indeed we found here the point of an arrowhead, such as they have not used for 2 centuries, and now know not how to make. The Indian picking up a stone, remarked to me "That very strange lock (rock)". It was a piece of hornstone, which, I told him, his tribe had probably brought here centuries before to make arrowheads of. He also picked up a yellowish curved bone by the side of our fire place, and asked me to guess what it was. It was one of the upper incisors of a beaver, on which some party had feasted within a year or 2. I found also most of the other teeth, and the skull &c.

We here dined on fried moose-meat. One who was my companion in my 2 previous excursions to these woods, tells me that when hunting up the Caucomgomoc about 2 years ago, he found himself dining one day on moose-meat, mud turtle, trout, and beaver, and he thought that there were few places in the world where these dishes could easily be brought together on one table.

After the almost incessant rapids and falls of the Madunkehunk (Height-of-Land, or Webster Stream), we had just passed through the dead-water of Second Lake, and were now in the much larger dead-water of Grand Lake, and I thought the Indian was entitled to take an extra nap here. Ktaadn, near which we were to pass the next day, is said to mean "Highest Land." So much geography is there in their names. The Indian navigator naturally distinguishes by a name those parts of a stream where he has encountered quick water and falls, and again, the lakes and smooth water where he can rest his weary arms, since those are the most interesting and memorable parts to him. The very sight of the *Nerlumskeechticook*, or Dead-Water Mountains, a day's journey off over the forest, as we first saw them, must awaken in him pleasing memories. And not less interesting is it to the white traveller, when he is crossing a placid lake in these out-of-the-way woods, perhaps thinking that he is in some sense one of the earlier discoverers of it, to be reminded that it was thus well known and suitably named by Indian hunters perhaps a thousand years ago.

Ascending the precipitous rock which formed this long narrow island I was surprised to find that its summit was a narrow ridge with a precipice on one side, and that its axis of elevation extended from N. W. to S. E., exactly like that of the great rocky ridges at the commencement of the Burnt Ground 10 miles north-westerly. The same arrangement prevailed here, and we could plainly see that the mountain ridges on the west of the lake trended the same way.

Splendid large hare-bells nodded over the edge and in the clefts of the cliff—and the blue berries (*Vaccinium Canadense*) were for the first time really abundant in the thin soil on its top. There was no lack of them henceforward on the East Branch. There was a fine view hence over the sparkling lake, which looked pure and deep, and had two or three, in all, rocky islands in it. Our blankets being dry, we set out again, the Indian as usual having left his gazette on a tree. This time it was we three in a canoe, my companion smoking. We paddled southward down this handsome lake, which appeared to extend nearly as far east as south, keeping near the western shore, just outside a small island, under the dark *Nerlumskeechticook* mountain. For I had observed on my map that this was the course. It was three or four miles across it. It struck me that the outline of this mountain on the southwest of the lake, and of another beyond it, was not only like that of the huge rock waves of Webster Stream, but in the main like Kineo, on Moosehead Lake, having a similar but less abrupt precipice at the southeast end; in short, that all the prominent hills and ridges hereabouts were larger or smaller Kineos, and that possibly there was such a relation between Kineo and the rocks of Webster Stream.

The Indian did not know exactly where the outlet was, whether at the extreme southwest angle or more easterly, and had asked to see my plan at the last stopping-place, but I had forgotten to show it to him. As usual, he went feeling his way by a middle course between two probable points, from which he could diverge either way at last without losing much distance. In approaching the south shore, as the clouds looked gusty, and the waves ran pretty high, we so steered as to get partly under the lee of an island, though at a great distance from it.

I could not distinguish the outlet till we were almost in it, and heard the water falling over the dam there.

Here was a considerable fall, and a very substantial dam, but no sign of a cabin or camp. The hunter whom we met at Telos Lake had told us that there were plenty of trout here, but at this hour they did not rise to the bait, only cousin trout, from the very midst of the rushing waters. There are not so many fishes in these rivers as in the Concord.

While we loitered here, Polis took occasion to cut with his big knife some of the hair from his moose-hide, and so lightened and prepared it for drying. I noticed at several old Indian camps in the woods the pile of hair which they had cut from their hides.

Having carried over the dam, he darted down the rapids, leaving us to walk for a mile or more, where for the most part there was no path, but very thick and difficult travelling near the stream. At length he would call to let us know where he was waiting for us with his canoe, when, on account of the windings of the stream, we did not know where the shore was, but he did not call often enough, forgetting that we were not Indians. He seemed to be very saving of his breath,—yet he would be surprised if we went by, or did not strike the right spot. This was not because he was unaccommodating, but a proof of superior manners. Indians like to get along with the least possible communication and ado. He was really paying us a great compliment all the while, thinking that we preferred a hint to a kick.

At length, climbing over the willows and fallen trees, when this was easier than to go round or under them, we overtook the canoe, and glided down the stream in smooth but swift water for several miles. I here observed again, as at Webster Stream, and on a still larger scale the next day, that the river was a smooth and regularly inclined plane down which we coasted. As we thus glided along we started the first black ducks which we had distinguished.

We decided to camp early to-night, that we might have ample time before dark; so we stopped at the first favorable shore, where there was a narrow gravelly beach on the western side, some five miles below the outlet of the lake. It was an interesting spot, where the river began to make a great bend to the east, and the last of the peculiar moose-faced *Nerlumskeechticook* mountains not far southwest of Grand Lake rose dark in the northwest a short distance behind, displaying its gray precipitous southeast side, but we could not see this without coming out upon the shore.

Two steps from the water on either side, and you come to the abrupt bushy and rooty if not turfy edge of the bank, four or five feet high, where the interminable forest begins, as if the stream had but just cut its way through it.

It is surprising on stepping ashore anywhere into this unbroken wilderness to see so often, at least within a few rods of the river, the marks of the axe, made by lumberers who have either camped here, or driven logs past in previous springs. You will see perchance where, going on the same errand that you do, they have cut large chips from a tall white-pine stump for their fire. While we were pitching the camp and getting supper, the Indian cut the rest of the hair from his moose-hide, and proceeded to extend it vertically on a temporary frame between two small trees, half a dozen feet from the opposite side of the fire, lashing and stretching it with arbor-vitæ bark, which was always at hand, and in this case was stripped from one of the trees it was tied to. Asking for a new kind of tea, he made us some, pretty good, of the checkerberry (*Gaultheria procumbens*), which covered the ground, dropping a little bunch of it tied up with cedar bark into the kettle; but it was not quite equal to the *Chiogenes*. We called this therefore Checkerberry-tea Camp.

I was struck with the abundance of the *Linnæa*

borealis, checkerberry, and *Chiogenes hispidula*, almost everywhere in the Maine woods. The wintergreen (*Chimaphila umbellata*) was still in bloom here, and *Clintonia* berries were abundant and ripe. This handsome plant is one of the most common in that forest. We here first noticed the moose-wood in fruit on the banks. The prevailing trees were spruce (commonly black), arbor-vitæ, canoe-birch, black ash and elms beginning to appear, yellow birch, red maple, and a little hemlock skulking in the forest. The Indian said that the white-maple punk was the best for tinder, that yellow-birch punk was pretty good, but hard. After supper he put on the moose tongue and lip to boil, cutting out the *septum*. He showed me how to write on the under side of birch bark, with a black spruce twig, which is hard and tough and can be brought to a point.

The Indian wandered off into the woods a short distance just before night, and, coming back, said, "Me found great treasure—fifty, sixty dollars' worth." "What's that?" we asked. "Steel traps, under a log, thirty or forty, I didn't count 'em. I guess Indian work—worth three dollars apiece." It was a singular coincidence that he should have chanced to walk to and look under that particular log, in that trackless forest.

I saw chivin and chub in the stream when washing my hands, but my companion tried in vain to catch them. I also heard the sound of bull-frogs from a swamp on the opposite side, thinking at first that they were moose; a duck paddled swiftly by; and sitting in that dusky wilderness, under that dark mountain, by the bright river which was full of reflected light, still I heard the wood-thrush sing, as if no higher civilization could be attained. By this time the night was upon us.

You commonly make your camp just at sundown, and are collecting wood, getting your supper, or pitching your tent while the shades of night are gathering around and adding to the already dense gloom of the forest. You have no time to explore or look around you before it is dark. You may penetrate half a dozen rods further into that twilight wilderness, after some dry bark to kindle your fire with, and wonder what mysteries lie hidden still deeper in it, say at the end of a long day's walk; or you may run down to the shore for a dipper of water, and get a clearer view for a short distance up or down the stream, and while you stand there, see a fish leap, or duck alight in the river, or hear a wood-thrush or robin sing in the woods. That is as if you had been to town or civilized parts. But there is no sauntering off to see the country, and ten or fifteen rods seems a great way from your companions, and you come back with the air of a much travelled man, as from a long journey, with adventures to relate, though you may have heard the crackling of the fire all the while,— and at a hundred rods you might be lost past recovery, and have to camp out. It is all mossy and *moosey*. In some of those dense fir and spruce woods there is hardly room for the smoke to go up. The trees are a *standing* night, and every fir and spruce which you fell is a plume plucked from night's raven wing. Then at night the general stillness is more impressive than any sound, but occasionally you hear the note of an owl further or nearer in the woods, and if near a lake, the semi-human cry of the loons at their unearthly revels.

To-night the Indian lay between the fire and his stretched moose-hide, to avoid the mosquitoes. Indeed, he also made a small smoky fire of damp leaves at his head and his feet, and then as usual rolled up his head in his blanket. We with our veils and our wash were tolerably comfortable, but it would be difficult to pursue any sedentary occupation in the woods at this season: you cannot see to read much by the light of a fire through a veil in the evening, nor handle pencil and paper well with gloves or anointed fingers.

FRIDAY, JULY 31.

The Indian said, "You and I kill moose last night, therefore use 'em best wood. Always use hard wood to cook moose-meat." His "best wood" was rock-maple. He cast the moose's lip into the fire, to burn the hair off, and then rolled it up with the meat to carry along. Observing that we were sitting down to breakfast without any pork, he said, with a very grave look, "Me want some fat," so he was told that he might have as much as he would fry.

We had smooth but swift water for a considerable distance, where we glided rapidly along, scaring up ducks and kingfishers. But as usual, our smooth progress erelong came to an end, and we were obliged to carry canoe and all about half a mile down the right bank, around some rapids or falls. It required sharp eyes sometimes to tell which side was the carry, before you went over the falls, but Polis never failed to land us rightly. The raspberries were particularly abundant and large here, and all hands went to eating them, the Indian remarking on their size.

Often on bare rocky carries the trail was so indistinct that I repeatedly lost it, but when I walked behind him I observed that he could keep it almost like a hound, and rarely hesitated, or, if he paused a moment on a bare rock, his eye immediately detected some sign which would have escaped me. Frequently *we* found no path at all at these places, and were to him unaccountably delayed. He would only say it was "ver strange."

We had heard of a Grand Fall on this stream, and thought that each fall we came to must be it, but after christening several in succession with this name, we gave up the search. There were more Grand or Petty Falls than I can remember.

I cannot tell how many times we had to walk on account of falls or rapids. We were expecting all the while that the river would take a final leap and get to smooth water, but there was no improvement this forenoon. However, the carries were an agreeable variety. So surely as we stepped out of the canoe and stretched our legs we found ourselves in a blueberry and raspberry garden, each side of our rocky trail around the falls being lined with one or both. There was not a carry on the main East Branch where we did not find an abundance of both these berries, for these were the rockiest places, and partially cleared, such as these plants prefer, and there had been none to gather the finest before us.

In our three journeys over the carries, for we were obliged to go over the ground three times whenever the canoe was taken out, we did full justice to the berries, and they were just what we wanted to correct the effect of our hard bread and pork diet. Another name for making a portage would have been going a berrying. We also found a few *Amelanchier*, or *service* berries, though most were abortive, but they held on rather more generally than they do in Concord. The Indian called them *Pemoymenuk*, and said that they bore much fruit in some places. He sometimes also ate the northern wild red cherries, saying that they were good medicine, but they were scarcely edible.

We bathed and dined at the foot of one of these carries. It was the Indian who commonly reminded us that it was dinner-time, sometimes even by turning the prow to the shore. He once made an indirect, but lengthy apology, by saying that we might think it strange, but that one who worked hard all day was very particular to have his dinner in good season. At the most considerable fall on this stream, when I was walking over the carry, close behind the Indian, he observed a track on the rock, which was but slightly covered with soil, and, stooping, muttered "caribou." When we returned, he observed a much larger track near the same place, where some animal's foot had sunk into a small hollow in the rock, partly filled with grass and earth, and he exclaimed with surprise, "What that?" "Well, what is it?" I asked. Stooping and laying his hand in it, he answered with a mysterious air, and in a half whisper, "Devil [that is, Indian Devil, or cougar]—ledges about here—very bad animal—pull 'em *locks* all to pieces." "How long since it was made?" I asked. "To-day or yesterday," said he. But when I asked him afterward if he was sure it was the devil's track, he said he did not know. I had been told that the scream of a cougar was heard about Ktaadn recently, and we were not far from that mountain.

We spent at least half the time in walking to-day, and the walking was as bad as usual, for the Indian being alone, commonly ran down far below the foot of the carries before he waited for us. The carry-paths themselves were more than usually indistinct, often the route being revealed only by the countless small holes in the fallen timber made by the tacks in the drivers' boots, or where there *was* a slight trail we did not find it. It was a tangled and perplexing thicket, through which we stumbled and threaded our way, and when we had finished a mile of it, our starting-point seemed far away. We were glad that we had not got to walk to Bangor along the banks of this river, which would be a journey of more than a hundred miles. Think of the denseness of the forest, the fallen trees and rocks, the windings of the river, the streams emptying in and the frequent swamps to be crossed. It made you shudder. Yet the Indian from time to time pointed out to us where he had thus crept along day after day when he was a boy of ten, and in a starving condition. He had been hunting far north of this with two grown Indians. The winter came on un-expectedly early, and the ice compelled them to leave their canoe at Grand Lake, and walk down the bank. They shouldered their furs and started for Oldtown. The snow was not deep enough for snow-shoes, or to cover the inequalities of the ground. Polis was soon too weak to carry any burden; but he managed to catch one otter. This was the most they all had to eat on this journey, and he remembered how good the yellow-lily roots were, made into a soup with the otter oil. He shared this food equally with the other two, but being so small he suffered much more than they. He waded through the Mattawamkeag at its mouth, when it was freezing cold and came up to his chin, and he, being very weak and emaciated, expected to be swept away. The first house which they reached was at Lincoln, and thereabouts they met a white teamster with supplies, who seeing their condition gave them as much of his load as they could eat. For six months after getting home he was very low, and did not expect to live, and was perhaps always the worse for it.

We could not find much more than half of this day's journey on our maps (the "Map of the Public Lands of Maine and Massachusetts," and "Colton's

Railroad and Township Map of Maine," which copies the former). By the maps there was not more than fifteen miles between camps, at the outside, and yet we had been busily progressing all day, and much of the time very rapidly.

For seven or eight miles below that succession of "Grand" falls, the aspect of the banks as well as the character of the stream was changed. After passing a tributary from the northeast, perhaps Bowlin Stream, we had good swift smooth water, with a regular slope, such as I have described. Low, grassy banks and muddy shores began. Many elms, as well as maples, and more ash trees overhung the stream, and supplanted the spruce.

My lily-roots having been lost when the canoe was taken out at a carry, I landed late in the afternoon, at a low and grassy place amid maples, to gather more. It was slow work grubbing them up amid the sand, and the mosquitoes were all the while feasting on me. Mosquitoes, black flies, &c., pursued us in mid-channel, and we were glad sometimes to get into violent rapids, for then we escaped them.

A red-headed woodpecker flew across the river, and the Indian remarked that it was good to eat. As we glided swiftly down the inclined plane of the river, a great cat-owl launched itself away from a stump on the bank, and flew heavily across the stream, and the Indian, as usual, imitated its note. Soon the same bird flew back in front of us, and we afterwards passed it perched on a tree. Soon afterward a white-headed eagle sailed down the stream before us. We drove him several miles, while we were looking for a good place to camp, for we expected to be overtaken by a shower,—and still we could distinguish him by his white tail, sailing away from time to time from some tree by the shore still further down the stream.

Some shecorways, being surprised by us, a part of them dived, and we passed directly over them, and could trace their course here and there by a bubble on the surface, but we did not see them come up. Polis detected once or twice what he called a "tow" road, an indistinct path leading into the forest. In the mean while we passed the mouth of the Seboois on our left. This did not look so large as our stream, which was indeed the main one. It was some time before we found a camping-place, for the shore was either too grassy and muddy, where mosquitoes abounded, or too steep a hillside. The Indian said that there were but few mosquitoes on a steep hillside. We examined a good place, where somebody had camped a long time; but it seemed pitiful to occupy an old site, where there was so much room to choose, so we continued on. We at length found a place to our minds, on the west bank, about a mile below the mouth of the Seboois, where, in a very dense spruce wood above a gravelly shore, there seemed to be but few insects. The trees were so thick that we were obliged to clear a space to build our fire and lie down in, and the young spruce trees that were left were like the wall of an apartment rising around us. We were obliged to pull ourselves up a steep bank to get there. But the place which you have selected for your camp, though never so rough and grim, begins at once to have its attractions, and becomes a very centre of civilization to you: "Home is home, be it never so homely."

It turned out that the mosquitoes were more numerous here than we had found them before, and the Indian complained a good deal, though he lay, as the night before, between three fires and his stretched hide. As I sat on a stump by the fire, with a veil and gloves on trying to read, he observed, "I make you candle," and in a minute he took a piece of birch bark about two inches wide and rolled it hard, like an allumette fifteen inches long, lit it, and fixed it by the other end horizontally in a split stick three feet high, stuck it in the ground, turning the blazing end to the wind, and telling me to snuff it from time to time. It answered the purpose of a candle pretty well.

I noticed, as I had done before, that there was a lull among the mosquitoes about midnight, and that they began again in the morning. Nature is thus merciful. But apparently they need rest as well as we. Few if any creatures are equally active all night. As soon as it was light I saw, through my veil, that the inside of the tent about our heads was quite blackened with myriads, each one of their wings when flying, as has been calculated, vibrating some three thousand times in a minute, and their combined hum was almost as bad to endure as their stings. I had an uncomfortable night on this account, though I am not sure that one succeeded in his attempt to sting me.

We did not suffer so much from insects in this excursion as the statements of some who have explored these woods in midsummer led us to anticipate—yet I have no doubt that at some seasons and in some places they are a much more serious pest. The Jesuit Hierosme Lalemant of Quebec, reporting the death of Father René Menard—who was abandoned, lost his way and died in the woods among the Outaoüax near Lake Superior in 1661 dwells chiefly on his probable sufferings from the attacks of mosquitoes when too weak to defend himself, adding that there was a frightful number of them in those parts "and so insupportable," says he, "that the 3 Frenchmen who have made that voyage, affirm that there was no other means of defending one's self, but to run always without stopping, and it was even necessary for 2 of them to be employed in driving off these creatures while the 3ᵈ wanted to drink, otherwise he could not have done it." I have no doubt that this was said in good faith.

AUGUST I.

I caught two or three large red chivin (*Leuciscus pulchellus*) early this morning, within twenty feet of the camp, which, added to the moose-tongue, that had been left in the kettle boiling over night, and to our other stores, made a sumptuous breakfast. The Indian made us some hemlock tea instead of coffee, and we were not obliged to go as far as China for it; indeed, not quite so far as for the fish. This was tolerable, though he said it was not strong enough. It was interesting to see so simple a dish as a kettle of water with a handful of green hemlock sprigs in it, boiling over the huge fire in the open air—the leaves fast losing their lively green color—and know that it was for our breakfast.

We were glad to embark once more and leave some of the Mosquitoes behind. We had passed the *Wassataquoik* without perceiving it. This, according to the Indian, is the name of the Main E. Branch itself, and not properly applied to this small tributary alone, as on the maps. We found that we had camped about a mile above Hunt's, which is on the east bank—and is the last house for those who ascend Ktadn on this side. We also had expected to ascend it from this point—but omitted it on account of the sore feet of my companion. The Indian however suggested that perhaps he might get a pair of moccasins at this place—and that he could walk very easily in them, and without hurting his feet, using several pairs of stockings—and he said beside, that they were so porous that when you had taken in water, it all drained out again in a little while. We stopped to get some sugar—but found that the family had moved away and the house was unoccupied except temporarily by some men who were getting the hay. They told us that the road to Ktadn left the river 8 miles above, and also that perhaps we could get some sugar at "Fisk's 14 miles below." I do not remember that we saw the mountain at all from the river. I noticed a seine here stretched on the bank, which probably had been used to catch salmon.

Just below this on the west bank we saw a moose-hide stretched and with it a bearskin, which was comparatively very small. I was the more interested in this sight because it was near here that a towns-man of ours when quite a lad and alone killed a large bear some years ago. Polis said that they belonged to Joe Aitteon, my last guide, but how he told, I don't know. He was probably hunting near and had left them for the day. Finding that we were going directly to Oldtown after all, he regretted that he had not taken more of the moose meat to his family, saying that in a short time, by drying it, he could have made it so light as to have brought away the greater part, leaving the bones. We once or twice inquired after the lip, which is a famous tit-bit, but he said, "That go Oldtown for my old woman; don't get it every day."

Maples grew more and more numerous. It was lowering, and rained a little during the forenoon, and, as we expected a wetting, we stopped early and dined on the east side of a small expansion of the river, just above what are probably called Whetstone Falls, about a dozen miles below Hunt's. There were pretty fresh moose-tracks by the water-side. There were singular long ridges hereabouts, called "horsebacks," covered with ferns. My companion having lost his pipe asked the Indian if he could not make him one. "O yer," said he, and in a minute rolled up one of birch-bark, telling him to wet the bowl from time to time. Here also he left his gazette on a tree.

We carried round the falls just below, on the west side. The rocks were on their edges, and very sharp. The distance was about three fourths of a mile. When we had carried over one load, the Indian returned by the shore, and I by the path; and though I made no particular haste, I was nevertheless surprised to find him at the other end as soon as I. It was remarkable how easily he got along over the worst ground. He said to me, "I take canoe and you take the rest, suppose you can keep along with me?" I thought that he meant, that while he ran down the rapids I should keep along the shore, and be ready to assist him from time to time, as I had done before; but as the walking would be very bad, I answered, "I suppose you will go too fast for me, but I will try." But I was to go by the path, he said. This I thought would not help the matter, I should have so far to go to get to the river-side when he wanted me. But neither was this what he meant. He was proposing a race over the carry, and asked me if I thought I could keep along with him by the same path, adding that I must be pretty smart to do it. As his load, the canoe, would be much the heaviest and bulkiest, though the simplest, I thought that I ought to be able to do it, and said that I would try. So I proceeded to gather up the gun, axe, paddle, kettle, frying-pan, plates, dippers, carpets, &c., &c., and while I was thus engaged he threw me his cow-hide boots. "What, are these in the bargain?" I asked. "O yer," said he; but before I could make a bundle of my load I saw him disappearing over a hill with the canoe on his head; so, hastily scraping the various articles together, I started on the run, and immediately went by him in the bushes, but I had no sooner left him out of sight in a rocky hollow, than the greasy plates, dippers, &c., took to themselves wings, and while I was employed in gathering them up again, he went by me; but hastily pressing the sooty kettle to my side, I started once more, and soon passing him again, I saw him no more on the carry. I do not mention this as anything of a feat, for it was but poor running on my part, and he was obliged to move with great caution for fear of breaking his canoe as well as his neck. When he made his appearance, puffing and panting like myself, in answer to my inquiries where he had been, he said, "Locks (rocks) cut 'em feet," and laughing added, "O, me love to play sometimes." He said that he and his companions when they came to carries several miles long used to try who would get over first; each perhaps with a canoe on his head. I bore the sign of the kettle on my brown linen sack for the rest of the voyage.

We made a second carry on the east side, around some falls about a mile below this. On the mainland were Norway pines, indicating a new geological formation, and it was such a dry and sandy soil as we had not noticed before.

As we approached the mouth of the East Branch, we passed two or three huts, the first signs of civilization after Hunt's, though we saw no road as yet; we heard a cow-bell, and even saw an infant held up to a small square window to see us pass, but apparently the infant and the mother that held it were the only inhabitants then at home for several miles. This took the wind out of our sails, reminding us that we were travellers surely, while it was a native of the soil, and had the advantage of us. Conversation flagged. I would only hear the Indian, perhaps, ask my companion, "You load my pipe?" He said that he smoked alder bark, for medicine. On entering the West Branch at Nickertow it appeared much larger than the East. Polis remarked that the former was all gone and lost now, that it was all smooth water hence to Oldtown, and he threw away his pole which was cut on the Umbazookskus. Thinking of the rapids, he said once or twice, that you wouldn't catch him to go East Branch again; but he did not by any means mean all that he said.

Things are quite changed since I was here eleven years ago. Where there were but one or two houses, I now found quite a village, with saw-mills and a store (the latter was locked, but its contents were so much the more safely stored), and there was a stage-road to Mattawamkeag, and the rumor of a stage. Indeed, a steamer had ascended thus far once, when the water was very high. But we were not able to get any sugar, only a better shingle to lean our backs against.

We camped about two miles below Nickertow, on the south side of the West Branch, covering with fresh twigs the withered bed of a former traveller, and feeling that we were now in a settled country, especially when in the evening we heard an ox sneeze in its wild pasture across the river. Wherever you land along the frequented part of the river, you have not far to go to find these sites of temporary inns, the withered bed of flattened twigs, the charred sticks, and perhaps the tent-poles. And not long since, similar beds were spread along the Connecticut, the Hudson, and the Delaware, and longer still ago, by the Thames and Seine, and they now help to make the soil where private and public gardens, mansions and palaces are. We could not get fir twigs for our bed here, and the spruce was harsh in comparison, having more twig in proportion to its leaf, but we improved it somewhat with hemlock. The Indian re-marked as before, "Must have hard wood to cook moose-meat," as if that were a maxim, and proceeded to get it. My companion cooked some in California fashion, winding a long string of the meat round a stick and slowly turning it in his hand before the fire. It was very good. But the Indian not approving of the mode, or because he was not allowed to cook it his own way, would not taste it. After the regular supper we attempted to make a lily soup of the bulbs which I had brought along, for I wished to learn all I could before I got out of the woods. Following the Indian's directions, for he began to be sick, I washed the bulbs carefully, minced some moose-meat and some pork, salted and boiled all together, but we had not patience to try the experiment fairly, for he said it must be boiled till the roots were completely softened so as to thicken the soup like flour; but though we left it on all night, we found it dried to the kettle in the morning, and not yet boiled to a flour. Perhaps the roots were not ripe enough, for they commonly gather them in the fall. As it was, it was palatable enough, but it reminded me of the Irishman's lime-stone broth. The other ingredients were enough alone. The Indian's name for these bulbs was *Sheepnoc*. I stirred the soup by accident with a striped maple or moose-wood stick, which I had peeled, and he re-marked that its bark was an emetic.

He prepared to camp as usual between his moose-hide and the fire, but it beginning to rain suddenly, he took refuge under the tent with us, and gave us a song before falling asleep. It rained hard in the night and spoiled another box of matches for us, which the Indian had left out, for he was very care-less; but, as usual, we had so much the better night for the rain, since it kept the mosquitoes down.

SUNDAY, AUGUST 2,

was a cloudy and unpromising morning. One of us observed to the Indian, "You did not stretch your moose-hide last night, did you, Mr. Polis?" Whereat he replied, in a tone of surprise, though perhaps not of ill humor: "What you ask me that question for? Suppose I stretch 'em, you see 'em. May be your way talking, may be all right, no Indian way." I had observed that he did not wish to answer the same question more than once, and was often silent when it was put again for the sake of certainty, as if he were moody. Not that he was incommunicative, for he frequently commenced a long-winded narrative of his own accord,—repeated at length the tradition of some old battle, or some passage in the recent history of his tribe in which he had acted a prominent part, from time to time drawing a long breath, and resuming the thread of his tale, with the true storyteller's leisureliness, perhaps after shooting a rapid,—prefacing with "we-ll-by-by," &c., as he paddled along. Especially after the day's work was over, and he had put himself in posture for the night, he would be unexpectedly sociable, exhibit even the *bonhommie* of a Frenchman, and we would fall asleep before he got through his periods.

Nickertow is called eleven miles from Mattawamkeag by the river. Our camp was, therefore, about nine miles from the latter place.

The Indian was quite sick this morning with the colic. I thought that he was the worse for the moose-meat he had eaten.

We reached the Mattawamkeag at half past eight in the morning, in the midst of a drizzling rain, and after buying some sugar set out again.

The Indian growing much worse, we stopped in the

north part of Lincoln to get some brandy for him, but failing in this, an apothecary recommended Brandreth's pills, which he refused to take, because he was not acquainted with them. He said to me, "Me doctor—first study my case, find out what ail 'em—then I know what to take." We dropped down a little further, and stopped at mid-forenoon on an island and made him a dipper of tea. Here too we dined and did some washing and botanizing, while he lay on the bank. In the afternoon we went on a little further, though the Indian was no better. "*Burntibus*," as he called it, was a long smooth lake-like reach below the Five Islands. He said that he owned a hundred acres somewhere up this way. As a thunder-shower appeared to be coming up, we stopped opposite a barn on the west bank, in Chester, about a mile above Lincoln. Here at last we were obliged to spend the rest of the day and night, on account of our patient, whose sickness did not abate. He lay groaning under his canoe on the bank, looking very woe-begone, yet it was only a common case of colic. You would not have thought, if you had seen him lying about thus, that he was the proprietor of so many acres in that neighborhood, was worth $6,000, and had been to Washington. It seemed to me that, like the Irish, he made a greater ado about his sickness than a Yankee does, and was more alarmed about himself. We talked somewhat of leaving him with his people in Lincoln,—for that is one of their homes,—and taking the stage the next day, but he objected on account of the expense, saying, "Suppose me well in morning, you and I go Oldtown by noon."

As we were taking our tea at twilight, while he lay groaning still under his canoe, having at length found out "what ail him," he asked me to get him a dipper of water. Taking the dipper in one hand, he seized his powder-horn with the other, and pouring into it a charge or two of powder, stirred it up with his finger, and drank it off. This was all he took to-day after breakfast beside his tea.

To save the trouble of pitching our tent, when we had secured our stores from wandering dogs, we camped in the solitary half-open barn near the bank, with the permission of the owner, lying on new-mown hay four feet deep. The fragrance of the hay, in which many ferns, &c. were mingled, was agreeable, though it was quite alive with grasshoppers which you could hear crawling through it. This served to graduate our approach to houses and feather-beds. In the night some large bird, probably an owl, flitted through over our heads, and very early in the morning we were awakened by the twittering of swallows which had their nests there.

MONDAY, AUGUST 3.

We started early before breakfast, the Indian being considerably better, and soon glided by Lincoln, and after another long and handsome lake-like reach, we stopped to breakfast on the west shore, two or three miles below this town.

We frequently passed Indian Islands with their small houses on them. The Governor, Aitteon, lives on one of them, in Lincoln.

The Penobscot Indians seem to be more social, even, than the whites. Ever and anon in the deepest wilderness of Maine you come to the log-hut of a Yankee or Canada settler, but a Penobscot never takes up his residence in such a solitude. They are not even scattered about on their islands in the Penobscot, which are all within the settlements, but gathered together on two or three,—though not always on the best soil,—evidently for the sake of society. I saw one or two houses not now used by them, because, as our Indian Polis said, they were too solitary.

The small river emptying in at Lincoln is the Matanawcook, which also, we noticed, was the name of a steamer moored there. So we paddled and floated along, looking into the mouths of rivers. When passing the Mohawk Rips, or, as the Indian called them, "Mohog lips," four or five miles below Lincoln, he told us at length the story of a fight between his tribe and the Mohawks there, anciently,—how the latter were overcome by stratagem, the Penobscots using concealed knives,—but they could not for a long time kill the Mohawk chief, who was a very large and strong man, though he was attacked by several canoes at once, when swimming alone in the river.

From time to time we met Indians in their canoes, going up river. Our man did not commonly approach them, but exchanged a few words with them at a distance in his tongue. These were the first Indians we had met since leaving the *Umbazookskus*.

At Piscataquis Falls, just above the river of that name, we walked over the wooden railroad on the eastern shore, about one and a half miles long, while the Indian glided down the rapids. The steamer from Oldtown stops here, and passengers take a new boat above. Piscataquis, whose mouth we here passed, means "branch." It is obstructed by falls at its mouth, but can be navigated with batteaux or canoes above through a settled country, even to the neighborhood of Moosehead Lake, and we had thought at first of going that way. We were not obliged to get out of the canoe after this on account of falls or rapids, nor, indeed, was it quite necessary here. We took less notice of the scenery to-day, because we were in quite a settled country. The river became

broad and sluggish, and we saw a blue heron wing-
ing its way slowly down the stream before us.

We passed the Passadumkeag River on our left and
saw the blue *Olamon* mountains at a distance in the
southeast. Hereabouts our Indian told us at length the
story of their contention with the priest respecting
schools. He thought a great deal of education and
had recommended it to his tribe. His argument in its
favor was, that if you had been to college and learnt
to calculate, you could "keep 'em property,—no other
way." He said that his boy was the best scholar in
the school at Oldtown, to which he went with whites.
He himself is a Protestant, and goes to church regularly in Oldtown. According to his account, a good
many of his tribe are Protestants, and many of the
Catholics also are in favor of schools. Some years
ago they had a schoolmaster, a Protestant, whom they
liked very well. The priest came and said that they
must send him away, and finally he had such influence, telling them that they would go to the bad
place at last if they retained him, that they sent him
away. The school party, though numerous, were
about giving up. Bishop Fenwick came from Boston
and used his influence against them. But our Indian
told his side that they must not give up, must hold
on, they were the strongest. If they gave up, then
they would have no party. But they answered that
it was "no use, priest too strong, we'd better give up."
At length he persuaded them to make a stand.

The priest was going for a sign to cut down the
liberty-pole. So Polis and his party had a secret meeting about it; he got ready fifteen or twenty stout
young men, "stript 'em naked, and painted 'em like
old times," and told them that when the priest and
his party went to cut down the liberty-pole, they were
to rush up, take hold of it and prevent them, and he

assured them that there would be no war, only a noise, "no war where priest is." He kept his men concealed in a house near by, and when the priest's party were about to cut down the liberty-pole, the fall of which would have been a death-blow to the school party, he gave a signal, and his young men rushed out and seized the pole. There was a great uproar, and they were about coming to blows, but the priest interfered, saying, "No war, no war," and so the pole stands, and the school goes on still.

We thought that it showed a good deal of tact in him, to seize this occasion and take his stand on it; proving how well he understood those with whom he had to deal.

The Olamon River comes in from the east in Greenbush a few miles below the Passadumkeag. When we asked the meaning of this name, the Indian said that there was an island opposite its mouth which was called *Olarmon*. That in old times, when visitors were coming to Oldtown, they used to stop there to dress and fix up or paint themselves. "What is that which ladies use?" he asked. Rouge? Red vermilion? "Yer," he said, "that is *larmon*, a kind of clay or red paint, which they used to get here."

We decided that we too would stop at this island, and fix up our inner man, at least, by dining.

It was a large island with an abundance of hemp-nettle, but I did not notice any kind of red paint there. The Olamon River, at its mouth at least, is a dead stream. There was another large island in that neighborhood, which the Indian called "*Soogle*" (i.e. Sugar) Island.

About a dozen miles before reaching Oldtown he inquired, "How you like 'em your pilot?" But we postponed an answer till we had got quite back again.

The *Sunkhaze*, another short dead stream, comes

in from the east two miles above Oldtown. There is said to be some of the best deer ground in Maine on this stream. Asking the meaning of this name, the Indian said, "Suppose you are going down Penobscot, just like me, and you see a canoe come out of bank and go along before you, but you no see 'em stream. That is *Sunkhaze*."

He had previously complimented me on my paddling, saying that I paddled "just like anybody," giving me an Indian name which meant "great paddler." When off this stream he said to me, who sat in the bows, "Me teach you paddle." So turning toward the shore he got out, came forward and placed my hands as he wished. He placed one of them quite outside the boat, and the other parallel with the first, grasping the paddle near the end, not over the flat extremity, and told me to slide it back and forth on the side of the canoe. This, I found, was a great improvement which I had not thought of, saving me the labor of lifting the paddle each time, and I wondered that he had not suggested it before. It is true, before our baggage was reduced we had been obliged to sit with our legs drawn up, and our knees above the side of the canoe, which would have prevented our paddling thus, or perhaps he was afraid of wearing out his canoe, by constant friction on the side.

I told him that I had been accustomed to sit in the stern, and lifting my paddle at each stroke, getting a pry on the side each time, and I still paddled partly as if in the stern. He then wanted to see me paddle in the stern. So, changing paddles, for he had the longer and better one, and turning end for end, he sitting flat on the bottom and I on the crossbar, he began to paddle very hard, trying to turn the canoe, looking over his shoulder and laughing, but finding it in vain he relaxed his efforts, though we still sped along a mile or two very swiftly. He said that he had no fault to find with my paddling in the stern, but I complained that he did not paddle according to his own directions in the bows.

Opposite the Sunkhaze is the main boom of the Penobscot, where the logs from far up the river are collected and assorted.

As we drew near to Oldtown I asked Polis if he was not glad to get home again; but there was no relenting to his wildness, and he said, "It makes no difference to me where I am." Such is the Indian's pretence always.

We approached the Indian Island through the narrow strait called "Cook." He said, "I 'xpect we take in some water there, river so high,—never see it so high at this season. Very rough water there, but short; swamp steamboat once. Don't you paddle till I tell you, then you paddle right along." It was a very short rapid. When we were in the midst of it he shouted "paddle" and we shot through without taking in a drop. Soon after the Indian houses came in sight, but I could not at first tell my companion which of 2 or 3 large white ones was our guide's. He said it was the one with blinds.

We landed opposite his door at about 4 P.M., having come some 40 miles this day. From the Piscataquis we had come remarkably and unaccountably quick, probably as fast as the stage on the bank, though the last dozen miles was dead water.

Polis wanted to sell us his canoe—said it would last 7 or 8 years—or with care perhaps 10—but we were not ready to buy it.

We stopped for an hour at his house, where my companion shaved with his razor, which he pronounced in very good condition. Mrs. P. wore a hat and had a silver brooch on her breast, but she was not introduced to us. The house was roomy and neat. A large new map of Oldtown and the Indian Island hung on the wall and a clock opposite to it. Wishing to know when the cars left Oldtown, Polis's son brought one of the last Bangor papers which I saw was directed to "Joseph Polis" from the office.

This was the last I saw of Joe Polis. We took the last train and reached Bangor that night.

Appendix.

THE prevailing trees (I speak only of what I saw) on the east and west branches of the Penobscot and on the upper part of the Allegash were the fir, spruce (both black and white), and arbor-vitæ, or "cedar." The fir has the darkest foliage, and, together with the spruce, makes a very dense "black growth," especially on the upper parts of the rivers. A dealer in lumber with whom I talked called the former a weed, and it is commonly regarded as fit neither for timber nor fuel. But it is more sought after as an ornamental tree than any other evergreen of these woods except the arbor-vitæ. The black spruce is much more common than the white. Both are tall and slender trees. The arbor-vitæ, which is of a more cheerful hue, with its light-green fans, is also tall and slender, though sometimes two feet in diameter. It often fills the swamps.

Mingled with the former, and also here and there forming extensive and more open woods by themselves, indicating, it is said, a better soil, were canoe and yellow birches (the former was always at hand for kindling a fire,—we saw no small white-birches in that wilderness), and sugar and red maples.

The Aspen (*Populus tremuloides*) was very common on burnt grounds. We saw many straggling white pines, commonly unsound trees, which had therefore been skipped by the choppers; these were the largest trees we saw; and we occasionally passed a small wood in which this was the prevailing tree; but I did not notice nearly so many of these trees as I can see in a single walk in Concord. The speckled or hoary alder (*Alnus incana*) abounds everywhere along the muddy banks of rivers and lakes, and in swamps. Hemlock could commonly be found for tea, but was nowhere abundant. Yet F. A. Michaux states that in Maine, Vermont, and the upper part of New Hampshire, &c., the hemlock forms three fourths of the evergreen woods, the rest being black spruce. It belongs to cold hillsides.

The elm and black ash were very common along the lower and stiller parts of the streams, where the shores were flat and grassy or there were low gravelly islands. They made a pleasing variety in the scenery, and we felt as if nearer home while gliding past them.

The above fourteen trees made the bulk of the woods which we saw.

The larch (Juniper), beech, and Norway pine (*Pinus resinosa*, red pine), were only occasionally seen in particular places. The *Pinus Banksiana* (gray or Northern scrub-pine), and a single small red oak (*Quercus rubra*) only, are on islands in Grand Lake, on the East Branch.

The above are almost all peculiarly Northern trees, and found chiefly, if not solely, on mountains southward.

II. FLOWERS AND SHRUBS.

It appears that in a forest like this the great majority of flowers, shrubs, and grasses are confined to the banks of the rivers and lakes, and to the meadows, more open swamps, burnt lands, and mountain-tops; comparatively very few indeed penetrate the woods. There is no such dispersion even of wild-flowers as is commonly supposed, or as exists in a cleared and settled country. Most of our wild-flowers, so called, may be considered as naturalized in the localities where they grow. Rivers and lakes are the great protectors of such plants against the aggressions of the forest, by their annual rise and fall keeping open a narrow strip where these more delicate plants have light and space in which to grow. They are the *protégés* of the rivers. These narrow and straggling bands and isolated groups are, in a sense, the pioneers of civilization. Birds, quadrupeds, insects, and man also, in the main, follow the flowers, and the latter in his turn makes more room for them and for berry-bearing shrubs, birds, and small quadrupeds. One settler told me that not only blackberries and raspberries, but mountain-maples came in, in the clearing and burning.

Though plants are often referred to primitive woods as their locality, it cannot be true of very many, unless the woods are supposed to include such localities as I have mentioned. Only those which require but little light, and can bear the drip of the trees, penetrate the woods, and these have commonly more beauty in their leaves than in their pale and almost colorless blossoms.

The prevailing flowers and conspicuous small plants of the *woods*, which I noticed, were: *Clintonia borealis, Linnæa,* checkerberry (*Gaultheria procumbens*), *Aralia nudicaulis* (wild sarsaparilla), great round-leaved orchis, *Dalibarda repens, Chiogenes hispidula* (creeping snowberry), *Oxalis acetosella* (common wood-sorrel), *Aster acuminatus, Pyrola secunda* (one-sided pyrola), *Medeola Virginica* (Indian cucumber-root), small *Circæa* (enchanter's nightshade), and perhaps *Cornus Canadensis* (dwarf cornel).

Of these, the last of July, 1857, only the *Aster acuminatus* and great round-leaved *orchis* were conspicuously in bloom.

The most common flowers of the *river* and *lake shores* were: *Thalictrum cornuti* (meadow-rue), *Hypericum ellipticum, mutilum,* and *Canadense* (St. John's-wort), horsemint, horehound, *Lycopus Virginicus* and *Europæus,* var. *sinuatus* (bugle-weed), *Scutellaria galericulata* (skull-cap), *Solidago lanceolata* and *squarrosa* East Branch (golden-rod), *Diplopappus umbellatus* (double-bristled aster), *Aster radula, Cicuta maculata* and *bulbifera* (water-hemlock), meadow-sweet, *Lysimachia stricta* and *ciliata* (loose-strife), *Galium trifidum* (small bed-straw), *Lilium Canadense* (wild yellow-lily), *Platanthera peramœna* and *psycodes* (great purple orchis and small purple-fringed orchis), *Mimulus ringens* (monkey-flower), dock (water), blue flag, *Hydrocotyle Americana* (marsh pennywort), *Sanicula Canadensis?* (black snake-root), *Clematis Virginiana?* (common virgin's-bower), *Nasturtium palustre* (marsh cress), *Ranunculus recurvatus* (hooked crowfoot), *Asclepias incarnata* (swamp milkweed), *Aster Tradescanti* (Tradescant's aster), *Aster miser,* also *longifolius, Eupatorium purpureum* especially lake shores (Joe-Pye-weed), *Apocynum Cannabinum* East Branch (Indian hemp), *Polygonum cilinode* (bind-weed), and others. Not to mention among inferior orders wool-grass and the sensitive fern.

In the water, *Nuphar advena* (yellow pond-lily), some *potamogetons* (pond-weed), *Sagittaria variabilis* (arrow-head), *Sium lineare?* (water-parsnip).

Of these, those conspicuously in flower the last of July, 1857, were: rue, *Solidago lanceolata* and *squarrosa, Diplopappus umbellatus, Aster radula, Lilium Canadense,* great and small purple orchis, *Mimulus ringens,* blue flag, virgin's-bower, &c.

The characteristic flowers in *swamps* were: *Rubus*

triflorus (dwarf raspberry), *Calla palustris* (water-arum), and *Sarracenia purpurea* (pitcher-plant). On *burnt grounds: Epilobium angustifolium,* in full bloom (great willow-herb), and *Erechthites hieracifolia* (fire-weed). On *cliffs: Campanula rotundifolia* (harebell), *Cornus Canadensis* (dwarf cornel), *Arctostaphylos uva-ursi* (bearberry), *Potentilla tridentata* (mountain cinquefoil), *Pteris aquilina* (common brake). At *old camps, carries, and logging-paths: Cirsium arvense* (Canada thistle), *Prunella vulgaris* (common self-heal), clover, herd's-grass, *Achillea millefolium* (common yarrow), *Leucanthemum vulgare* (white-weed), *Aster macrophyllus, Halenia deflexa* East Branch (spurred gentian), *Antennaria margaritacea* (pearly everlasting), *Actæa rubra* and *alba,* wet carries (red and white cohosh), *Desmodium Canadense* (tick-trefoil), sorrel.

The handsomest and most interesting flowers were the great purple orchises, rising ever and anon, with their great purple spikes perfectly erect, amid the shrubs and grasses of the shore. It seemed strange that they should be made to grow there in such profusion, seen of moose and moose-hunters only, while they are so rare in Concord. I have never seen this species flowering nearly so late with us, or with the small one.

The prevailing underwoods were: *Dirca palustris* (moose-wood), *Acer spicatum* (mountain maple), *Viburnum lantanoides* (hobble-bush), and frequently *Taxus baccata,* var. *Canadensis* (American yew).

The prevailing shrubs and small trees along the shore were: *osier rouge* and alders (before mentioned); sallows, or small willows, of two or three kinds, as *Salix humilis, rostrata,* and *discolor?, Sambucus Canadensis* (black elder), rose, *Viburnum*

opulus and *nudum* (cranberry-tree and withe-rod),
Pyrus Americana (American mountain-ash), *Corylus
rostrata* (beaked hazel-nut), *Diervilla trifida* (bush-
honeysuckle), *Prunus Virginiana* (choke-cherry),
Myrica gale (sweet-gale), *Nemopanthes Canadensis*
(mountain holly), *Cephalanthus occidentalis* (button-
bush), *Ribes prostratum*, in some places (fetid
currant).

More particularly of shrubs and small trees in
swamps: some willows, *Kalmia glauca* (pale laurel),
Ledum latifolium and *palustre* (Labrador tea), *Ribes
lacustre* (swamp gooseberry), and in one place
Betula pumila (low birch). At *camps and carries*:
raspberry, *Vaccinium Canadense* (Canada blueberry),
Prunus Pennsylvanica also along shore (wild red
cherry), *Amelanchier Canadensis* (shad-bush), *Sambucus pubens* (red-berried elder). Among those peculiar to the *mountains* would be the *Vaccinium
vitis-idæa* (cow-berry).

Of plants commonly regarded as *introduced* from
Europe, I observed at Ansel Smith's clearing, Chesuncook, abundant in 1857: *Ranunculus acris* (buttercups), *Plantago major* (common plantain), *Chenopodium album* (lamb's-quarters), *Capsella bursa-
pastoris*, 1853 (shepherd's-purse), *Spergula arvensis*,
also, north shore of Moosehead, in 1853, and elsewhere, 1857 (corn-spurrey), *Taraxacum dens-leonis*
—regarded as indigenous by Gray, but evidently introduced there—(common dandelion), *Polygonum
Persicaria* and *hydropiper*, by a logging-path in woods
at Smith's (lady's-thumb and smart-weed), *Rumex
acetosella*, common at carries (sheep-sorrel), *Trifolium pratense*, 1853 and 1857, carries, frequent
(red clover), *Leucanthemum vulgare*, carries (white
weed), *Phleum pratense*, carries, 1853 and 1857

(herd's-grass), *Verbena hastata* (blue vervain), *Cirsium arvense*, abundant at camps 1857 (Canada thistle), *Rumex crispus?*, West Branch, 1853 (curled dock), *Verbascum thapsus*, between Bangor and lake, 1853 (common mullein).

It appears that I saw about a dozen plants which had accompanied man as far into the woods as Chesuncook, and had naturalized themselves there, in 1853. Plants begin thus early to spring by the side of a logging-path,—a mere vista through the woods, which can only be used in the winter, on account of the stumps and fallen trees,—which at length are the roadside plants in old settlements. The pioneers of such are planted in part by the first cattle, which cannot be summered in the woods.

III. LIST OF PLANTS.

The following is a list of the plants which I noticed in the Maine woods, in the years 1853 and 1857. (Those marked * not in woods.)

1. Those Which Attained the Height of Trees.

Alnus incana (speckled or hoary alder), abundant along streams, &c.

Thuja occidentalis (American arbor-vitæ), one of the prevailing.

Fraxinus sambucifolia (black ash), very common, especially near dead water. The Indian spoke of "yellow ash" as also found there.

Populus tremuloides (American aspen), very common, especially on burnt lands, almost as white as birches.

Populus grandidentata (large-toothed aspen), perhaps two or three.

Fagus ferruginea (American beech), not uncommon, at least on the West Branch (saw more in 1846).

Betula papyracea (canoe-birch), prevailing every-where and about Bangor.

Betula excelsa (yellow birch), very common.

Betula lenta (black birch), on the West Branch, in 1853.

*Betula alba** (American white birch), about Bangor only.

Ulmus Americana (American or white elm), West Branch and low down the East Branch, i.e. on the lower and alluvial part of the river, very common.

Larix Americana (American or black larch), very common on the Umbazookskus, some elsewhere.

Abies Canadensis (hemlock-spruce), not abundant, some on the West Branch, and a little everywhere.

Acer saccharinum (sugar maple), very common.

Acer rubrum (red or swamp maple), very common.

Acer dasycarpum (white or silver maple), a little low on East Branch and in Chesuncook woods.

Quercus rubra (red oak), one on an island in Grand Lake, East Branch, and, according to a settler, a few on the east side of Chesuncook Lake; a few also about Bangor in 1853.

Pinus strobus (white pine), scattered along, most abundant at Heron Lake.

Pinus resinosa (red pine), Telos and Grand Lake, a little afterwards here and there.

Abies balsamea (balsam fir), perhaps the most common tree, especially in the upper parts of rivers.

Abies nigra (black or double spruce), next to the last the most common, if not equally common, and on mountains.

Abies alba (white or single spruce), common with the last along the rivers.

Pinus Banksiana (gray or Northern scrub-pine), a few on an island in Grand Lake.

Twenty-three in all (23).

2. *Small Trees and Shrubs.*

Prunus depressa (dwarf-cherry), on gravel bars, East Branch, near Hunt's, with green fruit, obviously distinct from the *pumila* of river and meadows.

*Vaccinium corymbosum** (common swamp blueberry), Bucksport.

Vaccinium Canadense (Canada blueberry), carries and rocky hills everywhere as far south as Bucksport.

Vaccinium Pennsylvanicum? (dwarf-blueberry), Whetstone Falls.

Betula pumila (low birch), Mud Pond Swamp.

Prinos verticillatus (black alder), '57, now placed with *Ilex* by Gray, 2d ed.

Cephalanthus occidentalis (button-bush).

Prunus Pennsylvanica (wild red cherry), very common at camps, carries, &c., along rivers; fruit ripe August 1, 1857.

Prunus Virginiana (choke-cherry), river-side, common.

Cornus alternifolia (alternate-leaved cornel), West Branch, 1853.

Ribes prostratum (fetid currant), common along streams, as Webster Stream.

Sambucus Canadensis (common elder), common along river-sides.

Sambucus pubens (red-berried elder), not quite so common, roadsides toward Moosehead, and on carries afterward, fruit beautiful.

Ribes lacustre (swamp-gooseberry), swamps, common, Mud Pond Swamp and Webster Stream; not ripe July 29, 1857.

Corylus rostrata (beaked hazel-nut), common.

Taxus baccata, var. *Canadensis* (American yew), a common under-shrub at an island in West Branch and Chesuncook woods.

Viburnum lantanoides (hobble-bush), common, especially in Chesuncook woods; fruit ripe in September, 1853, not in July, 1857.

Viburnum opulus (cranberry-tree), on West Branch; one in flower still, July 25, 1857.

Viburnum nudum (withe-rod), common along rivers.

Kalmia glauca (pale laurel), swamps, common, as at Moosehead carry and Chamberlain swamp.

Kalmia angustifolia (lamb-kill), with *Kalmia glauca*.

Acer spicatum (mountain maple), a prevailing underwood.

Acer striatum (striped maple), in fruit July 30, 1857; green the first year; green, striped with white, the second; darker, the third, with dark blotches.

Cornus stolonifera (red-osier dogwood), prevailing shrub on shore of West Branch; fruit still white in August, 1857.

Pyrus Americana (American mountain ash), common along shores.

Amelanchier Canadensis (shad-bush), rocky carries, &c.; considerable fruit in 1857.

Rubus strigosus (wild red raspberry), very abundant, burnt grounds, camps, and carries, but not ripe till we got to Chamberlain dam and on East Branch.

Rosa Carolina (swamp-rose), common on the shores of lakes, &c.

*Rhus typhina** (stag-horn sumac).

Myrica gale (sweet-gale), common.

Nemopanthes Canadensis (mountain holly), common in low ground, Moosehead carry, and on Mount Kineo.

Cratægus (*coccinea?* scarlet-fruited thorn), not uncommon; with hard fruit in September, 1853.

Salix (near to *petiolaris*, petioled willow), very common in Umbazookskus meadows.

Salix rostrata (long-beaked willow), common.

Salix humilis (low bush-willow), common.

Salix discolor? (glaucous willow).

Salix lucida (shining willow), at island in Heron lake.

Dirca palustris (moose-wood), common.

In all, 38.

3. *Small Shrubs and Herbaceous Plants.*

Agrimonia Eupatoria (common agrimony), not uncommon.

Circæa Alpina (enchanter's nightshade), very common in woods.

Nasturtium palustre (marsh cress), var. *hispidum*, common as at A. Smith's.

Aralia hispida (bristly sarsaparilla), on West Branch, both years.

Aralia nudicaulis (wild sarsaparilla), Chesuncook woods.

Sagittaria variabilis (arrow-head), common at Moosehead and afterward.

Arum triphyllum (Indian turnip), now *arisæma*, Moosehead carry in 1853.

Asclepias incarnata (swamp milk-weed), Umbazookskus River and after, redder than ours, and a different variety from our var. *pulchra*.

Aster acuminatus (pointed-leaved aster), the prevailing aster in woods, not long open on East Branch July 31st; two or more feet high.

Aster macrophyllus (large-leaved aster), common, and the whole plant surprisingly fragrant, like a medicinal herb, just out at Telos Dam July 29, 1857, and after to Bangor and Bucksport; bluish flower (in woods on Pine Stream and at Chesuncook in 1853).

Aster radula (rough-leaved aster), common, Moose-head carry and after.

Aster miser (petty aster), in 1853 on West Branch, and common on Chesuncook shore.

Aster longifolius (willow-leaved blue aster), 1853, Moosehead and Chesuncook shores.

Aster cordifolius (heart-leaved aster), 1853, West Branch.

Aster Tradescanti (Tradescant's aster), 1857. A narrow-leaved one Chesuncook shore, 1853.

Aster, longifolius like, with small flowers, West Branch, 1853.

Aster puniceus (rough-stemmed aster), Pine Stream.

Diplopappus umbellatus (large *diplopappus* aster), common along river.

Arctostaphylos uva-ursi (bear-berry), Kineo, &c., 1857.

Polygonum cilinode (fringe-jointed false buck-wheat), common.

Bidens cernua (bur-marigold), 1853, West Branch.

Ranunculus acris (buttercups), abundant at Smith's, Chesuncook, 1853.

Rubus triflorus (dwarf-raspberry), low grounds and swamps, common.

Utricularia vulgaris* (greater bladder-wort), Pushaw.

Iris versicolor (larger blue-flag), common Moose-head, West Branch, Umbazookskus, &c.

Sparganium (bur-reed).

Calla palustris (water-arum), in bloom July 27, 1857, Mud Pond Swamp.

Lobelia cardinalis (cardinal-flower), apparently common, but out of bloom August, 1857.

Cerastium nutans? (clammy wild chickweed).

Gaultheria procumbens (checkerberry), prevailing everywhere in woods along banks of rivers.

*Stellaria media** (common chickweed), Bangor.

Chiogenes hispidula (creeping snowberry), very common in woods.

Cicuta maculata (water-hemlock).

Cicuta bulbifera (bulb-bearing water-hemlock), Penobscot and Chesuncook shore, 1853.

Galium trifidum (small bed-straw), common.

Galium Aparine? (cleavers), Chesuncook, 1853.

Galium, one kind on Pine Stream, 1853.

Trifolium pratense (red-clover), on carries, &c.

Actæa spicata, var. *alba* (white cohosh), Chesuncook woods 1853, and East Branch 1857.

Actæa var. *rubra* (red cohosh), East Branch 1857.

Vaccinium vitis-idæa (cow-berry), Ktaadn, very abundant.

Cornus Canadensis (dwarf-cornel), in woods Chesuncook 1853; just ripe at Kineo July 24, 1857, common; still in bloom, Moosehead carry September 16, 1853.

Medeola Virginica (Indian cucumber-root), West Branch and Chesuncook woods.

Dalibarda repens (Dalibarda), Moosehead carry and after, common. In flower still, August 1, 1857.

Taraxacum dens-leonis (common dandelion), Smith's 1853, only there. Is it not foreign?

Diervilla trifida (bush honeysuckle), very common.

Rumex hydrolapathum? (great water-dock), common in 1857; noticed it was large seeded in 1853.

Rumex crispus? (curled-dock), West Branch 1853.

Apocynum cannabinum (Indian hemp), Kineo, *Bradford*, and East Branch 1857, at Whetstone Falls.

Apocynum androsæmifolium (spreading dogbane), Kineo, *Bradford*.

Clintonia borealis (Clintonia), all over woods; fruit just ripening July 25, 1857.

A *lemna** (duckweed), Pushaw 1857.

Elodea Virginica (marsh St. John's-wort), Moosehead 1853.

Epilobium angustifolium (great willow-herb), great fields on burnt lands; some white at Webster Stream.

Epilobium coloratum (purple-veined willow-herb), once in 1857.

Eupatorium purpureum (Joe-Pye-weed), Heron, Moosehead, and Chesuncook lake-shores, common.

Allium (onion), a new kind to me in bloom, without bulbs above, on rocks near Whetstone Falls? East Branch.

Halenia deflexa (spurred gentian), carries on East Branch, common.

Geranium Robertianum (Herb Robert).

Solidago lanceolata (bushy golden-rod), very common.

Solidago, one of the three-ribbed, in both years.

Solidago thyrsoidea (large mountain golden-rod), one on Webster Stream.

Solidago squarrosa (large-spiked golden-rod), the most common on East Branch.

Solidago altissima (rough hairy golden-rod), not uncommon both years.

Coptis trifolia (three-leaved gold-thread).

Smilax herbacea (carrion-flower), not uncommon both years.

*Spiræa tomentosa** (hardhack), Bangor.

Campanula rotundifolia (harebell), cliffs Kineo, Grand Lake, &c.

Hieracium (hawk-weed), not uncommon.

Veratrum viride (American white hellebore).

Lycopus Virginicus (bugle-weed), 1857.

Lycopus Europæus (water-horehound), var. *sinuatus*, Heron Lake shore.

Chenopodium album (lamb's-quarters), Smith's.

Mentha Canadensis (wild mint), very common.

*Galeopsis tetrahit** (common hemp-nettle), Olarmon Isle, abundant, and below, in prime August 3, 1857.

Houstonia cærulea (bluets), now *Oldenlandia* (Gray, 2d ed.), 1857.

Hydrocotyle Americana (marsh pennywort), common.

Hypericum ellipticum (elliptical-leaved St. John's-wort), common.

Hypericum mutilum (small St. John's-wort), both years, common.

Hypericum Canadense (Canadian St. John's-wort), Moosehead Lake and Chesuncook shores, 1853.

Trientalis Americana (star-flower), Pine Stream, 1853.

Lobelia inflata (Indian tobacco).

Spiranthes cernua (ladies' tresses), Kineo and after.

Nabalus (rattlesnake root), 1857; *altissimus* (tall white lettuce), Chesuncook woods, 1853.

Antennaria margaritacea (pearly everlasting), common, Moosehead, Smith's, &c.

Lilium Canadense (wild yellow lily), very common and large, West and East Branch; one on East Branch, 1857, with strongly revolute petals, and leaves perfectly smooth beneath, but not larger than the last, and apparently only a variety.

Linnæa borealis (Linnæa), almost everywhere in woods.

*Lobelia Dortmanna** (water-lobelia), pond in Bucksport.

Lysimachia ciliata (hairy-stalked loosestrife), very common, Chesuncook shore and East Branch.

Lysimachia stricta (upright loosestrife), very common.

Microstylis ophioglossoides (adder's-mouth), Kineo.

Spiræa salicifolia (common meadow-sweet), common.

Mimulus ringens (monkey-flower), common, lake-shores, &c.

Scutellaria galericulata (skullcap), very common.

Scutellaria lateriflora (mad-dog skullcap), Heron Lake, 1857, Chesuncook, 1853.

Platanthera psycodes (small purple-fringed orchis), very common, East Branch and Chesuncook, 1853.

Platanthera fimbriata (large purple-fringed orchis), very common, West Branch and Umbazookskus, 1857.

Platanthera orbiculata (large round-leaved orchis), very common in woods, Moosehead and Chamberlain carries, Caucomgomoc, &c.

Amphicarpæa monoica (hog peanut).

Aralia racemosa (spikenard), common, Moosehead carry, Telos Lake, &c., and after; out about August 1, 1857.

Plantago major (common plantain), common in open land at Smith's in 1853.

*Pontederia cordata** (pickerel-weed), only near Oldtown, 1857.

Potamogeton (pond-weed), not common.

Potentilla tridentata (mountain cinquefoil), Kineo.

Potentilla Norvegica (cinquefoil), Heron Lake shore and Smith's.

Polygonum amphibium (water-persicaria), var. *aquaticum*, Second Lake.

Polygonum Persicaria (lady's-thumb), log-path Chesuncook, 1853.

Nuphar advena (yellow pond-lily), not abundant.

Nymphæa odorata (sweet water-lily), a few in West Branch, 1853.

Polygonum hydropiper (smart-weed), log-path, Chesuncook.

Pyrola secunda (one-sided pyrola), very common, Caucomgomoc.

Pyrola elliptica (shin-leaf), Caucomgomoc River.

Ranunculus Flammula (spearwort, var. *reptans*).

Ranunculus recurvatus (hooked crowfoot), Umbazookskus landing, &c.

Typha latifolia* (common cat-tail or reed-mace), extremely abundant between Bangor and Portland.

Sanicula Marylandica (black snake-root), Moosehead carry and after.

Aralia nudicaulis (wild sarsaparilla).

Capsella bursa-pastoris (shepherd's-purse), Smith's, 1853.

Prunella vulgaris (self-heal), very common everywhere.

Erechthites hieracifolia (fireweed), 1857, and Smith's open land, 1853.

Sarracenia purpurea (pitcher-plant), Mud Pond swamp.

Smilacina bifolia (false Solomon's-seal), 1857, and Chesuncook woods, 1853.

Smilacina racemosa? (false spikenard), Umbazookskus carry (July 27, 1857).

Veronica scutellata (marsh speedwell).

Spergula arvensis (corn spurrey), 1857, not uncommon, 1853, Moosehead and Smith's.

Fragaria (strawberry), 1853 Smith's, 1857 Bucksport.

Thalictrum Cornuti (meadow-rue), very common, especially along rivers, tall, and conspicuously in bloom in July, 1857.

Cirsium arvense (Canada thistle), abundant at camps and highway sides in the north of Maine.

Cirsium muticum (swamp-thistle), well in bloom Webster Stream, August 31.

Rumex acetosella (sheep-sorrel), common by river and log-paths, as Chesuncook log-path.

Impatiens fulva (spotted touch-me-not).

Trillium erythrocarpum (painted trillium), common West Branch and Moosehead carry.

Verbena hastata (blue vervain).

Clematis Virginiana (common virgin's-bower), common on river banks, feathered in September, 1853, in bloom July, 1857.

Leucanthemum vulgare (white-weed).

Sium lineare (water-parsnip), 1857, and Chesuncook shore, 1853.

Achillea millefolium (common yarrow), by river and log-paths, and Smith's.

Desmodium Canadense (Canadian tick-trefoil), not uncommon.

Oxalis acetosella (common wood-sorrel), still out July 25, 1853, at Moosehead carry and after.

Oxalis stricta (yellow wood-sorrel), 1853, at Smith's and in his wood-path.

Liparis liliifolia (tway-blade), Kineo, *Bradford.*

Uvularia grandiflora (large-flowered bellwort), woods, common.

Uvularia sessilifolia (sessile-leaved bellwort), Chesuncook woods, 1853.

In all, 145.

4. Of Lower Order.

Scirpus Eriophorum (wool-grass), very common, especially on low islands. A coarse grass, four or five feet high, along the river.

Phleum pratense (herd's-grass), on carries, at camps and clearings.

Equisetum sylvaticum (sylvatic horse-tail).

Pteris aquilina (brake), Kineo and after.

Onoclea sensibilis (sensitive-fern), very common along the river sides; some on the gravelly shore of Heron Lake Island.

Polypodium Dryopteris (brittle polypody).

Woodsia Ilvensis (rusty Woodsia), Kineo.

Lycopodium lucidulum (toothed club-moss).

Usnea (a parmeliaceous lichen), common on various trees.

IV. LIST OF BIRDS

which I saw in Maine between July 24 and August 3, 1857.

A very small hawk at Great Falls, on Webster Stream.

Haliætus leucocephalus (white-headed or bald-eagle), at Ragmuff, and above and below Hunt's, and on pond below Mattawamkeag.

Pandion haliætus (fish-hawk or osprey), heard, also seen on East Branch.

Bubo Virginianus (cat-owl), near Camp Island, also above mouth of Seboois, from a stump back and forth, also near Hunt's on a tree.

Icterus phœniceus (red-winged blackbird), Umbazookskus River.

Corvus Americanus (American crow), a few, as at outlet of Grand Lake; a peculiar cawing.

Fringilla Canadensis (tree-sparrow), think I saw one on Mount Kineo July 24, which behaved as if it had a nest there.

Garrulus cristatus (blue-jay).

Parus atricapillus (chicadee), a few.

Muscicapa tyrannus (king-bird).

Muscicapa Cooperi (olive-sided fly-catcher), everywhere a prevailing bird.

Muscicapa virens (wood pewee), Moosehead, and I think beyond.

Muscicapa ruticilla (American redstart), Moosehead.

Vireo olivaceus (red-eyed vireo), everywhere common.

Turdus migratorius (red-breasted robin), some everywhere.

Turdus melodus (wood-thrush), common in all the woods.

Turdus Wilsonii (Wilson's thrush), Moosehead and beyond.

Turdus aurocapillus (golden-crowned thrush or oven-bird), Moosehead.

Fringilla albicollis (white-throated sparrow), Kineo and after, apparently nesting; the prevailing bird early and late.

Fringilla melodia (song-sparrow), at Moosehead or beyond.

Sylvia pinus (pine warbler), one part of voyage.

Muscicapa acadica (small pewee), common.

Trichas Marylandica (Maryland yellow-throat), everywhere.

Coccyzus Americanus? (yellow-billed cuckoo), common.

Picus erythrocephalus (red-headed woodpecker), heard and saw; and good to eat.

Sitta Carolinensis? (white-breasted American nut-hatch), heard.

Alcedo alcyon (belted kingfisher), very common.

Caprimulgus Americanus (night-hawk).

Tetrao umbellus (partridge), Moosehead carry, &c.

Tetrao cupido? (pinnated grouse), Webster Stream.

Ardea cærulea (blue heron), lower part of Penobscot.

Totanus macularius (spotted sandpiper or peetweet), everywhere.

Larus argentatus? (herring-gull), Heron Lake on rocks, and Chamberlain. Smaller gull on Second Lake.

Anas obscura (dusky or black duck), once in East Branch.

Anas sponsa (summer or wood duck), everywhere.

Fuligula albeola (spirit duck or dipper), common.

Colymbus glacialis (great Northern diver or loon), in all the lakes.

Mergus Merganser (buff-breasted merganser or sheldrake), common on lakes and rivers.

A swallow; the night-warbler? once or twice.

V. QUADRUPEDS.

A bat on West Branch; beaver skull at Grand Lake; Mr. Thatcher ate beaver with moose on the Caucomgomoc. A muskrat on the last stream; the red squirrel is common in the depths of the woods; a dead porcupine on Chamberlain road; a cow moose and tracks of calf; skin of a bear, just killed.

VI. OUTFIT FOR AN EXCURSION.

The following will be a good outfit for one who wishes to make an excursion of *twelve* days into the Maine woods in July, with a companion, and one Indian for the same purposes that I did.

Wear,—a check shirt, stout old shoes, thick socks, a neck ribbon, thick waistcoat, thick pants, old Kossuth hat, a linen sack.

Carry,—in an India-rubber knapsack, with a large flap, two shirts (check), one pair thick socks, one pair drawers, one flannel shirt, two pocket-handkerchiefs, a light India-rubber coat or a thick woollen one, two bosoms and collars to go and come with, one napkin, pins, needles, thread, one blanket, best gray, seven feet long.

Tent, six by seven feet, and four feet high in middle, will do; veil and gloves and insect-wash, or, better, mosquito-bars to cover all at night; best pocket-map, and perhaps description of the route; compass; plant-book and red blotting-paper; paper and stamps, botany, small pocket spy-glass for birds, pocket microscope, tape-measure, insect-boxes.

Axe, full size if possible, jackknife, fish-lines, two only apiece, with a few hooks and corks ready, and with pork for bait in a packet, rigged; matches (some also in a small vial in the waistcoat pocket); soap, two pieces; large knife and iron spoon (for all); three or four old newspapers, much twine, and several rags for dishcloths; twenty feet of strong cord, four-quart tin pail for kettle, two tin dippers, three tin plates, a fry-pan.

Provisions.—Soft hardbread, twenty-eight pounds; pork, sixteen pounds; sugar, twelve pounds; one pound black tea or three pounds coffee, one box or a pint of salt, one quart Indian meal, to fry fish in; six lemons, good to correct the pork and warm water; perhaps two or three pounds of rice, for variety. You will probably get some berries, fish, &c., beside.

A gun is not worth the carriage, unless you go as hunters. The pork should be in an open keg, sawed to fit; the sugar, tea or coffee, meal, salt, &c., should be put in separate water-tight India-rubber bags, tied with a leather string; and all the provisions, and part of the rest of the baggage, put into two large India-rubber bags, which have been proved to be water-tight and durable. Expense of preceding outfit is twenty-four dollars.

An Indian may be hired for about one dollar and fifty cents per day, and perhaps fifty cents a week for his canoe (this depends on the demand). The canoe should be a strong and tight one. This expense will be nineteen dollars.

Such an excursion need not cost more than twenty-five dollars apiece, starting at the foot of Moosehead, if you already possess or can borrow a reasonable part of the outfit. If you take an Indian and canoe at Oldtown, it will cost seven or eight dollars more to transport them to the lake.

VII. A LIST OF INDIAN WORDS.

1. *Katadn*, said to mean *Highest Land*. Rasles puts for mountain *Pemadené*; for *Grai, pierre à aiguiser, Kidadañgan*. (v. Potter.)

Mattawamkeag, place where two rivers meet. (Indian of carry.) (v. Williamson's History of Maine, and Willis.)

Molunkus.

Ebeeme, rock.

Noliseemack; other name, Shad Pond.

Kecunnilessu, chicadee.

Nipsquecohossus, woodcock.

Skuscumonsuk, kingfisher. Has it not the pl. termination *uk* here, or *suk*? } Joe.

Wassus, bear. *Aouessous*. Rasles.

Lunxus, Indian-devil.

Upahsis, mountain-ash.

Moose, (is it called, or does it mean, wood-eater?) *Mous*, Rasles.

Katahdinauguoh, said to mean mountains about Ktaadn.

Ebemena, tree-cranberry. *Ibimin, nar,* red, bad fruit. Rasles. } Joe.

Wighiggin, a bill or writing. *Aouixigan*,⎫ Indian of
"*Livre, lettre, peinture, écriture.*" Rasles. ⎭ carry.

Sebamook, Large-bay Lake. *Pegoua-*⎫
sebem; add *ar* for plural, *lac* or *étang.* ⎪ Nicholai.
Rasles. *Ouaṅrinaṅgamek, anse dans un* ⎬
lac. Rasles. *Mspame*, large water. Polis. ⎭

Sebago and *Sebec*, large open water.

Chesuncook, place where many ⎫
streams empty in. (v. Willis and Potter.) ⎪ Tahmunt,
Caucomgomoc, Gull Lake. (*Caucom-* ⎬ &c.
gomoc, the lake; *Caucomgomoc-took*, ⎪
the river, Polis.) ⎭

Pammadumcook.

Kenduskieg, Little Eel River. ⎫ Nicholai.
(v. Willis.) ⎭

Penobscot, Rocky River. *Pouapeskou*,⎫ Indian
stone. Rasles. (v. Springer.) ⎭ of carry.

Umbazookskus, meadow stream. ⎫
(Much-meadow river, Polis.) ⎪
Millinocket, place of Islands. ⎪
Souneunk, that runs between ⎬ Nicholai.
Mountains. ⎪
Aboljacarmegus, Smooth-ledge Falls ⎪
and Dead-water. ⎭

Aboljacarmeguscook, the river there.

Musketicook, Dead Stream. (Indian of
carry.) *Meskikou*, or *Meskikouikou*, a
place where there is grass. (Rasles.)
Muskéeticook, Dead water. (Polis.)

Mattahumkeag, Sand-creek Pond. ⎫ Nicholai.
Piscataquis, branch of a river. ⎭

Shecorways, sheldrakes. ⎫
Naramekechus, peetweet. ⎬ Polis.
Medawisla, loon. ⎭

Orignal, Moosehead Lake. (Montresor.)

Chor-chor-que, usnea.

Adelungquamooktum, wood-thrush.

Bematinichtik, high land generally. (Mountain, *Pemadené*, Rasles.)

Maquoxigil, bark of red osier, Indian tobacco.

} Polis.

Kineo, flint (Williamson); old Indian hunter (Hodge.)

Artoosoqu', phosphorescence.

Subekoondark, white spruce.

Skusk, black spruce.

Beskabekuk, the "Lobster Lake" of maps.

Beskabekukskishtook, the dead water below the island.

Paytaytequick, Burnt-Ground Stream, what Joe called *Ragmuff*.

Nonglangyis, the name of a dead-water between the last and Pine Stream.

Karsaootuk, Black River (or Pine Stream). *Mkazéouighen*, black. Rasles.

Michigan, fimus. Polis applied it to a sucker, or a poor, good-for-nothing fish. *Fiante* (?), *mitsegan*, Rasles. (Pickering puts the ? after the first word.)

Cowosnebagosar, Chiogenes hispidula; means, grows where trees have rotted.

Pockadunkquaywayle, echo. *Pagadaṅkouéouérre*. Rasles.

Bososquasis, moose-fly.

Nerlumskeechticook (or *quoik*?), (or *skeetcook*), Dead water, and applied to the mountains near.

Apmoojenegamook, lake that is crossed.

} Polis.

Allegash, hemlock-bark. (v. Willis.)

Paytaywecongomec, Burnt-Ground Lake, *Telos*.

Madunkehunk, Height-of-land Stream (Webster Stream).

Madunkehunk-gamooc, Height-of-land Lake.

Matungamooc, Grand Lake.

Uncardnerheese, Trout Stream.

Wassataquoik (or *-cook*), Salmon River, East Branch. (v. Willis.)

} Polis.

Pemoymenuk, Amelanchier berries. "*Pemouaïmin, nak*, a black fruit." Rasles. Has it not here the plural ending?

Sheepnoc, Lilium Canadense bulbs. "*Sipen, nak*, white, larger than *penak*." Rasles.

Paytgumkiss, Petticoat (where a small river comes into the Penobscot below Nickatow).

Burntibus, a lake-like reach in the Penobscot.

Passadumkeag, "where the water falls into the Penobscot above the falls." (Williamson.) *Pañsidañkioui* is, *au dessus de la montagne*. Rasles.

Olarmon, or *larmon*, (Polis) red paint. "Vermilion, paint, *Ourámañ*." Rasles.

Sunkhaze, "See canoe come out; no see 'em stream." (Polis.) The mouth of a river, according to Rasles, is *Sañghedétegoué*. The place where one stream empties into another, thus ⟨, is *sañktañoui*. (v. Willis.)

Tomhegan Brook (at Moosehead). "Hatchet, *temahígan*." Rasles.

Nickatow, "*Niketaoutegoué*, or *Niketoutegoué*, *rivière qui fourche*." Rasles.

2. *From WILLIAM WILLIS, on the Language of the Abnaquies. Maine Hist. Coll., Vol. IV.*

Abalajako-megus (river near Ktaadn).

Aitteon (name of a pond and sachem).

Apmogenegamook (name of a lake).

Allagash, a bark camp. Sockbasin, a Penobscot, told him, "The Indians gave this name to the lake from the fact of their keeping a hunting-camp there."

Bamonewengamock (head of Allagash), Cross Lake. (Sockbasin.)

Chesuncook, Big Lake. (Sockbasin.)

Caucongamock (a lake).

Ebeeme, mountains that have plums on them. (Sockbasin.)

Ktaadn. Sockbasin pronounced this Ka-tah-din, and said it meant "large mountain or large thing."

Kenduskeag, the place of Eels.

Kineo, flint, mountain on the border of Moosehead Lake.

Metawamkeag, a river with a smooth gravelly bottom. (Sockbasin.)

Metanawcook.

Millinoket, a lake with many islands in it. (Sockbasin.)

Matakeunk (river).

Molunkus (river).

Nicketow, *Neccotoh*, where two streams meet ("Forks of the Penobscot").

Negas (Indian village on the Kenduskeag).

Orignal (Montresor's name for Moosehead Lake).

Ponguongamook, Allagash, name of a Mohawk Indian killed there. (Sockbasin.)

Penobscot, *Penobskeag*, French *Pentagoet* or *Pentagovett*.

Pougohwakem (Heron Lake).

Pemadumcook (lake).

Passadumkeag, where water goes into the river above falls. (Williamson.)

Ripogenas (river).

Sunkhaze (river), Dead water.

Souneunk.

Seboomook. Sockbasin says this word means "the shape of a Moose's head, and was given to the lake which now bears the English name." *Howard* says differently.

Seboois, a brook, a small river. (Sockbasin.)

Sebec (river).

Sebago, great water.

Telos (lake).

Telasinis (lake).

Umbagog (lake), doubled up; so called from its form. (Sockbasin.)

Umbazookscus (lake).

Wassatiquoik, a mountain river. (Sockbasin.)

Judge C. E. Potter of Manchester, New Hampshire, adds in November, 1855:—

"*Chesuncook.* This is formed from *Chesunk*, or *Sehunk* (a goose), and *Auke* (a place), and means 'The Goose Place.' Chesunk, or Sehunk, is the sound made by the wild geese when flying."

Ktaadn. This is doubtless a corruption of *Kees* (high), and *Auke* (a place).

Penobscot, Penapse (stone, rock-place), and *Auke* (place).

Suncook, Goose-place, *Sehunk-auke.*

The Judge says that *schoot* means to rush, and hence *schoodic* from this and *auke* (a place where water rushes), and that *schoon* means the same; and that the Marblehead people and others have derived the words *scoon* and *scoot* from the Indians, and hence schooner; refers to a Mr. Chute.

THE END.

Index

Abbot (Me.), 88

Abenaki, church not, 7. *See also* Abnaquiois, Indians, Penobscot Indians

Abenaki Language, Dictionary of the, 139

Abenakis, gossip of, 136

Abies excelsa, 204. *See also* spruce, Norway

Abies nigra, 60. *See also* spruce, black

Abnaquiois, Jesuit expedition to the, 34. *See also* Abenaki

Aboljacarmegus, meaning of, 142

Aboljacarmegus Falls, 52; shooting, 74-75

Aboljacarmegus Lake, 46

Aboljacarmeguscook, meaning of, 142

Aboljacknagesic, meaning of, 142

Aboljacknagesic stream, 46, 54, 56

Acer striatum, 179. *See also* maple, striped; moose-wood

Adelungquamooktum, 168. *See also* wood-thrush

Adirondack country, moose in, 137

aianbé, 139

Aitteon, Governor [John], 149, 291

Aitteon, Joe, 85, 86, 189, 195, 211, 284, 320, 322; aids Thoreau's botanizing, 106; asks distance, 131; butchers moose, 116; calls moose, 101; cures moose-hide, 133; discusses Indian names, 140-42; disperses fire, 136; dress of, 90; eats viburnum, 105; examines moose signs, 110; finds

dead moose, 112; follows wounded moose, 111-13; leads moose hunt, 100-03; makes camp, 99; makes hunting horn, 137; makes moose call, 98; pitches canoe, 95; runs Pine-Stream Falls, 122; sees hedgehog, 117; skill in portaging of, 117; skins moose, 115-16; sleeps on river bank, 131; supports schools, 149; teaches Thoreau Indian words, 97; Thoreau meets, 89-90; Thoreau talks at night, 135; wanders off, 106

alder, hoary, 202; speckled, 96

alders, 98, 106

Allagash lakes, 72. *See also* Alleguash Lakes

Allagash River, 72; lumber of, 37. *See also* Allegash River

"Allegash and East Branch, The," 157-297

Allegash River, 235; effect of dam on, 231; head of, 211; intention to go down altered, 227; route of hunters, 161; Thoreau's party enters, 230; white-pine from, 145. *See also* Allagash River

Alleguash Lakes, 227. *See also* Allagash lakes

Allen, Ethan, 130

Alnus incana, 202. *See also* alder, hoary

Ambejijis Falls, 46, 76; path around, 47

Ambejijis Lake, 41, 42; beauty of, 44; boating on,

340　INDEX

Pamadumcook Lake, 27, 236; boating on, 41; loggers' use of, 43

Parish's Geography, 25

partridges, 106, 183; shot from buggy, 87

Passadumkeag (Me.), politicians at, 8

Passadumkeag River, 8, 294; passing the, 293

Passamagamet Falls, 46, 48, 76

Passamagamet Lake, 46

Passamagamet stream, 46

Passamaquoddy River, lumber of, 5

Paugus, 136, 222

Paytaytequick, 195. *See also* Ragmuff Stream

Paytaywecongomec Lake, 242. *See also* Telos Lake

Peaked Mountain, 230

peetweets, 132, 164

Pemoymenuk, 277. *See also service* berries

Pennyweight, Old John, 149

Penobscot, meaning of, 141

Penobscot Indians, fight with Mohawks, of, 292; home of, 83; sociability of, 291-92. *See also* Abenakis, Indians

Penobscot River, 36, 37, 141; altitude of, 94; arriving at over Northeast Carry, 188; ascending, 6-28; between Moosehead and Chesuncook, 105; carrying to, 93; crossing at Oldtown, 150; embarking on, 95, 189; end of ascent of, 55; falls of the, 4; Grand Falls of the, 28, 29; head of, 211; height-of-land above, 216; importance of, 82; lakes of, 3; length of, 72; main log boom on, 296; near source of, 246;

Northeast Carry to, 183; plan to ascend, 158; plan to return by, 159; returning to, 98, 131; sawmills on, 5; skill in ascending, 49; sources of, 175; white-pine coming down, 145. *See also* East Branch, West Branch

Penobscot Valley, 86

Pepe, 208

perch, red, 265, 267

Philadelphia (Pa.), 197

phosphorescent wood, 179-81

pickerel, 80

Pickering [John], 322

pigeon-woodpecker, 16, 25, 131. *See also* woodpecker, pigeon

pills, Brandreth's, 290

pine, 108; Banks', 268; grey, 268; higher uses of, 121; immortality of, 122; Labrador, 268; Norway, 286; now uncommon, 213; red, 209-10, 243, 269; scrub, 268; white, 21, 109, 209-10, 252. *See also* pine-trees, white-pine, white-pine-tree

Pine Stream, 109, 195; moose dead in, 112; returning down, 122

Pine Stream Dead-water, 109

Pine-Stream Falls, 122, 195-96

pine-forest, primitive, 153

pine-trees, stealing from public lands, 145

Pinus Banksiana, 268

Pinus resinosa, 243, 269. *See also* pine, red

pioneers, life of, 124-27; intelligence of, 22

pipe, of birch bark, 285

Piscataquis, meaning of, 142

Piscataquis Falls, 292

Editorial Appendix

Notes on Illustrations

Portrait of Thoreau   following page 376

Daguerreotype portrait of Thoreau by Benjamin D. Maxham, Worcester, Massachusetts, mid-June 1856. The following summer Thoreau was to make his third and final Maine expedition, the difficult canoe trip described in "The Allegash and East Branch."–Photocopy, Mr. Leonard F. Kleinfeld.

Map of Maine

A section of G. W. Coffin's "A Plan of the Public Lands in the State of Maine" (1835), the most reliable map of upper Maine available to Thoreau and the one he used on his Chesuncook and Allegash excursions. The portion reproduced includes all areas in what Thoreau called the "woods" proper through which he travelled in the expeditions of 1846, 1853, and 1857.–Public Record Office, London, C.O. 700 Maine 21.

"Chesuncook," a manuscript page of the
        Atlantic Monthly version

The last page, numbered 87, of the "Chesuncook" manuscript section that Thoreau sent to James Russell Lowell for the *Atlantic Monthly* on March 5, 1858. Text appears on page 122 of the present edition. The pencil mark after "tallow that" (line 12) is not authorial, but everything else on the page is in Thoreau's hand, including an erased pencil notation, "When the chopper" after "above me still," and the notice of continuation at the bottom. The *Atlantic*'s omission of the sentence beginning "It is as immortal as I am" caused the rupture of Thoreau's relationship with Lowell.–Houghton Library, Harvard University.

"The Allegash and East Branch," a page of the
        final draft

Text appears on pages 263-264 of the present edition.
Numerous pencil revisions by the author are discernible beneath the ink overdraft in Sophia Thoreau's
finer handwriting; but the page number and all save
one of the expansions of Thoreau's "Mt" and "mt(s)"
are in Sophia's hand only. The encircled "17A" in the
lower left corner refers to a folder in which this and
related leaves are stored.—Houghton Library, Harvard
University.

"Ktaadn," a page of the first version

A page of the 1848 *Union Magazine* publication of
"Ktaadn" with Thoreau's pencil corrections and revisions.—Berg Collection, New York Public Library.

Acknowledgments

So NUMEROUS are the persons who have contributed to this project and so diverse have been the forms of their assistance that I cannot hope to record my debts fully in this brief note. I express my gratitude, however inadequately, to the staff of the Miriam Lutcher Stark Library at the University of Texas, especially Mrs. June Moll and Mrs. Sally Leach; Mr. R. W. Franklin, Curator of the Abernethy Library of American Literature, Middlebury College; Mr. James Laughton, Curator of Manuscripts, Boston Public Library; Mr. Stuart C. Sherman, John Hay Librarian, Brown University; Mr. Herbert Cahoon and the staff of the Pierpont Morgan Library; Dr. Lola L. Szladits and the late John D. Gordan of the Berg Collection, New York Public Library; the staffs of the Houghton Library and the Henry E. Huntington Library and Art Gallery; Mr. Albert E. Lownes; John F. Jaques; Peter Swiggart; Lewis Leary; my Texas colleagues David DeLaura, William B. Todd, and Warner Barnes; and my fellow Thoreau editors, above all Editor-in-Chief Walter Harding.

Permission to use manuscripts and other unique materials in the preparation of this volume has been generously given by the Pierpont Morgan Library, the Berg Collection of the New York Public Library, the Boston Public Library, the Houghton and Widener Memorial libraries of Harvard University, the Henry E. Huntington Library, the Abernethy Library, the Brown University Library, and the Alderman Library of the University of Virginia.

I am particularly indebted to the University of Texas Research Institute for a summer grant in 1964, when I began my study of the *Maine Woods* manuscripts, and for supplementary funds in 1968-1969; to the John Simon Guggenheim Memorial Foundation, through whose generosity I was freed from other tasks for the academic year 1968-1969 to complete the major work on this volume; to the National Endowment for the Humanities; and to the Center for Editions of American Authors, whose Executive Committee awarded me a summer research fellowship in 1969 to bring the introductory matter and documentation into final form and to continue my related editorial work on Thoreau's journal.

And finally I thank my wife, Mickey, whose direct contributions to this seven-year enterprise have been extensive, and whose personal support surpasses all measure.

Textual Introduction

THE MAINE WOODS, Thoreau's second post-humous volume, was published by Ticknor and Fields of Boston on May 28, 1864. A composite work like its predecessor, *Excursions* (1863), *The Maine Woods* contained two narrative papers that had been published during Thoreau's lifetime, plus a third essay and an appendix of botanical and other data that now first appeared in print. Beyond question, however, Thoreau intended to issue the four parts as a single volume: he left a rough plan for the organization of the essays and a statement of their collective title, and he drew on all three chapters for his appendix materials. At the time of his death he was perfecting the third narrative, "The Allegash and East Branch." According to his friend William Ellery Channing his last intelligible words, spoken less than an hour before he expired on May 6, 1862, were "moose" and "Indians."[1]

The task of putting "The Allegash" in order and seeing the volume through the press fell to Channing and Thoreau's sister, Sophia. The contribution each made is difficult to assess. Sophia formalized some pencil revisions on the last working drafts by writing over them in ink (either before or after Thoreau's death, or both), and in all likelihood she transcribed at least part of "The Allegash" for Ticknor and Fields. Of Channing's role nothing specific has been recorded; he seems to have taken the publication lightly, for his copy of the first edition (now in the New York

[1] Channing, *Thoreau: The Poet-Naturalist* (Boston: Roberts Brothers, 1873), p. 319.

Public Library's Berg Collection) is pristine, and the inscription, "W. E. Channing From his grateful friend S. E. Thoreau," has been erased—presumably by Channing himself.

Questions of individual responsibility aside, the first edition *Maine Woods* was shoddily edited.[2] At several points in "The Allegash" a copyist or compositor misread Thoreau's handwriting ("beaked" for "headed," "bend" for "head," "*minatus*" for "*sinuatus*," "or the boat" for "on the bank," to name a few); and a passage amounting to two and a half pages of printed text was mislocated by some ten pages. This placement blunder, which caused a geographical shift of twenty miles forward and backward, and a temporal lurch of two days, could have resulted from the shuffling or dropping of the manuscript while Sophia was at work on it or after it had been delivered to Ticknor and Fields. The proofreader was evidently unfamiliar with upper Maine geography, and the error was to stand uncorrected and perhaps even unremarked for a quarter century, through no fewer than sixteen reimpressions from the original stereotype plates.

Despite Thoreau's weaknesses as a proofreader, it seems fair to assume that had he been able to supervise publication, the 1864 *Maine Woods* would have been a far more satisfactory volume. As it was, he lacked time before he died even to prepare a printer's-copy manuscript of "The Allegash." He revised "Ktaadn," expanding the text with several footnotes and major insertions. "Chesuncook" received minimal attention: Thoreau corrected an error or two, restored

2 It may also have been poorly set before stereotyping, for the Ticknor and Fields cost-books record an extraordinary hundred hours of labor, costing $48.20, for "Correcting" and "Correcting plates."

a sentence that had been expurgated in the first publication, added another sentence, and deleted a passage based on his misidentification of a bird species.
But the history of *The Maine Woods* begins some
fifteen years before those last revisions were drafted,
and eighteen before the appearance of the Ticknor
and Fields volume. It is a chronicle of experience,
composition, and publication spanning Thoreau's
most creative period.

"Ktaadn"

Thoreau alludes briefly in *Walden* to his having
spent "a fortnight in the woods of Maine" during his
second year's residence at the pond. He composed the
first draft of "Ktaadn" shortly after returning from
Bangor in mid-September 1846, and completed the
essay not long after his removal from Walden the
next autumn. On October 24, 1847, he wrote to
Sophia, who was visiting their Thatcher relatives in
Bangor, to thank her for accounts of trips to Mount
Katahdin that she had clipped and sent to him.[3] Two
months later he informed Emerson, then in England,
that he was about to read a Lyceum lecture on his
"expedition to Maine," and on January 12 he reported
that the lecture, which contained "many facts and
some poetry," had been well received by "a large
audience of men and boys." Thoreau had described,
offered, and perhaps already sent the finished essay
to Horace Greeley by April 3, 1848: on that date
Greeley volunteered to seek a more profitable outlet

[3] George A. Thatcher, Thoreau's cousin, had been one of
his companions on the trip to the mountain. The two others
not called by name in "Ktaadn" were Bangor men with lumber interests. Thoreau identifies them as "Lowell[l]" and
"Raish" (?—the writing is indistinct) in a draft of the essay.
Lowell is mentioned again in the 1853 journal.

for it than his own New York *Tribune*. Sending
Thoreau a $25 advance payment on the 17th, Greeley
observed, "It is rather long for my columns and too
fine for the million; but I consider it a cheap bargain,
and shall print it myself if I do not dispose of it to
better advantage." A month later the journalist expressed his hope of placing "Ktaadn" in "a new
magazine of high character that will pay," and
Thoreau, in his answering letter of May 19, again
hinted that Greeley himself publish it: "If more convenient the Maine article might be printed in the
form of letters; you have only to leave off at the end
of a day, and put the date before the next one."
Greeley's efforts must have borne fruit soon thereafter, for the first of five installments of "Ktaadn, and
the Maine Woods" appeared in the July issue of John
Sartain's *Union Magazine of Literature and Art*, edited
by Caroline M. Kirkland. Thoreau wrote to George
Thatcher on August 24, enclosing "the third part, as
they have chosen to call it, of that everlasting mountain story," and complaining that the *Union Magazine*
had failed to provide him with free copies for distribu-
tion despite a supposed agreement that it would. He
was unhappy, furthermore, about the serial publication, which he thought fragmented the narrative with
ill effect: "It should have been printed all together
in some large newspaper—then it would have gone
down in one dose by its very gravity."[4]

It would appear that Thoreau did not proofread
"Ktaadn, and the Maine Woods," for the essay contains many conspicuous errors which could hardly
have escaped his notice, such as "boys" for "bags,"

[4] Quotations from letters by and to Thoreau are taken from
The Correspondence of Henry David Thoreau, Walter Harding
and Carl Bode, eds. (New York: New York University Press,
1958).

"swallows" for "shallows," and "scows" for "æons."
Perhaps the *Union Magazine*'s tight printing schedule
and the distance between New York and Concord
precluded any opportunity for proofreading by the
author. Thoreau did, however, correct *Union Magazine* copy after the fact. On a set of "Ktaadn" pages
cut from the magazine and loosely sewn together—
possibly a copy he presented to a friend or relative—
he entered marginal corrections for some of the more
egregious blunders and made a few stylistic revisions
as well. The manuscript notations on this copy, which
is now in the Berg Collection, cannot be reliably
dated; but since they include none of the references to
sources published during the 1850s which Thoreau
incorporated in the 1864 publication, it would seem
that these notations were entered within a year or
two of the 1848 printing. At a later date, certainly
after 1851 and probably after 1857, he prepared
another set of *Union Magazine* "Ktaadn" pages to
serve as printer's copy for *The Maine Woods*. The later
set, now lost, contained most of the corrections and
revisions made on the Berg Collection copy and many
additional alterations. Included among these changes
were insertions of such length as to require supplementary sheets.

No textual significance is attached to "Ktaadn" extracts from the *Union Magazine* that were printed in
the New York *Tribune*, November 17 and 18, 1848,
and in *The Student*, January 1849.

"Chesuncook"

In September 1853 Thoreau made his second trip
to the Maine backwoods, again accompanied by
George Thatcher (who wanted to shoot a moose) and
guided by the Indian lumberman Joe Aitteon. From

his journal record he prepared a lecture about Moose-head Lake, which he read before the Concord Lyceum on December 14. Eleven months later, he advised the corresponding secretary of a lecture society that he was at liberty for the evening of December 5, 1854, "and will read you a lecture either on the Wild or on Moosehunting as you may prefer." The editors of Thoreau's correspondence conjecture that "a complete article of fifty-seven pages" sent by Thoreau to *Putnam's Monthly Magazine* on December 2, 1853 was probably "Chesuncook." If this submission was a narrative of Thoreau's second Maine excursion, however, it was a much shorter version than the one he published in 1858. It may have been the "Moose-head Lake" lecture of the same month, but no manuscript of an *Ur*-"Chesuncook" or other evidence has been found to support the conjecture.

When in January of 1858 James Russell Lowell, editor of the new *Atlantic Monthly*, solicited a Maine narrative for his magazine, Thoreau had already made his third excursion and had written at least an initial draft of "The Allegash and East Branch." Either directly or through Emerson, Lowell asked Thoreau for the more recent account, but the author demurred on the grounds that his guide Joe Polis, "whose words & deeds I report very faithfully," might read it and take offense. He offered instead the "Chesuncook" account, "the subjects of which are the Moose, the Pine Tree, & the Indian," and told Lowell that it ran to "about one hundred manuscript pages." In producing fair copy for the *Atlantic*, however, he far exceeded his estimate. The first half, sent to Lowell on March 5, 1858, totaled eighty-seven manuscript pages. Thoreau then judged the remainder (on which he was still working) as "about 50 pages," but this portion must have covered at least as many sheets as the first.

In the letter accompanying the first package of "Chesuncook" manuscript (from 84.1 to 122.20 in the present edition) Thoreau made his earliest recorded suggestion that the Maine narratives would be gathered as a book. "I reserve the right," he advised Lowell, "to publish it in another form after it has appeared in your magazine." He also specifically requested that the proofs be sent to him "on account of Indian names, &c." The first installment (from 84.1 to 108.34) appeared in the June issue—to Thoreau's annoyance, for he had been given neither proofsheets nor notice of a publication date in time to insist that they be sent. He wrote to Lowell on May 18, "The proofs, for which I *did* ask in the note which accompanied the ms, would have been an all sufficient 'Bulletin.'" His manuscript had, in fact, been rather freely modified in the *Atlantic* offices, and he may have feared that similar liberties, or worse, would be taken with the rest. On the same date he sent Lowell the second half of the manuscript with another request to be allowed "a sight of the proofs." Proofsheets for the second installment, scheduled for the July issue, were duly delivered to Thoreau, who made some restorations "of comparatively little importance" and one major one. A sentence on the immortality of the pine tree had been marked for deletion and Thoreau instructed that the cancellation be reversed.[5] By June 22 Thoreau had received the

---

[5] Information about both Lowell's editorial markings and Thoreau's instructions on these proofsheets, which have not survived, is obtained from Thoreau's letter to Lowell, June 22, 1858. It is not inconceivable that some differences between the second installment and the corresponding section of extant fair copy were changes ordered by Thoreau on the proofs.

new number and found that the pine-tree sentence was missing. Abandoning both courtesy and grammar, he shot off an angry note to Lowell: "When I received the proof of that portion of my story printed in the July number . . . I was surprised to find that the sentence—'It is as immortal as I am, and perchance will go to as high a heaven, there to tower above me still.' . . . have been crossed out, and it occurred to me that, after all, it was of some consequence that I should see the proofs; supposing, of course, that my 'Stet' &c in the margin would be respected. . . . However, I have just noticed that that sentence was, in a very mean and cowardly manner, omitted. . . . If you do not sanction [the omission]— or whether you do or not—will you do me the justice to print that sentence, as an omitted one, indicating its place, in the August number?" Although the request had the weight of a demand, Lowell ignored it. There is no extant correspondence between the two men about the third and last installment. Since Thoreau's hiking trip to the White Mountains took him out of Concord from July 2 until noon on the 19th, he may have entrusted the reading of third-installment proof to another. We may be fairly certain, however, that this section (130.36 through 156.34 in the present edition) contains no major changes from the lost fair copy. Thoreau wrote twice more to Lowell, on September 1 and October 4, 1858, icily asking that the *Atlantic* pay him the $198 owed for the essay. The pine-tree sentence, slightly revised from its original form, was restored in the 1864 *Maine Woods*, and an *Atlantic* passage about the myrtle warbler was deleted for reasons discussed in a textual note. Only seven further substantive changes were made from the *Atlantic* version, and of these only two are indubitably authorial. The marked

Atlantic "Chesuncook" pages that served as printer's copy for the posthumous volume have disappeared.

"The Allegash and East Branch" and "Appendix"

Thoreau's ambitious excursion to the headwaters of the Allagash River and down the wild East Branch Penobscot, which he would record in his third Maine essay, was undertaken on short notice in the summer of 1857. He informed Thatcher on July 11 that he wished to begin "within 10 days," and asked whether Thatcher's son Charles would be one of the party. He had also invited Eben Loomis of Cambridgeport and expected him to accept, though as it turned out Loomis did not make the journey. "If Charles cannot go," Thoreau wrote, "we may find another man here, or possibly take an Indian. A friend of mine [apparently H. G. O. Blake] would like to accompany me, but I think that he has neither woodcraft nor strength enough." When Thoreau set out for Bangor on July 20, his companion was Edward Hoar, a longtime Concord acquaintance. For a guide they employed the Indian aristocrat Joe Polis.

That Thoreau had completed the basic work on "The Allegash" by the time he sent "Chesuncook" to James Russell Lowell is indicated by his correspondence and by certain manuscript remains. He reported to Thatcher on January 1, 1858, that he had "written out a long account" of the excursion, "part of which I shall read to our Lyceum—but I do not know how soon I shall print it." Three weeks later he told Lowell that for the sake of his relationship with Polis he could not provide an "Allegash" article, but not long after the final "Chesuncook" installment appeared in the *Atlantic* he wrote to George William Curtis of *Putnam's,* "I am glad if you are not weary of the Maine Woods, partly because I have another and a larger slice to come."

For "Chesuncook" Thoreau drew upon various journal passages related to or inspired by the 1857 trip, and in "The Allegash" he incorporated some material from the 1853 Maine journal. Didactic passages on the need for conservation that were to appear separately in "Chesuncook" and "The Allegash" occur contiguously in fragmentary drafts that seem to date from Thoreau's composition of "Chesuncook" in the late winter and spring of 1858. Just after the pine-tree sentence in the preserved fair-copy section of "Chesuncook" Thoreau wrote in pencil, and then erased, "When the chopper"; a passage in "The Allegash" dealing with the lumberman's blindness to the unmarketable values of trees includes a sentence beginning "When the chopper would praise a pine. . . ."

From surviving "Allegash" drafts in the Henry E. Huntington Library and the Houghton Library of Harvard University it is apparent that when Thoreau died he left something very much like a finished (though not a fair) copy of the last essay. Cancelled passages on these sheets do not appear in the 1864 publication, the order of paragraphs is final, and the wording duplicates that of the first edition in all but a few particulars. The essay's title was determined at a late stage: on the ten-page Huntington draft of the beginning of the piece Thoreau wrote "The Allegash and Webster Stream East Branch," and then cancelled "Webster Stream." The before-mentioned organization plan in the Houghton Library has "The Allegash and Webster Stream," with "Webster Stream" struck out and "East Branch" entered in Sophia Thoreau's hand. Late draft comparable to the Huntington manuscript in its similarity to the published chapter survives among the Houghton worksheets for eighteen whole or partial pages of first-edition text. Six continuous sections of "The Allegash" are represented in these manuscripts. Like the Huntington fragment, they are ink drafts with pencil cancellations and insertions in Thoreau's autograph. Another hand—Sophia Thoreau's—has rewritten many pencil notations in ink. Sophia also expanded abbreviations and numerals, and occasionally changed the wording where no revision is discernible in the pencil substratum. Clearly those sheets on which Sophia's markings appear are the last versions on which her brother was able to work; and it is usually irrelevant whether she set her hand to them before or after his death.[6] The highest importance, then, attaches to these Huntington and Houghton library leaves, for they are all that remain of Thoreau's last draft of "The Allegash and East Branch."

The 1864 *Maine Woods* "Allegash" text was set from a manuscript, now lost, which was at least partially copied from Thoreau's last draft; the scribe was probably Sophia. Although the Huntington and Houghton leaves were apparently superseded by non-authorial copies, the remainder of the printer's manuscript may have been fairly clean pages in Thoreau's hand that Sophia thought it unnecessary to transcribe. This hypothesis is elaborated in part two of the textual introduction.

[6] The exceptions include erasures of pencil revisions, for which responsibility cannot be assigned, and a few alterations entirely in Sophia's hand that might just possibly have been dictated by Thoreau. It is inconceivable that he himself recopied these pages. Moreover, if a copy prepared by his sister was read to him or set before him, he could not have been able to correct it effectively, for the 1864 text corresponding to these last-draft pages contains variations that result from a copyist's misreadings of Thoreau's hand. Sophia's own penmanship is perfectly legible.

Given the large number of errors and nonauthorial changes in the printed "Allegash" as compared with the extant last-draft fragments, one would expect the "Appendix," had it been set from working manuscript recopied after Thoreau's death, to contain many more errata than it does. If Thoreau's last "Appendix" manuscript was reasonably clean and legible, there would have been no need to transcribe it for the printer; if the manuscript was rough, an intervening stage of transmission by a scribe would have introduced a multitude of blunders. But despite its technical character, the 1864 "Appendix" is a fairly accurate publication. (Most of the mistakes which do exist are misspellings of Indian terms in the final section, terms which, even in Thoreau's most careful longhand, could easily have been misread by a compositor. This section also contains print duplications of a Thoreauvian abbreviation, underscored "Mt.," which Sophia regularly expanded when she retouched pages of Thoreau's manuscript and which she would presumably have expanded in a transcription.) The present editor therefore believes that Thoreau's last "Appendix" manuscript was not subjected to an intermediate transcription, but served directly as printer's copy for the Ticknor and Fields text. Nothing remains of an "Appendix" printer's copy, in either Thoreau's or another's hand.

The botanical portions of the "Appendix" derive from Thoreau's scattered notations on Maine trees, flowers, and shrubs in the "Chesuncook" and "Allegash" journal drafts, and more particularly from a four-page prose section on plant habitats and a ten-page formal plant list, both in the 1857 journal and dated, respectively, October 3 and 8. The bird and quadruped lists were drawn from the "Chesuncook" and "Allegash" journal narratives and/or from the

printed "Chesuncook" text and Thoreau's late "Allegash" drafts. "Outfit for an Excursion" is anticipated
by a letter about routes, costs, provisions, and equipment for a Maine river trip, which Thoreau sent to
Thomas Wentworth Higginson on January 28, 1858.
Related manuscripts include detailed lists of equipment and supplies drafted in the journal for July 19,
1858, and August 9, 1860, just after Thoreau's trips
to the White Mountains and Mount Monadnock. Another version of the 1858 journal list was sent on
July 15, 1861, to a Worcester minister planning a
mountain excursion. In preparing "A List of Indian
Words," the final "Appendix" section, Thoreau employed his working copies of the *Union Magazine*
"Ktaadn" and the *Atlantic Monthly* "Chesuncook,"
plus his late "Allegash" draft: the order of Indian
terms and place-names closely follows that of their
appearance in the three finished essays. He also consulted the 1853 and 1857 Maine journals for a few
terms not included in the essay texts. No manuscript
copy by Thoreau has been found for most of the
definitions he extracted from printed works on Abnaki
language; he may have transcribed directly from these
sources when he wrote fair copy of the "List."

The Maine Woods

The 1864 first edition of *The Maine Woods* was
printed from stereotype plates in an impression of
1,450 copies.[7] The plates were cast and printed by
Welch, Bigelow and Company for Ticknor and Fields,
and the volume was bound in cloth of various colors
and designs. Its pages, 16mo in size, collate [*i-viii*],

[7] Details about the production of *The Maine Woods*, the
first printing, and reimpressions through 1880 are taken from
the manuscript cost-books of Ticknor and Fields, volumes 4-11
(Houghton Library MS Am 1185.6).

[1]2-328. Page *iii* is the titlepage, page *iv* bears the copyright and imprint, page *v* identifies the prior publication of the first two essays, and page *vii* is a table of contents. Pages *i*, *vi*, and *viii* are blank; page *ii* contains a priced list of "Mr. Thoreau's Writings." "Ktaadn" begins on page 1, "Chesuncook" on page 85, "The Allegash and East Branch" on page 161, and the "Appendix" text on page 307. Page 305, unnumbered, is a simple titlepage for the "Appendix." The gatherings collate π^4 1-13^{12} 14^8, and are also signed π^4 A-T^8 U^4. A twenty-four-page publisher's list, dated either April 1864 or June 1864, and printed from independent plates or type, is bound in after the text.

In August of the same year an impression of 520 copies was made, called the "Second Edition" on the copyright page; the two copies consulted lack advertising matter at the end and prices in the list of Thoreau's writings. Subsequent impressions—consecutively numbered "editions"—were ordered by Ticknor and Fields in October 1865 (520 copies, titlepage dated 1866) and July 1868 (290 copies). Apart from normal print wear, the only changes noticeable in the plates through these impressions are the alterations of publication date and "edition" designation and the removal after 1866 of the list facing the titlepage. A printing of 100 copies is recorded for March 1871, but no actual copy has been located; since the firm's title changed during that year from Fields, Osgood and Company to James R. Osgood and Company, the impression may bear either name. The next impression was made in 1872 and consisted of 104 copies, the titlepage bearing the device and publisher's title of James R. Osgood and Company. Between the 1868 and 1872 impressions a further alteration occurs: the table of contents is moved to page *v* and the note on prior publication to page *vii*. This rearrangement was

to prevail in all subsequent printings. Impressions of
150 copies each were produced for Osgood in October
1873, September 1875, and July 1877. The firm's
name was changed in 1878 to Houghton, Osgood and
Company, and an undated cost-book entry, presumably for that year, records an impression of 174
copies. This would have been the "tenth edition" by
the Ticknor line's designations, but no copy has been
located. However, a copy of the next impression bears
the legend "Tenth Edition" and the date 1880; the
cost-book records the printing of 175 copies in January 1880. The 1878 (?) and 1880 entries do not
duplicate one another, and it is impossible to tell,
until a copy is found, whether the former printing
was issued as a second "ninth edition" or under some
other designation. Type batter continued: the loss of
a dot from the series after "List of Birds" in the 1880
table of contents is a convenient reference for confirming later printings from the plates.

With the organization of Houghton, Mifflin and
Company in 1880 the cost-book record ceases, so that
the size of later *Maine Woods* impressions cannot be
determined. They came, however, with increasing
frequency, stimulated perhaps by the touring and
sporting boom Maine enjoyed in the 1880s. In 1881,
preserving the "edition" sequence, Houghton, Mifflin
printed the "eleventh." No copies of the next two impressions have been discovered, but the present editor has examined a "fourteenth" dated 1883, a "fifteenth" probably of 1884, and a "sixteenth" probably
of 1885.[8] The "seventeenth edition" can be dated be-

[8] William Ellery Channing asserts in a footnote in the enlarged edition of *Thoreau: The Poet-Naturalist* (F. B. Sanborn,
ed. [Boston: Charles E. Goodspeed, 1902], p. 8) that *The Maine
Woods* had gone through sixteen "editions" in 1883. But
Channing must have misremembered this detail. It is surprising enough that the publishers issued four impressions in

tween late 1885 and early 1887 on the basis of advertisements, bound in at the end, for published and pending volumes in Houghton, Mifflin's American Men of Letters and American Statesmen series.

The next impression located by the present editor (in three copies) is dated 1889 but lacks an edition designation, as do all later printings from the Ticknor and Fields stereotypes. Between the "seventeenth edition" and the 1889 impression the plates were significantly altered. The misplaced "Allegash" material on pages 282-285 of the earlier printings was properly positioned following the sentence "We made a second carry . . . below this" on (original) page 295. Whoever ordered the correction probably had access to Thoreau's manuscripts, for the revised paragraphing follows that in the journal. The changes were effected with minimal typesetting but a great deal of surgery on the plates for pages 282-295. That portion of original page 285 containing the dateline "Friday, July 31" and the following nine-line paragraph was excised and soldered onto page 282, replacing "On the mainland . . . took the wind out." Next, the plates for the remaining lower part of original page 285, all of pages 286-294, and page 295 through the sentence "I bore the sign . . . voyage" were counted out into normal thirty-three line pages, divested of their running heads, page numbers, and signatures, and cut and soldered into new pages. A paragraph was then freshly set that contained the first sentence of the short paragraph on original page 295 ("We made . . . below this") and the one-sentence paragraph on original page 282 ("On the mainland . . . noticed before").

---

three years (the eleventh through fourteenth, 1881-1883); it is hardly credible that the next two were made in the same year as the fourteenth.

This new section was affixed to the last of the re-
formed pages described above. Now the final seven
lines of original page 282, all of page 283, and all but
the last line of page 284 were shorn of their running
heads and page numbers, sliced to appropriate new
lengths, and rejoined into pages. In a second resetting
of matter, the last line of original page 284, the first
three lines of page 285, and the sentence on page 295
beginning "It rained hard" were combined into a new
paragraph, and the section was attached to the last
of the re-formed pages after "I stirred . . . an emetic."
This newly set section also included the final two
lines on page 295, although they did not need reposi-
tioning. Finally, the old running heads and page numbers were soldered onto the re-formed and doctored
pages, which could now be properly located in the
forme. The final product is remarkably neat: the
unaided eye cannot detect the differences in spacing
between those lines originally at the bottom of one
page and those originally at the top of the next, as
compared to the spacing of lines adjacent in both the
original and the corrected plates.

In the course of these reorganizations, the workers
made three minor changes in the same sequence of
pages, apparently by adding slugs to the old metal. A
colon at the end of the line after "season" on page
282, just before the first relocated paragraph, had
been lost due to plate batter and was now replaced
with a semicolon. A hyphen was provided in the space
after "a" in "a berrying" on original page 286. On
original page 292 a hyphen after "per" at the end of the
line had been lost through plate wear; this was replaced. Hand collation of pages 282-295 from the original and corrected plates and Hinman machine collation where that was possible in these pages have

disclosed no other changes.[9] The 1889 printing was issued with new titlepage and copyright page, and impressions dated 1891 and 1892 were made from the corrected plates. The last was probably the final printing from the Ticknor and Fields stereotypes, as *The Maine Woods* was entirely recomposed the following year for the Riverside Edition of 1894.

Francis H. Allen, Thoreau's bibliographer and an editor of the 1906 Walden Edition, wrote prior to May 29, 1921, to another Thoreauvian, Edwin B. Hill, about the modification of the text. In a letter to Julian W. Abernethy on that date, Hill quoted Allen as follows:

> I want to ask if you know anything about an interpolation I discovered in the "Maine Woods" a few weeks ago. Some time between 1883 and the publication of the Riverside edition—probably in the Riverside edition itself, but I haven't seen anything later than 1883 in the old 12mo to refer to—there crept in about two pages of new matter. This is in the Allegash chapter under date of August 1. It begins with the sentence "On the mainland were Norway pines," etc. (second section of the paragraph beginning, "We made a second carry") and stops before the last sentence under the date of August 1, which begins "It rained hard." I suppose this must have been found in some draft of the chapter or bit of Thoreau MS, and put in to make it more complete. Perhaps it was one of Sanborn's contributions. . . .

Allen was mistaken, of course, about the source and nature of the change—it was by no means an "inter-

[9] One cannot rule out the possibility that the platemakers prepared molds from some or all of these corrected plates and cast new stereotypes (in which event soldering of the cut edges might not have been necessary). But except in the specified places no new type was used: the battered faces of the immediately preceding "editions" are reproduced in the corrected impression.

polation" of "new matter"—and in his conjecture about the change having first been made in the Riverside Edition. His guess that F. B. Sanborn was responsible for the alteration is probably also wrong. By 1950, in a pamphlet entitled *Thoreau's Editors: History and Reminiscence* (Thoreau Society Booklet, number 7), Allen had realized that the textual change was a relocation of misplaced matter rather than an interpolation; but he now asserted categorically that the correction was made in the 1893 resetting of *The Maine Woods* for the Riverside Edition, and he attributed it to Horace E. Scudder.

Despite its matrix of fallacies, Allen's last statement may be true. Scudder might have had access to Thoreau's journal, from which the correct paragraphing could be determined, and he might well have begun work toward the Riverside *Maine Woods* before the 1889 impression. Further, he would have had a lively enough interest in the form of the text to persuade the publisher to make expensive corrections in the worn old plates less than five years before an anticipated resetting of the entire volume. It is difficult to imagine, however, that Scudder (or whoever planned the changes) was the first to notice the dislocation; anyone who knows the geography of the area or who reads the original text with a Maine map before him should be struck by the spatial lurch forward and back. By a very conservative estimate, 5,000 copies had been printed from the original plates prior to 1889—approximately 3,700 are documented through the "tenth edition" of 1880, with which the production records end. Many of these copies doubtless served as backwoods Baedekers for sportsmen and tourists, since even before the 1880s the Maine wilderness was a fashionable vacation retreat. Was the publisher's attention ever called to the error during the period of the first seventeen "editions"? If it was, why was the correction not made sooner? Unfortunately, these teasing questions cannot be answered.

A lesser curiosity of the 1889 plate-alterations concerns Houghton, Mifflin's decision to make three small changes—the semicolon after "season," the hyphen in "a-berrying," and the line-end hyphen after "per"—while ignoring numerous errors of far greater significance elsewhere in "The Allegash." Perhaps, like the cat in "Chesuncook" which did not run up a tree, the corrector was "bewildered by the very crowd of opportunities." More likely he studied only those pages involved in the relocation of misplaced matter.

The Riverside Edition *Maine Woods*, copyright 1892 and 1893 by Houghton, Mifflin and Company, was published in large-paper and trade forms with the titlepage dated 1894. According to Francis Allen's *Bibliography of Henry David Thoreau* (Boston: Houghton Mifflin Company, 1908), the actual publication took place in 1893. Set from a marked copy of one of the corrected reimpressions of the Ticknor and Fields plates, the new edition has no textual authority. Most of its variations from the earlier text are matters of modernized or regularized style—for instance, "traveler" for "traveller," "*i.e.*," for "i.e." and "etc." for occasional "&c." The editor normalized certain inconsistencies of spelling (e.g., "batteau" vs. "bateau" and a few place-names), and corrected some obvious errors of punctuation and spelling. There is no evidence that he consulted manuscripts or other authoritative early materials. During recomposition several new errors of wording entered the text.

The Maine Woods was again completely reset for its appearance as the third volume of Houghton Mifflin and Company's Walden Edition of Thoreau in 1906. (This twenty-volume publication was also issued in large paper as the Manuscript Edition, with a leaf of Thoreau's autograph mounted in volume 1.) The 1906 *Maine Woods*, thought to have been edited by Francis Allen, was the most thoughtful edition so far published, and the last important text in the Boston line. Working from a strong and immediate knowledge of Thoreau's style, the editor regularized many spellings and word-divisions to the author's dominant forms. His grasp of botany and ornithology is reflected in numerous corrections of misprinted scientific names. He compared "The Allegash" with the 1857 journal record and corrected some blunders which might otherwise have escaped notice.[10] In doing so, however, he became overzealous, replacing phrases and sentences in his printed working copy with their journal equivalents where Thoreau's surviving later drafts duplicate or closely approximate the 1864-1894 readings. It is obvious that the Walden Edition editor did not use the Huntington and Houghton libraries' last-draft manuscripts; they may not have been known or available to him. But his most serious failing by modern editorial standards was to use a Riverside Edition *Maine Woods* as his copy-text, and thereby to perpetuate the nonauthorial stylistic details and the substantive corruptions introduced into that edition. Furthermore, the 1906 editor regularized some of Thoreau's phrases and compounds to forms that prevail in the early or rough journals (e.g., "wood-thrush" to "wood thrush," "fish-hawk" to "fish hawk") when in actuality Thoreau's preserved fair drafts and some later journal appearances

[10] The comparison might have been closer: he overlooked and perpetuated several discrepancies between the printed text and the journal draft that must have resulted from scribal or compositorial errors in the preparation of the first edition.

indicate his disposition toward the original printed forms. The regularization of accidentals itself runs counter to Thoreau's practice, for he tolerated variants of capitalization, word-division, spelling, and the like in rough drafts, fair copies, and authorially annotated imprints. Aside from his comparison of "The Allegash" with the journal, the 1906 editor seems not to have consulted accessible manuscripts or printed forms earlier than the Riverside text, and he failed to approach each of the four *Maine Woods* sections in terms of its own particular textual history and evidence. Again, a few new corruptions appear in the Walden Edition, though these are more than offset by corrections to "The Allegash" and "Appendix." The fresh authority of the 1906 *Maine Woods* "Allegash" is of no practical consequence to the present editor, since he has had access to all the manuscripts used by his 1906 predecessor, plus others that were not.

Various other complete and partial publications of *The Maine Woods*, by Houghton Mifflin itself and by different houses, derive from one or another of the three editions described above. Certainly the most peculiar of the derived texts is that edited by Dudley C. Lunt and published by W. W. Norton & Company, New York, in 1950. Lunt scissored the three essays and rearranged them as a single grand excursion in sixteen chapters, from Bangor to Moosehead Lake to Chesuncook and the Allagash Lakes, thence down the East Branch Penobscot to its junction with the West Branch, up the latter to Katahdin, and back downstream to Bangor. Lunt appended some journal passages relative to Thoreau's 1853 and 1857 excursions, drawing them from the Walden Edition *Journal*. The editor's intention was "to give to *The Maine Woods* a unity that is rooted in Thoreau's swing around the great sweep of the Ktaadn country"

Portrait of Thoreau

Map of
Maine

"Chesuncook," a manuscript page
of the *Atlantic Monthly* version

"The Allegash and East Branch,"
a page of the final draft

map. At sundown, leaving the river-road awhile for shortness, we went by way of Enfield, where we stopped for the night. This, like most of the localities bearing names on this road, was a place to name, which, in the midst of the unnamed and unincorporated wilderness, was to make a distinction without a difference, it seemed to me. Here, however, I noticed quite an orchard of healthy and well-grown apple trees, in a bearing state, it being the oldest settler's house in this region, but all natural fruit, and comparatively worthless for want of a grafter. And so it is generally lower down the river. It would be a good speculation, as well as a favor conferred on the settlers, for a Massachusetts boy to go down there with a trunk full of choice scions, and his grafting apparatus, in the Spring.

The next morning we drove along through a high and hilly country, in view of Cold-Stream Pond, a very beautiful lake, four or five miles long, and came into the Houlton road again, at Lincoln, forty-five miles from Bangor, where there is quite a village, for this country—the principal one above Oldtown. Learning that there were several wigwams here, on one of the Indian islands, we left our horse and wagon, and walked through the forest half a mile, to the river, to procure a guide to the mountain. It was not till after considerable search that we discovered their habitations—regular shanties, in a retired place, where the scenery was unusually soft and beautiful, and the shore skirted with pleasant meadows and graceful elms. We paddled ourselves across to the island-side in a canoe, which we found on the shore. Near where we landed, sat an Indian girl, ten or twelve years old, on a rock in the water, in the sun, washing, and humming or moaning a song meanwhile. It was an aboriginal strain. A salmon-spear, made wholly of wood, lay on the shore, such as they might have used before white men came. It had an elastic piece of wood fastened to one side of its point, which slipped over and closed upon the fish, somewhat like the contrivance for holding a bucket at the end of a well-pole. As we walked up to the nearest house, we were met by a sally of a dozen wolfish-looking dogs, which may have been lineal descendants from the ancient Indian dogs, which the first voyageurs describe as "their wolves." I suppose they were. The occupant soon appeared, with a long pole in his hand, with which he beat off the dogs, while he parleyed with us. A stalwart, but dull and greasy-looking fellow, who told us, in his sluggish way, in answer to our questions, as if it were the first serious business he had to do that day, that there *were* Indians going "up river,"—he and one other—to-day, before noon. And who was the other? Louis Neptune, who lives in the next house. Well, let us go over and see Louis to-

gether. The same doggish reception, and Louis Neptune makes his appearance—a small, wiry man, with puckered and wrinkled face, yet he seemed the chieferman of the two; the same, as I remembered, who had accompanied Jackson to the mountain in '37. The same questions were put to Louis, and the same information obtained, while the other Indian stood by. It appeared, that they were going to start by noon, with two canoes, to go up to Chesuncook, to hunt moose—to be gone a month. "Well, Louis, suppose you get to the Point, (to the Five Islands, just below Mattawamkeag,) to camp, we walk on up the west branch to-morrow—four of us—and wait for you at the dam, on this side. You overtake us to-morrow or next day, and take us into your canoes. We stop for you, you stop for us. We pay you for your trouble." "Ye!" replied Louis, "may be you carry some provision for all—some pork—some bread—and no pay." He said, "Me sure get some moose;" and when I asked, if he thought Pomola would let us go up, he answered that we must plant one bottle of rum on the top, he had planted good many; and when he looked again, the rum was all gone. He had been up two or three times: he had planted letter—English, German, French, &c. These men were slightly clad in shirt and pantaloons, like laborers with us in warm weather. They did not invite us into their houses, but met us outside. So we left the Indians, thinking ourselves lucky to have secured such guides and companions.

There were very few houses along the road, yet they did not altogether fail, as if the law by which men are dispersed over the globe were a very stringent one, and not to be resisted with impunity or for slight reasons. There were even the germs of one or two villages just beginning to expand. The beauty of the road itself was remarkable. The various evergreens, many of which are rare with us—delicate and beautiful specimens of the larch, cedar, arbor-vitæ, ball spruce, and fir-balsam, from a few inches to many feet in height, lined its sides, in some places like a long front yard, springing up from the smooth grass-plots which uninterruptedly border it, and are made fertile by its wash; while it was but a step on either hand to the grim untrodden wilderness, whose tangled labyrinth of living, fallen, and decaying trees,—only the deer and moose, the bear and wolf, can penetrate. More perfect specimens than any front yard plot can show, grew there to grace the passage of the Houlton teams.

About noon we reached the Mattawamkeag, fifty-six miles from Bangor by the way we had come, and put up at a frequented house, still on the Houlton road, where the Houlton stage stops. Here was a substantial covered bridge over the Mattawamkeag, built, I think they said, some

"Ktaadn," a page of the first version

(page 11). But this spatial reordering is a Pyrrhic success, which sacrifices true chronology and the stylistic and thematic integrity each essay displays in Thoreau's original format. Reviewing Lunt's edition (*Bulletin of the Massachusetts Audubon Society* 34 [May, 1950], 175-176), Francis Allen declared, "For me this [new] 'arrangement' is nothing but a stunt, and I can only hope that it will not be imitated."

2. MANUSCRIPTS

All four portions of *The Maine Woods* are represented by a liberal quantity of surviving manuscript material, mainly early drafts. For "Ktaadn" the most important document is a notebook formerly owned by Stephen Wakeman and now in the Berg Collection of the New York Public Library. Like Thoreau's other composition books of the mid- and late-1840s, the Berg Collection volume served both as a journal and as a draftbook for books and essays in progress. It has been cannibalized to some extent; of the 269 pages in Thoreau's original numbering, 20 full pages and parts of several others have been scissored out. The dated entries in the notebook run consecutively from April 17, 1846, on the first page, through December 2 [1846] near the end, but outside the "Ktaadn" section only five or six passages are dated. The bulk of the book is devoted to the "Ktaadn" drafts, which begin on page 79 and continue through page 241 with only four internal digressions. Three of these are brief philosophical passages; the fourth is a five-page reflection on savages and cookery, including a response to Melville's *Typee*. The "Ktaadn" draft begins with a nine-page capsule summary of the excursion, nothing more than a list of words and phrases under date headings for August 31 through September 10. The precise detail and telegraphic style suggest that Thoreau carried the notebook with him at least as far as Bangor and possibly all the way to the mountain. (The notebook is badly worn and almost disbound; but its condition does not necessarily betray field use in Maine.) On the next six pages (88-93) are drafts in random order of several passages that occur near the middle and end of the essay. Pages 94-97 record events and impressions on the noctural steamboat trip from Portland to Bangor that were not used in "Ktaadn" but contributed to the beginning of "Chesuncook." From page 97 onward the draft sequence essentially duplicates that of the excursion and the finished account. A pencil index to the "Ktaadn" passages occupies page 242; one isolated bit of "Ktaadn" text appears on page 253. For the most part, Thoreau wrote his first draft in ink and revised in both ink and pencil at different times. Occasionally in the revision Thoreau cross-refers by "V" (*vide*) and page numbers to the "new" or "next" notebook, where, it is apparent, he had written drafts of "Ktaadn" passages not represented in the Berg manuscript.[11]

A probable survival from the "next" notebook is a four-page draft of the conclusion of "Ktaadn," formerly in the private collection of Mr. Albert E. Lownes and now in the Brown University Library's Special Collections. Since the Lownes fragment includes working versions of a paragraph and a quatrain first printed in the 1864 first edition, as well as drafts of passages published in 1848, we may assume that the paragraph and the poem are contemporary with the 1846-1847 "Ktaadn" matter in the Berg Collection

11 This book may have been a wholly cannibalized volume of which only the covers are preserved in the Pierpont Morgan Library (MA 1823). A pencil index to part of the contents inside the front cover associates the book with *Walden* drafts of the period 1847-1849.

book and were included in the fair copy Thoreau sent
to Greeley. Their omission from the *Union Magazine*
version was perhaps dictated by considerations of
space: the text on the last page of the fifth *Union*
installment runs to the third possible type line from
the bottom.

Aside from these and the annotated *Union* pages,
only two manuscripts bearing directly on "Ktaadn"
have been discovered. The first is a quotation from a
newspaper that was incorporated into a footnote for
the 1864 *Maine Woods* "Ktaadn" chapter. It is written
on a loose sheet among some Huntington Library
fragments (HM 13182), labeled in another hand,
"Journal of 1849 P. 132-3." The second item is a
largely paraphrased extract from Lescarbot's *Histoire
de la Nouvelle-France* in a book of notes relating
mainly to Canada, Pierpont Morgan Library MA 595,
which dates from the early 1850s. Thoreau rewrote
the extract somewhat before inserting it in "Ktaadn"
for the 1864 publication.

The earliest manuscript for "Chesuncook" is the
steamer-trip passage in the 1846 Berg notebook. The
next is a journal entry dated November 26, 1850, in
the tenth Pierpont Morgan Library journal notebook,
which records information Thoreau secured from
some northern Indians sojourning in Concord. Portions of this entry are used in the Indian-camp section
of the finished essay. The largest continuous body of
manuscript is the Morgan Library journal sequence
(in volume 22) for September 16 through September
27, 1853: the first draft, with subsequent ink and
pencil revisions, of the "Chesuncook" account. In the
fair copy he submitted to the *Atlantic Monthly* Thoreau
also drew upon several other entries in the same journal notebook, dated in October and November 1853,

and others yet in volumes 29, 30, and 31 (for summer 1857 through early spring 1858). The Houghton Library Thoreau fragments, b MS Am 278.5, folder 17, include one or two worksheets for "Chesuncook" alone and others combining matter that would appear separately in "Chesuncook" and "The Allegash and East Branch."

For editorial purposes the extant portion of the 1858 "Chesuncook" fair copy is the most important manuscript. The eighty-seven numbered pages of Thoreau's first shipment of "Chesuncook" holograph cover roughly half the essay, from the beginning through the short paragraph commencing "Ere-long the hunters returned" (122.20 in the present edition). Pages 52 through 57, 59, 85, and a small portion of 60 have not been discovered. These involve, respectively, the material from "or eight feet" through "slender, spiring tops" (106.29-109.15), from "the shore" through "I heard" (109.31-110.9), from "lumber than man is" through "understands it aright" (121.9-121.25), and from "we had passed" through "with their" (110.15-110.17). Manuscript page 58 is in the Abernethy Library of American Literature, Middlebury College; the top third of page 60 is in the Lownes Collection at Brown University; page 76 is in the Boston Public Library; and page 86 is in the Clifton Waller Barrett Collection, Alderman Library, University of Virginia. The remaining pages, including the lower third of page 60, are in the Houghton Library.

The "Chesuncook" fair copy gives evidence of two distinct periods of preparation. Pages 27-28, 31-37, 40-47, 49, 58, 60-67, 72-73, 76-84, and 86-87, all on off-white paper, reflect an earlier draft stage than the remaining extant pages, which are on light blue paper. The latter portions have replaced original white-paper draft. Where blue and white sheets are adjacent, the text on the blue has been fitted to the continuation of text on the white, rather than the reverse: a blank space occurs at the bottom of the blue (e.g., pages 39, 48) or the text extends onto the verso of the blue (e.g., pages 26, 30); the text on the white sheet begins at the top and extends to the bottom of the page. The white sheets are working draft brought into final form by authorial cancellations and substitutions; the blue are true "fair copy." In the first page of manuscript on white paper, for example, there are as many corrections and revisions by Thoreau as on the first twenty-six sheets of blue. By rough count, 110 authorial changes occur in the entire manuscript, ranging from verbal cancellations and interlineations to revisions of punctuation (most often the replacement of dashes with commas), cancelled false starts, and pencilled substitutions of written-out numbers for arabic numerals. Over eighty percent of these are on white sheets. At several points Thoreau instructs the printer by writing "no break" or joining passages with a pencil line. In addition to Thoreau's changes and directions, the fair copy bears the stint-marks and signatures—Hennessy, Bates, and R. Lev. or R. Sev.—of the compositors who set "Chesuncook" for the *Atlantic*.

The Morgan Library journal, volumes 29 and 30, contains the ink first draft of "The Allegash and East Branch" with subsequent revisions in ink and pencil. The major portion occurs in the entries for July 20 through August 3, 1857, but lengthy draft passages also appear under September, October, and November journal dates. Thoreau drew one entry for "The Allegash" from the 1853 Maine journal. The important last-draft manuscripts in the Huntington and

Houghton libraries have already been described; besides final pages, the Houghton fragments include
a leaf of heavily revised working draft for "The
Allegash."

Numerous quotations, translations, and para-
phrases in Thoreau's "Extracts Relating to the Indians," eleven manuscript notebooks in the Morgan
Library, bear indirectly upon "Chesuncook," "The
Allegash," and the "Appendix." Yet only one or two
Indian-book extracts could be called drafts toward
final essay passages; and these passages are also represented by manuscript versions later than the Indian-book entries.

The journal drafts for the "Appendix" have already been identified. Beyond these there is only one
other manuscript, a three-page working draft among
the Houghton fragments. Marked "Under appendix or
omit?" by Thoreau and "Omitted relics" by Sophia,
it is a discussion of differences in temperature and
seasonal phenomena between Maine and Massachusetts, parts of which derive from journal entries for
August 3, 1857, October 28, 1853, December 2, 1853,
and October 5, 1857. A portion of the fragment appears in condensed form in "The Allegash," 163.20-25.

What remains of Thoreau's *Maine Woods* manuscripts is impressive in its extent and variety; scholars
can count themselves fortunate that so much has
been saved. The actual and probable losses should,
however, be tallied. The following manuscripts are
nowhere recorded as extant and if they do exist have
escaped systematic search by the present editor and
his colleagues on the Thoreau Edition staff:

1. the "Ktaadn" working drafts in the "new" or "next" notebook
2. loose working copy, if any, for the 1848 "Ktaadn" publication
3. the "Ktaadn" fair copy Thoreau sent to Horace Greeley, from which the *Union Magazine* text was set
4. the *Union* "Ktaadn" pages Thoreau revised to serve as 1864 *Maine Woods* printer's copy, plus slips or sheets on which he wrote out extended additions
5. the second half of the "Chesuncook" fair copy, from which the 1858 *Atlantic Monthly* publication was set
6. the 8 1/3 pages missing from the first half of that fair copy
7. the penultimate draft portions of "Chesuncook" replaced by final copy on blue paper
8. the marked proofs of the second installment of *Atlantic* "Chesuncook"
9. the set of *Atlantic* "Chesuncook" pages that Thoreau marked as printer's copy for the 1864 *Maine Woods*
10. any copies of *Union Magazine* "Ktaadn" or *Atlantic* "Chesuncook" on which Thoreau corrected errors before presenting them to friends
11. additional working drafts for "The Allegash"
12. the bulk of Thoreau's last draft of "The Allegash"
13. the last copy, probably fair copy, of the "Appendix"
14. Sophia Thoreau's transcription for Ticknor and Fields of all or part of "The Allegash" from Thoreau's last draft, and
15. proofsheets of the 1864 *Maine Woods* marked by Sophia or by Channing if the proofs were read against manuscripts by Thoreau.

The unlocated *Union* "Ktaadn" proofs and the proofs for the first and third *Atlantic* installments of "Chesuncook" are of lesser interest.

Among the Huntington Library manuscripts is a single leaf, catalogue number HM 956, resembling a titlepage mockup for a printer. It reads "Remaining Manuscript/ of/ *The Maine Woods*/ By/ Henry D. Thoreau/ With/ A Large Amount of Original Manuscript about/ the Maine Woods Not Included/ in the Printed Book/ and/ Entirely Unpublished." No *Maine Woods* manuscript accompanies this tantalizing title. The present editor suspects that it applies to the Huntington's ten-page "Allegash" last draft *plus* the late "Allegash" materials in the Houghton Library. At some time, certainly, the Houghton and Huntington last-draft sections were together, and the titlesheet might easily antedate their separation. Together, the two portions would make up a small book; the Huntington fragment alone would not.

The fact that Thoreau's last-draft "Allegash" manuscripts are concentrated in only two repositories invites a conjecture about the "Allegash" printer's copy sent after his death to Ticknor and Fields. If the surviving leaves had been part of that printer's copy, they would show signs of use by the compositors. Were this the case, furthermore, or were the entire last draft recopied for the printer, we might expect to find much more material, for the unlocated bulk of the manuscript had as strong a claim for preservation as the Huntington and Houghton remnants. The conclusion we are tempted to reach is that *only* the Huntington and Houghton drafts were recopied by Sophia or another scribe, the remainder of Thoreau's last draft being clean enough to serve as printer's copy with some clarifications and perhaps unwitting corruptions by Sophia. It is interesting also that the relatively legible Huntington fragment is the very beginning of "The Allegash." Might Sophia have begun to transcribe the entire essay, then lost heart or energy and decided to copy only the least readable pages of the bulky manuscript that remained? These are, of course, only speculations; but given the number and seriousness of the discrepancies between the surviving last-draft pages and their equivalents in the 1864 text, and the disquieting likelihood that comparable violations of Thoreau's style and meaning would have occurred in the recopying of the remainder, the hypothesis is a source of comfort. If most of "The Allegash" was set directly from Thoreau's draft, the 1864 text is truer to his final intentions—despite the difficulties of his penmanship—than if printer's copy was a complete posthumous transcription.

3. THEORY OF COPY-TEXT AND PRINCIPLES OF EMENDATION

Like the other volumes in THE WRITINGS OF HENRY D. THOREAU, and like all volumes in the nine other large projects proceeding under the auspices of the Center for Editions of American Authors, *The Maine Woods* is an unmodernized, purified, eclectic or critical text. The editorial theory and procedures by which this volume has been prepared conform essentially to those employed in the Centenary Edition of Hawthorne and the Northwestern-Newberry Edition of Melville.[12] The interested reader should consult the Center's working manual for all projects under its

[12] See Fredson Bowers, "The Centenary Texts: Editorial Principles," appended to the second and subsequent Hawthorne volumes, and pp. xxix-xlii of the first, *The Scarlet Letter* (Columbus: Ohio State University Press, 1962); also, the discussion of editorial procedures in each of the Melville volumes.

sponsorship, the *Statement of Editorial Principles* (1967). He should also examine several essays that explain the theory of copy-text more fully, subtly, and systematically than the present introduction does: W. W. Greg, "The Rationale of Copy-Text," *Studies in Bibliography* 3 (1950), 19-36; Fredson Bowers, "Current Theories of Copy-Text, with an Illustration from Dryden," *Modern Philology* 48 (1950), 12-20; Bowers, "Established Texts and Definitive Editions," *Philological Quarterly* 41 (1962), 1-17; and Bowers, "Some Principles for Scholarly Editions of Nineteenth-Century American Authors," *Studies in Bibliography* 17 (1964), 223-228. What follows in these pages is a capsule discussion concentrating on those aspects of the theory most pertinent to the editing of *The Maine Woods*.

An eclectic or critical text is not an exact transcription of a manuscript nor an exact reprint of any particular printed form of the text. It is, rather, that one of the documentary forms of the text over which the author exercised the greatest degree of control (e.g., a fair-copy manuscript, or a set of corrected proofs for the first printing if the fair copy is lost, or a first printed form if both fair copy and corrected proofs have disappeared), as emended by the editor to reproduce as nearly as possible the author's intentions. Such emendation derives for the most part from other relevant forms of the text, which the editor compares with the "copy-text" or form under the greatest amount of authorial control. The category of relevant or authoritative materials includes the author's working manuscripts and those printed forms of the text over which he demonstrably, or probably, exercised authority. It is crucial that the editor have access to all known relevant documents, for he selects his copy-text from among these, and uses the others ("pre-copy-texts"—usually working manuscripts—and "post-copy-texts"—usually revised reprints) to guide him in emendation.

Since some of his emendations will not derive from an authoritative document, but rather from independent editorial judgment, the editor must be familiar with the author's style both in working draft and fair copy, with his composition habits at the time he wrote the work, with external data bearing on the composition and first publication of the text, and, so far as possible, with the style norms of the editors, publishers, and printers to whom the first publication and later authoritative reprintings were entrusted.

The editor works at reconstructing that text which most nearly reproduces the author's intentions, and a form of the text of which the author would have approved. In principle these two criteria are one; in practice they sometimes fail to coincide. Henry Thoreau submitted rather careless fair copy and was a desultory proofreader and corrector. He tolerated or overlooked in "Chesuncook," and doubtless in "Ktaadn" as well, many compositorial and editorial changes in his text, ranging from house-style spellings and trivial regularizations of pointing to major alterations in sentence structure and wording. But toleration and neglect are negative, not positive, forms of authorial "approval"; and where, in the absence of fair copy, strong evidence exists to indicate a different authorial intention, the present editor has emended the text. On the other hand, Thoreau's "intention" was often imperfect. Even those texts that he could supervise closely contain more than a few errors—usually misspellings or miswritings, but sometimes even misrememberings of fact. For instance, in the copy-text of "Ktaadn," Thoreau's marked copy of the *Union Magazine* publication,

Thoreau did not correct the name "Holly" to "Holley." The misspelling is perpetuated in the 1864 *Maine Woods* version of "Ktaadn," over which Thoreau also exercised some control. As it happens, the name is correctly spelled in a pre-copy-text manuscript, but even if it were not, the emendation would be justified. A more interesting example is the editorial emendation, discussed in a textual note for 134.23, of "1588" in the "Chesuncook" copy-text to "1592" in the present edition, although the erroneous date "1588" occurs in the manuscript pre-copy-text and in the 1864 first-edition post-copy-text. Neither textual authority nor Thoreau's "intention" is the chief determinant for such emendations as "Holley" and "1592."

This edition of *The Maine Woods* is doubly or even trebly eclectic inasmuch as the copy-texts for each of the four component parts have been separately determined, and each part has been emended on the basis of its own documentary evidence. The edition does not derive as a unit from the first book publication, but rather from the forms of its component parts most completely under Thoreau's control. In the case of "Chesuncook," moreover, the copy-text is a composite of fair-copy manuscript and first printing where fair copy has disappeared; and while the basic copy-text for "The Allegash" is the 1864 first printing, Thoreau's final-draft fragments serve as copy-text for the portions of the narrative which they cover.

A primary assumption in modern textual theory is that the form closest in time to the author's composition is the most reliable in its "accidentals"—the details of punctuation, capitalization, word-division, spelling, and paragraphing. The accidentals of later printed forms, even those produced during the author's lifetime, are less authoritative. This is so because in most cases (Thoreau's *Maine Woods* chapters not excepted) a later printing is set from an earlier published form, even when the reprinting contains authorial revisions. As the text is reset, further house stylings may be imposed upon the accidentals, and new compositor's errors are introduced. In the choice of copy-text, therefore, the author's fair or final manuscript enjoys the highest priority, followed by (in this order) authorially corrected proofsheets for the initial printing, authorially corrected post-publication copy of the first printing, and unmarked first printed copy.

Though the copy-text has maximum general authority among relevant forms of the text with respect to accidentals, its substantives are not binding where they differ from the substantives of a later *relevant* printing. The later substantives are adopted if it can be argued from internal or external evidence that they issued from the author's hand. Otherwise, they are rejected as sophistications, errors, or indifferent modifications by a copyeditor or compositor, and are discussed in textual notes.

These two steps, the choice of copy-text from among the relevant forms, and the emendation of copy-text from other relevant forms or from the editor's independent judgment, are the heart of the editorial process. Accordingly, the editor is under strict obligation to identify his copy-text for the reader, to explain on what grounds he chose and validated it, and to document every change he makes from it. This documentation is of especial importance, for it enables the reader to backtrack the editorial labor to the original form of the copy-text, and to judge for himself the validity of any particular emendation.

The relevant forms of the texts of all four *Maine Woods* sections have already been identified, and the theory of copy-text on which this edition proceeds has been explained. That theory dictates the selection of the corrected *Union Magazine* "Ktaadn" pages in the Berg Collection as copy-text for the first chapter. In accordance with the emendation principles outlined above, 69 substantive changes judged to be authorial are incorporated from the 1864 first edition (16 others are rejected as nonauthorial). Since the Berg Collection document did not itself serve as printer's copy for the 1864 publication, two examples of the *Union* print have been collated on the Hinman machine to safeguard against possible variations within the impression. The copies so collated are University of Texas number 051 Sa77 and a personal copy, number H 771-775, in the collection of Walter Harding. The latter was issued in separate numbers, and the former perhaps in a whole bound volume. No differences whatever appeared in mechanical collation. Hand collation was performed, in duplicate, on the *Union Magazine* "Ktaadn" text and the 1864 first-edition version (TxU Z917.41 T391m and Harding number 458) to determine all changes made between the two printings. As a matter of scholarly interest and as a check upon the possibility of fresh (though posthumous) authoritative readings, the 1864 text was hand-collated against the Riverside Edition (TxU 818 T39m 1894) and the Walden Edition (TxU Z818 T39 A2) for "Ktaadn" and the remainder of the book as well. In addition, the copy-text was read against the surviving pre-copy-text drafts, the editor noting such meaningful variations as might have resulted from careless drafting of the fair copy or compositorial error in the setting of *Union Magazine* type. "Ktaadn" printer's copy for the present edition was prepared on a set of enlarged electroprints taken from the Harvard College Library copy of *Union Magazine* (P 392.11). As a final safeguard, the editor's duplicate printer's copy, which he read against proofs of the present printed text, was prepared on electroprints from the TxU copy.

Where Thoreau's fair copy of "Chesuncook" survives, it serves as copy-text in this edition. Elsewhere, as noted earlier, the copy-text is the 1858 *Atlantic Monthly* publication. The 1858 essay as a whole was hand-collated against the 1864 *Maine Woods* "Chesuncook," from which four substantive emendations were drawn, though five other verbal differences in the reprinting were rejected as nonauthorial. Rejected 1864 substantive readings are recorded in textual notes; but forty first-edition readings that simply perpetuate the *Atlantic* editor's unauthorized substantive changes from the fair copy are listed only in the Table of Textual Variations. Again two sets of *Atlantic Monthly* "Chesuncook" pages for the printed copy-text portions were collated on the Hinman machine: TxU number 051 At6 (apparently issued in separate numbers) and Milne Library, New York State University College at Geneseo, number 50625 (apparently issued in a whole bound volume). The only discrepancy that appeared in collation was type shift on one of the pages of the third installment. Printer's copy for "Chesuncook" in this edition consisted of the editor's typescript of the manuscript copy-text portion plus a set of enlarged electroprints for the remainder from the Harvard Library *Atlantic Monthly*, copy KF 564. As a further safeguard against unnoticed variations in the *Atlantic* impression, the editor's duplicate of the printed copy-text section was prepared on electroprints of the TxU *Atlantic*, and the latter was read against proofs of the present typesetting. The editor systematically compared his eclectic copy-text with "Chesuncook" working draft, and noted such significant differences as might have resulted from careless authorial transcription or from printer's error in the setting of the *Atlantic Monthly* text where fair copy does not survive.

The copy-text for most of "The Allegash and East Branch" and the entire "Appendix" is the 1864 first edition of *The Maine Woods*. For the "Allegash" sections based on Thoreau's final manuscript, the printer's copy was a typescript prepared by the editor. Typed printer's copy was also submitted for the Indian-vocabulary part of the "Appendix," where such extensive revisions were required that the use of marked electroprints seemed impractical. Printer's copy of the remainder of "The Allegash" and "Appendix" was prepared on a set of enlarged electroprints from Harvard College Library copy *AC85 T3912 864 ma (A), while the editor's duplicate and proofreading copy was based on TxU copy Z917.41 T391m. Both volumes contain the April 1864 advertisements. In identifying the changes in the Ticknor and Fields plates, the editor collated "The Allegash" and "Appendix" in the TxU first edition with a copy of the last (1892) impression, Western Reserve University Library, number 818.31 M12 cop. 1. The results, aside from losses caused by normal type batter, are reported in section one of this introduction. The altered pages (282-295) of the 1892 copy were compared with those of the impression of 1889, in which the plate changes first occur, and the impression of 1891. Next, pages 282-295 of the first printing were machine-collated against the "sixteenth edition" (1885?; TxU 818 T39m 1864rl), the comparison revealing nothing other than plate wear. A copy of the "seventeenth edition" (ca. 1886; Ohio State University El 140 T488M), subsequently located, was found by nonmechanical inspection to conform to the "sixteenth edition" and earlier impressions. Since Thoreau could not supervise the publication of "The Allegash" and "Appendix," the copy-texts were read with particular care against all surviving pre-copy-text manuscripts. Numerous substantive differences occur between the printed copy-texts of these sections and the journal drafts. The editor emended to the manuscript reading wherever the print was obviously defective or in error. Warned, however, by the example of the 1906 "Allegash," he chose not to adopt several indifferent substantive variants, only recording them in the end matter. To supply all such journal readings for first-edition substantives would be to assume that the early draft is generally closer to Thoreau's lost final manuscript pages than is the 1864 print—an assumption the editor does not hold. (If he did, moreover, he might have equal cause to adopt unimportant journal variants in "Ktaadn" and the portions of "Chesuncook" unrepresented by fair-copy manuscript.) And if the editor has erred in one or more of his decisions to reject minor "Allegash" and "Appendix" journal variants, he has erred on the side of caution, out of a basic respect for the copy-text, and with the assurance that the record in the end matter of this volume and the publication of the journal first draft in THE WRITINGS OF HENRY D. THOREAU will enable readers to judge the wisdom of his policy.

4. TYPES OF EMENDATION AND FORMS OF
   DOCUMENTATION

   1. Since the present edition is not intended as a facsimile of the copy-texts, such details of copy-text design as wide spacing in contractions, display capitals in mid-chapter, and unindented paragraphs (as at the openings of the *Union Magazine* "Ktaadn" installments) are not duplicated. Repetitions of Thoreau's title in the second and subsequent install-

ments of "Ktaadn" and *Atlantic Monthly* "Chesun-cook" are omitted, as are notices of continuation and termination in the magazine installments and at the end of the "Chesuncook" manuscript copy-text. The original pagination of the copy-texts, printer's signature markings, and smudges are of course disregarded; broken but legible letters and punctuation marks are treated as though they were whole. A printer's rule between the narrative and the conclusion of the "Ktaadn" copy-text has been changed to a wide space, as it was in the first edition, to conform to the treatment of a similar shift in "Chesuncook." In addition, the designer of the present volume has omitted the separate title page which preceded the "Appendix" in the 1864 format, has provided display capitals at the opening of "Chesuncook" and "The Allegash and East Branch" (where copy-text is Thoreau's manuscript), has altered the case of the "Ktaadn" and "Appendix" titles and of the datelines in "The Allegash," has deleted printer's rules between "Appendix" subsections, has changed the case and font of "Appendix" subtitles, and has moved all centered titles and subtitles to the left margin. No changes in the foregoing categories are recorded in the end matter.

2. Thoreau's thirty-eight ampersands, on both blue and white pages of the "Chesuncook" fair-copy manuscript, are here printed as "and." In the portions of "The Allegash" for which last-draft fragments are copy-text, "and" replaces the original ampersand eighty-nine times. Except at the beginnings of sentences, Thoreau used the ampersand as a shorthand sign for "and" in every type of construction where the word would be used, including adjective phrases ("steady & reliable"), noun phrases ("dogs & their instincts"), adverb phrases ("quickly & quietly"), compound predications ("he walked off . . . & searched"),

compound verb phrases ("to get a view . . . & then return"), and compound sentences ("The wood-thrush sang . . . & the laugh of some loons . . . came distinct over the lake"). Newspapers, periodicals, and books of the mid-nineteenth century, which the editor has examined in a survey of contemporary American print usage,[13] employ the ampersand only in commercial titles ("Harper & Brothers," etc.). On the assumption that Thoreau himself regarded it as merely the informal mark for the print form "and," the present editor has followed Thoreau's contemporary editors in converting the manuscript symbol to the word. In keeping with contemporary practice the *Union Magazine* printed "Somebody & Co.," a mock commercial title, in "Ktaadn": this form is preserved in the present edition. Thoreau's manuscript "&c." is also allowed to stand, since it was widely used in nineteenth-century printing, but the editor adds periods to "&c" where Thoreau forgot to supply them. The period was a standard part of the print form. Again supported by contemporary print usage, the editor provides periods after the abbreviations "St," "lbs," "Mrs," and points of the compass (e.g., "S W"). Thoreau's "Pm" has been printed "P.M." in this edition, and the abbreviation "ac." (common in Thoreau's manuscripts but nonstandard) is expanded to "according." Periods are added to "Mts" and "Mt" in formal place-names once in the "Chesuncook" fair-copy section and once in the "Allegash" text based on a Houghton Library fragment. Thoreau wrote out "mountain(s)" six times on the blue or fairer pages

[13] Periodicals and newspapers included in the survey are *American Journal of Science and Arts*, *Atlantic Monthly*, *Harper's New Monthly Magazine*, *North American Review*, *Union Magazine*, Boston *Evening Transcript*, *The Liberator*, and Portsmouth (N.H.) *Journal*. Books consulted include New York, Boston, Philadelphia, and Augusta, Maine imprints.

of "Chesuncook" and once on a white page, the instances including "mountain ash," "allied mountains," and "distant mountains." His usual form in journal drafts and rough worksheets was "mt(s)". Because of the fair-copy pattern of expansion, and because the editor found no printed examples of lower-case "mt(s)." in his survey of documents, he emends "mt ash" to "mountain ash" in a single "Chesuncook" appearance, from a white page. Thoreau wrote out "mountains" once in the Houghton last-draft "Allegash" fragments, revised the abbreviation to the expanded form in one other instance, and left "mt" or "mts" in six more. All six (none are parts of place-names) are expanded by the present editor.[14]

Thoreau's treatment of numbers in the "Chesuncook" fair copy reveals his distinct preference for spelled-out forms over arabic numerals everywhere except in dates. On the blue or fairer sheets he used numerals in each of four date references and in a single abbreviated reference to the hour ("5 P.M."),

[14] Ampersands are converted to "and" at 86.9, 86.20, 86.22, 86.33, 88.12, 89.9, 90.7, 90.14, 90.20, 90.26, 90.35, 91.2, 91.3, 91.8, 91.21, 92.27, 93.10, 93.25, 93.32, 98.4, 98.7, 99.11, 101.8, 102.28, 103.3, 105.19, 109.29, 109.30, 111.13, 111.35, 112.1, 112.29, 116.11, 116.18, 118.21, 118.22, 120.11, 120.13, 158.23, 158.28, 158.36, 159.26, 160.17, 226.17, 226.17, 226.19, 226.28, 226.29, 226.36, 227.11, 227.16, 228.16, 228.16, 228.24, 228.29, 229.11, 229.12, 229.24, 229.28, 229.29, 229.30, 229.32, 229.34, 230.1, 230.4, 264.6, 264.7, 264.12, 264.15, 265.1, 265.12, 265.16, 265.20, 265.23, 265.29, 265.31, 265.35, 266.1, 266.3, 266.4, 266.11, 266.14, 266.20, 266.20, 266.24, 266.27, 266.34, 267.1, 267.5, 267.10, 267.10, 267.12, 267.13, 267.15, 267.16, 267.21, 267.22, 267.29, 267.35, 268.4, 268.19, 268.22, 268.24, 269.4, 269.22, 270.26, 270.29, 270.30, 282.24, 282.28, 282.33, 282.36, 283.19, 283.21, 283.27, 283.33, 283.34, 284.3, 284.6, 284.12, 284.18, 296.21, 296.28, 297.1, 297.2, 297.3, 297.4; "&c" is emended to "&c." at 86.5, 86.5, 93.27, 98.17, 158.32, 226.22, 267.9, 268.34, 269.23. The other expansions and emendations of abbreviations are individually documented in the end matter for "Chesuncook" and "The Allegash and East Branch."

but spelled out 108 of 109 other cardinal numbers and fractions, including four specifications of the hour followed by "o'clock" (e.g., "ten o'clock").[15] The single ordinal number in the blue pages is also written out. Over one of the 108 spelled numbers, a large figure, Thoreau added the arabic in pencil without cancelling the words, but since even large numbers are spelled out elsewhere in the manuscript and in the *Atlantic* print where fair copy does not survive, dates excepted, the present editor ignores that pencilled alternative. On the rougher white sheets of the manuscript Thoreau spelled out only eight of fifty cardinal numbers and one of two ordinals in his original writing. When perfecting these white pages, he interlined the expanded forms for the remaining ordinal and thirty-two of the forty-two arabic cardinal numbers. He failed to cancel the arabic original of nine cardinal numbers. The present editor adopts the expanded forms of these nine, and emends the remaining eleven numbers which Thoreau left in arabic alone (one from a blue page, ten from white; none dates), in keeping with the author's pattern.[16]

Arabic numbers in the last-draft "Allegash" fragments are not emended here, since none of them are revised to word form in Thoreau's hand and since numerals occur occasionally in the first edition where it serves as copy-text.

    3. Authorial substantive changes from the copy-text in relevant later printings are adopted as explained in section three above.

---

[15] This count does not include "one," which Thoreau regularly spells out (dates again excepted) in the fair copy.

[16] Pencilled spelled-out forms interlined over uncancelled arabic numbers are adopted at 98.4, 98.5, 100.6, 101.9, 101.9, 111.33, 111.33, 113.25, 115.19; arabic numbers are emended by the editor to spelled forms at 88.17, 97.14, 98.30, 98.34, 100.30, 104.4, 105.26, 109.27, 111.17, 113.27, 120.22.

4. Typographical blunders and other positive errors of punctuation and spelling are corrected, whether they are nonauthorial, authorial, or of undetermined origin. The editor has checked unusual spellings against Thoreau's own lexicons, John Walker, *A Critical Pronouncing Dictionary . . . of the English Language* (New York: Collins and Hannay, 1823) and Noah Webster, *An American Dictionary of the English Language*.[17] Variant copy-text spellings which are listed by Walker or Webster are retained in the present edition unless there is strong evidence of house-styling, sophistication, or misreading by a scribe or compositor. Thoreau's variant spellings of Indian place-names are likewise allowed to stand. Together with the manuscript record, the maps and geographical reference works Thoreau consulted have been used to distinguish between scribal or printshop errors and authorial variant spellings. Certain place-names are spelled in two or more ways within the last-draft "Allegash" fragments; and Thoreau did not see fit to regularize all variant spellings when he revised "Ktaadn" and "Chesuncook" for the 1864 publication. Therefore the forms of the copy-texts have been retained. The more extreme, and possibly confusing, variations preserved in this edition are Allagash-Allegash-Alleguash; Ktaadn-Katadn-Ktadn; Nickatow-Nickertow-Nickatou; Olemmon-Olamon; Pongokwahem-Pongoquahem; and Sowadnehunk-Souadneunk-Souneunk.[18]

17 Thoreau's manuscript library list does not specify the edition of "Webster's Dictionary, Unabridged, 1 v." which he owned. The present editor has used the fifteenth edition (New York: N. and J. White, 1838).

18 On Thoreau's organization sheet for *The Maine Woods* among the Houghton Library fragments he directs that the Indian noun *"spokelogan"* should always be spelled thus, as it is in "The Allegash." But emendation of *"pokelogan"* in

For corroboration of botanical spellings in the copy-texts, the editor has consulted Thoreau's texts, the first (Boston and Cambridge: James Munro and Company, 1848) and second (New York: George P. Putnam & Co., 1856) editions of Asa Gray's *Manual of the Botany of the Northern United States.*

5. Demonstrable compositor's or copyist's mis-readings in the printed copy-texts are corrected. Such errors include incredible or implausible substantives and significant accidentals, and plausible readings that can be shown to be nonauthorial corruptions of more appropriate ones in manuscript pre-copy-text. In the "Allegash" copy-text, for example, Thoreau's journal draft terms "memorable" and "white-headed" appear as "more arable" and "white-beaked."

6. Less frequently, *probable* scribal or print-shop corruptions of Thoreau's normal accidentals are corrected. Because of Thoreau's pervasive inconsist-encies of capitalization, word-division, punctuation, tolerated spellings, and so on, in the journal drafts and fair copies alike, such emendation has been per-formed conservatively. To regularize copy-text acci-dentals to the statistically dominant forms in Thor-eau's manuscripts—a difficult task both practically and theoretically, since the manuscripts often dis-close no clear preference—would be to misrepresent Thoreau's normal, that is, inconsistent, texture. Reg-ularization of any sort, even to the dominant forms of a copy-text or to an inconsistent author's most frequent forms, constitutes a form of modernization the present edition avoids. The irregularity of acci-dentals reflects, then, both Thoreau's style and the

---

"Ktaadn" and "Chesuncook" has not been performed, since Thoreau toys in "Ktaadn" with the etymology of the term in its (perhaps) incorrect spelling.

nineteenth-century printshop policies that permitted such diversity.

We may fairly assume that many accidentals in the printed copy-texts are nonauthorial, but because of Thoreau's own inconsistency we can only rarely be sure *which* forms are impositions by a copyist, editor, or compositor. The present editor has attempted, with only limited success, to isolate the elements of house-styling in the *Union Magazine*, *Atlantic Monthly*, and the 1864 Ticknor and Fields *Maine Woods*. Capital-ized season names in a limited section of "Ktaadn," the spelling *"bateau(x)"* in the *Atlantic*, and the spelling (or word-choice?) "farther" instead of Thor-eau's habitual "further" throughout the 1864 printing are viewed by the editor as recurrent nonauthorial impositions. The evidence for emendation to authorial forms in these instances is presented in textual notes and emendation lists.

7. The editor has located Thoreau's sources for all but five of the direct quotations and for most of the paraphrased references in *The Maine Woods*. As a check against errors by a copyist or compositor, he compared these sources with the printed copy-texts and with manuscript notes and transcripts from the sources, where such manuscripts are extant. On the basis of this comparison, one substantive and one ac-cidental in "Ktaadn," two substantives in "Chesun-cook," and one significant accidental in "The Alle-gash" have been interpreted as nonauthorial blunders or authorial slips of the pen and have been emended to agree with the sources. One other emendation of a "Chesuncook" substantive, mentioned in part three of the Textual Introduction and discussed in the Textual Note for 134.23, corrects Thoreau's error in dating a source.

Thoreau's major printed source for information about the old Abnaki tongue in the "Appendix" was Sébastien Rasles, *A Dictionary of the Abnaki Language*, edited by John Pickering, *Memoirs of the American Academy of Arts and Sciences*, new series, I (1833). He seems to have gone through the *Dictionary* at least twice: in the tenth of his notebooks of Extracts Relating to the Indians (in the Pierpont Morgan Library) he filled fifteen pages with Abnaki words and definitions, including two used in "Chesuncook," but excluding most of those that appear in the "Appendix." His reference to Rasles in the journal for December 30, 1860, is probably contemporary with his work on the "List of Indian Words" in the "Appendix." One of Rasles' phonetic symbols, *n̈*, reproduced accurately in the Indian notebooks, was regularly rendered as *ü* in the printed "Appendix." Doubtless Thoreau's script *n* was mistaken for a *u* by the scribe or compositor, who could associate the diacritical with a vowel but not with a consonant. Such errors render portions of the Indian vocabulary useless, or worse, for readers of the "Appendix." Various other terms ascribed to Rasles, plus a few ascribed to other authorities, vary slightly from the source spellings and diacriticals in ways that suggest misreadings of the manuscript by a person ignorant of these sources. The present editor therefore alters fifteen terms in all from Rasles, four terms from William Willis, and three from C. E. Potter to the forms in their respective works on Abnaki language.[19]

[19] Thoreau uses the spelling "Rasles" in all known manuscript occurrences. While "Rale," the consistent form in the "Appendix," was a tolerated nineteenth-century spelling, the editor regards "Rale" as nonauthorial and emends twenty times to the older spelling of Thoreau's journals, the Indian notebooks, and the source.

Five substantive emendations in the "List of Indian Words" are derived from these reference works. Rasles' French *"écriture"* was corrupted to *"ceinture"* in the copy-text, and four copy-text definitions from Willis are patently incomplete, reflecting an unfinished Thoreau manuscript. These are expanded in the present edition for the sake of intelligibility.

Willis distinguishes between applications and definitions of Indian place-names by a system of parentheses or commas, which is violated in five of the copy-text entries from Willis and respected in the remainder. In the present edition Willis' significant pointing is adopted for the five confused entries. In seven entries where Rasles is cited to support or amplify a definition Thoreau received from an Indian informant, and in one where William Williamson is cited, the editor emends the copy-text's punctuation or capitalization in order to clarify the relationship between words and authorities. The clearer pointing adopted for these entries conforms to a pattern Thoreau employed frequently in other parts of the "List of Indian Words." Similarly, in the "Appendix" botanical lists, a misleading pattern of punctuation for five entries has been emended to conform to the clearer pointing system used in nine others. Thoreau designed the "Appendix" as an unambiguous and informative catalogue of facts. The present editor's emendations of "Appendix" copy-text, as outlined above, are intended to respect that authorial purpose.

This edition of *The Maine Woods* embodies the clear-text principle: no footnotes or bracketed interpolations save Thoreau's own interrupt the text. The documentation of individual editorial choices, and other apparatus, is placed at the end of the volume. The editor has arranged the apparatus into four chapter groups for the convenience of users of the edition. Thus, the complete end matter for "Ktaadn" precedes that for "Chesuncook," and so on. Each section of end matter is headed by a note explaining the basic format of the list or table and identifying the symbols used therein.

The first type of end matter for each *Maine Woods* section is the Textual Notes. In these notes the editor discusses the most problematical and least obviously grounded of his emendations and comments on rejected substantive readings from pre-copy-text or relevant post-copy-text documents. The Textual Notes are followed by the List of Emendations, in which all alterations of the copy-text in the present edition are cited, except those identified above as silent design changes. Because of the special nature of the "Ktaadn" copy-text, a list of all Thoreau's manuscript changes and annotations in the Berg Collection copy of *Union Magazine* "Ktaadn" appears after the List of Emendations for that chapter. A Table of Textual Variations is next provided for each part of *The Maine Woods*: it is a historical collation comprising all substantive variants from the present text in the relevant printed forms for that section. Variants of accidentals are recorded only when they alter the sense. Manuscript pre-copy-text substantives that might inadvertently have been corrupted in transmission to the copy-text are also set down here. The Table of Textual Variations enables the reader to reconstruct the substantives of the copy-text and later relevant printings. At the same time, it presents the reader with the full body of textual evidence, the alternatives from among which the editor has drawn what he regards as the wording closest to Thoreau's intention. The apparatus is concluded with two lists reporting, respectively, word-division at the end of the line in each copy-text and word-division at the end of the line in the present edition. Every instance of line-end hyphenation of a compound or possible compound in the copy-text required an editorial decision as to the form the construction would take in this text. Such judgments were based on other appearances of the term within the copy-text, and, where necessary, on evidence from manuscript drafts. The form recorded in the table (for example, "pow-wows," or "backwoods") is the form to which the editor resolved each line-end hyphenation. By coincidence, some few compounds are hyphenated at the end of the line in *both* the copy-text and the present edition: these are listed in the forms to which the editor has resolved them. The word-division list for THE WRITINGS OF HENRY D. THOREAU records those compounds hyphenated at the end of the line in this edition that appeared as hyphenated compounds in the copy-text. Terms divided at the end of the line in THE WRITINGS but not listed here were continuous in the copy-text. (Again, since the present typesetting occasionally duplicated copy-text line-end hyphenations, certain entries in and omissions from this list reflect editorial decisions.) The information provided in the second list will enable a reader to reconstruct copy-text forms that would otherwise be disguised, and will permit accurate transcription of the text for quotation and reprinting.

In keeping with the guidelines established by the Center for Editions of American Authors for all editions published under its auspices, this volume has been examined in printer's copy by an independent textual expert (Professor Hershel Parker), and has been proofread at least five times by three different individuals, including the present editor, in galley and page proof.

Ktaadn

Textual Notes

In the following comments on decisions to emend or not to emend, "copy-text" designates the Berg Collection copy of "Ktaadn, and the Maine Woods," cut from the 1848 *Union Magazine* and annotated in pencil by Thoreau. The uncorrected magazine text is abbreviated "UM." Reference to the 1864 *Maine Woods* is made by the symbol "ɪ" or the words "first edition." A "ɪɪɪ" signifies the 1906 Walden Edition *Maine Woods* text, in which one substantive emendation is anticipated. "BJ" stands for Thoreau's 1846 manuscript journal-workbook in the Berg Collection, with page references to Thoreau's original pagination rather than the pagination of the surviving pages.

4.26 and other articles: "Other" is a manuscript addition in the copy-text, not incorporated in ɪ. Since the copy-text form is distinctly superior to "and articles," it seems more likely that Thoreau forgot to enter the revision in his first-edition printer's copy (or that the compositor overlooked it) than that he decided to restore the UM reading.

7.2 abroad-steads: The copy-text's singular "abroad-stead" is corrected to plural, probably by Thoreau, in ɪ; and the hyphenation, which also first appears in ɪ, is consistent with Thoreau's treatment of this compound at BJ, p. 104.

7.6 Abenaki: "Abenaki's" in UM is emended by Thoreau to "Abenakis" in the copy-text—a form anticipated at BJ, p. 104. But since "Abenakis" as a collective singular nominative appears nowhere else among the manuscripts, and is approached only remotely in the form "Abnaquiois" ("Ktaadn," 34 n.), the emendation to Thoreau's later normal "Abenaki" in ɪ is probably authorial. It is also possible that Thoreau's manuscript cancellation in the copy-text was incomplete and was intended to include the *s* as well as the apostrophe.

8.36   spring: Some of the UM compositors respected Thoreau's normal lower-case treatment of season names, while others apparently capitalized because of personal preference: no house policy is discernible in the 1848 issues of the magazine. "Spring" is capitalized in the copy-text here and at 16.35, 21.3, 22.20, 26.14, and 33.19; "winter" at 16.35, 23.9, and 33.6; and "summer" at 16.36, 23.9, 33.1, and 34.1. All but the first "Spring" are located in the second UM installment. In each of these instances the BJ draft has the lower-case initial, except once where no draft survives; and in each instance the copy-text's capital is reduced in the first edition. Uncapitalized season names occur once in the first UM installment, once in the second, and ten times in the third through fifth.

12.26   caribou: Since Thoreau's normal spelling, "caribou," appears in the BJ draft of this passage (p. 124) and later in the copy-text at 38.15 and 81.4, as well as in the "Chesuncook" fair copy at 102.11, "carribou" here in the copy-text is probably a compositor's sophistication or error.

13.11   further: Of six instances of "further" in the copy-text, five, including this one, are changed to "farther" in the first edition. Thoreau's preference in the BJ draft was for "further," which occurs nine times as compared with one "farther" and one occurrence where the vowel is questionable. The spelling distinction corresponds to no distinction of sense. No strong argument can be made for seeing the copy-text's single "farther" (71.33) as nonauthorial (the draft of that passage contains neither form of the word) and it is retained in the present edition. But the five first-edition changes of "further" to "farther" in "Ktaadn" are consistent with the almost invariable rejection of Thoreau's "further" in "Chesuncook" and "The Allegash" by the editor of 1, and are viewed as nonauthorial by the present editor. See notes for "Chesuncook," 128.11, and "The Allegash," 161.10.

14.29   emigrant: Although the copy-text's "immigrant" seems more precise in this context, the emendation to "emigrant" in 1 is probably authorial. An *e* written above the first syllable of "immigrant" at BJ, p. 122, the draft of this passage, reveals Thoreau's vacillation between the two terms.

15.9 appeared: Thus in the copy-text and the BJ draft, p. 122. The emendation to "appears" in 1 is needlessly inconsistent with the tense of other verbs in the sentence, and probably reflects a compositor's error.

15.28 that map: Thus in the copy-text and the BJ draft, p. 124. The less specific reading in 1, "the map," is probably not an authorial emendation.

16.5 backwoods: The copy-text's possessive "backwood's" varies from both the draft of this passage (BJ, p. 125) and 17.30, where the conventional adjective "backwoods" appears. The same emendation is made from "backwoods'" at 30.14. In both places the first edition corrects to "backwoods."

19.4 hovel: The reading in 1, "hovels," is rejected as a probable compositor's error, since the plural disagrees with singular "chimney" and implicitly singular "latter" in the last clause of the sentence. The BJ draft, p. 129, has "hovel."

19.34 that: The indifferent change in 1 to "which" should probably be assigned to the compositor. Like the copy-text, the draft of this passage at BJ, p. 130, reads "that."

19.36 logger's: The copy-text's plural possessive disagrees with "his" and "he," governed by this noun, in the following sentence. In the BJ draft, p. 130, the plural is used throughout. Thoreau probably revised all three words to the singular in his fair copy, but his habitual carelessness in the placement of apostrophes may have caused the compositor to read "loggers'" here.

22.33 villager's: Thus in the copy-text, though corrupted to "villagers" in 1. The singular possessive comports with "his" (the pioneer's) in this comparison; the plural nominative does not.

23.17 economize: The copy-text's spelling, "economise," results from either a misreading or a sophistication by the compositor. Thoreau's normal "economize" (BJ, p. 133) is restored in 1. "Recognised" at 71.24 is likewise emended to "recognized" in 1 and in the present edition, with support from the draft, BJ, p. 229.

24.5 idler: Thus in the copy-text and BJ, p. 137.

The emendation to "idle" in 1 overlooks Thoreau's play on the commonplace phrase, and should probably be assigned to the compositor.

26.8   ceiling: Although no manuscript evidence survives for this passage, the copy-text's "ceilings" is manifestly in error. The emendation to "ceiling" is first made in III.

29.5   lain: Thoreau has the verb thus, correctly, at BJ, p. 147. The copy-text's "laid" is probably due to a compositor's error. For "lain" in the "Chesuncook" fair copy, see 104.24 and 117.6.

32.30   torrent's: The copy-text reads "torrents' "—almost certainly the result of a compositor's error or of careless placement of the apostrophe in the lost fair copy, for the plural disagrees with "it" in the next phrase. Neither the source of Thoreau's quotation nor a manuscript draft of the sentence has been located. The first edition's "torrent's" may well be an authorial emendation.

34 (footnote)   Even . . . p. 185.:   Added to the copy-text by Thoreau for the first edition. The present editor emends "Abenaquinois" to "Abnaquiois" on the assumption that Thoreau used the latter spelling in the lost manuscript of his footnote, as he did in quoting (precisely) from the *Relation de ce qui s'est passé . . . en la Nouvelle France . . . en 1647* (Paris: Cramoisy, 1648) in the ninth of his Indian Extract Books at the Pierpont Morgan Library. Since both the italicized phrase and the spelling "Abnaquiois" derive directly from the tenth chapter or "relation" of the 1647 *Relation* (misnumbered the ninth in the Paris imprint), Thoreau's "See also" is misleading. It may represent a compositor's blunder. Thoreau's citation of p. 185 is likewise obscure. Though the page falls in the middle of the tenth chapter, nothing to Thoreau's purpose appears on it. The extracts in the Indian Book offer no clue to Thoreau's intention.

34.9   loggers':   The copy-text's "logger's" deviates in number from Thoreau's "lumberers' " in the draft of this passage at BJ, p. 156. II emends to "loggers'." See the note for 19.36 above, and "loggers' camps" at 18.35.

35.4-5   supper even here, white: The copy-text's "supper, even here white" is thus emended in 1. Thoreau's draft of the passage at BJ, p. 158, supports this emendation by indicating that the color of the hot cakes ("rarely white") distinguished them from the usual cakes.

35.30-31 rapids: The plural form invited, if not required, by "some" appears in Thoreau's draft at BJ, p. 159. The copy-text reads "rapid."

38.18-39.2 "Row, brothers . . . favoring airs!": Thomas Moore's "A Canadian Boat-Song," a poem whose popularity is attested by Emerson's parody in his Harvard journal XVII, was probably quoted from memory in BJ, pp. 164, 253, and in Thoreau's lost fair copy for the *Union Magazine*. In the copy-text Thoreau entered two autograph corrections, both substantive. Fifteen additional changes appear in the first edition of *The Maine Woods*, indicating that a sufficiently interested person consulted a printed text of the poem. These alterations may well be authorial. Three are substantive emendations that restore the wording of the source (see Moore's *Poetical Works*, Galignani edition, Paris, 1829); nine of the twelve changes of accidentals also conform to Moore's text. The first edition reading, which varies from Moore in only nine casual accidentals, is adopted as most likely representing Thoreau's final intentions.

38.20 described: The first-edition reading, "describes," is rejected with some hesitation as an error or independent emendation by the compositor. Although numerous authorial changes from the 1848 text occur in this and the next paragraph of the 1864 printing (giving some weight to the possibility that Thoreau chose "describes"), the shift from "described" is indifferent at best, and perhaps weakens the sentence by introducing needless vagaries of tense.

39.13 a camp: Thus in the copy-text and the BJ draft, p. 165. The first edition emendation to "the camp" is rejected because it probably represents the compositor's deliberate or accidental change from "a camp," rather than an authorial alteration. While the substitution does not modify Thoreau's meaning, the additional "the" weakens the clause.

44.26 sawn: The 1864 first edition, where Thoreau added the two quotations from Michaux and the intervening sentence referring to Springer to the text of "Ktaadn," reads "drawn." No manuscript of the passage in Thoreau's hand has come to light. Thoreau's source is F. Andrew Michaux, *The North American Sylva*, a work first translated from the French by Augustus L. Hillhouse and later slightly revised and annotated by J. Jay Smith for publication in Philadelphia. The *Maine Woods* version of the passage resembles the several Hillhouse-Smith editions too closely to suggest an independent translation by Thoreau, though these editions contain slight textual variations among themselves. The printed form closest to Thoreau's may be found in volume 3, pp. 131-132, of the 1857 Philadelphia edition. Here, and in five other editions consulted by the editor, Michaux's "débités" is properly translated "sawn"; and one must conclude that the *Maine Woods* reading, "drawn," results from a copying error by Thoreau or a scribe, or from a typesetter's mistake.

45.18   loggers': The copy-text prints "logger's." The draft of this passage, at BJ, p. 179, has only "camp," but refers shortly thereafter to "the loggers . . . here." Thoreau probably intended the plural in the lost fair copy. Compare the emendation to "loggers' " at 34.9.

46.23   lake or: The copy-text's comma after "lake," not present in the manuscript at BJ, p. 190, badly confuses Thoreau's meaning by divorcing "lake" from "above" and by suggesting an apposition between "stream" and "river."

46.30   inlet: The copy-text's "outlet" clearly violates the sense of Thoreau's explanations and examples. No draft of this sentence has been located.

48.24   one's: The BJ draft at p. 184 is barely legible, but seems to read "ones"—a far more plausible reading than the copy-text's "our" since it clearly establishes the dialogue between the two boatmen who were "ambitious to do something more than usual" to impress their passenger. The copy-text reading, which might well result from a compositor's misinterpretation of the manuscript, makes the reference of "the other" obscure.

49.9   place, of: The omission of the comma in the copy-text radically alters Thoreau's meaning by forcing "of the whole Penobscot River" to modify "place." The author's intention is manifest in the draft at BJ, p. 185: at the worst place *in this fall*, the whole Penobscot River drops perpendicularly two or three feet at least.

50.32 wont: In the copy-text Thoreau cancelled "apt" and entered this term in the margin. The first edition's restoration of "apt" more likely results from Thoreau's or a compositor's oversight than from a reversal of the author's intention.

54.7 swum: The copy-text prints "swam." In the BJ draft, p. 203, the vowel is uncertain; but since Thoreau writes "having swum" in "The Allegash" 162.3, and since his lexicon lists only "swum" as the past participle, it seems likely (notwithstanding the example of Herman Melville) that "swam" is a compositor's misreading.

54.33 lopped: Thoreau's lexicon listed only this form of the past participle, and the lexicographer would presumably have accepted only "lopped" as the preterite. The copy-text's "lopt" deviates, furthermore, from "lopped" in the BJ draft, p. 203.

57.12 literally covered: The copy-text's comma after "literally" distorts Thoreau's meaning. In the manuscript version at BJ, p. 208, "literally" unequivocally modifies "covered."

66.12 that. Immeasurable: The copy-text's obviously incorrect reading, "that immeasurable" is emended in 1 to "that,—immeasurable." The present emendation derives from Thoreau's draft at BJ, p. 225, where his use of the fragmentary sentence is quite deliberate.

67.2 ridden: As a past participle the copy-text's "rode" was unacceptable to the authors of Thoreau's dictionaries, and Thoreau's adherence to "ridden" is apparent in the "Chesuncook" fair copy at 89.36.

71 (footnote) The bears . . . besmeared.: Thoreau added this footnote to the copy-text for the first edition. The awkwardness in the first sentence may result from an incomplete cancellation of "things on" in the fair copy for the note, but neither that manuscript nor any earlier draft survives to direct an emendation.

73.8-9. before: Thus in the copy-text, but "below" in Thoreau's source, the account by James Hodge in C. T. Jackson, *Second Annual Report on the Geology of the Public Lands of Maine and Massachusetts* (Augusta, Me., 1838), p. 68. In the absence of a manuscript draft, it is impossible to determine whether this relatively unimportant variation from Hodge is due to Thoreau's mistranscription or to a typesetter's error.

75.9   Table-Rock: A place-name, uncapitalized in the copy-text.

77.4   Sault de Ste. Marie: Thoreau uses the properly feminine "Ste." in the BJ draft, p. 239, and spells the first word with an *l* both there and in the Indian Extract Books. The copy-text reads "Saute de St. Marie."

80.31   forest: Emended in 1 from the copy-text's "forests," perhaps by Thoreau, perhaps accidentally by the compositor. "Grim forest" (81.7) tends to support the emendation.

81.1   wolves; in: The deletion in 1 of the copy-text's "and" before "in" clarifies the sentence structure and may well be authorial. On the other hand, the deletion of "and" before "at night" in the preceding phrase—also in 1—divorces "hooting" and "howling" from "resounding," which controls them grammatically. The present editor regards this omission as either inadvertent or non-authorial.

83.8   military: In the copy-text Thoreau struck through this word with a diagonal line and drew a question mark in the margin. Perhaps he intended to acknowledge that the Houlton Road was not called the "Military road" until near Lincoln (see 9.4); but in the absence of further marginal instructions or a revision in the first edition, no emendation is warranted.

List of Emendations

ALL changes from copy-text made by the present editor, except those specified as silent alterations of design in the Textual Introduction, are recorded in the following list. The left-hand column contains THE WRITINGS OF HENRY D. THOREAU reading with a parenthetical notation of the emendation source and other significant details; the right-hand column records the copy-text reading. Items marked with an asterisk (*) before the page/line citation are discussed in the Textual Notes. Other symbols used in the list are "UC" for the annotated copy of the *Union Magazine* "Ktaadn" printing in the Berg Collection (the copy-text); "I" for the 1864 first edition of *The Maine Woods*; "II" for the 1894 Riverside Edition and "III" for the 1906 Walden Edition *Maine Woods* texts where these anticipate substantive emendations made by the present editor; "Ed." for the editor in emendations not based on a "Ktaadn" working manuscript or relevant print; "Ref." (reference work) for a printed source employed by Thoreau; and "PE" for this edition of *The Maine Woods* in THE WRITINGS OF HENRY D. THOREAU, Princeton Edition. A wavy dash (~) in a copy-text reading stands for the word occupying this position in the PE reading to the left, and an inferior caret (ʌ) signifies the absence of a punctuation mark.

	PE reading	UC reading
3 (title)	Ktaadn. (I)	Ktaadn, and the Maine Woods./ By Henry D. Thoreau.
3.16	and to some (I)	and some
3.31-32	mosquitoes, and midges (I)	*lacking*

414

KTAADN

4.2	1836, (Ed.)	~ .
5.33	light and shapely (1)	exceedingly light and beautiful
5.35-36	shoulders, from twenty to thirty (1)	shoulders. They are from eighteen to twenty-five
6.5	commonly (1)	*lacking*
6.6	or other hard-wood (1)	*lacking*
6.7	inward are (1)	*lacking*
6.14-15	, or often in a single trip, (1)	*lacking*
6.35	shabby, (1)	~ ∧
* 7.2	abroad-steads (1)	abroadstead
* 7.6	Abenaki (1)	Abenakis [*possibly* Abenaki]
7.8	once a powerful tribe (1)	the ancient Tarrantines
7.19	seemed shallow (1)	seemed very shallow
8.7	was (1)	is
8.8	talked (1)	talk
8.9	could not (1)	cannot
* 8.36	spring (BJ, 1; also in five subsequent instances, all from the second *Union Magazine* installment)	Spring
9.2-3	a beautiful (1)	a very beautiful
9.4-5	Houlton road again, here called the Military road, at (1)	Houlton, here called the Military, road, again, at
9.12	small huts (1)	regular shanties
10.6-7	chief man (1)	chiefer man
11.6	larch, arbor-vitæ (1)	larch, cedar, arbor-vitæ
11.15	easily (1)	*lacking*
11.24	We had dinner (1)	After dinner

* 12.26	caribou (BJ)	carribou
13.20	was (1)	*lacking*
13.23	his customer (1)	him
13.35	canalés (BJ)	canalès
* 14.29	emigrant (1)	immigrant
* 16.5	backwoods (BJ, 1)	backwood's
16.35	winter (BJ, 1; also in two subsequent instances, both from the second installment)	Winter
16.36	summer (BJ, 1; also in three subsequent instances, all from the second installment)	Summer
18.28	the East Branch a (1)	the Seboois, or East Branch, a
18.28	large and (1)	quite
* 19.36	logger's (Ed.)	loggers'
20.10	and lichen (1)	*lacking*
20 n.	* Springer . . . get loose. (1; also an asterisk at "suggest.")	*lacking*
20.18	pork, often raw (1)	raw pork
21.22-23	East Branch (1)	Seboois
* 23.17	economize (BJ, 1)	economise
23.20	the upper part of (1)	*lacking*
23.28	(*Vaccinium Vitis-Idæa*) (1)	*lacking*
24.27	tomatoes (1)	tomatos
25.13-14	"yellow hammer," (1)	'yellow hammer,'
* 26.8	ceiling (Ed., III)	ceilings
28.33-34	lamprey-eels' or suckers' nests (1)	lamprey-eel nests
* 29.5	lain (BJ)	laid

30.14	backwoods (1)	backwoods'
32 n.	* The Canadians ... *fond.* (1; also an asterisk at "iron,")	*lacking*
32.12	, whom we did not know, (1)	*lacking*
32.18	for the most part (1)	at any rate
* 32.30	torrent's (1)	torrents'
33.8	team (1)	train
33.20	lichens (1)	moss
* 34 n.	* Even ... p. 185. (1; also an asterisk at "ice.")	*lacking*
34 n.	Abnaquiois (Ed., Ref.: emended from "Abenaquinois" in 1)	*lacking*
* 34.9	loggers' (BJ, II)	logger's
34.26	Holley (BJ)	Holly
* 35.4-5	supper ∧ even here, white (BJ, 1)	∼ , ∼ ∼ ∧ ∼
* 35.30-31	rapids (BJ)	rapid
37.3	St. (1)	St ∧
38.15	timid caribou (1)	timid red deer or caribou
* 38.18	fast, (1)	∼ ;
38.19	Rapids (1)	rapids
38.19	near ∧ (1)	∼ ,
38.19	past! (1)	∼ ,
38.22	a similar (1)	exactly this
38.25	Utawas' (1)	Utawa's
38.27	curl! (1)	∼ ;
38.28	But, (1)	∼ ∧
38.29	O ∧ (1)	Oh,
38.29	weary (1)	laboring
38.30	Utawas' (1)	Utawa's
38.30	moon, (1)	∼ ∧
39.1	isle! (1)	∼ ,
39.2	O grant (1)	Grant
39.2	heavens (1)	days

39.2	airs! (1)	~ .
43.17-22	He uses . . . side-	*lacking*
	walks. (1)	
43.19	ferruled (Ed., II:	*lacking*
	emended from	
	"feruled" in 1)	
43 n.-44 n.	* "A steady . . .	*lacking*
	shore."—Springer.	
	(1; also an	
	asterisk at	
	"others.")	
43.31-44.30	I quote . . . years."	*lacking*
	(1)	
* 44.26	sawn (Ed., Ref.:	*lacking*
	emended from	
	"drawn" in 1)	
* 45.18	loggers' (BJ)	logger's
* 46.23	lake ∧ (BJ)	~ ,
* 46.30	inlet (Ed.)	outlet
47.25-26	three to five or	five to eight
	six (1)	
47.28-29	, or else there are	*lacking*
	two at the bows	
	(1)	
* 48.24	one's (BJ)	our
* 49.9	place, (Ed., BJ)	~ ∧
49.29	alligators (1)	aligators
* 54.7	swum (Ed.)	swam
54.23-30	Lescarbot . . .	*lacking*
	numerous. (1)	
* 54.33	lopped (BJ)	lopt
55.8	flame (1)	fire
* 57.12	literally ∧ (Ed.,	~ ,
	BJ)	
58.2	sometimes one	twelve hundred
	thousand (1)	
58.3	five-foot (BJ, II)	five-feet
60.36	*Abies nigra* (1)	pinus nigra
61.18	dens (1)	nests
62.22	aerial (BJ, 1)	aeriel
62.28	fir-tree (1)	fire-tree
63.32	wind's (1)	winds'
65.26	on (1)	in

65.32	the East Branch (1)	the Seboois or East Branch
* 66.12	that. Immeasurable (BJ)	that immeasurable
* 67.2	ridden (Ed.)	rode
68 n.-69 n.	* "The spruce-tree ... bearing. (1; also an asterisk at "hand.")	*lacking*
71.24	recognized (BJ, 1)	recognised
* 71 n.	* The bears ... besmeared. (1; also an asterisk at "batteau.")	*lacking*
74 n.	* I cut ... woods." (1; also an asterisk at "breath.")	*lacking*
74.16	Falls. (1)	~ ∧
* 75.9	Table-Rock (Ed.)	table-rock
75.34	till night (1)	tillnight
76.1	almost (1)	*lacking*
* 77.4	Sault de Ste. Marie (Ed., BJ)	Saute de St. Marie
77.25-26	*cried*, when ... daylight, "Why (BJ, 1)	*cried* ∧ when ... daylight. "Why
78.27	musquash (1)	muskrats
78.29	musquash (1)	muskrats
79.20	musquash (1)	muskrat
79.24	face (1)	race
* 80.31	forest (1)	forests
* 81.1	wolves; in (1)	wolves; and in
81.2	mosquitoes (1)	mosquitos
81.13-22	What a place ... pines among. (1)	*lacking*

Thoreau's Manuscript Revisions in the Copy-Text

THE revised readings in UC, Thoreau's annotated copy of the *Union Magazine* "Ktaadn" pages in the Berg Collection, are listed in the left-hand column; the original UM (*Union Magazine*) readings are recorded in the column to the right. UC items marked with a dagger (†) were not adopted in the 1864 first edition of *The Maine Woods* (1).

	UC reading	UM reading
3 (title)	*deleted*	No. I./The Wilds of the Penobscot.
4.26	other †	*lacking*
5.4	this	the
6.4	rocks	rock
6.35-36	shabby forlorn, and cheerless	shabby and forlorn, cheerless
7.2	their	there
7.6	Abenaki (*or* Abenakis †)	Abenaki's
7.24	*deleted*	Military
8.18	asseverations	observations
9.4	Houlton, here called the Military, road, again (*further revised in* 1)	Houlton road again
10.6-7	chiefer man (*further revised in* 1)	chieferman
10.14-15	[to . . . Mattawamkeag,]	(to . . . Mattawamkeag,)
10.15-16	West Branch	west branch
10.17	or	on
10.21	so	no
11.34-35	*demand*—the . . . demand,—and †	*demand.* The . . . demand, and
12.20-21	shallows	swallows

12.35	man	war
13.4	sight. There	sight; and there
13.7	bags	boys
14.9	cones	canes
15.3	*deleted*	No. II./Life in the Wilderness.
15.6	Why ∧	~ ,
17.6-7	Mattaseunk	Mattascunk
17.9	tract	track
17.28	teach	learn
18.18	names	name
22.4-5	bounded abruptly on . . . river, by	bounded on . . . river, abruptly by
25.11	premises."	~ . ∧
25.18	other. ∧	~ ."
25.36	some of	*lacking*
26.1	were	was
27.23	Lakes	Lake
28.15	him	them
29.23-24	in pickle	in the pickle
31.16	busied	buried
31.24	this	the
34.22	*made*	*had*
34.23	*Liberty*	*liberty*
35.19	batteaux	batteau
35.24	*deleted*	No. III./Boating on the Lakes
37.4	Indian's	Indian
38.22	experience	description
39.1	prayers	prayer
39.2	airs	air
39.8	rill	rills
42.14	the	that
42.30	as Y	as: Y
45.23	tamping	camping
45.33	rest of the	whole
46.11	Pockwockomus	Pochwockomus
50.32	wont †	apt
51.32-33	batteaux	batteau
53.6	Sowadnehunk	Sowadnechunk
53.15	*deleted*	No. IV./The Ascent of Ktaadn.

55.33	arcs	areas
56.20	land ∧ still, very †	~ , ~ ∧ ~
59.25	cornel	cornet
60.33	Satan's ∧	~ ,
62.18	were	we
62.34	all together	altogether
63.8	mist. The	mist, the
69.32	*deleted*	No. v./The Return Journey.
72.24	Allagash †	Allegash
72.33	Allagash †	Allegash
79.17	æons	scows
82.9	head-waters	head-quarters
83.8	*cancelled, but with a marginal question-mark* †	military

Table of Textual Variations

THE following table lists all differences of substantives, and of accidentals whose effects are alterations of meaning rather than of form alone, between the text of the present edition and the relevant forms of "Ktaadn." In addition, the table includes a few substantives and significant accidentals in the manuscript drafts that may have been altered inadvertently by Thoreau in transcribing fair copy or by the compositor in setting the *Union Magazine* text.

The readings in the left-hand column are those of the present (Princeton) edition, PE (THE WRITINGS OF HENRY D. THOREAU). "UM" stands for *Union Magazine* "Ktaadn" without authorial revisions, "UC" for the annotated copy in the Berg Collection (the copy-text), and "I" for the 1864 first edition *Maine Woods*. Some PE readings are first anticipated in the unauthoritative 1894 Riverside Edition (II) or 1906 Walden Edition (III), as noted by these symbols. "BJ" represents Thoreau's 1846 journal-workbook in the Berg Collection. PE readings not accompanied by parenthetical reference to an earlier printed text are new in this edition.

Accidentals associated with substantive variants, but not in themselves significant, are ignored in the table entries. A wavy dash ($\sim$) in a variant listing designates the word occupying this position in the PE reading. An inferior caret ($_\wedge$) indicates an absent punctuation mark.

	PE reading	Variant readings
3 (title)	Ktaadn. (1)	Ktaadn, and the Maine Woods. By Henry D. Thoreau. (UM, UC)
3 (title)	*omitted* (UC, 1)	No. 1. The Wilds of the Penobscot. (UM)
3.16	and to some (1)	and some (UM, UC)
3.31-32	mosquitoes, and midges (1)	*lacking* (UM, UC)
4.26	other (UC)	*lacking* (UM, 1)
5.4	this (UC, 1)	the (UM)
5.14	perchance ∧ (UM, UC)	∼ , (1)
5.33	light and shapely (1)	exceedingly light and beautiful (UM, UC)
5.35-36	shoulders, from twenty to thirty (1)	shoulders. They are from eighteen to twenty-five (UM, UC)
6.4	rocks (UC, 1)	rock (UM)
6.5	commonly (1)	*lacking* (UM, UC)
6.6	or other hard-wood (1)	*lacking* (UM, UC)
6.7	inward are (1)	*lacking* (UM, UC)
6.14-15	or often in a single trip (1)	*lacking* (UM, UC)
7.2	abroad-steads (1)	abroadstead (UM, UC)
7.2	their (UC, 1)	there (UM)
7.8	once a powerful tribe (1)	the ancient Tarrantines (UM, UC)
7.19	seemed shallow (1)	seemed very shallow (UM, UC)
7.24	Houlton Road (UC, 1)	Houlton Military Road (UM)

8.7	was (1)	is (UM, UC)
8.8	talked (1)	talk (UM, UC)
8.9	could not (1)	cannot (UM, UC)
8.18	asseverations (UC, 1)	observations (UM)
9.2-3	a beautiful (1)	a very beautiful (UM, UC)
9.4	Houlton road again, here called the Military road (1)	Houlton road again (UM); Houlton, here called the Military, road, again (UC)
9.12	small huts (1)	regular shanties (UM, UC)
10.6-7	chief man (1)	chieferman (UM); chiefer man (UC)
10.17	or (UC, 1)	on (UM)
10.21	so (UC, 1)	no (UM)
11.6	larch, arbor-vitæ (1)	larch, cedar, arbor-vitæ (UM, UC)
11.15	easily (1)	*lacking* (UM, UC)
11.24	We had dinner (1)	After dinner (UM, UC)
12.20-21	shallows (UC, 1)	swallows (UM)
12.35	man (UC, 1)	war (UM)
13.4	sight. There (UC, 1)	sight; and there (UM)
13.7	bags (UC, 1)	boys (UM)
13.11	further (UM, UC)	farther (1)
13.20	shop was so (1)	shop so (UM, UC)
13.23	his customer (1)	him (UM, UC)
14.9	cones (UC, 1)	canes (UM)
14.27	grain, and (UM, UC, 1)	grain or (BJ)
14.29	emigrant (1)	immigrant (UM, UC)
15.3	*omitted* (UC, 1)	No. II. Life in the Wilderness. (UM)
15.6	Why ᴀ (UC, 1)	~ , (UM)
15.9	appeared (UM, UC)	appears (1)

15.28	that map (UM, UC)	the map (1)
16.5	backwoods (1)	backwood's (UM, UC)
17.9	tract (UC, 1)	track (UM)
17.28	teach (UC, 1)	learn (UM)
18.18	names (UC, 1)	name (UM)
18.28	the East Branch (1)	the Seboois, or East Branch (UM, UC)
18.28	large and (1)	quite (UM, UC)
19.4	hovel (UM, UC)	hovels (1)
19.34	that (UM, UC)	which (1)
19.36	logger's	loggers' (UM, UC, 1)
20.10	and lichen (1)	*lacking* (UM, UC)
20 n.	* Springer . . . get loose. (1)	*lacking* (UM, UC)
20.18	pork, often raw (1)	raw pork (UM, UC)
21.22-23	East Branch (1)	Seboois (UM, UC)
22.33	villager's (UM, UC)	villagers (1)
23.20	the upper part of (1)	*lacking* (UM, UC)
23.23	shad and (UM, UC, 1)	shad or (BJ)
23.28	(*Vaccinium Vitis-Idæa*) (1)	*lacking* (UM, UC)
24.5	idler (UM, UC)	idle (1)
25.36	some of (UC, 1)	*lacking* (UM)
26.1	were (UC, 1)	was (UM)
26.8	ceiling (III)	ceilings (UM, UC, 1)
27.23	Lakes (UC, 1)	Lake (UM)
28.15	him (UC, 1)	them (UM)
28.33-34	lamprey-eels' or suckers' nests (1)	lamprey-eel nests (UM, UC)
29.5	lain	laid (UM, UC, 1)
29.22	further (UM, UC)	farther (1)
29.23-24	in pickle (UC, 1)	in the pickle (UM)
29.24	was (UM, UC, 1)	were (BJ)

30.14	backwoods (I)	backwoods' (UM, UC)
31.16	busied (UC, I)	buried (UM)
31.24	this place (UC, I)	the place (UM)
32 n.	* The Canadians ... *fond.* (I)	*lacking* (UM, UC)
32.12	whom we did not know (I)	*lacking* (UM, UC)
32.18	for the most part (I)	at any rate (UM, UC)
32.30	torrent's (I)	torrents' (UM, UC)
33.8	team (I)	train (UM, UC)
33.20	lichens (I)	moss (UM, UC)
34 n.	* Even ... p. 185. (I)	*lacking* (UM, UC)
34.9	loggers' (II)	logger's (UM, UC, I)
34.22	*had made* (UC, I)	*had had* (UM)
35.4-5	supper ∧ even here, white (I)	~ , ~ ~ ∧ ~ (UM, UC)
35.19	batteaux (UC, I)	batteau (UM)
35.24	*omitted* (UC, I)	No. III. Boating on the Lakes (UM)
35.30-31	rapids	rapid (UM, UC, I)
37.4	Indian's (UC, I)	Indian (UM)
37.24	boats (UM, UC, I)	boat (BJ)
38.15	timid caribou (I)	timid red deer or caribou (UM, UC)
38.21	described (UM, UC)	describes (I)
38.22	experience (UC, I)	description (UM)
38.22	a similar (I)	exactly this (UM, UC)
38.29	weary (I)	laboring (UM, UC)
39.1	prayers (UC, I)	prayer (UM)
39.2	O grant (I)	Grant (UM, UC)
39.2	heavens (I)	days (UM, UC)
39.2	airs (UC, I)	air (UM)
39.8	rill (UC, I)	rills (UM)
39.13	a camp (UM, UC)	the camp (I)
40.9	forms (UM, UC, I)	form (BJ)
42.14	the tide (UC, I)	that tide (UM)

43.3	all together (UM, UC)	altogether (1)
43.17-22	He uses . . . sidewalks. (1)	*lacking* (UM, UC)
43.19	ferruled (II)	feruled (1); *lacking* (UM, UC)
43 n.-44 n.	* "A steady . . . Springer. (1)	*lacking* (UM, UC)
43.31-44.30	I quote . . . thirty years." (1)	*lacking* (UM, UC)
44.26	sawn	drawn (1); *lacking* (UM, UC)
45.18	loggers'	logger's (UM, UC, 1)
45.23	tamping (UC, 1)	camping (UM)
45.33	rest of the (UC, 1)	whole (UM)
46.23	lake ∧	~ , (UM, UC, 1)
46.30	inlet	outlet (UM, UC, 1)
47.25-26	three to five or six (1)	five to eight (UM, UC)
47.28-29	or else there are two at the bows (1)	*lacking* (UM, UC)
48.24	one's	our (UM, UC, 1)
49.9	place,	~ ∧ (UM, UC, 1)
50.32	wont (UC)	apt (UM, 1)
51.32-33	batteaux (UC, 1)	batteau (UM)
53.15	*omitted* (UC, 1)	No. IV. The Ascent of Ktaadn. (UM)
54.23-30	Lescarbot . . . numerous. (1)	*lacking* (UM, UC)
55.8	flame (1)	fire (UM, UC)
55.33	arcs (UC, 1)	areas (UM)
56.10	further (UM, UC)	farther (1)
56.20	land ∧ still, very (UC)	~ , ~ ∧ ~ (UM, 1)
58.2	sometimes one thousand (1)	twelve hundred (UM, UC)
58.3	five-foot (II)	five-feet (UM, UC, 1)
59.25	cornel (UC, 1)	cornet (UM)
60.36	*Abies nigra* (1)	pinus nigra (UM, UC)

61.18	dens (1)	nests (UM, UC)
62.18	were (UC, 1)	we (UM)
62.28	fir-tree (1)	fire-tree (UM, UC)
62.34	all together (UC, 1)	altogether (UM)
63.8	mist. The (UC, 1)	mist, the (UM)
63.24	further (UM, UC)	farther (1)
63.32	wind's (1)	winds' (UM, UC)
65.26	rest on (1)	rest in (UM, UC)
65.32	the East Branch (1)	the Seboois or East Branch (UM, UC)
66.12	that. Immeasurable	that immeasurable (UM, UC); that, —immeasurable (1)
68 n.-69 n.	* "The spruce-tree . . . bearing. (1)	*lacking* (UM, UC)
69.24	further (UM, UC)	farther (1)
69.32	*omitted* (UC, 1)	No. v. The Return Journey. (UM)
71 n.	* The bears . . . besmeared. (1)	*lacking* (UM, UC)
74 n.	* I cut . . . woods." (1)	*lacking* (UM, UC)
76.1	almost (1)	*lacking* (UM, UC)
77.25-26	*cried*, when . . . daylight, "Why (1)	~ ∧ ~ . . . ~ . ~ (UM, UC)
78.27	musquash (1)	muskrats (UM, UC)
78.29	musquash (1)	muskrats (UM, UC)
79.17	æons (UC, 1)	scows (UM)
79.20	musquash (1)	muskrat (UM, UC)
79.24	face (1)	race (UM, UC)
80.20	fair, (UM, UC)	~ ∧ (1)
80.22	laws, (UM, UC)	~ ∧ (1)
80.31	forest (1)	forests (UM, UC)
80.36	streams; and at (UM, UC)	streams; at (1)

81.1	wolves; in (1)	wolves; and in (UM, UC)
81.13-22	What a place . . . pines among. (1)	*lacking* (UM, UC)
81.20	live here still (1)	live my fill (Albert E. Lownes MS, Brown University); *lacking* (UM, UC)
82.9	head-waters (UC, 1)	head-quarters (UM)

Line-end Hyphenation

THE compounds or possible compounds in list A, below, are hyphenated at the end of the line in the "Ktaadn" copy-text. On the general grounds discussed in the Textual Introduction, page 404, the editor has resolved each to the form recorded in list A. List B records only those compounds hyphenated at the end of the line in this edition that should be transcribed with the hyphen in order to duplicate the copy-text forms.

LIST A

5.23	becalmed	41.31	thoroughfare
6.25	Oldtown	44.12	canoe-birch
7.10	pow-wows		[in insertion
9.7-8	wigwams		from first
9.16	island-side		edition]
10.17	to-morrow	46.18	dead-water
11.7	fir-balsam	49.33	overshoot
12.17	arrow-heads	51.21	poke-logs
13.17	hay-scales	52.11	notwithstanding
17.27	picture-books	55.11	arbor-vitæ
21.4	yellow-birch	57.16	full-grown
21.21	overlook	59.19	whereabouts
22.26	backwoods	60.8	daylight
24.10	long-handled	60.14	spruce-trees
25.27-28	everywhere	60.36	spruce-trees
27.15	buck-beans	61.32	side-hill
31.30	boatmen	63.11-12	rocking-stones
33.7	highway	64.2	cloud-works
33.10	sled-track	66.7	cranberries
33.11	evergreen	68.4	green-jacketed
35.8	puffballs	72.32	three-quarters
38.6	unearthly	76.11	reshingling
38.9-10	big-throated	77.16	playthings
41.15	thoroughfare	80.33	woodpecker

LIST B

6.23-24	woe-begone	44.12-13	arbor-vitæ
7.21-22	fish-hawk	45.2-3	table-land
9.27-28	wolfish-looking	59.21-22	mountain-ash
11.9-10	grass-plots	60.2-3	camping-
11.18-19	fifty-six		ground
18.32-33	Rock-Ebeeme	61.32-33	side-mountain
24.21-22	two-thirds	63.11-12	rocking-stones
28.11-12	bald-eagle's	72.28-29	seventy-five
31.9-10	water-spout	79.19-20	sweet-cake
36.30-31	lake-country	81.32-33	world-wide
38.9-10	big-throated	82.16-17	fishing-town
41.12-13	to-day		

Chesuncook

Textual Notes

FOR approximately the first half of "Chesun-cook" the copy-text is Thoreau's surviving printer's-copy manuscript; for the remainder, and where fair-copy leaves are missing within the first half, it is the original *Atlantic Monthly* publication (1858). Those portions of the present text based on fair copy are precisely identified in the Textual Introduction, page 380. The copy-text—manuscript or *Atlantic* ("AM")—is mentioned in the first of each series of notes on emendations or decisions not to emend in a given copy-text section. "I" represents the 1864 first edition of *The Maine Woods*, while "II" and "III" designate, respectively, the 1894 Riverside Edition and the 1906 Walden Edition *Maine Woods* texts. When emendation of a substantive or important accidental is anticipated in I, II, or III, or in AM where the copy-text is the manuscript, the note cites the print in which the change first appears. "MJ" stands for Thoreau's manuscript journal in the Pierpont Morgan Library, with references to entries by date.

84.4 1853: Although the copy-text and the AM publication read "185–" Thoreau's letters of January 23 and March 5, 1858, to James Russell Lowell, editor of the *Atlantic*, reveal that Thoreau preferred that the full date be printed. In the first letter, after declining Lowell's request for an account of his 1857 excursion, he offers an essay on the trip he had taken four years earlier, and remarks, "The date could perhaps be omitted, if in the way" (*The Correspondence of Henry David Thoreau* [New York: New York University Press, 1958], p. 504). Whether or not Lowell expressed an opinion about the date in his lost response, Thoreau made his preference plain in the March 5 letter accompanying the fair-copy portion of "Chesuncook," which here serves as copy-text: "If there is no objection you can print the whole date 1853" (*Correspondence*, p. 509). While Thoreau might not have filled out the date if he had read proof of the first installment (he was not given the opportunity), the emendation to "1853" in 1 is probably authorial.

97.15   north: Thoreau spells out terms for points of the compass, using lower-case initials, on the blue sheets of the copy-text. On the rougher white sheets, he twice uses his typical journal abbreviations, the capital initials alone, and interlines the spelled-out forms (with lower-case initials) in pencil revisions. In the present instance, from a white page, Thoreau first wrote "N   end" and then completed the word "North" without reducing the capital letter. AM emends to "north."

99.35-36   was moose: Thus in the copy-text and AM, consistent with the journal draft, MJ, September 16, 1853. The indifferent change to "was a moose" in the first edition is probably a compositor's error or sophistication.

100.29   crackling: From all appearances, a pencilled comma in the copy-text after this word is not Thoreau's—the symbol is differently formed and the pencil impression sharper and darker than Thoreau's in this manuscript. No comma appears here in AM.

104.15   night as: When Thoreau cancelled a phrase in the copy-text after "night" he forgot to strike the comma which introduced it. The comma is deleted in AM.

107.3   chicadee: The fair-copy manuscript is missing. At 97.18 and 97.19, Thoreau's normal "chicadee" was changed in AM to "chickadee," and doubtless AM's "chickadee" at this point results from the same emendation. The first edition regularly restores Thoreau's spelling.

114.1-5   [Indeed . . . woods.]:   This sentence was added to the text by Thoreau for the 1864 first edition. His use of brackets rather than parentheses, and his failure to combine the new material with the last sentence of the paragraph, suggest that the bracketed sentence may have been intended as a footnote. It is also possible that Thoreau had not finally decided whether, or how, to use this material, and therefore bracketed it in the margin of (or on a slip accompanying) the lost AM copy which served as printer's copy for the first edition. But in the absence of concrete evidence concerning Thoreau's intentions, the addition must be presented as it appears in 1.

118.14 trickled seemed: A pencil mark resembling a comma after "trickled" in the manuscript copy-text may not be authorial; if it is, it represents an incomplete setting off of the phrase "through which it trickled." No comma appears here in the MJ draft, September 17, 1853, and AM ignores the mark.

122.14-16 It is as immortal . . . above me still.: This sentence was "in a very mean and cowardly manner" omitted in AM. Thoreau had read proofsheets of the installment and thought his instructions to restore the sentence before publication would be honored. The fair copy's "for aught I know, will" is altered by Thoreau to "perchance will" for the first edition. He had already decided upon this change when he wrote to Lowell on June 22, 1858, berating him and the *Atlantic Monthly* for the "bigoted & timid" expurgation of the thought (*Correspondence*, pp. 515-516).

123.10 *Katahdinauguoh*: Spelled thus in Thoreau's source, Moses Greenleaf, *A Survey of the State of Maine* (Portland, Me.: Shirley and Hyde, 1829), p. 46; in the journal draft (MJ, September 18, 1853); and in the first edition "Appendix," 320.33. AM, the copy-text here and for the remainder of the essay, prints *"Katahdinauquoh."*

128.11 further: Thus in the copy-text, which respects Thoreau's normal practice hereafter in the second and third installments, though it had emended the fair copy's "further" to "farther" four times in the first installment and twice (including a "farthest") earlier in the second. The first edition follows AM's "farther" and "farthest" in the earlier instances and emends AM's "further" to "farther" here and in the remainder of the essay.

129.5 Sharps: No manuscript draft of this sentence survives, but the copy-text spelling, "Sharpe's," is authorial, appearing again in the unrelated first printings of "A Plea for Captain John Brown" and "The Last Days of John Brown." The inventor (1848) of the sliding-block breech-loading weapon to which Thoreau refers was Christian Sharps; and long arms based on his patents were designated "Sharps rifles" in contemporary manufacturing records, although the forms "Sharps'" and "Sharp's" also occur in some technical reports and military histories from the period 1850-1865. See Winston O. Smith, *The Sharps Rifle* (New York: William Morrow & Company, 1943). The first edition follows the copy-text; II emends to "Sharps'"; III offers "Sharp's."

130.10   then the self-same lake: Thus (with the hyphen absent from "self same") in the journal draft, MJ, October 26, 1853; the copy-text reads "there,—the self-same lake." Thoreau's "then" and "there" are often difficult to distinguish, and it would appear that the compositor misconstrued "then" in this instance and added the comma and dash. These changes produced an intelligible statement, though a less plausible one than the original.

134.23   1592:   The copy-text, like the journal draft, MJ, September 19, 1853, reads "1588." Thoreau doubtless had in mind Theodore de Bry's *Americæ Tertia Pars* (Frankfurt-on-Main, 1592), which contains numerous copper engravings of frameworks on which the natives of Brazil cooked the flesh of animals and men. The largest and most remarkable of these plates occurs at p. 179, illustrating chapter 9 of Jean de Léry's *Historia Navigationis in Brasiliam*. The text there treats of the construction of the *boucan* and the preparation of meat on it over a slow fire. Other engravings of human flesh on the *boucan* are located at pp. 71, 80, 89, and the titlepage. Thoreau read the Harvard College Library's copies of parts I-V of De Bry's great "Collection of Voyages" in the mid-1850s, taking five or six pages of notes from the "Brazil" volume alone in his Indian Extract Books (notebook 7). Thoreau's erroneous dating of the De Bry reference in "Chesuncook"—he had recorded it accurately in his Indian notes—probably resulted from his confusing, indirectly, the *Tertia Pars* with the famous quarto of Thomas Hariot's *A briefe and true report of the new found land of Virginia* (London, 1588). Unillustrated in this initial edition, Hariot's work was republished by De Bry in 1590, with De Bry's engravings based on watercolors by John White. White, or Wyth, or With, as his name is variously spelled, had spent a year at Raleigh's ill-fated Roanoke colony in Virginia. One of White's paintings, elaborated by De Bry for the 1590 "Virginia" volume, depicts a rectangular framework on which fish are being cooked. Latin and German translations of the English Hariot were issued by De Bry in the same year (1590), forming the first part of his monumental series. Though two of John White's designs were also used in De Bry's *Secunda Pars*, the "Florida" volume published in 1591, the "Brazil" illustrations are only tangentially indebted to White's work. Thoreau summarized Schoolcraft's remarks on White in his sixth Indian notebook, and recorded additional information about him in the ninth, while taking extended extracts from De Bry's English Hariot edition.

141.20 Cusabexsex: Thus in the manuscript draft, MJ, September 19, 1853, and on the Map of the Public Lands of Maine and Massachusetts. The AM reading, "Cusabesex," corresponds to no form of the name located by the present editor, and is probably not authorial.

142.2 son-in-law of Neptune: This individual, again called Neptune's son-in-law at 149.30-31 and identified as "Nicholai" in the "Appendix," is called "Peal Nicholai" in the journal draft, MJ, September 22, 1853. According to Fannie Hardy Eckstorm in *Old John Neptune and Other Maine Indian Shamans* (Portland, Me., Southworth-Anthoensen Press, 1945), p. 16 and *passim*, Peol Nicola was one of the illegitimate children of the Old Governor and Molly Molasses: he was also called Peol Molly and Peal Palassy. Among Neptune's legitimate sons a Piel Nicola Neptune is named by a twentieth-century informant, but nothing else is known of him (Eckstorm, p. 31). One of Neptune's daughters, Mary Malt, married Tomer Nicola; another, Tellis Annias, married a Nicola variously identified as Joseph, Mitchell, and "Nicola from S. John" by informants several generations later. Numerous possibilities of interpretation present themselves: (1) Tellis Annias' husband was named Peal, and it was with this Indian that Thoreau conversed; (2) Thoreau spoke with Tomer or Joseph/Mitchell Nicola but mistook his name or confused him with another Indian called Peal, Peol, or Piel; (3) Thoreau spoke with the legitimate *son* Piel Nicola Neptune and misunderstood his relationship to the Governor; (4) Thoreau spoke with the clever, highly verbal Peal (Peol) Molly Nicola, and either misunderstood his kinship with Neptune or was misinformed by the old man. Lending weight to this last possibility are Mrs. Eckstorm's impressive accounts of the guardedness of the Penobscots generally, and of the Neptune clan in particular, about their personal relations. Neither her grandfather nor her father, who had close dealings with the Governor and Molly, knew crucial details of Neptune's career as a politician and progenitor, or guessed at his powers of wizardry.

143.35   at once.:   The following passage in the copytext after "at once." is deleted in 1:

> At the carry-man's camp I saw many little birds, brownish and yellowish, with some white tail-feathers, hopping on the wood-pile, in company with the slate-colored snow-bird, (*Fringilla hiemalis*,) but more familiar than they. The lumberers said that they came round their camps, and they gave them a vulgar name. Their simple and lively note, which was heard in all the woods, was very familiar to me, though I had never before chanced to see the bird while uttering it, and it interested me not a little, because I had had many a vain chase in a spring-morning in the direction of that sound, in order to identify the bird. On the 28th of the next month, (October,) I saw in my yard, in a drizzling day, many of the same kind of birds flitting about amid the weeds, and uttering a faint *chip* merely. There was one full-plumaged Yellow-crowned Warbler (*Sylvia coronata*) among them, and I saw that the others were the young birds of that season. They had followed me from Moosehead and the North. I have since frequently seen the full-plumaged ones while uttering that note in the spring.

The deletion was almost certainly authorial. After he submitted the "Chesuncook" fair copy to the *Atlantic Monthly*, and indeed after he had revised the journal draft of his "Allegash" account at least once, Thoreau decided that the bird he had so long identified as the "myrtle bird" or "*tull-lull*" (*Sylvia coronata*: yellow-rumped warbler or golden-crowned warbler, according to Thoreau's edition of *Wilson's American Ornithology*, edited by T. M. Brewer, New York: H. S. Samuels, 1852, pp. 184-185, 694) was the white-throated sparrow. In MJ, January 15, 1858 he reports making the "myrtle bird's" note, "*ah- te te te te te te te te te*," for Dr. Samuel Kneeland, who informed him that it was the white-throated sparrow's song. He continued to refer to this bird as the "myrtle bird" in his journals through June 4, 1858, thereafter calling it the white-throated sparrow with apparent confidence (see MJ, July 5, 1858). He went back to earlier journal citations of "myrtle bird" and to some of the "Allegash" worksheets, where he corrected in pencil to "white-throated sparrow." For a related emendation in the "Allegash" copy-text see note for 193.13.

148.18 characters: In all three editions of Josselyn's *An Account of Two Voyages to New-England* used by Thoreau—the Harvard Library copy of the 1674 first edition, the 1675 second, and a reprint of the second in the *Collections of the Massachusetts Historical Society*, third series, III (1833)—the substantive reading is "characters." Since the copy-text reading, "character," implies a different sense of the term in changing from the plural to the singular, it cannot be regarded as deliberately authorial.

150.22 but-end: This is Thoreau's usual form for the term during this period, and the form listed in his lexicons. It occurs in the "Allegash" copy-text at 188.25, while "but" (end) occurs at 254.30 and twice in the journal draft for that passage. AM's "butt-end" here is emended in I to "but-end."

152.33 tops: Thoreau quotes precisely in MJ, October 21, 1852, from his source, William Gilpin's *Observations on the Western Parts of England*, second edition (London: T. Cadell and W. Davies, 1808), p. 331. The copy-text's "top" therefore seems to be nonauthorial.

156.32 recreation: The copy-text reads "re-creation," while the first draft (MJ, November 13, 1857) and a later version in a worksheet related to both "Chesuncook" and "The Allegash" (Houghton b MS Am 278.5, folder 17A) have the word as "recreation." Internal evidence argues as strongly for the hyphenated form as for the unhyphenated—that is to say, the pun might be emphasized for the reader from either of its aspects—but the manuscript record unequivocally supports "recreation." The *Atlantic* reading might have resulted from an editor's or compositor's emendation, or from the resolving of a line-end hyphenation of the term in the lost fair copy. The first edition divides at the end of the line, and II prints "recreation."

List of Emendations

ALL changes from copy-text made by the present editor, except those specified as silent alterations of design in the Textual Introduction, are recorded in the following list. The left-hand column gives THE WRITINGS OF HENRY D. THOREAU reading with a parenthetical notation of the emendation source and other significant details. The right-hand column records the reading in the copy-text—either the partial fair-copy manuscript in the Houghton Library or, where fair copy is lost, the 1858 *Atlantic Monthly* printing of "Chesuncook." These copy-texts are designated "MS" and "AM" respectively. Each series of readings from manuscript or *Atlantic Monthly* copy-text is identified by the proper abbreviation in parentheses after the first item of the group. Entries marked with an asterisk (*) before the page/line citation are discussed in the Textual Notes. Other symbols and abbreviations used in this list are "1" for the 1864 first edition of *The Maine Woods*; "MJ" for Thoreau's manuscript journal in the Pierpont Morgan Library; "Ed." for the present editor in emendations not based on a "Chesuncook" working manuscript or relevant print; "Ref." (reference work) for a printed source employed by Thoreau; and "PE" for this edition of *The Maine Woods* in THE WRITINGS OF HENRY D. THOREAU, Princeton Edition. An inferior caret ($_\wedge$) signifies the absence of a punctuation mark, and a wavy dash ($\sim$) in a copy-text reading stands for the word occupying this position in the PE reading to the left.

	PE reading	Copy-text reading
* 84.4	1853 (1)	185– (MS)
84.24	Don't (AM)	Dont
86.5	&c. (Ed.; also in 3 subsequent instances; see Textual Introduction, pp. 395-96)	&c ∧
86.9	and (AM; also in 37 subsequent instances; see Textual Introduction, pp. 394-96)	&
86.19	exhilarated (AM)	exhilirated
88.17	five (AM; also in 10 subsequent number references; see Textual Introduction, pp. 396-97)	5
90.35	St. Francis (AM)	St ∧ Francis
91.22	St. John (AM)	St ∧ John
91.28	wild (AM)	wilde
92.26	don't (AM)	dont
93.2	ash, (AM)	∼ ∧
93.21	all, (AM)	∼ ∧
93.29	lanceolata (MJ)	lanceolatus
94.17	Russell (AM)	Russel
94.18	nine hundred and sixty (AM)	960 nine hundred and sixty [*neither cancelled*]
97.5	from (AM)	from from
97.15	Mts. (Ed.)	Mts ∧
* 97.15	north (AM)	North
97.27	mountain ash (AM)	mt ∧ ash
97.29	creek (AM)	creak

98.4	twenty (AM; also in 8 subsequent number references; see Textual Introduction, pp. 396-97)	twenty 20 [*neither cancelled*]
100.25	swollen (AM)	swolen
* 100.29	crackling ∧ (AM)	~ , [*perhaps not Thoreau's comma*]
104.4	o'clock (AM)	'o'clock
* 104.15	night ∧ (AM, MJ)	~ , [*following matter cancelled*]
105.15	tea, (AM)	~ ∧
* 107.3	chicadee (1)	chickadee (AM)
113.5	swollen (AM)	swolen (MS)
* 114.1-5	[Indeed . . . woods.] (1)	*lacking*
115.35	ghastly (AM)	gastly
117.9	is, (AM)	~ ∧
* 118.14	trickled ∧ (AM, MJ)	~ , [*perhaps not a comma*]
118.21	columns, (AM)	~ ∧
* 122.15	perchance ∧ (1)	for aught I know,
* 123.10	*Katahdinauguoh* (MJ, Ref.)	*Katahdinauquoh* (AM)
123.36	batteaux (MJ)	*bateaux*
126.29	batteau (MJ)	*bateau*
* 129.5	Sharps (Ed.)	Sharpe's
* 130.10	then the (MJ)	there,—the
* 134.23	1592 (Ref.)	1588
* 141.20	Cusabexsex (MJ, Ref.)	Cusabesex
* 143.35	*omitted* (1)	At the carry-man's camp . . . spring.
144.17	batteau (MJ)	*bateau*
146.1	batteau (MJ)	*bateau*
* 148.18	characters (Ref.)	character
150.1	batteau (MJ)	*bateau*
* 150.22	but-end (1)	butt-end
* 152.33	tops (MJ, Ref.)	top
* 156.32	recreation (MJ)	re-creation

Table of Textual Variations

THE following table lists all differences of substantives, and of accidentals whose effects are alterations of meaning rather than of form alone, between the text of the present edition and the relevant forms of "Chesuncook." In addition, the table records a few substantives and significant accidentals in the manuscript drafts that may have been altered inadvertently by Thoreau in transcribing fair copy or by the compositor in setting the *Atlantic Monthly* text from now-lost portions of the fair copy.

The readings in the left-hand column are those of the present (Princeton) edition, PE (THE WRITINGS OF HENRY D. THOREAU). "MS" stands for the surviving "Chesuncook" fair copy, "AM" for the 1858 *Atlantic Monthly* printing, and "I" for the first edition of *The Maine Woods*. "MJ" designates Thoreau's manuscript journal in the Pierpont Morgan Library, of which volume 22, for 1853, contains the "Chesuncook" draft passages cited in this table. PE readings not accompanied by parenthetical reference to an earlier printed text are new in this edition.

Accidentals associated with substantive variants, but not in themselves significant, are ignored in the table entries. An inferior caret ($_\wedge$) indicates an absent punctuation mark.

	PE reading	Variant readings
84.4	1853 (I)	185– (MS, AM)
84.26	yet (MS, I)	get (AM)
85.1	blacker (MS)	boot-black (AM, I)
85.15	his bowels (MS)	the monster's bowels (AM, I)
86.5	&c., &c. (MS)	etc. (AM, I)
86.26	but mortised (MS)	but were mortised (AM, I)

87.28	one (MS)	a (AM, 1)
88.5	further (MS)	farther (AM, 1)
89.14	thought that she (MS)	thought she (AM, 1)
89.31	nor any (MS)	and no (AM, 1)
89.32	further (MS)	farther (AM, 1)
90.24	will (MS)	wish (AM, 1)
91.29	further (MS)	farther (AM, 1)
93.3-4	did not look as if they cared (MS)	looked as if they did not care (AM, 1)
93.25	last (?) a (MS)	last a (AM, 1)
93.27	&c., &c. (MS)	etc. (AM, 1)
95.12	place (MS)	suspected spot (AM, 1)
95.14	placed (MS)	set (AM, 1)
96.23	common and rarely the (MS)	*omitted* (AM, 1)
97.14	name, or (MS)	name, one or (AM, 1)
98.19	place (MS)	spot (AM, 1)
98.25	further (MS)	farther (AM, 1)
99.35-36	was moose (MS, AM)	was a moose (1)
100.8	made (MS)	making (AM, 1)
101.20	Working (MS)	They work (AM, 1)
101.21	letting (MS)	let (AM, 1)
101.21-22	grow, without (MS)	grow, and live without (AM, 1)
102.11	also the (MS)	also that of the (AM, 1)
102.11	and deer (MS)	and the deer (AM, 1)
102.19	was (MS)	is (AM, 1)
102.25	which afforded (MS)	affording (AM, 1)
103.11	inhabitant (MS)	inhabitants (AM, 1)
104.18	this (MS)	thus (AM, 1)
104.22	has (MS)	had (AM, 1)
104.33	on to (MS)	on (AM, 1)
105.9	chickaree (MS)	chickadee (AM, 1)
107.16	common (AM, 1)	commonest (MJ)
107.35	twenty (AM, 1)	25 (MJ)

110.24	furthest (MS)	farthest (AM, 1)
114.1-5	[Indeed . . . woods.] (1)	*lacking* (MS, AM)
114.14	an idea (MS)	some idea (AM, 1)
114.32	upwards (MS)	upward (AM, 1)
115.16	one inch (MS)	an inch (AM, 1)
116.1	*hide* (MS)	hide (AM, 1)
116.31	further (MS)	farther (AM, 1)
118.10-11	This was . . . main stream (MS)	This stream was . . . main one (AM, 1)
119.5-6	near to being . . . miss it, as possible (MS)	near as is possible to come to being . . . miss it (AM, 1)
121.17	use (AM, 1)	uses (MJ)
121.30	was (MS)	to have been (AM, 1)
122.14-16	It is as immortal as I am, and perchance will go to as high a heaven, there to tower above me still. (1)	It is as immortal as I am, and for aught I know, will go to as high a heaven, there to tower above me still. (MS); *omitted* (AM)
127.7	uses (AM, 1)	used (MJ)
128.11	further (AM)	farther (1)
128.13	further (AM)	farther (1)
130.10	then ∧ ∧ the	there,—the (AM, 1)
134.23	1592	1588 (AM, 1)
142.24	further (AM)	farther (1)
143.9	shave with (AM, 1)	shave a stick with (MJ)
143.35	*omitted* (1)	At the . . . spring. (AM)
148.18	characters	character (AM, 1)
152.33	tops	top (AM, 1)
153.20	further (AM)	farther (1)
156.32	recreation	re-creation (AM); re-/creation (1)

Line-end Hyphenation

THE compounds or possible compounds in list A, below, are hyphenated at the end of the line in the "Chesuncook" copy-texts. On the general grounds discussed in the Textual Introduction, page 404, the editor has resolved each to the form recorded in list A. List B records only those compounds hyphenated at the end of the line in this edition that should be transcribed with the hyphen in order to duplicate the copy-text forms.

LIST A

85.18	Whitehead	105.34	cranberry
85.31	moose-hunting	108.13	arbor-vitæs
86.24	fenceposts	109.3	pine-boards
86.30	zigzagged	111.28	reloaded
87.29	buttercups	113.9	horse-like
87.30	fire-weeds	114.12-13	cross-stake
88.12	mid-afternoon	115.6	moss-covered
89.3	semi-cylin-drical	118.2	standstill
		118.15-16	moonlight
90.7	methinks	119.14	extraordinary
90.24	life-boat	125.15	white-lead
90.35	moose-hides	127.18	black-ash
92.16	ere-long	131.20	frying-pan
93.27	bellwort	131.36	pigeon-woodpeck-er
93.36	evergreen		
96.1-2	cross-bars	132.1-2	white-pine
96.23	large-toothed	132.5	fish-hawk
97.17	woodpecker	134.17	headboard
97.31	crowfoot	139.21	last-mentioned
98.17	wool-grass	140.29-30	Large-Bay
98.33	Moosehorn	145.33	Oldtown
99.4	moose-hunting	148.13	fore-foot
102.29	moonlight	152.12	white-pines
103.26	fungus-like	154.6	meeting-house
103.33	overthrow	154.22	pear-trees
105.19	Moosehead	156.4-5	woodman's

LIST B

84.28-29	sea-sickness	128.30-31	moose-hunting
85.25-26	a-moose-hunting	132.1-2	white-pine
87.6-7	hay-caps	133.27-28	log-camp
90.17-18	India-rubber	140.29-30	Large-Bay
93.2-3	arbor-vitae	143.23-24	moose-meat
93.33-34	arbor-vitae	145.17-18	forest-warden
95.35-36	bird's-eye	147.8-9	frock-coat
96.1-2	cross-bars	148.30-31	son-in-law
96.33-34	half-drowned	149.30-31	Four-pence-ha'penny
97.5-6	south-east	153.21-22	pine-forest
114.12-13	cross-stake	154.5-6	town-house
126.4-5	ice-house	154.10-11	willow-rows

The Allegash and East Branch

Textual Notes

COPY-TEXT for the bulk of this essay is the 1864 first edition of *The Maine Woods*, but the surviving fragments of Thoreau's final draft in the Huntington and Houghton libraries serve as copy-text for the corresponding portions of the narrative. The copy-text—"I" or "first edition," or a Huntington or Houghton manuscript—is briefly identified in the first of each series of notes on emendations or decisions not to emend in a given copy-text section. The symbols "II" and "III" represent, respectively, the 1894 Riverside Edition and the 1906 Walden Edition *Maine Woods* texts. When a substantive or important accidental emendation is anticipated in II or III (or, as is once the case, in the corrected 1889 impression of the first-edition plates), the note cites the printing in which the change first appears. "MJ" stands for Thoreau's manuscript journal in the Pierpont Morgan Library, with references to entries by date.

158.32 clothing: Above the last three letters of this word in the copy-text (Huntington Library HM 13199) the letters "es" are written in the darker ink used by Sophia Thoreau. The original reading is not cancelled, and there is no indication of Thoreau's pencil beneath the interlinear ink reading.

160.31 nine: Thoreau observes in the first draft (MJ, July 23, 1857) that the stage fare was three dollars per person; see also his estimate of the cost of transportation of an Indian and a canoe from Oldtown to Moosehead Lake in the "Appendix," 320.9-11. In all likelihood the (first-edition) copy-text's "two" at this point results from a misreading of the numeral 9 in the lost last draft, for Thoreau's 2 closely resembles a 9 with its large upper loop and sometimes perfunctory horizontal stroke at the end.

161.10   further: The copy-text reads "farther" here and twenty-seven times subsequently (including one "farthest") in "The Allegash." "Further" occurs only once, at 184.20. Of the twenty-eight instances of the *a* form in 1, three are unquestionable editorial emendations of Thoreau's "further" in surviving last-draft passages, and eighteen more vary from "further" in the corresponding journal draft passages. Manuscript equivalents are lacking for only seven first-edition *a* readings. Since Thoreau uses "further" invariably in the "Allegash" working manuscripts and last-draft remains, all these *a* readings where 1 is the copy-text are regarded as editorial sophistications and regularizations. They are emended to Thoreau's "further" in the present edition. See notes for "Ktaadn," 13.11, and "Chesuncook," 128.11.

161.18   dress: While the copy-text's "address" is a plausible reading, the manuscript draft (MJ, July 23, 1857) runs "a handsome and gentlemanly dressed man with a faultless toilet." Thoreau uses "manners" rather than "address" to describe Leonard's behavior both in the draft and at 161.24 below. Thus "address" is almost surely a copyist's or compositor's misreading of "dress."

163.22   ringing: Although the copy-text's "singing" is plausible, Thoreau's usual term for the sounding of toads was "ringing," as the word appears in the manuscript draft, MJ, July 23, 1857. Two other drafts of the passage, MJ October 5, 1857, and a Houghton Library worksheet (b MS Am 278.5, folder 17B), have "ring of toads." Thoreau's initial *r* and *s* before *i* are often almost indistinguishable. III emends to "ringing."

166.19-20   The Indian thought that the mother had perhaps been killed.:   Lacking in the copy-text; added in the present edition from the journal draft, MJ, July 24, 1857. The conjunction with which the following sentence begins is functionless and the concluding clause about Kineo's protection of the ducks is not fully coherent in the absence of a statement about their vulnerability. Since no later draft has been located, the editor can come no nearer to Thoreau's intention than the journal version of this passage.

169.7 putting *m*: Thus in the journal draft (March 5, 1858) and in a worksheet among the Houghton Library fragments (folder 17D). The copy-text has "putting *ne*"—clearly the result of a misreading of Thoreau's manuscript by a copyist or compositor. III corrects to "putting *m*."

172.13-14 succeeded: The journal draft (MJ, July 24, 1857) has "succeeding" in this sentence, as does the copy-text; but the structure of the clause demands the past tense here.

177.4-5 to the *V. Pennsylvanicum*, our: Thus in III, which emends from the copy-text's bewildering "to (the *V. Pennsylvanicum*) our." The journal draft, MJ, July 24, 1857, omits the parentheses. If the copy-text's pointing duplicates that in a later draft by Thoreau, as it probably does, the parentheses there were a compositional device indicating Thoreau's doubt as to whether he would include or cancel the enclosed material. Such marks occur frequently in the working drafts.

184.29 north, south, east, west: Thoreau's imperfect last copy probably read "N. S. E. W."—the reading which occurs in the copy-text. With III, the present editor expands the abbreviations to the forms appropriate in a quotation of Polis' speech.

193.13 that State: The following sentence appears after "State" in the copy-text: "Wilson did not know where they bred, and says, 'Their only note is a kind of chip.'" Throughout the journal drafts of the "Chesuncook" and "Allegash" excursions Thoreau uses the name "myrtle bird" for the species he calls "white-throated sparrow" in the first edition. Thoreau's discovery of his error, and his correction of late drafts at some time after mid-1858, are discussed in the note for "Chesuncook," 143.35. This reference to Wilson in "The Allegash," silently deleted in III, is a part of the "myrtle bird" complex that Thoreau forgot to cancel in his lost final draft, or that was cancelled but accidentally restored by a scribe or compositor. Wilson's quoted and paraphrased remarks may be found on p. 185 of *American Ornithology* in the section on *Sylvia coronata*, the myrtle bird.

193.16 darkest: The journal first draft and a revision of the sentence, both in MJ, October 5, 1857, read "darkness." The copy-text's "darkest" is also plausible and may result from authorial revision in a later draft, though the possibility of a copyist's or compositor's misreading cannot be ruled out.

195.22 *Paytaytequick*: When recording Indian terms in the journal drafts, especially in their first occurrences, Thoreau formed his letters deliberately and sometimes spaced slightly between syllables, apparently for the sake of clarity. Such spacing appears after the first and second syllables of *"Paytaytequick"* at MJ, July 26, 1857. The copy-text reading, *"Pay tay te quick,"* may reflect a similar caution in the lost final draft; but the name is recorded as a single word in the "Appendix," 322.16. III emends here to the continuous form.

196.3 batteau: Thoreau consistently spelled this word with two *t*'s in both rough and fair copy. The house spelling "bateau(x)" imposed upon the "Chesuncook" fair copy by the *Atlantic* editor or compositors seems to have directed the choice of "bateau(x)" by Ticknor and Fields in printing "The Allegash." The present editor restores Thoreau's spelling here and at three subsequent points in this essay, drawing the emendations from specific draft appearances in two of the four instances.

199.14 *sketch*: This reproduction of Thoreau's drawing in the journal draft (MJ, July 26, 1857) replaces the words "[The figure of a bear in a boat]" in the copy-text. In the lost draft from which the first edition was set directly, or which served as the basis of a posthumous fair-copy transcription, these words clearly served as *instructions*—not as text. If they were textual in nature, they would pointlessly duplicate information already given in the two sentences near the end of the paragraph, "It was surmounted . . . to copy it."

201.6 blanket: Thus in two journal drafts of the passage, MJ, July 26 and October 5, 1857. The copy-text's "blankets" probably results from a misreading of Thoreau's lost final manuscript. At 159.25-27 Thoreau makes it clear that the Indian's bedding—for a summer trip at least—consisted of only one blanket. Likewise, a single blanket is prescribed for the traveller in the "Appendix" equipment list, 319.3-4. At 260.21 the present editor again emends "blankets" to the singular form in the journal draft, MJ, July 29, 1857.

201.34-35 *Caucomgomoc-took*; there: The journal draft (MJ, July 26, 1857) begins a new sentence with "There" and places no special emphasis on the preceding name or phrase. The pointing in the copy-text, "*Caucomgomoc-took!* there", probably reflects a misreading of Thoreau's lost final draft. III emends the exclamation point to a semicolon.

202.33 kingfisher, tweezer bird or: The copy-text's erroneous "kingfisher (tweezer bird), or" is thus corrected (with the further emendation of a hyphen in "tweezer bird") in III. In the journal draft, MJ, July 26, 1857, Thoreau isolates "tweezer bird or" in pencil parentheses, indicating his doubt as to whether to include the phrase. A similar set of parentheses may have occurred in a later draft and led to the blunder in the copy-text.

219.34 "swamping" it: In the copy-text the quotation is closed after "it," though the pronoun is not part of the expression Thoreau here defines. His source, John Springer's *Forest Life and Forest Trees* (New York: Harper & Brothers, 1851), p. 84, speaks of "swamping" but not of "swamping it." No quotation marks are employed in the journal draft, MJ, July 27, 1857. III emends as in the present edition.

227.5 north-west, containing: Thoreau's last draft, Houghton Library b MS Am 278.5, folder 17A, is the copy-text for this passage. It is heavily revised in pencil here, and was apparently left in an imperfect condition. The ink original of the sentence begins, "Also a township many miles further north-west was indicated to us, containing the highest land thereabouts." Thoreau cancelled the first word and interlined in pencil, "At Bangor we had been told of." "Was" and the first syllable of "indicated" were later cancelled and "It" inserted after "north-west" in the darker ink and handwriting of Sophia Thoreau. Thoreau's revision at the beginning of the sentence required an adjustment of the original predicate, and from all appearances, including the irresolute cancellation of "was in-," Sophia chose the first edition's awkward wording, "northwest; it was indicated to us as containing," while at work on the manuscript after her brother's death.

228.1   undistinguished: This is the ink original reading in the last-draft copy-text. The word "obscure" is interlined in pencil as an alternative, but neither term is cancelled. The first edition prints "undistinguished."

230.5-8   When the state . . . a university.:   The original version of this sentence is found in MJ, March 9, 1858, and an intermediate draft appears in another context on a rough worksheet in Houghton folder 17D. In the Houghton last draft, copy-text for this passage, the sentence is a marginal pencil insertion entirely in the hand of Sophia Thoreau. A caret and paragraph mark between "Nature's leave!" (228.22) and Thoreau's indented "The wilderness" are also apparently in Sophia's handwriting, and the sentence appears there in the first edition. But the paragraph beginning "The wilderness" is plainly continuous with the conclusion of the last: both treat of the damage done by damming the streams and lakes. (See also the first draft, MJ, November 5, 1857.) This continuity is seriously disrupted by the observation on state grants of land to academies and universities. It fits naturally, however, at the end of the paragraph contrasting true culture with the gross learning of the "Anglo-American." In the last draft of that paragraph (folder 17A), cancelled passages on the culture-barbarism theme that follow it end with two authorial notes in pencil: "Strange &c" and, almost illegibly, "The State —[?] V S."

234.34   *margaritacea*:   The spelling *"margaraticea"* in the first edition, the copy-text here, may result from Thoreau's error in the lost final draft, since the name is so misspelled in the journal draft, MJ, July 28, 1857.

236.5   forks at: Thus in the journal draft, MJ, October 6, 1857. The copy-text's "forks of the" is obviously in error and nonauthorial, for Nickatou, the name of an island at the junction of the East and West Branches, means "the forks," as Thoreau observes in "Ktaadn," 18.17.

238.4   and we under: The copy-text's "and we ran under," which confounds the sentence structure, may result from an imperfect or forgotten cancellation in the lost final draft. The journal draft (MJ, July 28, 1857) reads "compelled us to get under the edge of the dam & under the canoe," the second "under" being a pencilled addition.

243.19-20 in a deserted log hut: The journal drafts, MJ, October 7 and 31, 1857, specify that the bread was found in a hut; see also MJ, July 29, 1857: "Here was a deserted log hut." The copy-text's implausible "on a deserted log" (a log might be abandoned, but not deserted) doubtless results from a misreading of the lost manuscript by a copyist or compositor.

246.28 1853:   The erroneous date in the copy-text, "1854," probably reflects Thoreau's own *lapsus* in the lost final copy, for the journal draft (MJ, July 29, 1857, insert) reads "at Old-town in '54." The conversation to which Thoreau refers is recorded in the journal for October 26, 1853.

251.11 path: Thus in the journal draft, MJ, July 29, 1857, and in III, which emends from the copy-text's "paths." The plural not only obscures the fact that Thoreau and Hoar used the same trail here, but also disagrees with "it" at the end of the sentence.

258.22-23 trees (not of rocks) for: Thus in the journal draft, MJ, July 29, 1857 (a pencil interlineation). The copy-text's "trees, without rocks, for" probably results from a misreading of Thoreau's manuscript, for later in the paragraph Thoreau says he searched for Hoar along that section of shore, "thinking he might be concealed behind a rock."

263.36 *Nerlumskeechticook*:   The original ink reading in Thoreau's final draft (Houghton fragments, folder 17A) is "*Nerlumskiticook.*" When making pencil revisions, Thoreau cancelled the first *i*, drew a caret under it, and added some letters above, which Sophia went over in ink thus: "kech." The pencil substratum is now illegible, but this name is spelled with two *e*'s by Thoreau in a cancelled phrase immediately after the present appearance, from which Sophia might have deduced the correct spelling as she recopied the page for the printer: the first edition reads "*Nerlumskeechticook.*" This is also the form prescribed by Thoreau on a worksheet (folder 17C) bearing the titles of the three chapters and of the book as a whole, plus the spellings of two Indian terms: "always . . . 'Nerlumskeechticook.[']" The worksheet was consulted by Sophia, for it contains matter in her handwriting.

264.8-11   The dark . . . around it.:   In the final draft Thoreau wrote, "The dark mts about it were seen through a glaucous mist, and the brilliant white stems of canoe-birches, mingled with other woods, rose around." Revising in pencil, he cancelled "mts" and entered "mountains" above, placed a caret after "canoe-birches" and added some matter above the line, added "the" after "with," cancelled "rose," and added "it" at the end of the sentence. All these revisions were confirmed by Sophia in dark ink. She construed the interlinear matter after "canoe-birches" as "were seen," but the pencil substratum is now illegible. When Sophia recopied the page for the printer, she disregarded (as does the present editor) three original marks of punctuation that were rendered inappropriate by the revision: commas after "canoe-birches" and "woods" and a period after "around." By accident or design, however, she also disregarded the interlinear "were seen," which does not appear in the first edition.

265.35   fallen red maples: Thoreau first wrote "fallen timber—red maples &c," and then cancelled "timber" and "&c" in pencil. The uncancelled and now superfluous dash before "red" was disregarded in the preparation of first-edition copy by Sophia, as it is in the present edition.

269.30   brought: Thoreau cancelled this word lightly in pencil and interlined "collected" above. The latter word was then erased, but whether by Thoreau or by another it is impossible to tell. The first edition prints "brought."

274.8-9   black ash . . . to appear,:   The first-edition copy-text's confusing parentheses around this phrase probably reflect an imperfect late draft. In the journal draft (MJ, July 30, 1857) Thoreau first wrote "black ash, & elms which began to appear"; he then isolated "black ash, & elms" with parentheses, expressing his indecision, and queried above the line, "or after?" See note for a similar survival of doubt-marks in the copy-text at 177.4-5.

280.22   then: Thus in the copy-text. The reading in the journal draft (MJ, July 31, 1857) is uncertain, but may be "there"—a somewhat more appropriate word in this context. In the absence of more convincing evidence, however, the present editor does not emend.

284.10 salmon.: Copy-text is the Houghton final draft, folder 17A. After "salmon" Thoreau wrote in pencil, "This house &c"—designating the insertion of a sentence beginning with those words. No such sentence appears on other last-draft pages or in the first edition. Thoreau's reference may be to an erased pencil passage of sentence length on this page of the final draft, of which the first words alone are barely legible. They seem to read "This house." In MJ, August 1, 1857, Thoreau observes, "This house is on the E bank," but that information about Hunt's was supplied in the first sentence of the copy-text paragraph, where it formed part of the basic ink writing.

286.13-14 "Locks (rocks): Copy-text is the first edition, where " 'Rocks (locks)' " confuses Thoreau's rendering of Polis' speech. The journal draft has only " 'Rocks' " (MJ, August 1, 1857). Compare " 'lock (rock)' ", from Thoreau's final draft, at 269.15.

286.21 east: The journal draft, MJ, August 1, 1857, distinctly reads "E"; the copy-text has "west." Whether or not the lost final draft from which the first edition derives followed the journal, it is reasonable to assume that the earlier reading is the correct one.

286.22-288.32 On the mainland . . . falling asleep.: This material, amounting to two and a half pages in the copy-text, was erroneously placed at 276.7, with "On the mainland" inset as a paragraph. In the corrected reimpressions beginning with that of 1889 the material was moved to the place it occupies in the journal draft (MJ, August 1, 1857) and in the present edition. "On the mainland" is made the last sentence of the paragraph, as in the journal, by the unknown corrector. For a discussion of this major copy-text error, its discovery, and its correction, see the Textual Introduction, 356, 370-74.

289.2-3 August 2, / was: The copy-text has a dash after "2," at the right margin, and capitalizes "was." "Was" is also indented as a paragraph. Thoreau's apparent intention was to link the date-line and the beginning of the entry more closely than this. The journal draft has "Sunday Aug 2nd" on one line and a deliberate fragment, "A cloudy and unpromising morning," inset on the next. Thoreau later added "was" in pencil to the right of "2nd." The copy-text creates the false appearance of a fragment; this treatment is probably not authorial.

291.26-27   lives on one: Thus in the journal draft, MJ, August 3, 1857. The copy-text's "lives in one" (which probably results from a misreading of Thoreau's manuscript) distorts the sense, for "in" is intelligible only if "one" refers to "houses." The Governor, however, lived *on* one of the Indian islands in the Penobscot, situated within Lincoln township.

293.23   Fenwick: In point of fact the Bishop of Boston at the time of the liberty-pole fracas may have been John Bernard Fitzpatrick, rather than his predecessor, Benedict Joseph Fenwick. In *Old John Neptune*, p. 168n., Fannie Hardy Eckstorm declares that "Fenwick is a slip for Fitzpatrick." Thoreau's journal draft, MJ, August 3, 1857, has the same reading as the copy-text, and the slip (if it was an error) could have been Polis'. The chronology of the school dispute is vague and the nineteenth-century documentation scarce and partly colored by private interests. Mrs. Eckstorm's evidence suggests a date in the late 1840s or early 1850s for the liberty-pole episode. Fitzpatrick, third Bishop of Boston, succeeded Fenwick upon the latter's death on August 11, 1846; both men took a lively interest in Maine missionary activities.

294.29   Olamon: Thus in the journal draft, MJ, August 3, 1857, and in II, which emends from the copy-text's "Olarmon." The error probably resulted from memorial contamination by *"Olarmon"* (Island) and *"larmon"* in the preceding long paragraph.

295.29   stroke, getting: The journal draft reading, adopted in III, is "stroke give it a twist in order to steer the boat only getting" (MJ, August 3, 1857). The questionable grammar of the copy-text version raises the possibility that a portion of the sentence, duplicating or resembling that in the journal, was accidentally dropped. If this material was present in a later draft and was cancelled by Thoreau, he may or may not have remembered to alter "getting" to "get." In the absence of any firm evidence of authorial intention, the present editor is unwilling to attempt substantive emendation.

List of Emendations

ALL changes from copy-text made by the present editor, except those specified as silent alterations of design in the Textual Introduction, are recorded in the following list. The left-hand column gives THE WRITINGS OF HENRY D. THOREAU reading with a parenthetical notation of the emendation source and other significant details. The right-hand column records the reading in the copy-text—either the 1864 first edition of *The Maine Woods* or the surviving fragments of Thoreau's last "Allegash" draft in the Huntington and Houghton libraries. These copy-texts are designated "I," "MS Huntington," and "MS Houghton" respectively. Each series of readings from manuscript or first-edition copy-text is identified by the proper abbreviation in parentheses after the first item of the group. Entries marked with an asterisk (*) before the page/line citation are discussed in the Textual Notes. Other symbols and abbreviations used in this list are "I [1889-1892]" (in a single source notation) for the impressions between 1889 and 1892 from the first-edition plates; "II" for the 1894 Riverside Edition and "III" for the 1906 Walden Edition where these anticipate a substantive emendation or important accidental emendation made by the present editor; "MJ" for Thoreau's manuscript journal in the Pierpont Morgan Library; "Ed." for the present editor in emendations not based on an "Allegash" working manuscript or anticipated in I; "Ref." (reference work) for a printed source employed by Thoreau; and "PE" for this edition of *The Maine Woods* in THE WRITINGS OF HENRY D. THOREAU, Princeton Edition. A wavy dash (~) in a copy-text reading stands for the word occupying this position in the PE reading to the left, and an inferior caret (∧) signifies the absence of a punctuation mark.

	PE reading	Copy-text reading
157.18	blacksmith, (1)	∼ ∧ (MS Huntington) ["who . . . blacksmith" *an interlinear insertion*]
157.19	rock. (1)	rock;
158.22	$2 oo (Ed.)	$200
158.23	dollar and (1; also in 4 subsequent instances in MS Huntington; see Textual Introduction, pp. 394-96)	dollar &
158.25	o'clock (1)	'o'clock
158.32	&c. (1)	&c ∧
159.7	friend's (1)	friends'
* 160.31	nine (Ed.)	two (1)
* 161.10	further (MJ)	farther
161.12	Ristigouche (MJ, II)	Pistigouche
* 161.18	dress (MJ)	address
161.32	further (Ed.)	farther
* 163.22	ringing (MJ, III)	singing
163.23	seasons (MJ)	season
* 166.19-20	The Indian . . . killed. (MJ)	*lacking*
168.32	*reality* (MJ, III)	*realility*
168.34	is, (Ed., II)	∼ ∧
* 169.7	putting *m* (MJ, Houghton worksheet, III)	putting *ne*
169.9	*m–ar* (Houghton worksheet)	*m ar*
170.22-23	lake, and she (MJ, III)	lake, she
172.2	it! (MJ)	∼ .

* 172.13-14	succeeded (Ed.)	succeeding
173.6	further (MJ)	farther
* 177.4-5	the V. *Pennsyl-vanicum,* our (MJ)	(the V. *Pennsyl-vanicum*) our
181.20	*retorts* (MJ)	retorts
182.36	further (Ed.)	farther
184.21	side hill (MJ)	side-hill
* 184.29	north, south, east, west (Ed.)	N. S. E. W.
185.26	exactly, (MJ)	~ ∧
186.20	curve (MJ)	course
189.6	we (MJ)	he
190 n.	Rasles' (Ed.)	Rasle's
* 193.13	*omitted* (Ed., III)	Wilson . . . chip."
194.10	further (MJ)	farther
194.26	there's (MJ)	ther 's
195.6	*Beskabekukskish-tuk* (MJ)	*Beska bekuk-skishtuk*
* 195.22	*Paytaytequick* (Ed.)	*Pay tay te quick*
195.27	white-headed (MJ, III)	white-beaked
195.30	*Nonglangyis* ∧ (MJ)	~ ,
* 196.3	batteau (MJ)	bateau
198.30	further (MJ)	farther
* 199.14	*sketch* (MJ)	*lacking*
199.14	*omitted* (MJ, Ed.)	[The figure of a bear in a boat.]
199.21	*Niasoseb* ∧ (MJ)	~ .
199.22	Joseph ∧ (MJ)	~ .
199.23	*elioi* (MJ, III)	*clioi*
199.26	*onke* (MJ, III)	*ouke*
199.28	*quambi* (MJ)	quambi
200.30	further (MJ)	farther
* 201.6	blanket (MJ)	blankets
201.28	further (MJ)	farther
201.33	*Caucomgomoc-took* (MJ)	*Caucomgomoctook*
* 201.34	*Caucomgomoc-took;* (Ed.)	~ !

* 202.33	kingfisher, tweezer bird ∧ or (Ed., III)	kingfisher (tweezer bird), or
210.25	batteau (MJ)	bateau
210.36	poled (MJ, III)	polled
210.36	part (MJ, III)	point
211.15	head (MJ, III)	bend
211.26	John's (Ed.)	Johns
213.7	further (MJ)	farther
214.8	further (Ed.)	farther
* 219.34	"swamping" it, (Ref., III)	"swamping it,"
222.2	Telos (MJ, II)	Tebos
226.16	very (1)	Very (MS Houghton)
226.17	and (1; also in 83 subsequent instances in MS Houghton; see Textual Introduction, pp. 394-96)	&
226.20	blanket. (1)	~ —
226.22	&c. (1; also in 3 subsequent instances in MS Houghton; see Textual Introduction, pp. 395-96)	&c ∧
227.1	St. John's (1)	St ∧ Johns
227.23	lake, (1)	~ ∧
227.24	water, (1)	~ —
227.25	them, (1)	~ ∧ ["some . . . them" an interlinear insertion]
227.35	blazoned. (1)	~ —
228.8	St. (1)	St ∧
229.21-22	log, the . . . corpse, (1)	~ ∧ ~ . . . ~ ∧ ["the . . . corpse" an interlinear insertion]
230.1	Spenser (1)	Spencer

* 230.5-8	When the state . . . university. (Ed.)	[*sentence placed by Sophia Thoreau at 228.22*]
230.7	land; (1)	$\sim$ $_\wedge$
230.7	academy, (1)	$\sim$ $_\wedge$
230.8	university. (1)	$\sim$ $_\wedge$
230.10	about (MJ, 1)	about about
232.15	further (MJ)	farther (1)
233.9	further (MJ)	farther
234.33	abundant, (Ed.)	$\sim$.
234.33	*sinuatus* (MJ, III)	*minatus*
* 234.34	*margaritacea* (Ed.)	*margaraticea*
235.2	furthest (Ed.)	farthest
235.14	were (MJ)	was
* 236.5	forks at (MJ)	forks of the
236.9	Vegetation (MJ)	vegetation
* 238.4	*omitted* (Ed.)	ran
238.23	raised were still (MJ)	raised still
241.31	*shecorways* (MJ)	*she-cor-ways*
242.26	*Paytaywecongomec* (MJ)	*Paytaywecomgomoc*
* 243.19-20	in a deserted log hut (Ed.)	on a deserted log
243.23	further (Ed.)	farther
243.27	further (Ed.)	farther
* 246.28	1853 (Ed.)	1854
247.22-23	*Madunkehunk* (MJ)	*Madunkchunk*
247.23-24	*Madunkehunk-gamooc* (MJ)	*Madunkchunk-gamooc*
248.4	simple (Ed.)	sim ple
249.6	batteau (Ed.)	bateau
* 251.11	path (MJ, III)	paths
255.13	further (MJ)	farther
* 258.22-23	trees (not of rocks) (MJ)	trees, without rocks,
258.36	further (MJ)	farther
259.3	further (MJ)	farther
260.21	blanket (MJ)	blankets
261.27	further (MJ)	farther

261.33	further (MJ)	farther
263.35	mountains (Ed.)	mts ∧ (MS Houghton)
263.35	side—(MJ)	∼ ∧
* 263.36	*Nerlumskeechti-cook* (Houghton worksheet, 1)	*Nerlumskechticook* [?]
264.1	Mt. (Ed.)	Mt ∧
264.3	elevations (1)	elevation
264.6	*mooc* (1)	mooc
* 264.8-11	canoe-birches ∧ . . . woods ∧ . . . around ∧ (1)	∼ , . . . ∼ , . . . ∼ .
264.18	mountain (1)	mt ∧
265.9	moose!" (1)	∼ ! ∧
265.19	neighborhood (1)	neighbor-hood [?]
* 265.35	fallen ∧ (1)	∼ —
266.34	we (1)	We
267.9	spruce—(MJ)	∼ ∧
267.9	&c.—(Ed.)	&c ∧ ∧
267.19	lbs. (Ed.)	lbs ∧
267.19	lbs. (Ed.)	lbs ∧
268.9	S.W. (Ed.)	S ∧ W ∧
268.10	mountains (1)	mts ∧
268.12	mountains (1)	mts ∧
268.28	cooking, (1)	∼ .
268.34	Pine, (1)	∼ ∧
269.23	skull ∧ (Ed.)	∼ .
269.33	Madunkehunk (MJ)	Madunkchunk (1)
270.6	falls (MJ)	forks
270.8	memorable (MJ)	more arable
270.23	N.W. (Ed.)	N ∧ W ∧ (MS Houghton)
270.23	S.E. (Ed.)	S ∧ E ∧
270.26-27	mountain (1)	mt ∧
* 274.8-9	∧ black . . . appear, ∧ (Ed.)	(∼ . . . ∼ ,) (1)
274.14	lip (MJ)	lips
274.20	dollars' (Ed., III)	dollars ∧
275.7	further (MJ)	farther
275.30	further (MJ)	farther
277.5	that (Ed., II)	tnat

278.19	cougar]—ledges (MJ, III)	cougar] lodges
280.36	further (Ed.)	farther
282.27	Menard (Ref., 1)	Mènard (MS Houghton) [*accent possibly in another hand*]
282.27-28	abandoned, (1)	~ ∧
282.31	himself, (1)	~ .
282.33	insupportable," says he, "that (1)	~ ∧∧ ~ ~ ∧∧ ~ ["says he" *an interlinear insertion*]
282.35	one's self (1)	onesself
283.23	according (1)	ac.
283.24	E. (MJ)	E ∧
283.34	feet, (1)	~ ∧ ["& without . . . feet" *an interlinear insertion*]
284.7	Fisk's (1)	Fisks
284.8	mountain (1)	mt ∧
284.17	guide, (1)	~ ∧
284.17	don't (Ed.)	dont
* 286.13-14	Locks (rocks) (Ed.)	Rocks (locks) (1)
* 286.21	east (MJ)	west
* 286.22-288.32	On the mainland . . . falling asleep. (MJ, 1 [1889-1892])	[*placed at* 276.7]
286.27	signs (MJ)	sign
* 289.2-3	August 2, / was (MJ)	August 2,— / Was ["Was" *inset as paragraph*]
290.7	further (MJ)	farther
290.11	further (MJ)	farther
* 291.27	on (MJ)	in
292.4	Matanawcook (MJ)	Matanancook
292.29	batteaux (Ed.)	bateaux
294.22	use (MJ)	used
* 294.29	Olamon (MJ, II)	Olarmon

295.5	me (MJ)	we
296.4	according (Ed.)	accord ing
296.26	P.M. (Ed.)	P ∧ m ∧ (MS Houghton)
296.32	10–(Ed.)	10.
296.36	Mrs. (1)	Mrs ∧
296.36	hat (MJ, 1)	h [*remainder torn away*]
297.1	breast, (MJ, 1)	breas [*remainder torn away*]
297.2	The (MJ, 1)	[*torn away*]
297.3	large new (MJ, 1)	la [*remainder torn away*]
297.3	Indian Island (MJ, 1)	Indian [*remainder torn away*]
297.4	opposite (MJ, 1)	op [*remainder torn away*]
297.5	cars (MJ, 1)	c [*remainder torn away*]
297.8	This (1)	[*torn away*]
297.8	took the (MJ, 1)	[*all but final letter torn away*]
297.9	night (MJ, 1)	[*all but final letter torn away*]

Table of Textual Variations

THE following table lists all differences of substantives, and of accidentals whose effects are alterations of meaning rather than of form alone, between the text of the present edition and the relevant forms of "The Allegash and East Branch." In addition, the table records a few substantives and significant accidentals in the working manuscripts that may have been altered inadvertently by Thoreau in preparing final copy or changed by a copyist or compositor after Thoreau's death.

The readings in the left-hand column are those of the present (Princeton) edition, PE (THE WRITINGS OF HENRY D. THOREAU). "MS Huntington" and "MS Houghton" designate the surviving final draft fragments, and "I" represents the 1864 first edition of *The Maine Woods*. Some PE readings are emendations first anticipated in the 1889-1892 impressions from first-edition plates (I [1889-1892]) or the 1906 Walden Edition (III), as noted by these symbols. "MJ" stands for Thoreau's manuscript journal in the Pierpont Morgan Library, of which volumes 29 and 30, for 1857, contain the "Allegash" draft passages cited in this table. PE readings not accompanied by parenthetical reference to an earlier printed text are new in this edition.

Accidentals associated with substantive variants, but not in themselves significant, are ignored in the table entries. A wavy dash ($\sim$) in a variant listing designates the word occupying this position in the PE reading. An inferior caret ($\wedge$) indicates an absent punctuation mark.

	PE reading	Variant reading
157.19	a rock (MS Huntington)	the rock (1)
157.20	us (MS Huntington)	me (1)
158.28	reliable (MS Huntington)	trustworthy (1)
159.6	Polis (MS Huntington)	the Indian (1)
159.7	friend's (1)	friends' (MS Huntington)
160.13	stages ∧ (MS Huntington)	∼ , (1)
160.31	nine	two (1)
161.10	further	farther (1)
161.18	dress	address (1)
161.32	further	farther (1)
163.22	ringing (III)	singing (1)
163.23	seasons	season (1)
166.19-20	The Indian . . . killed.	*lacking* (1)
168.32	*reality* (III)	*realility* (1)
169.7	putting *m* (III)	putting *ne* (1)
170.22-23	lake, and she (III)	lake, she (1)
172.13-14	succeeded	succeeding (1)
173.6	further	farther (1)
175.4	sources (1)	source (MJ)
177.5	earliest (1)	earlier (MJ)
180.35	fires (1)	fire (MJ)
181.20	*retorts*	retorts (1)
182.36	further	farther (1)
184.21	side hill	side-hill (1)
185.6	straight to camp (1)	straight camp (MJ)
185.26	exactly,	∼ ∧ (1)
186.20	curve	course (1)
189.6	we	he (1)
193.13	*omitted* (III)	Wilson . . . chip." (1)
193.16	darkest (1)	darkness (MJ)
194.10	further	farther (1)
195.27	white-headed (III)	white-beaked (1)

195.30	*Nonglangyis* ∧ (III)	~ , (I)
198.1	greater (I)	great (MJ)
198.30	further	farther (I)
199.14	*sketch*	[The figure of a bear in a boat.] (I)
199.23	*elioi* (III)	*clioi* (I)
199.26	*onke* (III)	*ouke* (I)
200.30	further	farther (I)
201.6	blanket	blankets (I)
201.28	further	farther (I)
202.33	kingfisher, tweezer bird ∧ or (III)	kingfisher (tweezer bird), or (I)
203.8	rivers (I)	river (MJ)
204.30	purpose (I)	purposes (MJ)
210.36	poled (III)	polled (I)
210.36	part (III)	point (I)
211.15	head (III)	bend (I)
213.7	further	farther (I)
214.8	further	farther (I)
226.24	main, was hardly (MS Houghton)	main hardly (I)
226.25	or an (MS Houghton)	and an (I)
226.32	north-westerly (MS Houghton)	northeasterly (I)
226.33	discerned (MS Houghton)	discovered (I)
227.5	further (MS Houghton)	farther (I)
227.5	north-west, containing	northwest; it was indicated to us as containing (I)
227.9	now (MS Houghton)	*lacking* (I)
227.16	Polis (MS Houghton)	the Indian (I)
228.5	further (MS Houghton)	farther (I)
230.5-8	When the . . . university.	*placed at* 228.22 (I)
230.10	about (I)	about about (MS Houghton)

232.15	further	farther (1)
233.9	further	farther (1)
234.33	*sinuatus* (III)	*minatus* (1)
235.2	furthest	farthest (1)
235.14	were	was (1)
236.5	forks at	forks of the (1)
238.4	we under	we ran under (1)
238.23	raised were still	raised still (1)
240.16	behind (1)	before (MJ)
243.19-20	in a deserted log hut	on a deserted log (1)
243.23	further	farther (1)
243.27	further	farther (1)
246.28	1853	1854 (1)
246.36	source (1)	sources (MJ)
249.12	by wet (1)	by being wet (MJ)
249.28-29	by the way (1)	on the way (MJ)
251.11	path (III)	paths (1)
253.34	could (1)	would (MJ)
255.13	further	farther (1)
258.22-23	(not of rocks)	without rocks (1)
258.36	further	farther (1)
259.3	further	farther (1)
260.19	was by this (1)	was now (MJ)
260.21	blanket	blankets (1)
261.27	further	farther (1)
261.33	further	farther (1)
263.30	yellow land Lily (MS Houghton)	wild yellow lily (1)
264.3	elevations (1)	elevation (MS Houghton)
264.8	ripples (MS Houghton)	ripple (1)
264.11	were seen (MS Houghton)	*lacking* (1)
264.17	loons (MS Houghton)	loon (1)
264.24	of Ambejijis (MS Houghton)	of the Ambejijis (1)
264.26	3/4 down (MS Houghton)	down three quarters of (1)
264.27	a line (MS Houghton)	*lacking* (1)

264.31	crashing (MS Houghton)	crushing (1)
264.35	dream (MS Houghton)	dreams (1)
266.16	She's (MS Houghton)	She is (1)
266.21	scored (MS Houghton)	scarred (1)
266.25	completely (MS Houghton)	*lacking* (1)
267.6	as usual to obtain (MS Houghton)	to find (1)
268.21	saying (MS Houghton)	and said (1)
268.36-269.3	which is . . . 10 feet high (MS Houghton)	*lacking* (1)
269.22	other (MS Houghton)	*lacking* (1)
270.6	falls	forks (1)
270.8	memorable	more arable (1)
270.24	ridges (MS Houghton)	ridge (1)
274.14	lip	lips (1)
275.7	further	farther (1)
275.30	further	farther (1)
278.19	ledges (III)	lodges (1)
280.36	further	farther (1)
282.20	attempt (1)	attempts (MJ)
282.21	in this (MS Houghton)	on this (1)
282.27	René (MS Houghton)	Reni (1)
282.29	Outaoüax (MS Houghton)	Ontarios (1)
283.30-31	sore feet of my companion (MS Houghton)	chafed feet of one of my companions (1)
283.33-34	them, and without (MS Houghton)	them without (1)
283.34	using (MS Houghton)	wearing (1)
284.5	us (MS Houghton)	me (1)

284.6	above, and also (MS Houghton)	above; also (1)
284.15	when (MS Houghton)	then (1)
284.16	Polis (MS Houghton)	The Indian (1)
284.17	don't (MS Houghton)	do not (1)
284.20	after all (MS Houghton)	*lacking* (1)
286.13-14	Locks (rocks)	Rocks (locks) (1)
286.21	east	west (1)
286.22-288.32	On the mainland . . . falling asleep. (1 [1889-1892])	*placed at* 276.7 (1)
286.27	signs	sign (1)
289.34	drizzling (1)	mizzling (MJ)
290.7	further	farther (1)
290.11	further	farther (1)
291.27	on one	in one (1)
294.22	use	used (1)
295.5	me	we (1)
295.29	stroke, getting (1)	stroke give it a twist in order to steer the boat only getting (MJ)
296.26	P.M. (MS Houghton)	in the afternoon (1)
296.29	on the bank (MS Houghton)	or the boat (1)
297.8	last I (MS Houghton)	last that I (1)

Line-end Hyphenation

THE compounds or possible compounds in list A, below, are hyphenated at the end of the line in the "Allegash" copy-texts. On the general grounds discussed in the Textual Introduction, page 404, the editor has resolved each to the form recorded in list A. List B records only those compounds hyphenated at the end of the line in this edition that should be transcribed with the hyphen in order to duplicate the copy-text forms.

LIST A

160.17	threadbare	216.10-11	"highlands"
166.3	southwest	217.34	outlook
168.22	bluebirds	219.3	cedar-top
172.23	Whereupon	220.4	road-makers
174.4	headway	225.30	east-southeast
175.8	overcast	227.6	thereabouts
177.2	harebells	230.32	southwest
177.15	twayblade	232.23	carrying-places
182.23	myself	235.22	snow-shoes
184.2	overtaken	235.30	guide-board
186.15	southwesterly	240.28-29	meadow-mouse
188.10	empty-handed	241.2	shed-shaped
188.18	spruce-bark	241.3	Yankee-baker
189.27	camping-place	243.20	Yankee-baker
191.12	birch-bark	249.24	lumbermen
191.36-192.1	thun- der-shower	250.5	northeasterly
		254.27	golden-rod
195.2	rememberum	256.32-33	rock-waves
196.7	canoe-birch	259.14	near-sighted
196.28	water-fowl	262.31	overtook
197.32	northwest	264.36	fisherman
197.33	south-southeast	266.5	upside
203.14	birch-bark	267.27	sometimes
207.35	water-lily	270.25	north-westerly
208.7	night-hawks	271.16	hereabouts
214.26	black-flies	276.12	rock-maple
215.16	northeasterly	276.22	erelong

277.13	forenoon	215.19-20	insect-wash
284.34	moose-tracks	218.21-22	seventy-five
287.29	tent-poles	222.28-29	light-colored
289.5	moose-hide	223.3-4	moose-flies
289.14	long-winded	225.12-13	low-flying
289.19-20	story-teller's	233.20-21	east-southeast
289.25	Frenchman	235.27-28	half-mile
290.15	thun-der-shower	238.21-22	thunder-storm
		240.20-21	arbor-vitæ
293.5	southeast	255.36-256.1	fire-weed
294.16	Greenbush	256.32-33	rock-waves
		268.20-21	gun-case
		272.5-6	moose-hide
	LIST B	279.1-2	starting-point
163.12-13	purple-fringed	280.20-21	mid-channel
165.35-36	wood-pewee	280.30-31	white-headed
169.16-17	bow-arrow	284.11-12	moose-hide
174.36-175.1	hay-caps	285.21-22	river-side
178.2-3	ridge-pole	287.15-16	stage-road
184.7-8	bear-haunted	288.29-30	moose-hide
189.25-26	thun-der-shower	289.19-20	story-teller's
		289.31-32	moose-meat
191.2-3	stub-ends	290.12-13	lake-like
207.32-33	wool-grass	291.3-4	to-day
214.17-18	forest-path	294.27-28	hemp-nettle

Appendix

Textual Notes

COPY-TEXT for the "Appendix" is the 1864 first edition of *The Maine Woods*. The symbol "III" represents the 1906 Walden Edition *Maine Woods* text in one note for a substantive emendation anticipated in that edition. "MJ" stands for Thoreau's manuscript journal in the Pierpont Morgan Library, with references to entries by date.

303.21 Ansel: This spelling in the copy-text and the journal draft, MJ, October 8, 1857, varies from "Ansell" in the "Chesuncook" draft and copy-text (123.34, 127.2), but neither form seems more certain than the other.

303.33 1853 and 1857, carries, frequent: The copy-text reading, "1853, and carries frequent," is an obvious error; in the journal draft (MJ, October 8, 1857) Thoreau specifies "53 & 7" as the years when he noticed this plant, and "On carries &c frequent" as the locale.

304.3 1853 (curled: A question-mark in the margin at this item in the journal draft, MJ, October 8, 1857, almost surely applies to the identification, rather than the date. Since *Rumex crispus* is queried at the beginning of the citation here, the copy-text's question-mark after "1853" is regarded as inadvertent and misleading.

305.6 *Betula alba**: In the journal draft, MJ, October 8, 1857, Thoreau marks this species as one not found in the backwoods. According to the notation at the head of the "List of Plants," it should therefore be asterisked. The copy-text lacks the asterisk here and in four later entries for plants Thoreau observed only near the settlements and marked for special treatment in the draft list.

306.10 *Pennsylvanicum*? (dwarf-blueberry): The copy-text reads "*Pennsylvanicum* (dwarf-blueberry?)," but Thoreau's query applies to his identification of the species rather than to the appropriateness of the common name. His clearer pattern of scientific name-question mark-common name, to which this and four later entries are emended, occurs originally nine times in the "Appendix."

308.30 East Branch: The copy-text's "South Branch" is an obvious error for "East Branch," where Thoreau was on July 31, 1857.

309.21-22 Smith's, Chesuncook: The copy-text adds "dam" after "Smith's" but there was no dam at this settlement. The journal draft, MJ, October 8, 1857, reads simply "Smith's." In the journal for September 18, 1853, Thoreau notes buttercups along the Chesuncook shore near Smith's. He may have intended the word "farm" for this "Appendix" entry.

310.28-29 common in 1857 . . . 1853.: The copy-text places "common" after "1853," probably reflecting an unclear printer's-copy manuscript. In the journal draft (MJ, October 8, 1857) "57" is a careted insertion immediately after "common" and before the other information. A comma after "1853" in the copy-text is deleted as required by this emendation.

315.28 145: Thus in the copy-text; but the number of plants totals only 143 unless one counts the white *Epilobium angustifolium* and *Nabalus altissimus*, neither of which is set off as a separate entry. The first of these is a sport, rather than a species or variety. The second is a species; presumably the reference with which the entry begins, "*Nabalus* (rattlesnake root)," designates *N. albus*.

317.1 *Cooperi*: Thoreau spells the name thus, in agreement with *Wilson's American Ornithology*, in "The Allegash," 208.8. The copy-text here reads "*Cooperii*."

318.15 A swallow . . . twice.: In the copy-text this material is illogically placed between *Colymbus glacialis* and *Mergus Merganser* (both identified species), and is not indented as a separate entry.

319.5 Tent, six: The copy-text's "*Tent,—six*" implies a parallelism with the categorical paragraph beginnings, "*Wear,—*" and "*Carry,—*" above. The present editor's emendation is made on the model of "Axe, full size" at the next paragraph indentation.

320.16 mountain *Pemadené*: "Mt. Pemadene," the copy-text reading, obscures Thoreau's meaning and almost certainly results from his usual abbreviation of "mountain" (underscored "mt") in the lost manuscript from which the first edition derives. A similar emendation is made at 322.4. The accent in *Pemadené* is present both in Thoreau's source, Sébastien Rasles, *A Dictionary of the Abnaki Language in North America*, edited by John Pickering, *Memoirs of the American Academy of Arts and Sciences*, new series, 1 (1833), pp. 375-574, and in Thoreau's notes from Rasles in the tenth Indian Extract Book. Other terms from Rasles in the "List of Indian Words" are emended to the forms in Thoreau's source: see the Textual Introduction, pp. 401-02.

322.3 *Bematinichtik:* Thus in the journal, MJ, July 24, 1857. A misreading of Thoreau's manuscript resulted in the copy-text spelling, "*Bematruichtik.*" "*Beskabekuk-skishtook,*" "*Nonglangyis,*" "*Bososquasis,*" and "*Apmoo-jenegamook,*" later in the "List of Indian Words," have also been emended to the forms in "The Allegash" and its drafts from copy-text misspellings probably attributable to the compositor. At 323.28, the present editor follows III in correcting "ho, see" to "no see," the wording in "The Allegash," 295.6, and the journal draft. Although the spelling "*Nerlumskeechtcook*" at 322.32 may well be authorial, the editor respects Thoreau's instruction, "always . . . 'Nerlumskeechticook,'" on the organization sheet for *The Maine Woods* among the Houghton Library fragments (b MS Am 278.5, folder 17C).

322.7-8 (Williamson); old Indian hunter (Hodge.): The copy-text obscures Thoreau's meaning by printing "(Williamson; old Indian hunter). (Hodge.)" The first definition, "flint," comes from William D. Williamson, *The History of the State of Maine* (Hallowell, Me.: Glazier, Masters & Co., 1832), I, 96 n. James Hodge writes that "Mt. Kenio receives its name from that of an old Indian, who formerly lived and hunted in its vicinity," in C. T. Jackson's *Second Annual Report of the Geology of the Public Lands* (Augusta, Me., 1838), p. 60.

322.25 (?),: A comma, lacking in the copy-text, is supplied after the closing parenthesis for clarity by the present editor. "*Fiante*" is an older French form of the word for dung, as "*fimus*" is the Latin.

324.6 *Allagash,* a bark camp: Thus in Willis, "The Language of the Abnaquies, or Eastern Indians," *Collec-*

tions of the Maine Historical Society, IV (1856), p. 104. The copy-text reads *"Allagash* (a bark camp)." Willis uses parentheses immediately after Indian names to set off their *applications;* he does not isolate *definitions* in parentheses. The present editor also emends the pointing of four later entries in order to restore Willis' distinction, and he emends the spellings of four Indian names from Willis to conform to the source. Two of the spelling variants in the copy-text are clearly nonauthorial.

324.15 pronounced: Thus in Willis, p. 105. Since the copy-text's "pronounces" disagrees in tense with "said," it would seem to be a copyist's or compositor's error. Substantive readings from Willis—"border of Moosehead Lake," *"Pentagoet* or *Pentagovett,"* and "lake which now bears the English name' "—are added in the present edition to incomplete entries. The copy-text readings, "border, &c.," *"Pentagoet,* &c.," and "lake,' &c.," suggest that Thoreau intended to fill out the entries in his lost final draft, or that he expected an editor to consult Willis and complete these phrases for the 1864 publication.

325.22 *Sehunk:* The source of this passage is C. E. Potter, "Appendix to 'Language of the Abnaquies,' " *Collections of the Maine Historical Society,* IV (1856), p. 189. A misreading of Thoreau's hand resulted in the misspelling *"Schunk"* here and twice afterward in the copy-text.

List of Emendations

ALL changes from copy-text made by the present editor, except those specified as silent alterations of design in the Textual Introduction, are recorded in the following list. The left-hand column gives THE WRITINGS OF HENRY D. THOREAU reading with a parenthetical notation of the emendation source and other significant details. The right-hand column records the reading in the copy-text, the 1864 first edition of *The Maine Woods* (1). Entries marked with an asterisk (*) before the page/line citation are discussed in Textual Notes. Other symbols and abbreviations used in this list are "III" for the 1906 Walden Edition where it anticipates a substantive emendation or important accidental emendation made by the present editor; "MJ" for Thoreau's manuscript journal in the Pierpont Morgan Library; "Ed." for the present editor in emendations not based on an "Appendix" working manuscript; "Ref." (reference work) for a printed source employed by Thoreau; and "PE" for this edition of *The Maine Woods* in THE WRITINGS OF HENRY D. THOREAU, Princeton Edition. A wavy dash ($\sim$) in a copy-text reading stands for the word occupying this position in the PE reading to the left, and an inferior caret ($_\wedge$) signifies the absence of a punctuation mark.

	PE reading	I reading
300.33	1857 (MJ)	1858
301.22	especially $_\wedge$ (MJ)	apparently,
302.11	herd's (MJ, III)	herds
* 303.33	1853 and 1857, carries, (MJ)	1853, and carries $_\wedge$
303.35	1853 and 1857 (Ed., III)	1853 – 7

* 304.3	1853 ∧ (Ed.)	~ ?
* 305.6	*alba** (Ed.)	~ ∧
306.6	*corymbosum** (Ed.)	~ ∧
* 306.10	*Pennsylvanicum?* (dwarf-blue-berry ∧) (Ed.)	~ ∧ (~ ?)
306.13	*verticillatus* (Ed., III)	*verticillata*
306.13	alder), '57 (Ed.)	alder, '57)
306.24	as Webster (MJ)	on Webster
307.26	Chamberlain (Ed.)	Cham berlain
308.5	*discolor?* (glaucous willow ∧) (Ed.)	~ ∧ (~ ~ ?)
* 308.30	East Branch (Ed.)	South Branch
* 309.21-22	Smith's, Chesun-cook (MJ)	Smith's dam, Chesuncook
309.34	*nutans?* (clammy wild chick-weed ∧) (Ed.)	~ ∧ (~ ~ ~ ?)
310.8	*Aparine?* (cleav-ers ∧) (Ed.)	~ ∧ (~ ?)
* 310.28-29	common in 1857 ... 1853. (MJ)	in 1857 ... 1853, common.
311.1	A *lemna** (Ed.)	A *lemna* ∧
312.3	*tetrahit** (Ed.)	~ ∧
312.19	*cernua* (MJ, III)	*cernuus*
312.31	*Dortmanna** (Ed.)	~ ∧
313.18	*monoica* (MJ, III)	*monocea*
314.24	*racemosa?* (false spikenard ∧) (Ed.)	~ ∧ (~ ~ ?)
314.25	1857 (MJ)	1853
315.22	and in his (MJ)	and his
316.24	Seboois (Ed.)	Schoonis
* 317.1	*Cooperi* (Ed., Ref.)	*Cooperii*
318.10	*albeola* (Ref., III)	*albicola*
* 318.14-15	rivers. [⌁] A swallow ... twice. (Ed.: *relocation*)	lakes. A swallow ... twice. [⌁] *Mergus*
* 319.5	Tent, six (Ed.)	*Tent,—six*
320.15	*Land.* (Ed.)	~ ,

320.15	Rasles (Ed.; also in 19 subsequent instances; see Textual Introduction, p. 401 n.)	Rale
* 320.16	mountain (Ed.)	*Mt.*
320.16	*Pemadené* (Ref.)	*Pemadene*
320.17	*Kidadañgan* (Ref.)	*Kitadaügan*
320.28	bear. *Aouessous* (Ed.)	bear, *aouessous*
320.32	*Mous* (Ed.)	*mous*
320.35	*Ibimin* (Ref.)	*Ibibimin*
321.1	writing. *Aouixigan* (Ed.)	writing, *aouixigan*
321.1	Indian (Ed.)	Ind'n
321.2	*écriture* (Ref.)	*ceinture*
321.3	Lake. (Ed.)	~ ,
321.3-4	*Pegouasebem* (Ref.)	*Peqouasebem*
321.5	*Ouañrinañgamek* (Ref.)	*Ouaürinaügamek*
321.11	*Caucomgomoc-took* (Ed.)	*caucomgomoc-took*
321.16	*Pouapeskou* (Ref.)	*Puapeskou*
321.16	Indian (Ed.)	Ind'n
321.17	Rasles. (v. Springer.) (Ed., Ref.)	(Rale v. Springer.)
321.26	*Musketicook* (Ed.)	*Muskiticook*
* 322.3	*Bematinichtik* (Ed.)	*Bematruichtik*
322.4	Mountain, (Ed.)	*Mt.* ∧
* 322.7-8	(Williamson); old . . . hunter ∧∧ (Hodge.) (Ed., Ref.)	(Williamson ∧; old . . . hunter). (Hodge.)
322.14	*Beskabekukskish-took* (Ed.)	*Beskabekuk shishtook*
322.18	*Nonglangyis* (Ed.)	*Nonlangyis*
* 322.25	(?), (Ed.)	(?) ∧
322.27	*hispidula*; (Ed.)	~ ,
322.30	*Pagadañkouéouérre* (Ref.)	*Pagadaükoueouérré*

322.31	*Bososquasis* (Ed.)	*Bororquasis*
322.32	*Nerlumskeechti-cook* (Ed.)	*Nerlumskeechtcook*
322.35	*Apmoojenegamook* (Ed.)	*Apmoojeuegamook*
323.12	berries. (Ed.)	~ ,
323.13	*Pemouaïmin* (Ref.)	*Pemouaimin*
323.13	fruit." Rasles. (Ed.)	fruit. Rale."
323.24-25	*Pañsidañkioui* (Ref.)	*Paüsidaükioui*
323.27	*Ourámañ* (Ref.)	*Ouramaü*
323.28	no see (Ed., III)	ho, see
323.30	*Sañghedétegoué* (Ref.)	*Saüghedétegoue*
323.31	*sañktaüoui* (Ref.)	*saüktaüoui*
323.32	Brook (Ed.)	Br.
323.32	Hatchet (Ed.)	*Hatchet*
323.32-33	*temahígan* (Ref.)	*temahigan*
323.34	*Niketaoutegoué* (Ref.)	*Nicketaoutegué*
323.34	*Niketoutegoué* (Ref.)	*Niketoutegoue*
* 324.6	*Allagash*, a . . . camp (Ed., Ref.)	*Allagash* (a . . . camp)
324.9	(head of Allagash), (Ed., Ref.)	, head of Allagash,
* 324.15	pronounced (Ref.)	pronounces
324.17	*Kenduskeag*, the . . . Eels. (Ed., Ref.)	*Kenduskeag* (the . . . Eels).
324.18	*Kineo*, flint, (Ed., Ref.)	*Kineo* (flint),
324.18-19	border of Moosehead Lake. (Ref.)	border, &c.
324.27	*Neccotoh* (Ed., Ref.)	Neccotoh
324.33-34	*Pentagoet* or *Pentagovett* (Ref.)	*Pentagoet*, &c.
324.35	*Pougohwakem* (Ref.)	*Pougohwaken*

325.3	*Ripogenas* (Ref.)	*Ripogenus*
325.7-8	lake which now bears the English name." (Ref.)	lake," &c.
325.12	*Sebago,* great water. (Ed., Ref.)	*Sebago* (great water).
325.14	*Telasinis* (Ref.)	*Telasiuis*
325.17	*Umbazookscus* (Ref.)	*Umbazookskus*
* 325.22	*Sehunk* (Ref.)	*Schunk*
325.23	Sehunk (Ref.)	Schunk
325.29	*Sehunk-auke* (Ref.)	*Schunk-auke*

Table of Textual Variations

THE following table lists all differences of substantives, and of accidentals whose effects are alterations of meaning rather than of form alone, between the text of the present edition and the only relevant form of the "Appendix," the 1864 first edition of *The Maine Woods* (copy-text). Also recorded is one significant accidental from working manuscript that may have been altered inadvertently by Thoreau in preparing final copy or changed by a copyist or compositor after Thoreau's death.

The readings in the left-hand column are those of the present (Princeton) edition, PE (THE WRITINGS OF HENRY D. THOREAU). "1" represents the first edition, and "MJ" stands for Thoreau's manuscript journal in the Pierpont Morgan Library, of which volume 30, for 1857, contains the "Appendix" variant cited in the table. Two PE readings are emendations first anticipated in the 1906 Walden Edition (III), as noted by that symbol. PE readings not accompanied by parenthetical reference to an earlier printed text are new in this edition.

Accidentals associated with substantive variants, but not in themselves significant, are ignored in the table entries. A wavy dash ($\sim$) in a variant listing designates the word occupying this position in the PE reading, and an inferior caret ($_\wedge$) indicates an absent punctuation mark.

	PE reading	Variant reading
300.4-5	*protégés* (1)	*protegées* (MJ)
300.33	1857	1858 (1)
301.22	especially	apparently (1)
303.33	1853 and 1857, carries	1853, and carries (1)

304.3	1853	1853? (1)
305.6	*alba** (also in 4 subsequent entries)	~ ₄ (1)
306.24	as Webster	on Webster (1)
308.30	East Branch	South Branch (1)
309.21	Smith's	Smith's dam (1)
310.28-29	common in 1857 ... 1853	in 1857 ... 1853, common (1)
311.1	A *lemna* (III)	A *lemna* (1)
314.25	1857	1853 (1)
315.22	and in his	and his (1)
316.24	Seboois	Schoonis (1)
320.16	mountain *Pemadené*	*Mt. Pemadene* (1)
321.2	*écriture*	*ceinture*
322.4	Mountain, *Pemadené*	*Mt. Pemadené*
323.28	no see (III)	ho, see (1)
324.15	pronounced	pronounces (1)
324.18-19	border of Moose-head Lake	border, &c. (1)
324.33-34	*Pentagoet* or *Pentagovett*	*Pentagoet*, &c. (1)
325.7-8	lake which now bears the English name."	lake," &c. (1)

Line-end Hyphenation

THE compounds or possible compounds in list A, below, are hyphenated at the end of the line in the "Appendix" copy-text. On the general grounds discussed in the Textual Introduction, page 404, the editor has resolved each to the form recorded in list A. List B records only those compounds hyphenated at the end of the line in the present edition that should be transcribed with the hyphen in order to duplicate the copy-text forms.

LIST A		LIST B	
298.8	arbor-vitæ	301.9-10	meadow-sweet
300.12	mountain-maples	301.16-17	snake-root
300.24	checkerberry	302.1-2	water-arum
301.9-10	meadow-sweet	303.3-4	bush-honeysuckle
301.13	purple-fringed	303.6-7	button-bush
302.13	white-weed	303.24-25	*bursa-pastoris*
302.29	hobble-bush	312.10-11	John's-wort
303.31	lady's-thumb	313.4-5	lake-shores
303.32	sheep-sorrel	316.18-19	bald-eagle
306.26	river-sides	319.7-8	pocket-map
306.28	roadsides	319.33-34	India-rubber
310.19	Moosehead	319.34-35	water-tight
314.35	highway	320.6-7	twenty-five
315.22	wood-path	322.18-19	dead-water
318.21	muskrat		
319.11	tape-measure		
319.15	waistcoat		
319.31	India-rubber		

DATE DUE